Egypt as a Woman

# Egypt as a Woman

*Nationalism, Gender, and Politics*

Beth Baron

UNIVERSITY OF CALIFORNIA PRESS
*Berkeley · Los Angeles · London*

University of California Press
Berkeley and Los Angeles, California

University of California Press, Ltd.
London, England

Portions of chapters 1, 3, and 8 have appeared previously in different form as "The Making of the Egyptian Nation," in *Gendered Nations: Nationalism and Gender Order in the Long Nineteenth Century,* ed. Ida Blom, Karen Hagemann, and Catherine Hall (London: Berg, 2000), 137–58; "Nationalist Iconography: Egypt as a Woman," in *Rethinking Nationalism in the Arab World,* ed. James Jankowski and Israel Gershoni (New York: Columbia University Press, 1997), 105–24; and "An Islamic Activist in Interwar Egypt," in *Iran and Beyond: Essays in Middle Eastern History in Honor of Nikki R. Keddie,* eds. Rudi Matthee and Beth Baron (Costa Mesa, Calif.: Mazda, 2000), 201–20.

Library of Congress Cataloging-in-Publication Data

Baron, Beth.
    Egypt as a woman : nationalism, gender, and politics / Beth Baron.
        p.    cm.
    Includes bibliographical references and index.
    ISBN 978-0-520-25154-0 (pbk : alk. paper)
        1. Women—Egypt—Political activity.
    2. Women—Middle East.   3. Gender identity—Egypt.
    4. Nationalism—Egypt.   5. Feminism—Egypt.
    6. Egypt—Politics and government.   I. Title.
HQ1793.B368   2005
305.4'0962—dc22                              2004008294

Manufactured in the United States of America

16   15   14   13   12   11   10   09   08   07

10   9   8   7   6   5   4   3   2

The paper used in this publication meets the minimum requirements of ANSI/NISO Z39.48-1992 (R 1997) (*Permanence of Paper*).

*To Neta, Talya, and Yitzhak*

# Contents

# Illustrations

# Acknowledgments

In a decade-long exploration of gender and nationalism, I incurred many debts, only some of which can be acknowledged here. Librarians and archivists in Egypt, England, and the United States have made this work possible. Michael Hopper and Alice Deyab at Harvard University's Widener Library opened doors (and closets), and allowed me to read through their collection of Arabic women's periodicals. Thanks as well to librarians at Dar al-Kutub in Egypt, Princeton University's Firestone Library, the Library of Congress, and to the Controller, H. M. Stationery Office, for permission to quote crown copyright material in the Public Record Office in London.

Funding for research came from a National Endowment for the Humanities Summer Stipend (1993) and an American Council of Learned Societies Fellowship (1995–96). This work was also supported by grants from the City University of New York PSC-CUNY Research Award Program and the Simon H. Rifkind Center for the Humanities and Arts at the City College of New York.

Much of the rewriting was done while I was a visiting fellow in the Department of History at Princeton University. Special thanks to Robert Tignor for arranging that stay, for commenting on the manuscript, and for helping to launch the biweekly Egypt Seminar, which met in Princeton in 1999–2000. That group mourns the premature passing of one of its members, Magda al-Nowaihi. Among the participants, Jane Hathaway and Ron Shaham read large chunks of the manuscript, helping to sharpen ideas; and Eve Troutt Powell encouraged me to combine questions on gender with inquiries into race.

The comments of organizers and participants in workshops over the past decade proved invaluable. Israel Gershoni has given me multiple opportunities to present work, for which I am most grateful. I would also like to acknowledge Lila Abu-Lughod, Bishara Doumani, Avner Giladi, Karen Hagemann, Catherine Hall, James Jankowski, Donald Quartaert, Amy Singerman, Dror Ze'evi, and the late Mine Ener for invitations to present work in progress. Zachary Lockman, Afsaneh Najmabadi, and Ehud Toledano, among others, took the task of commenting on papers seriously.

Other colleagues who deserve a special thanks for reviewing drafts of the manuscript include Arthur Goldschmidt Jr., who helped clarify some of the details; Donald Reid, who raised important points; and Elizabeth Thompson, whose suggestions for revisions were invaluable. As always, Nikki Keddie has been a trusted reader, mentor, and friend. Gene Garthwaite helped feed and rejuvenate me at critical moments. And Iris Agmon, Annette Aronowicz, Dina Le Gall, and Leslie Peirce listened, prodded, and pushed.

Frank Grande, chair of the Department of History at CCNY during most of the writing of this book, gave tremendous support in numerous ways, which will always be remembered. His successor, Lou Masur, had faith in the project. The team at the Middle East and Middle Eastern American Center at the CUNY Graduate Center—Mehdi Bozorgmehr and Anny Bakalian—have demonstrated the virtues of collaboration through intense times in New York City.

My students have taught me far more than they realize. Among them, Malek Abisaab introduced me to debates on nationalism, Marios Fotiou gave me insights into issues of class, and Sara Pursley sharpened my thinking on class and gender and helped prepare the bibliography for production.

Lynne Withey at the University of California Press patiently supported this project over the long haul. Readers for the Press pushed me to strengthen the arguments of the book. Julie Brand and Rachel Berchten ably guided me through production; Peter Dreyer polished the final version. I also wish to thank the University Seminars at Columbia University for their help in publication. The ideas presented have benefitted from discussions in the University Seminar on Women and Society.

This book was conceived shortly after the birth of my twin daughters and has grown with them. There is no greater pleasure than being "Umm al-banat," the mother of girls: Neta and Talya have given me the gift of better understanding the rhetoric and reality of motherhood. Yitzhak Nakash made both mothering and writing more pleasurable. And my own parents showed their support in many ways.

The theme of memory, and forgetting, winds through *Egypt as a Woman*. There are many people who helped make this book possible. Although I may not have acknowledged them here by name, their contributions have not been forgotten.

# Note on Transliteration

Transliteration is not an exact science. I have more or less followed the system of transliteration adopted by the *International Journal of Middle East Studies*, which reduces diacritics to a minimum. I have deviated from this system to use accepted English spelling for well-known place-names and people, such as "Cairo" and "Farouk." For early members of the Mehmed Ali dynasty, I have favored a Turkish transliteration to signal their Ottoman context. In references, I have retained the spelling of names used in the original documents, which may be crucial in locating the source in a file. Thus, whereas I refer to "Safiyya Zaghlul" in the text, variations such as "Saphia Zaghloul" appear in the notes. For authors who published in Arabic and English, alternate spellings of their names may occur; but the standard Arabic transliteration of their name for their Arabic works has been retained in the bibliography to facilitate finding their works in catalogues.

# Introduction

Unrest broke out in Egypt in March 1919 when the British, who had occupied the autonomous Ottoman province in 1882 and declared it a protectorate at the outset of World War I, arrested and deported leaders of the Wafd (literally, delegation) who sought to present Egyptian demands for independence at peace talks in Paris. Diverse groups in the city and countryside, including urban elite women, staged protests. Inspired by what came to be known as the revolution of 1919, Mahmud Mukhtar sculpted a work called *Nahdat Misr* (The Awakening of Egypt), which shows a peasant woman lifting her veil from her face with her left arm and placing her right arm on the back of a sphinx as it rises up on its forelegs (see figure 6). Juxtaposing Egypt's ancient pharaonic glory with her modern awakening, Mukhtar's sculpture thus depicts modern Egypt as a woman. The work captured the public imagination, and the campaign to have the model sculpted in monumental size accelerated in the wake of the British unilateral declaration of Egyptian independence (with points reserved for future negotiation). The press closely followed the progress of the carving of *The Awakening of Egypt* in a public square in front of the railroad station. The government planned a big ceremony for the unveiling of the statue in 1928, to which foreign dignitaries and local notables were invited, and over which King Fu'ad presided. But by the latter's explicit orders, and with few exceptions, Egyptian women were barred from the ceremony.[1]

The almost complete absence of women from a national ceremony celebrating a sculpture in which a woman represented the nation epitomizes

1

the paradox faced by women nationalists. Scholars have noted "the inverse relationship between the prominence of female figures in the allegorization of nation and the degree of access granted women to the political apparatus of the state."[2] They have also had varying assessments of the impact of national discourses on women. While some argue that familial rhetoric discursively included women in the nation, others stress women's less than full citizenship in the nation-state. A middle position sees gendered nationalist discourses as "Janus-faced," facilitating women's political participation and at the same time constricting their roles and restricting their emancipation.[3]

*Egypt as a Woman* explores the connections between gendered images of the nation and the politics of women nationalists. It starts with the making of the nation in the nineteenth century and ends with the eclipse of a generation of political activists in the 1940s. The book's methodology sets literary discourses and visual culture firmly in sociopolitical contexts. At the same time, it combines several strands of scholarship, including writings on collective memory,[4] debates on nationalism, and the injection of gender into these debates,[5] and conceptualizations of women's political culture.[6]

## COLLECTIVE REMEMBERING AND FORGETTING

The histories of national struggles have generally been written by nationalist elites. In supplying these texts, historians have played a central role in nation-building and myth-making and have only recently begun to deconstruct some of the myths. The texts generally present a unified story of the nationalist struggle and are meant to provide the nation with a shared understanding of the past. The narrative and its embedded myths are thus part of the glue that binds the collective. The protagonist in the story is the nation itself, and the story shows how the nation awakens culturally and politically, throws off the occupier or ancien régime, and becomes independent.

Nationalist narratives generally identify an external enemy, heroes, a vanguard party, and pivotal moments. The narratives written about nationalist movements are by necessity neater than the actual events. For purposes of promoting unity behind a particular leader or group, counternarratives are silenced, marginalized, or incorporated in shortened form into the nationalist narrative. These counternarratives tend to be those written, or remembered, by opposition groups, members of the lower classes, minorities, and women. Their versions of the past often focus on different characters and events or give them a different twist. Scholars of women's history tried early on to include women in nationalist narratives or to produce counternarratives, but they remained ambivalent about nationalist movements, which many feminists ultimately found disappointing.

Forgetting is a crucial part of constructing nationalist narratives, as episodes and actualities that might divide the collective or show internal dissent and conflict are suppressed.[7] Other memories simply fade, not having been recorded. The theme of remembering and forgetting runs throughout this work, suggesting that memory functions as a linchpin between cultural images and political actions. As the details of women's political activism were suppressed or forgotten, what remained, or were remembered, were female symbols. This work asks: How were women incorporated into the collective memory? Which women? What literary and visual tools were used to trigger collective memories? To what extent did women become "sites" of memory themselves, symbols of an event or movement? Do women become symbols because they have already been excluded, or are they excluded because they are symbols? How do women, by crafting memoirs and commemorating certain events, seek to reshape history and memory?

Among the most forgotten women are those of the lower classes. Working-class and peasant women initiated their own political actions, and the latter often came to represent the nation. Yet this work focuses for the most part on elite women at a time when elites dominated nationalist politics. The politics of lower-class women, and their production and reception of images, deserves its own study, one that would cover the post-1952 period. The politics of royal women and nationalist representations of the monarchy also fall outside the main purview of this work.

## GENDERING NATIONALISM

Egypt appears to have the most natural of all nationalist pedigrees. Anchored in the ancient world, it presumably had fixed boundaries for millennia, continuous settlement of a people on a land, and a river system that bound the people together. The story seems simple: a nation that once boasted one of the great empires was occupied by a series of foreigners, but "awakened" in the modern period to wage a struggle for independence. According to this narrative, Muhammad 'Ali (r. 1805–48), the "founder of modern Egypt," set the nation on the path toward independence.[8]

Influenced by the theoretical debates on nationalism in which modernists (also known as constructionists) argue that nations are modern constructs and stress the importance of myths, symbols, and discourses in "imagining," "inventing," or "constructing" the nation, historians of Egypt have offered new accounts of Egyptian nationalism, including its origins. They have argued that Mehmed Ali Pasha (as Muhammad 'Ali was known in Turkish, the language of his administration and household) should be seen as an Ottoman *vali* (governor) who harbored dynastic ambitions rather than designs for an independent nation.[9] Scholars point to the 'Urabi revolt (1881–82), which ended in British occupation, or the anti-colonial movement that surfaced in the 1890s, as the earliest stirrings of Egyptian nationalism.[10] They have analyzed the rich reservoir of pharaonic, Roman, Hellenistic, Coptic, Arab, Mamluk, and Ottoman layers from which Egyptian nationalists drew myths and symbols, and have discussed nationalist and religious identities.[11] Egypt's relationship to the Sudan—part of a Nile Valley entity in the nationalist view—has been scrutinized and reassessed as an imperialist enterprise.[12]

Standard accounts of Egyptian nationalism paid little attention to women activists, or mentioned them only to signify the breadth of the movement, until Margot Badran corrected the view that women were bit players in her study *Feminists, Islam, and Nation: Gender and the Making of Modern Egypt* (1995).[13] In that book, Badran chronicles the feminist movement launched by Huda Sha'rawi (1879–1947) and examines the activities of feminist nationalists. She shows how secular feminists in the first half of the twentieth century assumed agency and worked to advance the cause of women through a rethought Islam and reconfigured nation. Drawing on women's records and documents, she traces the emergence of an indigenous feminism and argues that these women were militant nationalist feminists. *Egypt as a Woman* builds on Badran's pioneering book, broadening the cast of characters, incorporating diverse theoretical and cultural approaches to nationalism, and offering some new interpretations. This work also builds on a rich corpus of works by colleagues who have explored various aspects of the nationalist debates on women and the family, as well as on my own *The Women's Awakening in Egypt* (1994), which focused on female intellectuals at the turn of the century and their interest in family, reform, and nation-building.[14]

Nationalists everywhere have used an array of family metaphors, resulting in a rhetoric that provides a key to understanding the emotive power of nationalism. The use of kin idioms by women as well as men in nationalist discussions reveals something of the transformations within families, the debates about gender relations, and ideas about the nation and nationalism. The nation, according to its proponents, was "one family" descended from the same roots with shared blood. Young men, the foot soldiers of the nation, were its "sons," and young girls became its "daughters." At the head of the nationalist movement generally loomed a dominating "father" figure or group of "founding fathers." Nationalists hoped to replicate the sense of belonging and loyalty experienced within the family on a national scale. The rhetoric strove to create a sense of the relatedness of people who were otherwise strangers and often separated by ethnicity, race, class, and religion. Asserting that the nation, whatever its ethnic origins, was a family was meant to generate bonds and ensure unity. In short, the nation became a family writ large, a fictive household, with elites at its head.

The mobilization of familial rhetoric for political purposes was not invented by nationalists. Imperial family idioms, like subsequent nationalist ones, were meant to inspire love, loyalty, and obedience. In an example of imperial paternalism, the Ottoman sultan Abdul Hamid II (r. 1876–1909) staged gift-giving and other ceremonies to present himself as a caring father.[15] Yet nationalists used family metaphors more widely than their predecessors, stressed fraternal over paternal ties, introduced "mothers" as important actors, and based their ideal on the bourgeois family.

Maternal imagery proved particularly prevalent in nationalist literatures across the world. Women spoke of themselves, and were spoken of, as "Mothers of the Nation." They were ascribed the role of biologically and culturally reproducing the nation and used this role to claim entry into the public arena.[16] In similar processes, individual women such as Indira Gandhi, Winnie Mandela, and Safiyya Zaghlul (1876–1946) became known respectively as the mothers of India, South Africa, and Egypt, which gave them great political clout.[17] Maternal rhetoric sometimes coincided with calls for the protection of the rights of women and children and the rudiments of a welfare state, what some historians have labeled "maternalism."[18] Yet rhetoric and social policy were not always, or even often, consistent.

Debates on family structure and family idioms—both part of the nationalist discourse of the family—are an almost universal component of nationalism and an integral dynamic regardless of whether the movements were anti-colonial or of another variety. When nationalists used family metaphors, they drew on local meanings and hoped to reshape family relationships along modern lines that better suited nation-states grounded in capitalist relationships. This was not just mimicry of the West, or reaction to a Western critique, but something that arose from internal impulses as well as external influences.[19] Egyptian nationalists keenly interested in reconfiguring the family along modern bourgeois lines promoted the cult of domesticity articulated in the women's press and elsewhere since the late nineteenth century.[20] Mona Russell pursues this idea, looking at how the new capitalist system recast women formerly engaged in household production as consumers and educated marital partners.[21] Clarissa (Lisa) Pollard argues that both men and women were domesticated and links the domestic to the political in innovative ways in charting the family politics of Egypt through 1919.[22] Nationalists sought to undermine women's and men's homosocial bonds, as well as women's ties to their natal families, which all challenged the new model of companionate marriage.[23]

The prevalence of familial metaphors in nationalist rhetoric inside and outside Egypt should not obscure their different uses, particular resonances, and varied receptions. Familial metaphors could be used to reinforce, or undermine, family hierarchies based on age and gender. Maternal, paternal, and fraternal jargon had different echoes in households of varying sizes and shapes. Members of a household made up of multiple wives or concubines, a few generations, and grown siblings would have understood the meaning of family differently than members of a nuclear unit. Family forms changed over time, varied between regions and across classes, and were experienced differently by men and women.

When male and female Egyptian nationalists used a constellation of family metaphors at the end of the nineteenth century, they had their own realities and ideals. Unfortunately, we know much more about the ideals than the realities, for little work has been done on Egyptian family structure in the modern period.[24] It has been assumed that the cult of domesticity targeted the newly emerging middle classes, but the size and composition of this group is not that clear. Given low literacy rates— 8 percent of Egyptian men and only 0.2 percent of Egyptian women in 1897[25]—the turn-of-the-century literature must have targeted as broad a spectrum of the population as possible. This would have included, as in nearby Lebanon, peasants on the rise, as well as wealthier families that were reorganizing along more modern lines.[26] Even the household of the khedive (or viceroy under the Ottoman sultan) Tawfiq (r. 1879–92) showed a clear shift to monogamy.[27]

Chapter 1 of *Egypt as a Woman* highlights the transformations of elite households in the long nineteenth century, with particular emphasis on the roles of slavery and ethnicity in this process. The unraveling of these households led to a crisis in the family by the end of the century and influenced nationalist debates on gender relations. Nationalists who attempted to redefine the shape of the family were thus often trying to steer changes already under way or engineer further changes. Their family discourses targeted various groups and operated on both the micro and macro levels, ranging from debates about the shape of an individual family to the rhetoric of the nation as a family.

Once the nation was envisioned as a family, the concept of family honor could easily be appropriated as the basis for national honor. Chapter 2 charts the process whereby nationalists used such oral media as ballads, poetry, and speeches to disseminate the notion of family-national honor. The honor discourse derived from and reinforced cultural ideals of masculinity, and was activated particularly in time of war and revolution. Honor came to define the parameters of the collective and was at the core of its identity: those who shared honor belonged to the nation; those who did not or were not ready to defend and avenge national honor would be excluded.[28]

National honor worked as a concept because at more or less the same time as the notion of national honor emerged, the nation was imagined as a woman. "Nation" has multiple meanings and can refer to a group of people associated with a particular land who seek sovereignty over that territory, or the territory itself. For a variety of reasons, nationalists often depicted the nation in artistic representations as a woman. Like family rhetoric, this was not a new phenomenon, but rather one that had deep roots. The depiction of political abstractions in female forms goes back to antiquity. (Mosaics of the Hellenistic period, for example, show Egypt as a woman.) This may be because land is easily feminized in peasant societies due to its link with fertility. Yet fertility was not the only trigger; morality and deities also acted to inspire female imagery. Thus Iceland, Russia, and India evoked the "Motherland" and represented the country as female in depictions.[29] In addition, female imagery was adopted by empires as well as their colonies. Imperial centers such as Holland, England, and France were rendered as a woman, along with colonies such as Australia, Canada, New Zealand, and South Africa.[30] Yet the practice was not universal or consistent, and some nations were gendered both male and female. The classic example is England / Great Britain, where John Bull and Victoria were used as imagery.

Arabic has different terms for the territory or homeland (*watan*) and for the collective community or people (*umma*).[31] *Watan* is gendered male and *umma* is gendered female, and the term for Egypt (*Misr*) is also gendered female. Theoretically, the Egyptian nation could have been gendered male or female in representations. Chapter 3 examines the process by which Egypt came to be gendered as a woman in paintings, monuments, and cartoons, as well as on postage stamps. By grounding Egyptian iconography in historical contexts, the chapter highlights general patterns and divergences and attempts to tie images of Egypt to real political actors and events. It shows how symbols changed over time, in different media, and across the political spectrum.

Nationalism is a modern phenomenon, made possible by modern technologies. Much attention has been paid to the importance of print culture, specifically periodicals, in constructing the nation. Yet given low literacy rates in places such as Egypt, the role of oral and visual media in this process should be stressed. Most Egyptians would have heard or seen nationalist dramas, not read about them. Nationalist iconography, and representations of Egypt as a woman, became familiar in part through their wide dissemination in photographs in the press and elsewhere. Photography was one of the first modern media used by nationalists and a necessary precursor to some of the others, especially film and television.[32]

Chapter 4 examines how photography, and photojournalism in particular, played a special role in constructing the Egyptian nation. Photography changed the way individuals looked at the world and at one another. It transformed space, since images from and of diverse places could be assembled together, and photographs began to occupy spaces in homes, on walls, and in rituals. It stopped time, as scenes could be arranged, frozen, and preserved to shape memories. It liberated the arts, since painters, sculptors, and other artists could work from photos. In short, photography proved to be a tremendous tool for Egyptian nationalists, allowing them to publicize the activities of nationalist leaders and to create and disseminate new symbols.

NATIONALISMS AND FEMINISMS IN THE MIDDLE EAST

Early scholars of Middle Eastern women's history had ambivalent attitudes toward nationalism. While they recognized the almost complete absence of women in nationalist accounts and sought to correct the oversight, they were at the same time critical of movements that denied women full citizenship once certain nationalist goals had been achieved. In short, while celebrating nationalist struggles and female participants, they condemned the outcomes and male nationalists.

Some scholars have disapproved of the way this debate has been framed. Marnia Lazreq, for example, takes issue with the view that sees Algerian women as "duped into joining the nationalist movement by unscrupulous men who later did not share with them the spoils of independence." Lazreg stresses women's agency and "rational response" to an irrational colonial situation. Women were not passive participants who were mobilized to fight and then sent home, she argues. Rather, women willingly chose to fight against the colonial power and achieved their primary goal. That a secondary one—advancing women's rights—eluded them needs to be considered separately.[33]

Women's rights movements in the Middle East (and elsewhere) emerged as part of nation-state building, or in reaction to it, and histories of women's rights movements, nationalism, and anti-colonialism invariably became intertwined.[34] Yet not all women nationalists were feminists, and even among those who gave high priority to the struggle for women's rights, not all agreed on what those rights ought to entail and whether the path should be a secular or a religious one. Feminism and nationalism need to be examined both in relation to each other and apart.

Male nationalists had different agendas when struggling for power and once in power. Struggling for power, they sought to mobilize women, exploit their energies, and channel their contributions. Once these men came to control state institutions, however, the ground rules for the engagement of women changed. Almost everywhere that male nationalists achieved power, they blocked women's political path: women could not vote, run for office, or join political parties. Competing male politicians continued to use the rhetoric of nationalism but denied women benefits, jobs, and promised reforms. Women's relationship to the nationalist movement and to the state, whether colonial or postcolonial, must be disentangled, and the nation-state pried apart to understand the important shift that took place at this juncture.

The question of "which struggle to fight first" preoccupied activists, theorists, and historians for some time, giving rise to varied analyses and answers. While lamenting what Middle Eastern women did not gain from male nationalists, scholars need to explore the alternative political culture that women developed. For, in spite of the obstacles, women devised their own forms and forums for shaping the national polity. In looking at women's political culture, a dynamic picture emerges as women alternated between and among partisan, feminist, Islamist, social, and other politics in the name of nation-building.

WOMEN'S POLITICAL CULTURE IN EGYPT

There were precedents for elite women's political activity in Egypt. Jane Hathaway has shown that women in the eighteenth century acquired authority and legitimacy by cementing alliances between elite households, anchoring the household as "a sort of family matriarch," and guarding the household wealth. "The wife of a grandee lived in the thick of political intrigue and was likely to be a skilled political operator herself." The political influence of these ladies, she explains, outlived the deaths of their husbands and sons. As widows, "they assumed a sort of elder stateswoman or dowager status from which the households and factions to which they belonged derived prestige."[35] Women had maneuvered within the context of rivalries between elite households for positions of power and often came to control the wealth in a family because of their greater longevity. They devised successful strategies for maximizing their influence within the politics of households.

We know more about elite women's politics in eighteenth-century Egypt than in the nineteenth century, when Mehmed Ali centralized power in his own household and founded a dynastic state.[36] In the late nineteenth century, elite women began to organize collectively, generating a new women's political culture. Transformations in women's political culture from 1880 to 1950 paralleled key changes in the Egyptian landscape, notably the British occupation of 1882, the revolution of 1919, nominal independence in 1922, and the 1952 overthrow of the monarchy.

In the period from 1882 to 1922, male and female nationalists devised different political responses to the British colonial presence. Men's political culture was characterized by newspapers, parties, and a legislative assembly noted more for its oratory than its legislation. During this period, elite men oscillated between cooperation with British authorities in administering the state and opposition to colonial rule. Gender segregation mandated that middle- and upper-class women start women-only organizations and institutions, which gave them autonomy to pursue their own agendas. A vibrant women's press emerged, followed by the formation of a variety of women's associations. Groups such as Jam'iyyat Tarqiyat al-Mar'a (the Society of Woman's Progress, 1908) devised programs that had social welfare, educational, and proto-feminist components. These groups pressed for expanded education, reform of family law, and women's rights in secular or religious terms.[37] Chapter 1 of *Egypt as a Woman* includes a discussion of aspects of women's political culture prior to 1919.

In the wake of the revolution of 1919 and failed negotiations, Great Britain unilaterally awarded Egypt semi-independence in 1922, giving male politicians greater control of the state. The constitution of 1923 granted the king broad executive and legislative powers; restricted the Senate to the upper classes; and gave the Senate veto power over the

Chamber of Deputies, whose membership was confined to literate males. Women were denied the vote in a system established to promote the interests of upper-class men. Party infighting, palace autocracy, and British manipulation soon paralyzed men's political culture. As male politicians jockeyed for position, little, if any, attention was given to social reform.

Women's political culture expanded its repertoire of nationalist activities in the transition to semi-independence. Elite women's demonstrations in the revolution of 1919 marked a more public turn in organizing. In the early 1920s, middle- and upper-class women formed a variety of organizations, including the Women's Wafd, the Society for Egyptian Ladies' Awakening, Mothers of the Future, and the Egyptian Feminist Union. Like earlier associations, these groups pursued programs that fused social welfare, education, and feminist goals, but they did so more visibly and on a larger scale in the interwar years. To the earlier objectives were added new concerns, such as eliminating legalized prostitution and clamping down on drug and alcohol abuse. Women's political culture showed remarkable creativity and adaptability during this period.

Part 2 of *Egypt as a Woman* focuses on the nationalist component of women's political culture from 1919, considering the activities of female nationalists, as well as how they were remembered. It looks at what has been identified as "the space for women's political agency" in the nationalist movement and "the cracks in the political dominance of men."[38] In conceptualizing women's nationalist activity as part of women's political culture, we can see where women succeeded in inserting wedges in the cracks and widening them, and where they felt constrained and fell back on other options. The main protagonists are a group of women, mostly wives and daughters of pashas and beys (titles of the elite), who themselves were women of means with their own resources. Their careers stretched well beyond those of their husbands, who tended to be quite senior to them in years, and whom they often outlived.[39] Many of these female protagonists are often referred to here after first mention by first rather than last name. This is because using their surnames, which are often male names, seems both confusing and inconsistent with my purpose of restoring women to history and recovering erasures from the past.

Chapter 5 starts with the story of the "ladies' demonstrations" of 1919, sketching how they became part of the nationalist collective memory. Chapter 6 turns to a profile of the single most powerful woman in this period, Safiyya Zaghlul (wife of the nationalist leader Sa'd Zaghlul), who played the maternalist card and carved out a special role for herself as the "Mother of the Egyptians." In chapter 7, the attempts by partisan women to overcome divisions and keep the Women's Wafd intact are examined, as are attempts by women journalists to build alliances with male party leaders. Chapter 8 follows the career of Labiba Ahmad (1870s–1951), whose activism included journalism, radio addresses, and frequent travel to the Arabian peninsula to promote an Islamic version of Egyptian nationalism.

These chapters illuminate the ways in which elite women, despite their lack of full citizenship, crafted a vibrant political culture that complemented men's political culture. They organized collectively in various forms (auxiliary parties and private associations) to produce multiple products (such as journals and speeches) and services (health, education, and welfare) that filled vacuums and plugged holes. Individual women worked to patch up political differences, advise ministers on social matters, and act as representatives at home and abroad. Whether they championed feminist, Wafdist, Islamist, or social politics, or some combination, they saw their work as part of the nationalist endeavor and their efforts as part of nation-building.

Most of the protagonists here came of age around the turn of the century and left politics to a younger, more radical generation around the time of World War II or shortly thereafter. That is when we leave them. From the 1940s, Egyptian political culture shows important shifts, as class tensions and religious-secular divides came to the foreground. The politics of the new generation, and the nationalist images created by them, deserve their own study.[40]

While this book is neatly divided into two sections, with part 1 exploring images of the Egyptian nation and part 2 examining the politics of women nationalists, the relationship between gendered images and political activists proves complex. Female actors figure in the first half of the book, which gives background to women's nationalist activities prior to 1919 and shows how women helped to construct discourses and symbols. Symbols and discourses spill over into the second half of the book, where the women of March 1919 became symbols of the revolution, Safiyya Zaghlul emerged as a national icon, women activists deployed a maternal rhetoric, and Labiba Ahmad promoted images of the "new Islamist woman." Cultural images and political action became interwoven. Yet somehow the symbols endured and are better remembered than the political actors.

# Images of the Nation

PART I LOOKS AT IMAGES OF THE NATION against the backdrop of social transformations. The unraveling of elite Ottoman-Egyptian households in the nineteenth century helped to pave the way for the making of a national family. Nationalists debated the contours of the family and used metaphors of the nation as a family to promote a bourgeois family ideal and guide transformations already under way. At the same time, nationalists elevated the notion of family honor to a national plane in order to develop a rhetoric of national honor. Visual images were used to illustrate these notions and to mobilize the collective. In nationalist iconography, Egypt was almost invariably imagined and presented as a woman. Representations of Egypt as a woman emerged over the course of several decades, overcoming social obstacles and paralleling the unveiling of Egyptian women. Photography played a key role in disseminating images of nationalist leaders and women activists as well as the nation as a family and as a woman. Part I captures the role of women nationalists in inspiring, producing, and adapting nationalist metaphors and symbols.

CHAPTER ONE

# Slavery, Ethnicity, and Family

The origins of nations have been intensely debated by scholars. A consensus has emerged among most historians that nations are "constructed," "invented," or "imagined" in the modern period.[1] Yet they are not invented from thin air. Rather, nationalists are bound by the cultural materials at hand, the ethnicities on the ground, and socioeconomic circumstances. Some "ethnies" develop into nations, others are absorbed into a larger national project, and still others languish or disappear.[2] Gender analysis challenges some of the presumptions about the construction of nations and argues that gender is crucial in the production and reproduction of ethnic and national identities. The primary site of this production and reproduction is the family.

At the turn of the twentieth century, the "Woman Question"—a debate about gender roles in the family and society—preoccupied Egyptian nationalists. These same nationalists deployed an array of family metaphors to smooth over ethnic and other differences and build a sense of collective identity. This chapter looks for the roots of the turn-of-the-century debate on the "Woman Question" in social changes of the long nineteenth century, a century that began in Egypt with the French occupation (1798 to 1801) and ended at the outset of World War I (1914), when Egypt became a British protectorate.[3] It connects the transformations in elite households, particularly those caused by the end of harem slavery, with the making of the nation and nationalist discourses. The perceived crisis of the family at the turn of the century, it argues, must be seen in the context of changing Ottoman-Egyptian households, as well as an emerging bourgeoisie. Many of the female nationalists whom we shall later encounter were products of these multi-ethnic Ottoman-Egyptian households. Yet the Ottoman-Egyptian past and its ethnic diversity were effectively repressed from the collective memory and historical accounts.

Family and ethnicity played crucial roles in the making of the nation in multiple ways. Obviously, other factors proved critical in this process, including new economic opportunities (such as the prominence of cotton as a cash crop), the rise of rural notables, the secularization of law and education, the development of new professional classes, and the growth of a modern state apparatus that was increasingly autonomous from Istanbul. As these factors have been dealt with elsewhere at great length, they will not be pursued here.[4]

## THE TRANSFORMATION OF ELITE HOUSEHOLDS

One key to understanding the origins of the modern Egyptian nation lies in the structural changes of the elite. In nineteenth-century Egypt, the members of this elite were Turkish speakers who had polyglot slaves in their households. During the nineteenth century, the upper-class Ottoman-Egyptian household—one of the most important social formations—unraveled.[5] Elite households, which were smaller-scaled versions of the Ottoman sultan's household, were composed of a patriarch, his children, single or multiple wives and concubines, eunuchs, domestic slaves, and other retainers and relatives. A multi-ethnic unit, members of the household came from different parts of the Ottoman Empire or beyond—Central Asia or sub-Saharan Africa. A major factor contributing to the transformation of elite households was the demise of harem slavery. Although some Egyptian nationalists continued to defend African slavery (mostly of domestic laborers) until the end of the nineteenth century, the end of harem slavery (concubinage of Circassians, Georgians, and others) coincided with the emergence of nationalism. In short, foreign-born slave mothers could not be entrusted with raising good patriots.

At the beginning of the nineteenth century, the Albanian-born Mehmed Ali (Muhammad 'Ali) became recognized as the Ottoman governor (*vali*) of Egypt in the struggle that followed the French withdrawal from Egypt. He eventually won the right to bequeath the position to his sons. The local Ottoman elite over which he presided remained bound by their loyalty to his house, their commitment to serve in Egypt, and a sense of belonging to an imperial Ottoman tradition. Ottoman was not an ethnic but rather a cultural and supra-ethnic identity. Composed of multiple ethnicities—Albanians, Bosnians, Circassians, Ethiopians, Georgians, Greeks, Sudanese, Turks, and others—and coming from diverse Ottoman territories, this elite spoke Turkish—and thus were often identified as Turks rather than Ottomans—while the Egyptian population they ruled spoke Arabic. The Ottoman-Egyptian ruling elite numbered about ten thousand men and women, and its men monopolized political posts.[6]

A core component of the Ottoman-Egyptian elite, especially those who rose to high positions of power, were male military slaves (kul) purchased at a young age by powerful persons to be raised in their households, trained, and launched on careers in the army and the bureaucracy, who were eventually manumitted. In the late eighteenth century, Georgians were the dominant group; in the nineteenth century, Circassians from the Caucasus region became prominent. The former slaves took pride in their slave pasts, which were seen as providing them with social mobility. Their slave backgrounds bound them to one another, as well as to their former owners and their owners' households. In Egypt in the mid-nineteenth century, a government official could think of only two ministers who were not manumitted slaves and predicted that those two might not last long in their positions. Although he may have exaggerated, ex-slaves were clearly quite prominent in the political elite.[7]

The Ottoman elite reproduced itself through reliance on the institution of female harem slaves and a household structure patterned on that of the Ottoman sultan. Just as young boys were purchased and groomed for military or bureaucratic service in the capital or provinces, young Circassian and Georgian girls were purchased and groomed to serve as concubines or wives in the households of the Ottoman-Egyptian elite. Some were kidnapped and others were taken as prisoners in war; many Circassian girls were also sold by their parents, who were themselves often agricultural slaves, to improve their lot in life. While Circassians constituted only a minority of slaves imported into the Ottoman Empire (the majority of female slaves were African), they served as a linchpin in the elite social system. In purchasing Circassian concubines or receiving them as gifts, Circassian men in Egypt and elsewhere could keep their ethnic identity intact, and local Ottomans of other backgrounds could keep their distance from the native population. Sometimes these concubines or slave partners came from the household of Mehmed Ali or his sons, who in this way sought to cement bonds of loyalty. Ismail (r. 1863–79), for example, bound officers to the court by having them marry slaves from his harem. By the late 1870s, at least fifty officers had married Circassian and other slaves from the palace.[8]

The house of Mehmed Ali was also not averse to drawing on free Egyptian talent, and, in time, those Egyptians tapped patterned their households on that of the *vali* (and thus by extension the household of the Ottoman sultan in Istanbul). The Pasha, as he was known to many, incorporated Egyptians trained in languages and other skills into the bureaucracy as technocrats, and his son Said (r. 1854–63) allowed the sons of village officials to become army officers up to a certain rank. In addition, rural notables increasingly served in the provincial government. Rural notables had benefited from Mehmed Ali's policies, unlike the poorer peasants, who had suffered under his rule. They set up large joint households to enhance their economic and political status, and helped enact legislation in 1858 and 1869 to strengthen these households. That legislation gave the family head authority to manage the family's land and property jointly to avoid fragmentation.[9] These new rural notables often marked their entry into the Ottoman elite by purchasing Circassian slaves.

Consider Muhammad Sultan, the "King of Upper Egypt," who rose to prominence in mid-century as a provincial governor and crowned his achievements as president of the Chamber of Delegates established by Ismail in 1866. Serving the viceroys faithfully, he increased his holdings to over 13,000 feddans by 1882, becoming the largest landowner in the region around Minya.[10] His household included a wife, a Circassian concubine (Iqbal), several eunuchs, and Egyptian and Circassian companions for his children. In 1879, Iqbal bore a daughter, Huda, who became one of the leading female nationalists and the founder of the Egyptian Feminist Union in the interwar period. Huda (Sha'rawi) relates in her memoirs that her widowed grandmother had left the Caucasus with Iqbal and four other children at mid-century, part of the wave of Circassians pushed by Russian expansion and the contingencies of conflict to migrate to the Ottoman Empire in the 1850s and 1860s. Unable to support all the children in Istanbul, Huda's grandmother sent Iqbal to live with a relative in Egypt. When that relative's wife blocked the plan, Iqbal stayed in the home of the patron who had transported her; she later joined the household of Muhammad Sultan as a concubine.[11] References to Circassian slave mothers abound among the elite; but only fragments of their lives—like that of Iqbal's—are revealed in memoirs, court records, *waqf* (trust) documents, police registers, and biographical notes.[12] The female slave experience has generally been suppressed from the collective Egyptian memory along with the Ottoman past.[13]

In the course of the nineteenth century, the composition of the elite underwent a significant transformation as two paths converged. On one path, native Egyptians from the rural notability became upwardly mobile, increasing their landholdings and finding new opportunities for government employment, as Arabic joined French and Turkish as an official language from mid-century on. Egyptian notables and a growing corps of technocrats increasingly replaced those sent from Istanbul in the administration. When Turkish-speaking members of the governing elite left Egypt for Istanbul and elsewhere, they were not replaced by military slaves. On another path, the entrenchment of the Mehmed Ali dynasty enhanced the sense of Egypt's separateness from Istanbul and, along with other factors, generated greater local ties on the part of Ottoman-Egyptian officials. The latter set down roots and increasingly intermarried with notables and professionals, which in turn further anchored Ottoman-Egyptian identity. Ottoman-Egyptians who stayed put and upwardly mobile Egyptian notables no longer imported harem slaves or eunuchs to guard them. The two paths converged in part because the abolition of slavery cut off the supply of harem slaves and altered marriage patterns among the elite.[14]

The abolition of slavery in the Ottoman Empire occurred piecemeal over the second half of the nineteenth century. In the face of British pressure to eliminate all forms of slavery, Ottoman officials enacted a series of reforms, not all of which immediately took force or held. Edicts at mid-century in Istanbul and Cairo prohibited the trade in black slaves but not slavery itself, an important loophole. Demand remained high, particularly during the cotton boom in Egypt in the 1860s, and the decrees against slave trading were, on the whole, ineffective. Ottomans resisted tampering with harem slavery in particular, for it sustained the household structure. In general, reform of personal status law, especially that regarding women, lagged behind other spheres. This was in part intended to pacify conservative religious forces in the face of wide-ranging educational and legal reforms. In 1877, the British and Egyptian governments signed a Convention for the Suppression of the Slave Trade that delayed the prohibition of the trade in white slaves for seven more years. But harem slavery died out as the sources dried up: it had become almost impossible to procure young white girls after Circassian migrants had been settled in the Ottoman Empire for a few decades.[15] A central tool in cementing personal loyalty to the Mehmed Ali dynasty was eliminated, too. Although a much more limited pool of daughters could be used, the khedives had to come up with alternative strategies.

The Ottoman historian Dror Ze'evi has linked the abolition of slavery to the dissolution of elite identity and the formation of official nationalism in the center of the Ottoman Empire:

> Whether or not the *kul* involved in the process realized that they were cutting off the branch they were sitting on, this was the end result of the series of events. By abolishing slavery the core of the Ottoman elite abolished its own definition, its own terms of reference. . . . in fact the old elite retracted and made way for a new one. . . . the *kul* became a dinosaur, an obsolete remnant of a disappearing way of life.[16]

Ze'evi argues that the new elite that arose to supplant the old one in Istanbul sponsored state nationalism. In a similar process, the new Arabic-speaking elite that arose in Egypt in the second half of the nineteenth century challenged the old Turkish- and Circassian-speaking elite, as well as growing European dominance of Egyptian affairs, and sponsored an anti-imperialist nationalism.

In brief, the end of harem slavery helped "Egyptianize" the Ottoman-Egyptian elite, which increasingly intermarried with the local population. The new nation would not be built on households that included harem slaves from the Caucasus, retainers from Central Asia, concubines from Ethiopia, eunuchs from Africa, and patriarchs from Anatolia or the Balkans. The Circassian slaves and their descendants would be absorbed into the new elite, and the new nation would be constructed around bourgeois families—Muslim, Copt, and Jewish—grounded in Egyptian territory. The transition from empire to nation-state was reflected on the micro level as large, multi-ethnic elite households were reconstituted as models for the nation.

The end of slavery played a crucial part in the transformation of large Ottoman-Egyptian households and sexual relations within those households.[17] Other factors contributed to the process as well: these elite households had been the central loci of politics in Ottoman Egypt when the Ottoman state was decentralized.[18] Seeking to concentrate power in their dynasty, Mehmed Ali and his successors eliminated rival centers of power that posed a threat. The politics of Ottoman-Egyptian households gave way to a new political culture. Rural notables and their urban professional offspring would merge with the old Ottoman-Egyptian elite. The new elite would seek a share in governing the state and would subsequently lead the nationalist movement.

## "EGYPT FOR THE EGYPTIANS!"

The ʿUrabi movement of 1881–82 can be seen as the outcome of stresses created in the process of transformation in elite identity as Arabophone groups on the rise sought a share in power with the older dominant elite.[19] Ahmad ʿUrabi (1841–1911), the son of a village shaykh from the region of Zaqaziq, emerged as the leader of a group of Egyptian army officers. When cuts in the officer corps threatened Egyptian officers rather than their Ottoman-Egyptian counterparts, the Egyptian officers acted. ʿUrabi later explained:

> The practice in Egypt was to tend to discriminate by race. And so all the promotions, decorations and rewards went to those of the Circassian race, since they were from the Mamluks [slaves], the paid retainers of either the Khedivial family, or of the aristocracy who were in turn also Mamluks of the Khedivial family. After this faction came that of the Turks and others who were not Egyptians, along with those of mixed origins. Thereafter came those Egyptian by race.[20]

The army's challenge to the government started with military grievances but soon developed wider political ramifications. Discontent with European intervention and with Khedive Tawfiq (r. 1879–92), who had replaced Ismail at the behest of the foreign powers, crystallized around ʿUrabi and his circle. Rural notables led by Muhammad Sultan (Huda Shaʿrawi's father) called for a constitution that would give them a greater role in central government and would check the autocratic rule of the khedive. The rural notables and army officers thus found common cause, for the moment, under the slogan "Egypt for the Egyptians!"

ʿUrabi had little time to launch his reform program, which apparently included the suppression of domestic slavery. (His own wife was the daughter of Prince Ilhami's wet nurse, who was of slave origin, and she had grown up in Khedive Ismail's harem.)[21] In March 1882, Wilfred Blunt wrote to the British Anti-Slavery Society on behalf of the "National Party of Egypt" to explain their views: "I have received the most positive assurances from Arabi [ʿUrabi] Bey, the Minister of War, that he will cooperate loyally in this work, and he has authorized me to say that he will not rest until the stigma of slavery is entirely removed from the Egyptian community."[22] Blunt distinguished between the past promises of "the Turk" in Egypt, and the proposals of "the Egyptian." Yet whether ʿUrabi was sincere or could be effective is uncertain, for some of the most prominent ʿUrabists had a mixed record on slavery. For example, Mahmud Pasha al-Barudi (a prominent ally of ʿUrabi, a nationalist poet, and, at the time, prefect of the Cairo police) presided over a household in which a Circassian slave stated, in an appeal to the British consulate for a certificate of manumission, that Barudi's wife had had her tied up and beaten.[23]

When the British invaded Egypt in the summer of 1882 to put down the 'Urabi revolt, a number of Ottoman-Egyptian officials and wealthy rural notables joined Tawfiq in seeking British protection, including Muhammad Sultan. But the bulk of the population seemed to support 'Urabi's stand, and 'Urabi found "some of his most patriotic and powerful adherents" in Egyptian harems, according to his lawyer, A. M. Broadley. "The National cause, even in its earlier stages, was warmly espoused by the great majority of Egyptian ladies." One princess from the khedivial family reportedly told Broadley, "We saw in Arabi ['Urabi] a deliverer, and our enthusiasm for him knew no bounds."[24] The anti-Tawfiq sentiment within the khedivial family can be explained partially by rivalries and resentment regarding his succession. Observers would repeat the theme of strong "harem" support for the nationalists in the coming decades.

'Urabi rallied the population with appeals to *al-din wa al-'ird wa al-watan* (faith, honor, and homeland). He declared a *jihad* (holy war), but did not exclude Copts or Jews from the enterprise. "The Egyptian nation," 'Urabi later wrote, "for all its variety of religious affiliation, did indeed do its duty in defense of the homeland."[25] Indeed, one of the earliest Egyptian spokesmen of the nationalist movement was an Egyptian Jewish dramatist and journalist named Ya'qub Sanu'a, whose cartoons satirized the khedivial family.[26] Throughout the conflict, 'Urabi continued to affirm his loyalty to the Ottoman sultan, Abdul Hamid (r. 1876–1909). The latter, feeling besieged by nationalist movements in the Balkans and concerned by reports of nationalist activity in the Levant, was wary of outbreaks of nationalism of Arab or any other variety in the empire. He did not send troops to Egypt either to subdue 'Urabi or to help him, and the British speedily defeated the Egyptian army and occupied Egypt.[27]

The British occupation reinforced the territorial integrity of Egypt by effectively cutting the province off from the Ottoman center and transforming it into a "veiled protectorate" under the control of Sir Evelyn Baring, later Lord Cromer, British agent and consul general from 1883 to 1907.[28] The occupation accelerated the transformation in elite identity already under way, definitively suppressing slavery and further Egyptianizing the Ottoman-Egyptian elite. The British built up an infrastructure of roads and communication that linked the country for economic purposes, but it had political repercussions, because it tied villages to towns and towns to cities. The British thus unintentionally aided in the making of the Egyptian nation, the existence of which they were often at pains to deny. Indeed, in documents such as the census of 1897, they were keen to stress the ethnic and religious diversity of Egypt. The Egyptian elite, on the other hand, increasingly stressed the unity of the nation, mapping its ethnic-racial boundaries and determining the place of Sudanese, Bedouins, Syrians, and Copts, among others, within the national entity. Family metaphors were increasingly used to create bonds among the disparate parts of the nation.

## THE SUDAN, RACE, AND EMPIRE

At about the same time that the British occupied Egypt, the Egyptians lost their grip on the Sudan. Ottoman-Egyptian administration of the Sudan stemmed from the days of Mehmed Ali, whose conquest of the Sudan had ostensibly been in the name of the sultan, and who appointed military governors from among the Ottoman-Egyptian elite. Ismail had enlisted American and British officers to lead Egyptian troops in the expansion and administration of African territory under Egyptian control. As part of Egypt's "civilizing" role, Ismail consented to the prohibition of the slave trade in the Sudan, although the prohibition was often ineffective. In 1881, as the 'Urabi movement gained momentum in Egypt, a young religious leader in the Sudan known as the Mahdi, or "rightly guided one," rallied followers against Ottoman-Egyptian rule. Among the backers of the Mahdi (Muhammad Ahmad) were merchants and clerics who saw the attempt to eliminate the lucrative slave trade in the 1870s as an assault on Islamic law and their livelihoods, and who also opposed Ottoman-Egyptian taxation policies. By 1885, the Mahdi's forces had seized Khartoum, routed the remaining Egyptian troops, killed the ranking British officer, General C. G. Gordon, and established an independent Islamic state.[29]

Egyptian nationalists did not let go of the Sudan so easily. As Eve Troutt Powell convincingly demonstrates, the idea of the Sudan as part of Egypt had become embedded in the nationalist imagination. Herein lay a central paradox: Egyptian nationalists fought European imperialism at the same time that they sought to regain control of the Sudan and to hold on to their own empire. Powell shows how this battle was fought metaphorically over the bodies of female slaves. In August 1894, the occupation government intercepted six Sudanese women destined for

domestic slavery in the homes of four prominent pashas, one of whom—
the president of the Legislative Council—had earlier called for the dissolution of the Slave Trade Bureau. The military trial pitted the British
defenders of the slave women's right to freedom against the nationalists
and their assertion of the pashas' right to buy slaves as an act of "rescue." "Each side fought over these tired women in ragged clothing with
the same ideologies and slogans with which they fought over the Sudan
itself," Powell writes. The trial ended in the acquittal of two pashas, and
a brief sentence for the third (while a fourth was tried separately). The
British tried to close loopholes: a convention in 1895 and a special decree
in 1896 enacted stiffer penalties for buyers of slaves.[30] A key feature of
the elite Ottoman-Egyptian household—African domestic slaves—thus
became unattainable. Elite Egyptian households replaced them with servants, who were often of peasant background.

As slavery died a slow death within Egypt, British-led Egyptian forces
reconquered the Sudan in 1898. Egypt was now both colonized by the
British and a colonizer of the Sudan. Yet the British quickly sought to
erode Egyptian control of the Sudan, and in 1899, they established the
Anglo-Egyptian Condominium—a partnership founded on Egyptian
funds and British military commanders—to govern the Sudan. The link-
age of the Sudan and Egypt in a Nile Valley entity nonetheless remained
a tenet of Egyptian nationalists, who did not want to see their empire
dismembered. Nationalists used family metaphors to stress the bonds
of the Sudanese and Egyptians. Ahmad Lutfi al-Sayyid, ideologue of
Hizb al-Umma (Party of the Nation), founded in 1907, spoke, for example, of the Egyptians and Sudanese as "brothers, or as cousins, all from
one mother."[31]

The Sudan of nationalist rhetoric contrasted with that of nationalist representations, for the rhetoric emphasized male bonds, while the
representations showed female bodies. The Sudan in post–World War I
cartoons often appeared as a highly sexualized, nearly naked black
woman with exaggerated facial and sexual features. Egypt, on the other
hand, appeared as a light-skinned, modestly dressed, and veiled upper-
class woman of Ottoman-Egyptian descent.[32] Egyptians tried to incorporate the Sudanese, whether male or female, into the national family
as "minors," wards to be tamed and civilized. Within the Egyptian-
Sudanese "household," elite Egyptians played the patriarch and
Sudanese took the role of domestic slaves and servants. But the British
aborted the plan and encouraged the Sudanese to develop their own
nationalist aspirations.

## BEDOUINS, IDENTITY, AND LOYALTY

Mehmed Ali had seen the Arabic-speaking nomadic and semi-nomadic tribes of Egypt as troublesome and had aggressively sought to settle them. This policy included forced settlement, detribalization, and assimilation through co-opting shaykhs. Large tracks of land were registered in the names of shaykhs, who in effect transferred their loyalties from their tribes to the new class of wealthy landowners. Evidence of socioeconomic differentiation and new attachments came with the marriages of shaykhs outside of the tribe to rich peasants, townspeople, the ruling elite, and even in some cases to Circassian women. Once again, women were crucial in the maintenance, reproduction, and transformation of identity. As shaykhs became large landowners, the rest of the tribe seemingly disappeared into the settled population. The social historian Gabriel Baer considers the settling of tribes "one of the most radical changes in Egypt's social structure during the nineteenth century."[33]

That process was far from complete in 1882, and both the British and the 'Urabists sought the support of the Bedouins. At the critical moment, most of the tribes of Lower and Middle Egypt supported 'Urabi. A few, however, gave important aid to the British. Alexander Schölch argues that, for the most part, the Bedouins retained their separate identity, privileges, and tribal organization through 1882, and that they acted in their own interests rather than in the perceived interests of a "national" grouping.[34]

Under the British occupation, and with the strengthening of the state, renewed efforts were made to integrate the Bedouins into Egyptian society. They were counted separately, along with other groups, in the census of 1897, which listed over half a million semi-nomadic and nomadic Bedouins (a figure Schölch sees as highly inflated) in a population of over nine and a half million Ottoman subjects in Egypt.[35] Bedouin groupings that survived the century intact continued to practice tribal law until at least World War I, although the state did not usually recognize it.[36] Bedouins of the Sinai and Western deserts remained apart from Egyptian society, but others became more integrated over time and more engaged in the national movement. Among the founders of the Umma Party, a party of large landowners, one finds 'Abd al-Sattar Bey al-Basil, a tribal shaykh from the Fayyum. In keeping with marital trends discussed above, he had chosen an educated middle-class schoolteacher, Malak Hifni Nasif, as his (second) wife. Malak subsequently became distinguished as a writer under the penname "Bahithat al-Badiya" (Searcher in the Desert). After her death, Basil married one of the daughters of Labiba Ahmad.[37]

## SYRIANS AND NATIONALITY

Syrians played a critical role in the intellectual and political life of Egypt
from the 1870s on, pioneering the Egyptian press and serving in the government. Syrians launched some of the most important early newspapers, including the pro-French *al-Ahram* and the pro-British *al-Muqattam*.
They started the women's press as well, with journals such as *al-Fatah*,
*Anis al-Jalis*, and *Fatat al-Sharq*.[38] Yet Syrians and Egyptians did not
always see eye-to-eye on the issue of nationalism. Although language
was one of the cultural factors that differentiated Arabic-speaking Egyptians from Turkish-speaking Ottomans, it did not always tie Arabic speakers together. This was due to different spoken dialects and to factors such
as religion and sectarianism. Egyptian nationalists showed little interest
in the early Arab nationalism (or "Easternism") of Syrians who opposed
Ottoman rule, and in contrast they appealed to the Ottoman government for aid against the British occupation. Moreover, the Egyptian
nationalists showed outright hostility to some of the Syrians in their midst
who supported the British occupation. The conflict helped to sharpen
Egyptian territorial identity and the sense of separate nationality.

Egyptians resented Syrian competition for posts in the administration
and British officials' preference for them. Those officials reportedly told
Cromer in 1890 that they "cannot get on without a certain number of
Syrians; that the Syrians are much the most intelligent employes [*sic*] in
their offices; that the young Egyptians who are sent to them are so igno-
rant and incompetent as to be quite useless."[39] Egyptians argued that
each part of the Ottoman Empire, especially Egypt, had a nationality of
its own and sought to restrict government posts to those of Egyptian
nationality. Cromer conceded that from "an ethnological point of view"
the statement might be partially true; but he denied that such a thing as
an Egyptian nationality existed legally. Many of the Syrians who won
government posts were Christians, and Cromer characterized the conflict
as one pitting Muslim against Christian. Yet the unity of Egyptian Copts
and Muslims in calling for restrictions on Syrians in government employment belied this assessment. Eventually, certain residency requirements
were imposed on Syrians, who continued nonetheless to fill a high per-
centage of administrative posts.[40] In short, Syrians were not "brothers"
in "one family," or even cousins, but rather more like unwanted guests.

Egyptians complained loudly in the press about those Syrians who
took stands against the "nation." In speeches from 1896, Mustafa Kamil
(1874–1908), a young lawyer and nationalist leader, began to attack

the "intruding foreigners," which was code for Syrians.[41] The friction
between Syrians and Egyptians continued until World War I, after which
it subsided as Egyptians gained semi-independence. Syrian immigrants
and their children were either absorbed—like migrants from other
Ottoman provinces before them—or left the country. Labiba Hashim
(1882–1952) presents an interesting example. A Maronite from Beirut,
she migrated to Egypt at the turn of the century, founded *Fatat al-Sharq*
in Cairo in 1906, and took off for Damascus after the war to serve as
a school inspector in the short-lived Faysali Arab nationalist government. When that government collapsed, she traveled to South America,
launched a journal there, and then returned to Egypt to edit *Fatat al-
Sharq* until World War II.[42] Children of immigrants often assimilated
more quickly than their parents. Iskander Makariyus, a child of Greek
Orthodox Syrian immigrants, preferred Egyptian to Arab nationalism
and maintained an ardent Egyptian nationalist line in his *al-Lata'if al-
Musawwar*, founded in 1915.

Egyptian nationalist calls for more Arabic-language education in state
schools should not be confused with Arab nationalist sympathies at turn
of the century. Arabic was a component of Egyptian identity but not its
sole determinant. The elite had become increasingly Egyptianized and
rejected or absorbed other elements, whether Turkish-speaking Ottomans
or Arabic-speaking Syrians, on their own terms.

## COPTS AND PHARAONIC EGYPT

At the heart of Egyptian national identity lay a perception of common
descent, of shared lineage, of the relatedness of the community. But which
past would Egyptian nationalists draw from—pharaonic, Hellenic, Coptic, Arab, Mamluk, Ottoman—to craft that lineage and shape national
narratives? Copts claimed direct descent from the ancient Egyptians of
pharaonic times and stressed that they were the real Egyptians, not late-
comers like the Arab tribes who had conquered Egypt. Descent may have
been imagined, and the actual story quite muddled, but the sense of relatedness, of shared blood, had real power. Egyptian nationalists used various strategies to fuse the lines of Copts and Muslims and create a single
lineage of ancient pedigree.

Religious minorities in the Ottoman Empire had been treated as "pro-
tected peoples," a category of subjects who paid a special *jizya* tax and
faced certain restrictions. In the nineteenth century, they had their own
corporate structure as a *millet* (religious community) and collectively

enjoyed a degree of autonomy. Religious leaders ran communal affairs and administered the religious laws and courts that covered many aspects of life.[43] Anthony Smith has suggested that these millets were premodern ethnies that had the potential to become separate nations.[44] And quite a few Christian groups in the empire—from the Serbs and Greeks in the Balkans to the Maronites in Mount Lebanon—pushed for autonomy or independence. Yet not all chose this route. Although high concentrations of Copts existed in Upper Egypt (in areas such as Asyut, they formed a quarter of the population), and they made up 5 to 20 percent of the population in Egypt depending on who counted and when, they did not push for their own state. At the same time, the emerging Egyptian state sought to increase the rights, responsibilities, and ties of religious minorities to the state. At mid-century, new laws eliminated the *jizya* tax on non-Muslims and introduced compulsory army service, from which Copts had previously been exempt.[45]

The end of slavery did not shake up the internal structure of Coptic families in the same manner as that of Muslim households. In the nineteenth century, Asyut had been the gateway for slaves brought from the south. Some Copts had profited from the slave trade and had owned domestic slaves. But their religion did not permit them to practice concubinage, and they could easily switch from slaves to wage-earning servants for household labor. With Egypt's integration into the world market, some Copts, like Muslims, accumulated large landholdings and formed part of the rural notability. This group became increasingly secularized in the second half of the century. Coptic notables and professionals began vying with the religious hierarchy for leadership of the community and control of its institutions, and the elite were receptive to nationalist appeals. Coptic clerks also proved receptive, given their experience with the British occupation, which eroded the monopoly held by Copts for centuries on positions in the Egyptian financial administration.

Incorporating the Copts into the nation gave contemporary Egyptians a bridge back to the "golden age" of pharaonic times and an apparent physical link to ancient Egyptians. Mustafa Kamil could thus describe the nation at the turn of the century as "one family" descended from the ancient Egyptians.[46] This enlarged the body of material from which nationalists could draw their symbols, myths, and models. Some of the earliest representations of the Egyptian nation—as early as the 1880s— were of pharaonic women (see figure 1), and such images were very common in postwar cartoons.[47] "Egyptian women used to study science, speak from pulpits, and govern the empire when women in other countries were still in a state of slavery and misery," wrote Malaka Sa'd, the Coptic editor of *al-Jins al-Latif*, of women in this golden age.[48] Evidence of Egypt's glorious past was used to advance calls for women's progress together with national revival.

Relations between Copts and Muslims fluctuated. By 1907, competing nationalist visions had crystallized into two major political parties. A more secular version of nationalism gained currency among a group of large landowning provincial notables. Rather than immediate evacuation, this group called for a gradual path to independence and for cooperation with the British authorities so that reforms could be enacted and limits placed on the khedive's authority. Its leading ideologues were educated in law or similar subjects in Europe and adopted the model of secular nationalism current in the West. Their Umma Party attracted Coptic notables, who saw promise in its platform. Mustafa Kamil led a more religiously inflected movement, which galvanized students and others of the urban middle classes. He called for the immediate evacuation of the British, while simultaneously preaching loyalty to the Ottoman sultan/caliph. His Watani Party combined territorial affinity with religious identity, although he clearly emphasized the former.[49]

Shortly after launching the party, Mustafa Kamil died, and under his successor, Muhammad Farid (1868–1919), the party became more stridently pan-Islamic and anti-Coptic. In a heated atmosphere, a young Watani Party sympathizer assassinated the Coptic prime minister Butrus Ghali in 1910. Relations between the Muslim and Coptic communities reached a low point. The British subsequently muzzled the press and drove Farid and other leading Watanists into exile. Their policy was to suppress those they labeled "fanatic" nationalists, while encouraging the "moderates," the large landowners of the Umma Party who spoke a secular language they could understand.

The new elite wrestled with the ethnic boundaries of the nation—whether to include Sudanese, Bedouins, Syrians, and Copts—in a process of selection, integration, and homogenization common in nation-building. A discourse of the nation as a family emerged to smooth this process. The issue of whether to include or expel other minorities—Greeks, Armenians, and Jews—would await later resolution.

## DEBATING THE FAMILY CRISIS

Women and men debated a bundle of issues at the turn of the century touching on female education and work; seclusion and veiling; marriage

and divorce; and other similar topics. Collectively, these topics constituted what has often been called the "Woman Question." These debates
have been analyzed in the context of nationalism, feminism, and modernity, and have been linked directly to the British occupation. Leila
Ahmed, for example, sees the main protagonist, Qasim Amin, as "the
son of Cromer and colonialism," a vessel for colonialist rhetoric during the British occupation.[50] Lila Abu-Lughod argues that Amin's vision
of conjugal marriage, derived from the West, effectively subjected a
woman to her husband and children by undermining women's homosocial bonds.[51] And Clarissa Pollard suggests that the "Woman Question"
is not about women at all, but rather is linked to broader family politics. Men, as well as women, were domesticated through these debates
and taught proper roles.[52]

The "Woman Question" cannot be divorced from transformations in
Egyptian society across the long nineteenth century, in particular the
unraveling of elite Ottoman-Egyptian households and the rise of a new
middle class. The Egyptian "Woman Question" thus needs to be set in
the broader Ottoman context. And the debates in turn-of-the-century
Cairo should be seen in conjunction with those in Istanbul and elsewhere,
as well as being in part a product of the British occupation, "Western-
ization," and nationalist family politics. Reformers throughout the empire
criticized elite family structures in order to find solutions to a perceived
family crisis, in part precipitated by the abolition of harem slavery.[53]

Harem slavery was a defining feature of nineteenth-century elite
Ottoman-Egyptian households. Its abolition helped speed the end of the
harem system and threw the entire household structure into disarray.
Concubines and freeborn women of the Ottoman-Egyptian elite may
have had different origins, but they had lived similar lives, secluded within
the harem, served by domestic slaves, and guarded by eunuchs. After the
abolition of harem slavery, the harem system slowly and sometimes
painfully disintegrated. Patterns of socialization and social roles were
reworked in the process. What would an elite household now look like?
What roles would different members play within the family? Who would
be pressed into service from the outside?

Female and male intellectuals worked out their answers in the press
from the 1880s and in the women's press from the 1890s on. Syrian
Christian women editors opened the pages of their monthlies to a range
of writers. Egyptian Copts and Muslims soon began their own Arabic
journals, with such titles as *al-Jins al-Latif* (The Gentle Sex, 1908), *Tarqiyat al-Mar'a* (Woman's Progress, 1908), and *Fatat al-Nil* (Daughter

of the Nile, 1913). In spite of their diverse ethnic and religious backgrounds, or perhaps because of them, these writers evolved a common format and focused mostly on domesticity. They pushed a bourgeois family ideal: a conjugal marriage based on love, a mother dedicated to raising her children, a wife frugally managing her household, and an attentive father. Female intellectuals called for girls' education, which stood at the center of the "women's awakening" in Egypt, yet they differed on the degree to which they endorsed veiling and seclusion. They discussed the management of the servants who replaced domestic slaves within the household and suggested ways to confine their roles in the new family structure.[54]

The debate became especially vocal at the turn of the century with the publication of two books by Qasim Amin (1863–1908): *Tahrir al-Mar'a* (The Emancipation of Woman, 1899) and *al-Mar'a al-Jadida* (The New Woman, 1900). Amin stepped right out of the old Ottoman-Egyptian elite. His father, Muhammad Bey Amin Khan, had been an Ottoman governor in Kurdistan and had subsequently received a land grant in Egypt. There he married into an elite family and became a high-ranking officer in Ismail's army, a member of the Turkish-speaking officer corps. Qasim Amin's secular education was capped by a law degree in France, and he returned to Egypt to take up a judicial post, joining the circle of reformers working with the British. His marriage to a daughter of the Turkish admiral Amin Tawfiq reaffirmed his status as a member of the Ottoman-Egyptian elite.[55] Yet the world he had been born into had been transformed. The Ottoman-Egyptian elite had solidified its local roots and become increasingly Egyptianized. At the same time, it looked to Europe, rather than Istanbul, for political models and social solutions. This class traveled to Europe, mixed with Westerners, and often profited from foreign trade ties. Amin found inspiration in Europe, and his bourgeois vision closely corresponded with that of the editors of Arabic women's journals. He pushed for a package of girls' education, conjugal marriage, unveiling, and an end to seclusion, arguing that educated women would help the nation develop, a theme articulated in the women's press.[56]

Rebuttals to Amin came from religious nationalists such as Mustafa Kamil, Fatima Rashid, and her husband Muhammad Farid Wajdi. While they endorsed women's education, they opposed some of Amin's other reforms, arguing that Islamic culture should provide models for women and the family. This group generally came from the middle classes, not the highest ones, where harem slavery had been most widely practiced, and continued to look to Istanbul for models and to Mecca for spiritual sustenance. Families that had been most touched by the end of harem slavery may ultimately have been more open to new models than sections of the middle class, which seem sometimes to have aspired to the older models.

The "Woman Question" illuminated a cultural split between the two nationalist camps, a split that became clearer with the emergence of the Watani and Umma parties. Gender thus became the fault line along which cultural adjustments were worked out in Egyptian nationalism. Religious and secularly-oriented nationalists used the "Woman Question" as the field upon which they pitched their battles over the cultural content of Egyptian nationalism.

One of the most contentious aspects of the "Woman Question" was marriage: Should families arrange marriages? Should the couple be allowed to meet beforehand? Should romantic love have any role in the relationship?[57] Safiyya Fahmi (1876–1946), daughter of the Ottoman-Egyptian politician Mustafa Fahmi (who had a long record of cabinet appointments before and after the British occupation), was married to Sa'd Zaghlul, an ambitious lawyer about twenty years her senior, at the age of eighteen. Labiba Ahmad (1870s–1951) was married to another ambitious lawyer, 'Uthman Murtada. Huda Sultan was married to her cousin and guardian, 'Ali Sha'rawi, at the age of thirteen after her father had died to keep the family lands intact. These female notables played prominent roles in the nationalist movement. Their arranged marriages in the 1890s followed established patterns of forming political alliances between households (a role previously played by slave women as well) or consolidating property within families.

Attitudes toward arranged marriages shifted in some circles as the couple became the center of the family in the rhetoric of the new cult of domesticity. One familial dispute taken to trial sparked a national debate. In 1904, Safiyya al-Sadat, the youngest daughter of Shaykh 'Abd al-Khaliq al-Sadat (a popularly revered leader of the descendants of the Prophet), challenged convention and against her father's wishes married Shaykh 'Ali Yusuf, the editor of al-Mu'ayyad, an anti-British newspaper, founded in 1889, that supported palace positions and received backing from 'Abbas Hilmi II. Shaykh 'Ali Yusuf came from a humble background but had risen to national prominence, becoming a member of the General Assembly. Having amassed wealth, he sought a new marriage to a woman from a notable household, and Safiyya had caught his attention. Her father agreed to the match but postponed the wedding for years. Safiyya then took matters into her own hands and agreed to go ahead with the ceremony in the home of a relative; she claimed that she was of age and able to give her own consent to the union. Upon learning of their marriage contract, however, al-Sadat went to a religious court to have the marriage annulled on the grounds that 'Ali Yusuf had deluded her into marriage and that he was of inferior social standing to a family descended from the Prophet. The court ruled in favor of al-Sadat and annulled the marriage. Safiyya returned home only after a secret agreement had been worked out that she could marry 'Ali Yusuf in her father's presence after some time had elapsed.[58]

The court case became a national drama, drawing heavy coverage in the press and sparking heated exchanges among nationalists. Lines were drawn on ideological and political grounds. Conservatives generally sided with al-Sadat and his right to determine his daughter's future. Reformers favored a woman's right to have some say in her marriage and greater social mobility for women. The controversy led to a major rift between Mustafa Kamil, who supported al-Sadat and attacked his rival 'Ali Yusuf in the pages of *al-Liwa'*, and the khedive, who intervened in support of his propagandist.[59] The case touched core cultural issues, challenging social hierarchies and patriarchal authority. The Egyptian nation showed cracks and fissures, which nationalists tried to mend. The road from ethnie to nation was a rocky one involving the renegotiation of power relations and fundamental social structures. The scandal was as much about "a couple's right to choose" as about marrying across class and caste lines.

New conceptions of marriage coincided with attacks on gender segregation. The maintenance of separate spaces (the harem) and special dress (the veil) for women had been an important feature of Ottoman-Egyptian households. Architectural styles and clothing fashions began to change; many elite women adopted Western dress, which they concealed with long cloaks when they went outdoors. The face veil remained one of the last vestiges and main markers of the old Ottoman order, and it increasingly became a symbol of cultural contention. In response to foreign critiques and attacks by Egyptian reformers, religious nationalists defended the veil. "This veil is not a disease that holds us back. Rather, it is the cause of our happiness," wrote Fatima Rashid in 1908. "And we shall guard it carefully and do all that concerns us from behind this beloved veil, which is our symbol and the symbol of our Muslim grandmothers."[60]

The face veil worn by the Egyptian elite in the early twentieth century was a white one that had originated in Istanbul. (Egyptian peasants had their own style of veiling: they pulled a head scarf across the face when the situation warranted.) A trend toward unveiling among the elite had begun: minority women stopped veiling, younger girls never started, and veils became lighter over time. Religious nationalists continued to support veiling as a sign of modesty and moral virtue, as women became markers of cultural purity. The cover of the journal al-'Afaf (Modesty), founded in 1910, had initially carried the picture of an Egyptian peasant woman with an transparent head scarf drawn across her face; but to reaffirm its position, the editor subsequently blotted out the woman's facial features below her eyes.[61] The more secularly oriented nationalists, on the other hand, adopted the veil as a cultural symbol with a markedly different meaning, as a sign of backwardness. "Women are not the only ones who are veiled in Egypt," asserted 'Abd al-Hamid Hamdi, the editor of the newspaper al-Sufur (Unveiling), founded in 1915. "We are a veiled nation."[62] The veil became a metaphor for both backwardness and virtue as women came to symbolize the nation, as we shall see in chapter 3.[63]

## "MOTHERS OF THE NATION"

Hoping to fuse ethnies and overcome divisions, male and female nationalists adopted a variety of kinship idioms. As men became "sons" and "brothers," women became "Mothers of the Nation." This identified women as the bearers and rearers of its future citizens. Female teachers, journalists, and activists produced and disseminated this rhetoric in schools, publications, and associations. Those who emphasized the role of women as "Mothers of the Nation" argued that the nation would only advance with girls' education and women's progress. Only educated mothers would imbue their sons with love for the nation. "It is upon you, tenderhearted mother, to instill into your son respect for his beloved nation, which has no dignity without him. The glory of this nation and its misery are in your hands," wrote Fatima Rashid in 1908 in an article on "Nationalism and Woman" in her journal Tarqiyat al-Mar'a.[64] Writers occasionally pointed to the assumed etymological links between umm (mother) and umma (community, nation) and stressed their special connection.[65]

Depicting women, particularly elite women, as "Mothers of the Nation" gave them a maternal authority to engage more openly in society and politics, and they returned repeatedly to that source of authority as well as to a moral authority.[66] In letters to the British and circulars to the nation, activists often presented themselves as "Mothers of the Nation." Stressing their commonalities as mothers (or mothers-to-be) helped them to forge alliances across religious and ethnic lines. The language transcended class, while simultaneously reinforcing class hierarchies with its maternalism.

Elite women's political culture from the turn of the century on developed in settings such as schools, salons, and associations, or in the pages of the press, rather than in the street, as it would in 1919. Whereas women in elite Ottoman-Egyptian households had been educated in harem "in-house" schools, girls from well-to-do homes now went to new state and private schools, and nationalist rhetoric was used to justify the transition. Girls' schools became sites of plays, ceremonies, and speeches that often had nationalist content. And schoolgirls became one of the earliest female groups to stage public protests. After the British declared martial law in November 1914, for example, many girls in the government secondary schools carried black rosettes as a sign of protest, mirroring the black ties worn by male students.[67]

Graduates and more mature women formed a variety of associations, which became important springboards to political action. These associations ranged from intellectual societies to social welfare organizations, and recruited membership and leadership from the middle and upper strata of society. Many elite women chose to contribute to the national endeavor by founding or funding philanthropic works. This was especially so in times of crisis. For example, during the Balkan Wars in 1911–12, a "Muslim Egyptian Ottoman woman" urged others to donate funds to the Ottoman war effort.[68] Social welfare associations served to incorporate older women who were past school age into the nationalist movement and politicized them by drawing them into "national service." Associations linked women in elite households in a common cause.

The Watani Party established a tradition of allowing women to participate in its meetings from its inception. Fikriyya Husni, a teacher who later played a prominent role in the revolution of 1919, recalled attending meetings of the party as a young girl with her father.[69] Muhammad Farid's daughter, who corresponded with him in his exile and urged him to return home to face a trial (and likely imprisonment), noted that students at the Saniyya girls' school strongly supported the party. She later suggested that a women's auxiliary to the Watani Party had existed before the war.[70] Labiba Ahmad, the daughter of a Cairene doctor and wife of a pasha, supported the Watani Party and was known for her speeches and activism. The Umma Party had its own female adherents, including Malak Hifni Nasif, who spoke in the party hall to a large female audience.[71]

Activities in schools and associations spilled over into the press, and vice versa, as the press became an instrument for socializing and politicizing readers. Female intellectuals acted as publicists for nationalist ideas in the women's press and elsewhere. They reported on the new activities and debated national reforms in social and cultural spheres. In essays in the pages of publications, women discussed nationalist issues such as the language of instruction in the new schools, the nationality of teachers, and the dangers of marrying foreign (in this case European) women.[72] Marrying within the group, the national family, remained a concern of Egyptian nationalists.

At the outset of World War I, British observers noted a "sub-current of hostility" to the change in regime (the replacement of Khedive 'Abbas Hilmi II with Sultan Fu'ad) that was "especially powerful in the 'Hareems.' "[73] Elite women's prewar activities, legitimized by maternal rhetoric, set the stage for the visible role they would play in the revolution of 1919. Then the "Mothers of the Nation" would march.

Over the long nineteenth century, the elite in Egypt underwent a metamorphosis, from Ottoman-Egyptian to Egyptian. Harem slavery, and the purchase of Circassians in particular, had been crucial in maintaining elite identity for Ottoman-Egyptians, or in demonstrating it for ambitious Egyptians replicating the household structure of the khedivial courts. The abolition of slavery and marrying locally sped the transformation of the ethnic composition of the elite. This meant both that more Egyptians had climbed into the elite and that Ottomans were becoming more assimilated into the Egyptian population. Their Egyptian-born descendants became Arabic speakers, and, although they may personally have been proud of their ancestry, they publicly renounced the Ottoman past.[74]

The nationalist movement arose in part in reaction to ethnic tensions created in the transition, as Arabic speakers pushed for promotions in the army and more power in the central government. While the 'Urabi movement itself was aborted, the underlying transformation of the elite was completed in the following decades. At the end of the long nineteenth century, the Egyptian nationalist elite was made up of vestiges of the old Ottoman-Egyptian order and a strong rural notability.[75] The elite, male and female, led the nationalist movement and mapped the boundaries of the Egyptian nation. They included Bedouins, Copts, and some Syrians in the nation and attempted to include Sudanese. Sovereignty over the Sudan, a onetime source of domestic slaves, remained a tenet of Egyptian nationalists, but the British edged the Egyptians out, and Sudanese were ultimately excluded from the Egyptian nation.

Nationalists juxtaposed a family rhetoric of the nation with debates about the family. These debates grew out of transitions elite households had undergone in the long nineteenth century and marked the emergence of a new bourgeoisie. The "Woman Question" became a front line in the struggle among Egyptians to define and defend a national culture. Nationalists deployed family metaphors to accomplish the work of binding the nation together and assigning roles. Muslims and Christians could not literally join in one family, but they could do so figuratively. Here the familial metaphors produced by male and female nationalists helped the two communities—and other minorities—to combine lineages. This gave Egyptians a myth of continuity from antiquity to the present. Female activists became "Mothers of the Nation," with a special nurturing and protective mission.

CHAPTER TWO

# Constructing Egyptian Honor

All nations, it seems, have a national honor to defend. Yet just as nations are not givens, but rather communities built around ethnic, economic, linguistic, religious, and other ties, so too national honor must be seen as a modern construct and a crucial element in the making of collective memory. Nationalists worked at promoting a sense of national honor using the cultural materials and social relations at hand. The concept thus had distinct resonances and a broad range of meanings depending on the region and period. Knowing more about national honor and the notions upon which it is based should help us to understand the phenomenon of nationalism and the bonds of nations better.[1]

National honor developed in Egypt against the backdrop of imperial intervention and occupation, and was used as a mobilizing strategy to resist foreign control. Nationalists elevated the concept of family honor, which was based on female purity, to a national plane, and honor became a larger communal affair. Indeed, the formulation worked in reverse as well. The nation had an honor to defend, and those who shared honor made up the nation. National honor made sense, it worked, because Egyptians were imagined as a family, and nationalist rhetoric constantly reinforced this notion of the collective. At the same time, as we shall see in chapter 4, Egypt was represented as a woman whose honor had to be defended.

Nationalists tapped into the regional code of family honor, appropriated it, and redirected the passion behind it for their own purposes. This chapter explores how nationalists interpreted and remembered various events through the prism of honor and its opposites, humiliation and shame. Over time, national honor became an important bedrock of collective memory. Nationalists used classical and colloquial language and multiple forms of oral and other media—speeches, proclamations, poems, plays, songs, and so on—to solidify and spread a notion of national honor. Female nationalists participated in the production of this rhetoric at the same time that they strove to cleanse it of its sexual connotations.

FAMILY HONOR

Anthropologists have pioneered the study of honor in the Mediterranean. They have noted that honor can mean many things, and the confusion is multiplied when foreign words with varying shades of meaning are reduced in English translation to the one word "honor."[2] Moreover, words change over time, mean different things in different contexts, and vary from colloquial to literary usage. In Arabic, *'ird* (honor, good repute, dignity), *sharaf* (high rank, nobility, distinction, eminence, dignity, honor, glory), and *karama* (nobility, generosity, honor, respect) are the words most frequently used to express the concept.[3] Yet the words have different connotations: *karama* implies nobility and generosity; *sharaf* suggests rank and social prestige, can be augmented or diminished, and should be defended by men; *'ird*, can only be lost or redeemed and is mostly connected with a woman's body.[4]

Honor in the Arab world was a collective affair. The entire family's honor—and in this context, "family" means those related by blood through the male line—resided in the conduct of its women. A girl's hymen had to be intact so that on the night of her wedding, her husband, a woman from her tribe, or a village midwife could perforate it and give proof to the community of the girl's virginity. Premarital relations leading to a loss of virginity or extramarital affairs and other infringements of the modesty of a girl or woman carried a heavy price. Immodest actions dishonored the family, metaphorically tainting the family blood, which could only be "cleansed" or redeemed by loss of life. The spilling of blood washed away the shame or dishonor. According to the code of honor, an agnatic blood relative of the woman—her father, brother, father's brother, or his son (who might also be her husband in a region where cousins on the paternal side frequently married)—should kill her to redeem his honor. Yet honor crimes—the killing of the girl—could be avoided through quickly marrying off a girl, hiding her, or suppressing the evidence. What was not publicly acknowledged need not be acted upon.[5]

Honor codes everywhere seemed to place value in women's bodies and female virtue. Yet significant differences in honor practices emerged, with some cultures emphasizing protecting women and others focused on policing women. In Northern Europe, men fought one another over insults to honor, putting their own lives at risk. In the Mediterranean and Middle East, on the other hand, women who had dishonored male relations were the targets of male violence.[6] Within the Middle East, different males (husbands or agnatic relatives) were designated to police and punish women. Differences in honor practices gave rise to variations in discourses of national honor.

Our picture of honor practices in nineteenth-century Egypt remains sketchy. From the time of Mehmed Ali, the emerging Ottoman-Egyptian state sought greater control over criminal justice and issued new penal codes. This was part of a reform strategy to codify law, centralize power, and institute broad social controls. This meant that the state increasingly intervened in the family to prosecute crimes related to issues of honor (such as rape and adultery) that had previously been resolved through Islamic courts or according to tribal-customary law. The Egyptian Penal Code of 1875 further removed criminal matters from the Islamic courts, and the new penal code based on French-derived law adopted in 1883 completed the process of secularizing criminal law.[7] When nationalists from the 1880s spoke of honor, they evoked a concept imbedded in customary law and practice, which the state increasingly sought to control. Through its interventions, the state tried to replace the father or brother as the guardian of the family, freeing him, as it were, to protect the nation. Family honor thus underwent transformations in this period, as the family came under increasing state control. One major shift was the appropriation of the concept of honor by the nationalists.

## INVASION AND OCCUPATION: HONOR AND HUMILIATION

When Khedive Tawfiq issued a proclamation in July 1882 dismissing 'Urabi as minister of war, 'Urabi answered with his own proclamation to the Egyptian people. He accused the khedive, after the latter had called for British help, of betraying his country and his people to the enemy. 'Urabi asserted that the people were not ready to surrender to the British without a fight, and that it was the duty of the Egyptian army to fight steadfastly for "faith, honour, and the homeland" (*al-din wa al-'ird wa al-watan*).[8] Balancing religious and territorial loyalties, 'Urabi used honor to mobilize his compatriots. He later claimed that: "The

Egyptian nation, for all its variety of religious affiliation, did indeed do its duty in defense of the homeland. The people offered themselves and their sons, volunteering willingly, and did spend their wealth for the sake of honor [sharaf] and the nation [al-watan]."[9] 'Urabists linked honor to watan, which is the masculine noun for nation, rather than to umma, the feminine noun.[10] For example, 'Abd Allah al-Nadim, one of 'Urabi's propagandists, called a play that he subsequently wrote and staged at a boys' school al-Watan.[11]

When Mustafa Kamil delivered the speech announcing the formation of the Watani Party on October 22, 1907, he made multiple references to honor. Yet as this was now a country under occupation, he also referred to honor's opposites: humiliation, insult, and shame. Mustafa Kamil began his remarks professing his love for the nation—"Can an Egyptian ever be over-ardent in his love of his country?"[12]—but he quickly shifted from romantic images of the nation as the beloved to images of the nation as receptacle of honor. "Traitors dare to state publicly and shamelessly that they have accepted the Occupation as a domination and the British as masters. They have the audacity to attack the patriots who demand the restitution of the honor and dignity of Egypt."[13] It was no longer a matter of steadfastly defending Egypt's honor; Egypt's honor had to be restored. Those who would restore it were the real patriots and rightful leaders. Kamil appealed to British promises and honor as well as to Egyptian aspirations.[14]

Mustafa Kamil elaborated the insults and injustices Egyptians had endured under occupation. "They have atrociously insulted us and hurled false accusations against us. One of their leading politicians, Lord Cromer, has found it compatible with his politeness and his experience not to leave Egypt without insulting its inhabitants."[15] But the Dinshaway incident stood out as the greatest of all injustices. In June 1906, British army officers en route from Cairo to Alexandria accidentally shot and wounded the wife of the local prayer leader in the village of Dinshaway near Tanta while pigeon-shooting. This caused a struggle between villagers and officers, with casualties on both sides. One soldier died on the march back to camp as the result of head wounds or sunstroke, and soldiers returning to the scene killed a bystander. The British reaction was swift and severe: after a hastily held trial at which three British officials sat, the court sentenced four villagers to hang, many to imprisonment with hard labor, and others to public flogging.[16] "Does not Dinshaway alone suffice to prove for all time that the English have mercilessly inflicted on the Egyptians a humiliation that will never be forgotten," asked Mustafa

Kamil, "a humiliation concerning which there can be no two opinions among impartial men?"[17]

Poets and balladeers expressed Egyptians' outrage over Dinshaway. A colloquial narrative ballad conveyed the rural villagers' version of the story:

> The problem started with a woman—an Arab—in the barn.
> One of the English loaded his gun and fired.
> In order to shoot pigeons, they let fly upon the hill,
> And so he burnt the woman, also her barn and her father's house.
> Up came her son and said, "Such deeds bring shame ['ar] upon me.
> Shall I not take revenge, by the claims upon us of the Prophet and of this
>     Lord of ours?" . . .
> Those who were hanged have died, and from the lashes blood ran,
> Something that indeed brings tears to the people, the sons of the Fatherland
>     [awlad al-watan].[18]

The ballad told the tale in a form that often dealt with honor crimes, and it cast the incident in a familiar frame: the injury to the woman dishonored her family. Yet it extended that frame, showing that the incident touched the people, the "sons of the fatherland."

The poet Ibrahim Hafiz, an Umma Party sympathizer, published a poem in classical Arabic days after the executions at Dinshaway:

> Kill well if you withhold pardon. Was it punishment you sought or
>     revenge?[19]

Egyptian poets often produced works in the wake of events that inspired them or that had national repercussions. Like the ballads of the countryside, classical poems were frequently memorized and recited in cafes and homes and were an important medium for communicating social and political dissent. When possible, they were also published in the press. Hafiz followed with other poems that year, earning the title "the nationalist poet and publicist of Dinshaway in the world." These poems, according to one scholar, were "effective in widening and deepening the feeling of national humiliation which was brought to the surface by the Dinshaway incident."[20] The poet Ahmad Shawqi, who was associated with the khedive (and known as the "Prince of Poets," but called by his detractors the "Poet of Princes") published poems on Dinshaway some time after the event:

> A shame ['ar] and a curse the atrocities of Dinshaway washed by this [the
>     Khedive's] pure hand.[21]

Here, the poet also set the event in the honor-shame, 'ird-'ar, frame. Ballads and poems helped transform the Dinshaway incident into a crucial cornerstone of the collective national memory. Over time it became the subject of a novel, a censored play, and a film, all of which had their own specific contexts and audiences, and together served to shape the memory of the event as an insult to national honor.[22]

Balladeers and poets praised the nationalist leaders; at the same time, nationalist leaders spoke of the importance of the production of patriotic verse. In 1910, Muhammad Farid, Mustafa Kamil's successor, wrote an introduction to a collection of poems by 'Ali al-Ghayati, whose views often reflected those of the Watani Party. Farid praised rural poets who composed ballads about Dinshaway, and called for songs extolling patriotism rather than romantic love. Moreover, he suggested a need to redirect love from an unnamed beloved toward love of the nation.[23] Al-Ghayati had taken up the theme of love, sending "Greetings to the Nile" from a "passionate lover."[24] The Nile embodied Egypt for the patriotic poet. But elsewhere al-Ghayati, the "poet of the people," spoke of humiliation and vengeance: "Does the occupying power believe that we are a nation who, accepting peace, cannot show hostility? / Or does the oppressor believe that we bear humiliation and will not seek vengeance?"[25]

That the British also recognized the importance of poetry in resisting the occupation was clear: they had al-Ghayati's book confiscated; tried the poet, Farid, and Shaykh 'Abd al-'Aziz Jawish (who also wrote an introduction to the collection) for political crimes; and sentenced the three to prison terms, which were evaded through exile. Ballads and poetry were important disseminators of nationalist sentiment precisely because they operated on the emotive level.

## WAR AND REVOLT: THE RAPE OF THE NATION

British imperial troops used Egypt in World War I as a base for actions in the region and established a defense of the Suez Canal against a probable Ottoman attack. The British feared that Ottoman advances might spark an Egyptian uprising, and their fears were fanned by propaganda such as that carried by prisoners captured by one patrol. The letters confiscated called for assistance from the Ottoman Empire to "relieve us of these oppressors." The Egyptians tried to rally their "brethren in religion" by emphasizing the "submission of the faithful to the pride of the infidel" and the rape of the "women of the faithful."[26] The rapes here were meant to enrage Ottoman Muslim brothers for the insult to the community. Honor could be tied to the religious community as well as the territorial collective, or some combination thereof. Various movements appropriated the concept of family honor, all claiming to protect it.[27] Appeals to honor based on violations of women could be used to include as well as exclude religious and ethnic communities within the nation. Rumors circulated that "the English have taken all the Armenian women and girls and locked them up for the use of the soldiers." This was meant to win over Armenians to the national cause after attacks on Armenians by Muslims and was in the context of multiple reports of rapes by British soldiers.[28]

The rape of women in the midst of war or political turmoil has historically been seen as a by-product of war and chaos. Yet rape by an enemy had political as well as personal consequences. The dishonor to the woman and her family became a collective dishonor; her body became a metaphor for a communal or national disgrace. This is what occurred in the midst of the revolution of 1919 in Egypt. In March 1919, in the wake of the war and with the arrest of the leaders of the Wafd, protests against the British occupation spread from the capital to the provinces. Peasants cut railroad lines, attacked and killed British personnel traveling by train, and raided British munition stores. The military authorities used British soldiers who had been stationed in Egypt during the war to put down the revolt. Investigations were later held when the soldiers who reimposed order on several specific villages were accused of committing atrocities.

A couple of hours after midnight in the early morning of 25 March in the villages of Badrashin and al-'Aziziyya, which were just to the south of the capital, two teams of nearly one hundred Australian soldiers under British officers mounted a search for arms and munitions. Inhabitants reported that during the search, the soldiers set houses on fire, looted valuables, assaulted women, and killed three men and a woman. "The latter I heard was beaten to death because she refused to be defamed by British soldiers," an Egyptian sergeant major of the Badrashin police force reported to investigators taking statements a couple of days after the event. He continued, "the rest of the [Egyptian] policemen complained that their houses were searched and robbed while their women were assaulted and treated indecently." According to the mayor of Badrashin, the woman killed was 'Aliyya, wife of a blind shaykh. The subchief of guards from al-'Aziziyya said in his statement, "They ill-treated the women in an infamous manner and raped others. The people would conceal this fact in shame of permanent disgrace."[29]

A similar sequence of events occurred over the course of two days— 30 and 31 March—in the village of Shubak. British troops accompanying a construction train entered the village to disarm peasants after unarmed soldiers had been attacked, and the troops in turn wreaked havoc in the village. A military court of inquiry was assembled at Qasr al-Nil Barracks in Cairo in June and July to hear the charges, which included the murder of a shaykh and four notables. This time the female rape victims, or their surviving relatives, came to court to testify. The widow Umm al-Bint Sayyid Muhammad, mother of three, stated, "I heard the soldiers were coming so I locked the door. We slept all night in the house. Next morning after sunrise two soldiers came to my house. They broke the door open. One of them went upstairs and the other remained on the ground floor and violated me there. . . . The man in the tarboush [an Egyptian official] asked me if the soldiers had violated me and I was so ashamed to own to it that I denied it."[30] 'Aisha Bint Mit-walli stated, "One of the soldiers saw my head behind the bedding. . . . This soldier took me by the hair and pulled me to the floor. . . . The soldier lifted up my shirt. He slipped off his shorts and laid with me. I at once shouted and the brother of my husband came into the room to help me and another soldier shot him with a rifle."[31] Muhammad al-Kurdi testified, "The soldiers forced the door open and entered my house. They pointed rifles at me. My sister who is a virgin was standing by and a soldier came up to her and pushed her. He threw her on the ground. He then violated her. Another soldier who was close by also attempted to violate her. She escaped this soldier and ran away and this second soldier then shot her."[32]

The military court collected testimony surrounding the charges that seven women had been raped at Shubak. In its summation, the court noted, "It is unfortunate that Lieut. Norrington and all his platoon have been demobilized and gone to the U.K. and were therefore unable to give evidence to meet the charges." Nonetheless, the court dismissed the testimony of the villagers as "not worthy of belief" and essentially made up of lies.[33] The court accepted the argument of the advocate for the military authorities of "the inherent improbability that a soldier would commit such an offence while a number of his comrades was watching." He also expressed bewilderment at the delay in reporting the rapes, seeing it as part of a conspiracy to fabricate testimony.[34] The court did not consider that the women's initial denial of attacks was not surprising given the disgrace that raped women would have faced, and that they might have agreed to testify only when the scale of the attacks and numbers of victims turned out to be so large. Two discourses of honor—that of the colonizer and colonized—intersected through these trials. British military honor, which pitted officers against unruly soldiers, had been called into question.

The village rapes had an immediate impact on urban politics. When female teachers in Egyptian government girls' schools went out on strike in early April, the "rape of women" at Badrashin, al-'Aziziyya, Shubak, and other villages stood at the top of a long list of "atrocities committed recently by the English" that they had compiled.[35] In May, an Arabic circular from the students to "the Bridegroom" appeared, criticizing Sultan Fu'ad's decision to marry at this moment:

> At the time when the nation is making funerals under the whips of the executioner, amid her burning villages that are running with the blood of her children the martyrs, and at the time when the voices of the nation go up to heaven weeping for the smirched honour of her women . . . there, in the Bustan Palace—the house of ill repute—from that den arise the cheers and shouts of feasting in order to celebrate a Sultanic wedding by means of which (Foad) may indulge in honourable fornication, respect his religion, and exchanges illegal acts for legal.[36]

The rapes—and "[be]smirched honour"—had become a cause for general sorrow, contrasting with the celebration—and suspect honor—in the sultan's household. (Fu'ad's daughter by his first wife was rumored to have had an illicit relationship with a man who refused to marry her; the man's brother subsequently agreed to salvage the situation, for which he was generously rewarded.)[37]

An Arabic pamphlet that circulated that June in Cairo calling for a boycott of British commerce also evoked the village rapes:

> The anger has started in Showbak and El Azizia where women were roaming about going from place to place and trying to find shelter in the underground and underneath beds and they could not find a shelter. Whereas wolves (soldiers) rushing after them with the threat of their weapons, rifles, committed adultery [rape] with them, and they were crying for help but without avail. . . . The voice of Allah for those women who have been assaulted as well as the blood which has been poured.[38]

Another circular making the rounds that month, and signed by the central committee of al-Azhar, asked Egyptian women to boycott the goods "of those beasts who [have been] encouraged by our generous manner and have rewarded our generosity with bullets, the violation of our women and the burning of our villages."[39]

In late June, while the British military court in Egypt was still hearing testimony, Sa'd Zaghlul presented claims for Egyptian independence at the Paris Peace Conference and affixed affidavits concerning the events at Shubak and other villages as evidence of British misrule. Although the military court denied the allegations, the accounts of eyewitnesses and victims were subsequently circulated abroad and reprinted in the American press in August, to the chagrin of British officials.[40] Egyptian nationalists used the village incidents to mobilize public opinion. To this end, the rapes of score(s) of women in specific villages became the rape of Egyptian women—"our women"—in general, and the sorrow of individual families became the "weeping" of the collective for "the [be]smirched honour of her women." The rape of women in general could in a further transformation metaphorically become the "rape of the nation," which by 1919 was depicted as a woman.

The memory of the village rapes lived on well after the event. The daughter of the doctor of Fu'ad's bodyguards raised the matter of the violation of the women of Badrashin in a private conversation with a foreign woman with official connections three years later.[41] Over thirty years later, the novelist Naguib Mahfouz included an account of the incident in *Bayna al-Qasrayn* (Between the Two Palaces, 1956), the first novel of a trilogy depicting the life of a middle-class Cairene family from 1917 to 1944. (Mahfouz had spent four years researching background for the work, which was written in the 1940s).[42] The character Shaykh Mutawalli gives the news of what had occurred in the villages of al-'Aziziyya and Badrashin. Details of time, place, and numbers match the evidence in the contemporary British documents: "Two or three hours after midnight when the people were sleeping, a few hundred British soldiers armed to the teeth surrounded the two towns." In the homes of the village mayors, "they penetrated the women's quarters, where they plundered the jewelry and insulted the women. They dragged them outside by their hair, while the women wailed and called for help, but there was no one to help them." The soldiers then stormed the homes of village notables, where they "attacked the women in a most criminal fashion, after killing those who tried to defend themselves. They beat the men violently. Then they moved out of the towns, leaving nothing precious untouched and no honor ['ird] undefiled." Finally, "The soldiers formed a ring around the burning villages to wait for the wretched inhabitants, who rushed off in every direction. . . . Then they detained the women to strip them of their jewelry and divest them of their honor. Any woman who resisted was killed. Any husband, father, or brother who lifted a hand to protect them was gunned down."[43] Mahfouz's inclusion of an account of this episode suggests that the village rapes, like the earlier Dinshaway affair, had become embedded in the collective memory and were crucial in the construction of national honor.

SEMI-INDEPENDENCE: PROSTITUTION AND SHAME

The notion of national honor had taken root: novelists described it, poets composed verse about it, and dramatists produced historical plays that focused on a golden age—pharaonic or Islamic—and extolled the virtue of honor.[44] National honor continued to be anchored in ideas and practices surrounding family honor, which varied over time and by place. Yet rape under occupation proved only one threat to family-national honor. The proliferation of prostitution, legalized and regulated under the British occupation, and sometimes sustained by British soldiers, proved another. Both rape and prostitution brought dishonor to a woman's family; but in the case of prostitution, the woman was apparently a willing party, and she sometimes paid a high price in punishment.

The details of one of the most famous crimes of honor, in which a brother kills a sister who turned out of desperation to prostitution, have been preserved in the narrative ballad of Shafiqa and Mitwalli. The ballad existed in "countless versions," according to Pierre Cachia, who collected various samples. The incident upon which they are based supposedly took place in Upper Egypt in 1925.[45] After Mitwalli was drafted into the army, the story goes, he quickly rose through the ranks and began training recruits. One day a newly inducted soldier claimed that he had been with Mitwalli's sister in the prostitutes' quarter of Asyut. Mitwalli asked for a leave to return to Girga, his village, where he verified that his sister had left home. Shafiqa, who had been seduced by the son of the village mayor, had become a licensed prostitute in Asyut. Mitwalli found her there:

> He went for a bayonet he had brought with him from the Army.
> With his hand on the girl, he slit her throat, dragging her to extinction—the
>      [right] abode for her.
> He kept cutting off her flesh and throwing [it] from the balcony,
> Saying: "We have folded shame ['ar] away! No longer can the deviant
>      deride us. . . .
> Have meat for nothing, dogs of Asyut!"[46]

At his trial, Mitwalli spoke of the shame that he had had to uproot. According to the ballad, the judge pronounced a verdict of not guilty: "You have honoured Girga, and illumined protective men."[47]

The ballad celebrates Mitwalli and the honor he sought to defend, making of the story a classic crime of honor and cautionary social tale. Yet it was not an isolated incident. The interwar press carried multiple stories of prostitutes killed by relatives who said they had acted to restore family honor.[48] Officials trying these cases proved sympathetic to the relatives and gave them lightened sentences.

The Egyptian state continued to allow prostitutes to practice their trade so long as they were licensed. Yet the presence of licensed prostitutes not only offended the families from which they had come; it outraged groups that ranged across the political spectrum, from the Muslim Brotherhood to the Egyptian Feminist Union. These groups and others argued that the presence of legalized prostitution in Egypt dishonored the nation and made its abolition a priority.[49] But the campaign to abolish prostitution faced many obstacles. The British had issued detailed regulations for legalized prostitution in 1905, building their policy upon Ottoman-Egyptian precedents. It was difficult to overturn this policy, for under the Capitulations granted foreign powers by the Ottoman Empire and still in effect in interwar Egypt, brothel owners could claim foreign protection and avoid prosecution under Egyptian law. Little could be done to combat prostitution until the Montreux Agreement of 1937 phasing out the Capitulations had gone into full effect in 1949. State officials subsequently declared prostitution illegal.[50]

Rhetoric against prostitution filled the press in the interwar years.[51] Feminists began their crusade against prostitution in the 1920s, in tandem with Muslim leaders, and Islamists took up the call for its elimination in their platform in the 1930s. Motivated by the exploitation of women that prostitution represented, feminists spoke of the moral repercussions and health implications of the trade. An unnamed writer in the Cairo weekly *al-Hisan* in 1926 applauded the campaign against prostitution—"the selling of a woman's honor and dignity"—and called on parliament to act on this matter "to ennoble the nation and to purify the country of this disgrace."[52] Islamic activists such as Labiba Ahmad criticized the official sanctioning of prostitution, in a country in which Islam was the state religion, when Islamic law did not allow it. In the early 1920s, she had responded to tales about girls being drawn into prostitution in Egypt by opening an institute to teach poor girls skills. In the early 1930s, she repeatedly demanded an end to officially sanctioned prostitution.[53] The Muslim Brothers also called for stopping "clandestine and overt" prostitution.[54] A contributor to the Muslim Brothers' publication *al-Ikhwan al-Muslimun* reiterated, "For forty years the honor *[karama]* of Misr and her purity have been stained with the disgrace of the dishonor of legalized prostitution licensed by the Muslim Egyptian government."[55]

Combating legalized prostitution became a central mission for nationalists of different stripes in this period. The campaign had tactical advantages: feminists, who were themselves fearful of being labeled "prostitutes" for unveiling and mixing in society, could forge a broad alliance with religious representatives and take the moral high ground. Their campaign might disarm their critics: how could they be "prostitutes" if they were fighting prostitution? For Islamists, it was an important test of the commitment of individual politicians and parties to Islam. Yet it was clear that the hands of the government were tied by the Capitulations. The campaign against prostitution thus became an important front in the war for complete sovereignty. Islamists and paramilitary groups such as the Greenshirts moved the front into the prostitutes' quarters, staging demonstrations in favor of abolition.[56] In this war, the presence of licensed and unlicensed prostitutes—"dishonorable women"—became a national blemish which had to be removed.

A bone of contention between Egyptian nationalists and British officials in the interwar years, prostitution became a major source of stress during the two world wars. As the numbers of British troops stationed in Egypt multiplied, so too did the numbers of foreign and native prostitutes. During World War I, a rampage through a prostitutes' quarter in Cairo by Australian soldiers, who burned houses and damaged property, earned them infamy.[57] By World War II, most British forces had been relocated to the Suez Canal zone, but troops still frequented the major cities. Naguib Mahfouz captures the dilemma created by British soldiers soliciting Egyptian prostitutes in his *Zuqaq al-Midaqq* (Midaq Alley, 1947). In the novel, written and set in the early 1940s, Hamida, a girl with high material expectations, is seduced by an Egyptian pimp, who then establishes her as a prostitute. 'Abbas, the man to whom she had been engaged, who had gone off to work for the British to earn money for their marriage, finds her in a bar "sitting amidst a crowd of [English] soldiers. One stood behind her pouring wine into a glass in her hand, leaning towards her slightly as she turned her head towards him. Her legs were stretched on the lap of another soldier sitting opposite her and there were others in uniform crowding around her, drinking boisterously." The scene does not end well: after an enraged 'Abbas hurls a glass at Hamida, the soldiers fall on him and beat him to death.[58]

Seduction became a metaphor for British-Egyptian relations in cartoons during the interwar period as British officials and Egyptian politicians continued to negotiate Egypt's status. John Bull or the British High Commissioner tries to seduce Egypt, imagining that she can be had for a price. But Egypt is no courtesan and, in spite of the entreaties, she turns down Great Britain's offers.[59] Debates over prostitution—

real and metaphoric—proved central to the notion of national honor in this period.

## FEMALE IMAGES AND WOMEN ACTIVISTS

The nation was a collective, with a collective memory of humiliation and honor derived from notions of family honor. Notions of family and national honor varied over time and in different contexts and could be used in reference to internal and external cultural and political threats. Representing the nation as a woman helped to reinforce the concept of national honor, as we shall see in chapter 3. In cartoon imagery, a female Egypt sometimes speaks of national honor. In an image in *al-Lata'if al-Musawwara* in 1927, John Bull (Great Britain) asks the Egyptian nation (a pharaonic woman) if they have become friends. With arms crossed, she defiantly answers, "The matter hinges on my satisfaction, honor [*karama*], freedom, and independence."[60] In a *Ruz al-Yusuf* cartoon from 1929, another pharaonic woman speaks of her honor and rights.[61]

Women collectively also became a repository of national honor. For example, Mustafa Kamil's brother, 'Ali Fahmi, notes that the Egyptian woman had "demonstrated her nationalist affection . . . love for nation [*jins*], land, and national honor [*sharaf*]." The daughters of the nation were thus half its guardians and "the basis of its honor [*'irdihu wa-sharafihu*]."[62] He links, as do women activists, women's struggle in the nationalist movement with their struggle for women's progress, but he uses a different language and imagery than they do.

Female nationalists spoke and wrote of national honor, further disseminating the concept. Yet their writings contrast in some respects with those of male nationalists. While the former oscillated between the terms *karama*, *sharaf*, and *'ird*, the women writers and speakers chose terms that stressed dignity and social rank and shied away from the term *'ird*, which had sexual connotations. Thus, while cartoonists occasionally put the terms *karam* or *'ird* in abstract Egypt's mouth, or in the same frame, real women activists and intellectuals chose not to use the latter term.

Fatima Rashid was one of the first female intellectuals to take up the theme of women and the nation. In an article on "Nationalism and Woman" published in her *Tarqiyat al-Mar'a* in 1908, she argued that educated women in their capacity as mothers had a duty to spread nationalist sentiment. For "they have no honor [*karama*] without the honor of their nation," and the responsibility for spreading this sentiment to their sons was upon them.[63] Fatima was instrumental in carving out a role for women in the nationalist movement as "Mothers of the Nation" in the early 1900s.

Labiba Ahmad frequently wrote of *karamat Misr* (Egypt's honor) in the 1920s and 1930s. In an article objecting to the export of Egyptian dancers to Europe, she declared, "We all must be conscious of the meaning of national pride *[al-'izza al-qawmiyya]*, the meaning of the distinction *[sharaf]* of defending the honor of the nation *[karamat ummatihu]*, the meaning of having responsibility for protecting the glory of the homeland *[majd al-watan]*."[64] Just as the family had to protect their honor vis-à-vis other families, the nation had to defend its honor and uphold its reputation vis-à-vis other nations. Labiba discussed both Egyptians abroad and foreigners in Egypt. Multiple words with varying connotations were used for the collective—*qawm* (tribe, nation), *umma* (community, nation), *watan* (fatherland, homeland)—and each in turn was coupled with words that could be translated as honor.

This sort of language spanned the political spectrum. The secular feminist Munira Thabit subtitled a piece on the front page of her periodical *al-Amal* "The Nation Defends Its Freedom and Honor *[karama]*."[65] Huda Sha'rawi also used this language in penning petitions and letters to the British authorities. In one such letter, written in 1924, the group—in this case a boycott committee—was "defending our national honor *[karama]* by making these resolutions." Throughout the document, the metaphor of violation of honor appears.[66] Twenty years later, when a letter was sent under Huda's signature and that of other activists (among them Zaynab al-Ghazali and Fatima al-Yusuf), to protest British support for a corrupt cabinet, similar language appears: "It is very distressing that your Ambassador should take such action and interfere in our internal affairs, aiming not at the victory of the Egyptian people but at their defeat and the lowering of their nobility *[karama]*."[67]

Women nationalists used family metaphors, attacked prostitution, and discussed national honor, but they shied away from notions of national honor grounded in female sexuality and connected to their bodies. They sought to displace honor from the female body and protect women, whose lives were sometimes imperiled by the notion. This probably stemmed from both class positioning and gender sensitivities, and one wonders if a similar selective use of language occurred among women nationalists in other Arabic-speaking countries. On the other hand, male politicians, who had a social base that reached into the lower classes and out into the countryside, favored a concept of national honor (*'ird*) that had mass masculine appeal.

Films show the culmination of the elevation of family honor to a national plane. In the 1980s film *Shafiqa wa-Mitwalli*, directed by the female filmmaker Su'ad Hasan, the heroic soldier and disgraced prostitute of the 1920s were transplanted back to the 1860s. The cautionary social tale became a political critique of elites and imperialists. Mitwalli, conscripted into the army, witnesses the deprivations and deaths of Egyptians forced to dig the Suez Canal. Meanwhile, Shafiqa, left at home and nearly starving, succumbs to the advances of the mayor's son, who soon loses interest in her. Rather than descend into prostitution and poverty, she becomes the mistress of a bey and then a pasha, and in the process views the treachery of the Egyptian aristocracy and its cooperation with European imperialists. She clearly represents an "innocent Egypt" abused and then "prostituted" by the powerful and wealthy. Shafiqa in time becomes sickened by the corruption she has witnessed and returns to her village to await her fate at the hands of her brother. Mitwalli arrives and prepares "to redeem his honor" with his sword. Yet the film rescripts the tale's ending: at the last moment, Mitwalli hesitates and offers forgiveness. But reconciliation is not to be, for Shafiqa has seen too much and is shot from a carriage sent by the pasha to silence her. She dies in her brother's arms. The film suggests that a fallen woman can be redeemed through forgiveness. Rather than undermine the notion of honor, however, it turns the classic family honor tale into a saga of national honor.

From the 1880s on, nationalists began to elevate the concept of family honor to the national plane, using the rhetoric of honor to mobilize the population. In the following decades, they built on family metaphors and female images of the nation to strengthen a sense of national honor in the face of occupation and humiliation. Murder in the village of Dinshaway in 1907 became a national insult. The rape of tens of villagers in 1919 by British soldiers became the rape of "our women" and subsequently, the rape of the nation, a dishonor shared by the collective. The presence of hundreds of prostitutes became the prostitution of the nation and a symbol of its shame. Family honor and national honor had become inextricably linked and continued to have a dialectical relationship.

Family and national honor continued to be intertwined as honor defined the nation, setting its boundaries and marking its inclusions and exclusions. Different groups used the notion to solidify their own sense of community. In 1950, King Farouk's sister Fathiyya, who was living abroad, married a Copt without her brother's permission. The Muslim Brothers subsequently threatened to send assassins after the groom to avenge the king's honor, which was by extension theirs. With their offer, the Muslim Brothers by implication excluded Copts from the collective.[68]

The conflation of family honor and national honor, as well as religious honor, is obviously not unique to Egypt. We need to know more about the construction of national honor in other cases to make broad comparisons and to test what is specific to the Middle East, the Arab world, and Egypt. In Egypt, the underlying colonial conditions, political arrangements, and family relations generated a discourse built on shame as much as honor. The discourse of national honor helped to reify the notion of family honor and strengthened ideals of female virginity. Before the 1952 revolution, female intellectuals tried to transform the discourse by stressing a concept of honor associated with rank and dignity, rather than one tied to female sexuality. A subsequent strategy, seen in the film *Shafiqa wa-Mitwalli,* was to offer forgiveness in cases of family honor and to channel the rage that often accompanied it onto the political plane and into national honor. However, the celebration of national honor would make family honor that much more difficult to deconstruct.

# CHAPTER THREE

# Nationalist Iconography

A nation is an abstraction. That is, it has no material form. Yet ever since the rise of nationalism, the nation has been represented visually. The nation is thus an "imagined community" that is sometimes imagined in human form.[1] The purposes of this iconography are clear: images of the nation were meant to reaffirm the unity of the collective and give the concept of nationhood greater immediacy. In societies such as those of the Middle East, they were also meant to disseminate the idea of nationalism to broad segments of the population who remained illiterate. When the nation was personified, it appeared as either a male or female figure, with the latter predominating. The selection and subsequent attributes associated with the chosen figure give insight into a particular nationalist movement and its ideal of the nation.

Egypt (*Misr*) or the Egyptian nation (*al-umma al-Misriyya*)—both the territory and the collective—came over time and with few exceptions to be depicted as a woman.[2] Explanations of why this is so vary. A folkloric practice of thinking of the nation as a woman (Bahiyya) might have influenced artists, but the nationalists could have broken with this tradition. Both *Misr* and *umma* are feminine nouns, yet artists could have depicted *al-watan* (homeland), a masculine noun, instead. The idea of representing the nation as a woman, like the idea of nationalism itself, might have come from abroad. Derived from the European model in general or the French republican precedent (Marianne) in particular, it would be one more example of an almost universal practice.[3] Yet there were

important exceptions; some nations were rendered as male—England's
John Bull and the United States's Uncle Sam, for example—or had both
male and female icons.[4] But perhaps the question of why Egypt was
depicted as a woman is not so important as the process by which this
occurred, what sort of woman was chosen, and what these images ultimately tell us about race, class, and gender in Egypt.

Significant obstacles existed to representing the Egyptian nation as a
woman, most notably the fact that until the early 1920s, most elite
women did not expose their faces in public. This chapter considers the
context of creation of visual representations of the Egyptian nation, their
intended meanings, and their reception by Egyptian audiences. Egyptian
iconography was generated under diverse circumstances by a variety of
artists and others for multiple audiences. Often it was to memorialize
moments, movements, or particular men, and was tied to collective memory. The implicit argument is that nationalist iconography would have
reached a broad segment of the population, in part through photographic
reproductions, and operated on a visceral level.

## EARLY CARTOONS

Some of the earliest images of the Egyptian nation came from the pen of
Ya'qub Sanu'a, a nationalist educated in part in Italy and invariably influenced by the arts there. Sanu'a was a man of many talents. In the early
1870s, he wrote and produced plays, and he is credited with founding
native Egyptian theater. In 1877, he started a satirical weekly called *Abu
Naddara Zarqa'* (The Man with the Blue Glasses). Only fifteen issues of
the handwritten journal appeared before an angry Khedive Ismail expelled
Sanu'a from Egypt. Sanu'a then took up residence in Paris, where he continued to produce his journal under various titles for decades, adding
French to the colloquial Arabic.[5]

Sanu'a's journal circulated widely in its early days according to contemporary observers. Blanchard Jerrold wrote that the satire in the second
issue "was so thoroughly to the taste of the public, that the paper was sold
in immense quantities. It was in every barrack, in every Government-office.
In every town and village it was read with the liveliest delight." Jerrold
claimed that the journal subsequently "found its way into every village,
and was read universally." If they could not read, he explained, the *fellah*
"learned to listen with delight to the satire of the Abou Naddarah."[6] After
his exile, Sanu'a had the banned journal smuggled back into Egypt: copies
were hidden in the pages of art books and large journals or in the luggage

of Egyptian travelers (with one poor woman carrying the journal home in her bedding).[7] It is hard to know how many people read *Abu Naddara*. Circulation has been variously estimated, with 3,300 per issue being a plausible figure.[8] Because papers were passed from hand to hand and read aloud, scholars of the Arabic press suggest that circulation numbers ought to be multiplied for a more accurate accounting of actual distribution.[9] And to readers and listeners, we must add viewers, for Sanu'a introduced cartoons to the Egyptian public.[10]

Sanu'a himself often appeared in the cartoons, sometimes in the garb of a shaykh and always wearing glasses, the perennial observer. His cartoons incessantly attacked Khedive Ismail and his successors, as well as ministers and foreign officials. John Bull and representations of other European nations also made frequent appearances in the pages of *Abu Naddara*, where they were easily caricatured.[11] Sanu'a depicted the Egyptian nation in various guises. One series of cartoons showed Egypt as a cow (occasionally with the head of the Sphinx) being milked dry by ministers and by the European powers or sucked by foreigners.[12] Egypt also appeared as a donkey: Ismail sat astride the animal as his sons and associates beat it.[13] The satirist also occasionally used *ibn al-balad* (son of the village) characters to represent Egypt, or the quintessential Egyptian, and these were always male.

Sanu'a represented Egypt as a woman on a few occasions and at least twice as an ailing pharaonic queen. The first cartoon appeared in 1883. "Cholera: The Eleventh Plague of Egypt" shows a dying queen reclining on the ground, surrounded by male figures representing European powers. To the left of the queen, the viewer sees a destroyed Alexandria; to her right, the defeat of the Egyptian army at Tel al-Kabir at the hands of the British. After hearing what others have to say, England adds, "I first brought war. Today I bring you cholera."[14] The second cartoon, which appeared a year later, shows "The Killing of a Nation" (figure 1). Here Egypt sits in a chair on a stage with Prime Minister Nubar on one side and Lord Cromer, who is trying to force her to take a drug, on the other, with both grabbing her arms. On one side of the stage, Khedive Tawfiq digs her grave, and on the other, women mourn over the graves of their husbands and children. Figures representing Europe, the Ottoman Empire, and Balkan nations witness the scene from boxes in the theater. Egypt asks the sultan to save her from the "two doctor-assassins."[15]

In depicting the nation as a pharaonic queen, Sanu'a drew on Egypt's ancient heritage, unearthed in excavations, strengthening the foundation myth of the nationalists, who fought with the British for control over

Figure 1. "The Killing of a Nation": Sir Baring (Lord Cromer) forces Egypt to drink poison, while Nubar holds her arm and Khedive Tawfiq prepares her grave. *Abu Naddara* 8 (1884): 142.

that past and the actual antiquities. Sanu'a, who was Jewish, may have found pre-Islamic representations particularly appealing as symbols, as did Egyptian Copts, for presumably all Egyptians could identify with them. Sanu'a may also have chosen a pharaonic queen precisely because there were few female alternatives. He showed Egypt as a fully veiled woman with face covered in 1894: a woman representing Egypt stands next to women representing Russia and France, and confronts a female Britannia (figure 2).[16] But the contrasts are compelling and show the artistic and ideological limitations of depicting Egypt as a fully cloaked woman. Countries calling for national independence generally made claims to being modern, but a fully veiled woman did not convey modernity. Sanu'a himself was a man of liberal ideas who had criticized the situation of women in Egyptian society in his plays and attacked institutions such as polygamy. Yet until the debate on veiling had taken off, he could not easily use contemporary women as representations of Egypt, and he did not depict many women. The image of a veiled Egypt was not, in any case, repeated in the pages of *Abu Naddara*.[17]

Figure 2. A veiled Egypt, with Russia and France at her side, confronts England. *Abu Naddara* 18 (1894): 50.

The importance of visual matter in *Abu Naddara* should not be underestimated, given the low literacy rates of the day. But would viewers have easily understood the cartoons? A knowledge of Egyptian and European politics would seem important, and the captions in Egyptian dialect (and French) under the cartoons clarified meanings. But the cartoons could have been appreciated on a number of levels, for they caricatured familiar figures and drew on local humor. Verbal antecedents to the cartoon could be found in indigenous Egyptian humor: folktales (in particular the Goha repertoire), proverbs, *zajal*s (rhymed prose), and *nukta*s (verbal cartoons or jokes).[18] Still, one should not assume that illiterate Egyptians had a visual literacy and understood the signs and symbols used in cartoons. Reading pictures was a skill that had to be learned.[19]

Sanu'a's significance diminished with the emergence of Mustafa Kamil and a younger generation of nationalists with an Islamic tilt who worked from Egypt. These men eventually developed their own organs, such as Kamil's newspaper *al-Liwa'*, which did not initially favor the cartoon as political expression or carry photographs for that matter. With the odd exception, cartoons receded from the press until after World War I.[20] This may have been a matter of Mustafa Kamil's style, Islamic conventions, the absence of illustrators with a bent toward humor, a focus on a more literate audience, or British censorship. For other early images of

the nation, we must turn to other art forms. When we return to cartoons
later, we shall see that the advent of illustrated periodicals, which carried photographic spreads and are discussed in chapter 4, enhanced the
potential of cartoons to criticize politicians. By then, the latter had become
more easily recognized.

## PICTURES, PAINTINGS, AND POSTERS

Mustafa Kamil's initial strategy, like that of Sanu'a, had been to appeal
to the French to pressure the British to leave Egypt peacefully. When
Mustafa Kamil presented the president of the French Chamber of Deputies
with a petition in 1895 requesting French aid in evicting the British from
Egypt, he also gave him a painting entitled *Appel au secours du Peuple
égyptien à la France, libératrice des nations* (Appeal for Help from the
Egyptian People to France, Liberator of Nations) (figure 3). This work,
reproduced in 'Ali Fahmi Kamil's biography of his brother, and later in
'Abd al-Rahman al-Rafi'i's book on the nationalist leader, depicts Egypt
as a captive of the British. In the foreground, an Egyptian with clothes
stripped to the waist sits with back to the viewer and hands chained; the
chains are held in the claws of the British lion, lying to the right; and to
the right of the lion sits a bare-chested soldier, sword in hand, eye on
Egypt, and one foot in the Nile. Behind this group, an Egyptian *effendi*
(gentleman) wearing European dress and a fez hands a document to an
allegorical woman symbolizing France and justice. To his left, stand a
group of male Egyptians wearing fezzes and turbans, waving the
Ottoman-Egyptian flag; and to the right, women representing nations
that the French had helped to achieve independence observe the scene.[21]
The figure representing Egypt is ambiguous: the physique appears to be
that of a man, but 'Ali Fahmi Kamil reported that it was a woman.[22] A
woman would be consistent with the other nations rendered as women
in the picture. Although her partial nakedness might be considered shocking, it is only implied and not revealed, because her back is towards us.
Women appear here as representations of nations, but not in the crowd
as members of the nation or as its leaders.

   The work was probably completed by a Frenchman commissioned by
Mustafa Kamil, the khedive, or some member of his entourage. Folk
painting existed in Egypt, but the first generation of professional Egyptian painters was still in its infancy. Thousands of copies were made of
the picture and distributed to the international press, and some circulated in Egypt and appeared in the press there.[23] Egyptian nationalists

Figure 3. *Appel au secours du Peuple égyptien à la France, libératrice des nations* (Appeal for Help from the Egyptian People to France, Liberator of Nations). 'Ali Fahmi Kamil, *Mustafa Kamil Basha fi 34 Rabi'an* (Cairo, 1908–11), vol. 3.

were clearly influenced by foreign conventions for the rendering of nationalist images, but they also sought to adapt them to the local context.

Some of these conventions appear in a poster of Mustafa Kamil's funeral procession that was published in the press at the time of his death (figure 4). In the poster, students from the schools of law and medicine escort Mustafa's Ottoman-style coffin (his fez rests on top); a picture of the deceased is set in the upper left-hand corner; two cherubs fly above the coffin in the center; and a mourning Egypt, who points to the coffin, looms to the right. This allegorical Egypt is more Roman-looking than pharaonic. She has pyramids on her breast-plate, and Egypt written in Roman letters below. The spectators shown are mostly men in turbans, fezzes, and Western hats; but the crowd contains a few women, too. A woman represents the nation, but women are not major participants or prominent observers. Still, they have not been left out of the nationalist scene altogether.[24]

Figure 4. Poster of Mustafa Kamil's funeral procession with a weeping ancient
Egypt. *Sijill al-Hilal al-Musawwar* (Cairo, 1992), 1: 454–55.

Inspired by the events of the revolution of 1919—elite women's street
demonstrations and rural women's protests—and influenced by the Mex-
ican muralists, the artist Muhammad Naji painted a vibrant tableau that
year. The monumental oil on canvas bears the title *The Awakening of
Egypt, or the Procession of Isis,* and contains pharaonic and rural motifs.
In it Egypt is represented as the queen-goddess Isis. She rides alongside
the Nile in a chariot drawn by a water buffalo, surrounded by male and
female peasants, traders, scholars, artisans, and entertainers. The procession is slow and colorful, suggesting historic motion and the march
toward independence. Originally shown in Paris, the contemporary art
capital of the world, Naji's mural was hung in the hall of the Egyptian
parliament in the mid-1920s.[25] It was theoretically on display for the
Egyptian public, but the number of viewers of the original work would
have been limited. Most women were denied access to the parliament in
its early years, and the parliament itself was closed down under certain
governments. Yet photos of the work appeared in the illustrated press
both before and after it had been hung. Thus, even if Egyptians did not
visit Cairo or the parliament, many could still see images of the picture.[26]

Paintings, pictures, and posters in the 1920s and 1930s showed Egypt
as a woman. In one oil painting that appeared photographed in the press,
Sa'd Zaghlul rescues Egypt from the jaws of a shark. In another, which
hung over the desk of the Wafd Party president Mustafa al-Nahhas, a

peasant woman wrapped in a flag represents Egypt.[27] Unlike cartoons, which were printed on newsprint and replaced weekly, and were thus quite ephemeral, these paintings hung on walls and were meant to be longer-lasting. Some found prominent places, in the parliament or party head-quarters, and their images were reproduced in the press; a few others were stored or forgotten. More permanent than cartoons, they may have been less enduring and less prominent than images carved in stone or bronze.

## MONUMENTS AND SCULPTURES

After Mustafa Kamil's death in 1908, a committee raised funds to cre-ate a memorial and commissioned the famous French sculptor Leopold Savine to produce a bronze statue (figure 5). The work was made under the direction of Mustafa's brother, 'Ali Fahmi Kamil, who was also a member of the committee, along with Muhammad Farid and Isma'il Sabri.[28] The statue depicts Mustafa Kamil standing erect, delivering a speech. He places his left hand on top of a bust of the Sphinx, which evokes Egypt's past glory, and points down with his right hand. The extended forefinger of his right hand draws us to the pedestal of the statue: a bronze relief shows a seated young peasant woman, with head covered but face unveiled, of slightly smaller dimensions than Mustafa Kamil. Entrapped in the square space, she represents Egypt under British occupation. Left hand to her ear, she listens to the speaker.[29]

The statue of Mustafa Kamil was delivered to Egypt in early 1914, on the eve of the war, and in the midst of the debate discussed in chap-ter 1 on whether or not Egyptian women ought to remove their face veils. Both sides of this debate had come to see veiled women as symbols of the nation, either of its backwardness or its purity.[30] The irony of the appearance of a woman as the representative of Egypt on the pedestal of the statue commemorating Mustafa Kamil is that he was against unveil-ing. To be sure, peasant women had never worn the same sort of face covering that urban elite women had. They dressed modestly and cov-ered their heads, and if needed, they drew the head scarf across their face. Their work in the fields and elsewhere made strict veiling and the seclu-sion that it suggested impractical. Still, in bronze, a peasant woman with uncovered face represented the nation in its struggle for independence.

By the time the monument had arrived in Egypt, Muhammad Farid was in exile and the Watani Party in disarray. Although the statue was origi-nally intended as a public memorial, it was barred from public exhibition by the British and the Khedive. It was erected instead in the courtyard

Figure 5. Statue by Leopold Savine of Mustafa
Kamil set on a pedestal with a relief of a peasant
woman, 1914. ʿAbd al-Rahman al-Rafiʿi, *Mustafa
Kamil: Baʿith al-Haraka al-Wataniyya, 1892–1908*,
5th ed. (Cairo, 1984).

of the Mustafa Kamil School, where it was officially unveiled for the
public in 1921. Nearly two decades later, it was moved to a public square
named for Mustafa Kamil and ceremoniously unveiled once again. When
moved to the public square, the statue of Mustafa Kamil was placed on
a stone pedestal, separating it from the original base but making it visible from a greater distance. Pictures of the monument appeared in the
press on both occasions, giving the image wide exposure.[31]

Figure 6. Model of Mahmud Muhktar's 1920 sculpture *The Awakening of Egypt (Nahdat Misr)*. Cover of *al-Nahda al-Nisa'iyya,* April 1928.

The Mustafa Kamil statue was overshadowed in the 1920s by Mahmud Mukhtar's sculpture *The Awakening of Egypt (Nahdat Misr)*. Mukhtar, who had shown a talent for sculpting as a village youth, became one of the first graduates of the School of Fine Arts, opened in 1908, and went on to Paris to continue his studies. Inspired by the revolution of 1919, as Naji had been, he carved a small-scale *The Awakening of Egypt,* which won a French prize in 1920. Photographs of the model appeared on the cover of such journals as *al-Nahda al-Nisa'iyya* (The Women's Awakening) (figure 6).[32]

Enthusiasm for Mukhtar's success abroad spurred a campaign to have the sculpture carved in monumental size. Egyptians followed the progress of the project closely through the decade, as photographs and drawings of the image became familiar in the press. However, the costly project was not without its critics. The satirical pro-palace weekly *al-Kashkul* parodied Mukhtar's effort to complete the statue in cartoons. The sculpture was finally presented to the public with great fanfare in 1928, when it was unveiled in the square in front of the Cairo train station. As mentioned in the introduction, few women were allowed to attend the opening ceremony.[33]

The work juxtaposes two images: the Sphinx rising and a peasant woman unveiling. The elements of the Mustafa Kamil statue, which was also produced in France, are thus repeated, only the man himself is missing. The Sphinx and the woman both represent Egypt: the Sphinx rising suggests a rebirth of Egypt's ancient grandeur; the peasant woman lifting her veil symbolizes the liberation of the modern nation. The linking of the two figures—the woman's hand rests on the Sphinx's head—connect antiquity to the present.[34] The sculpture thus reinforced nationalist claims to territorial continuity, a common theme in the rhetoric of nation-building. Interestingly, the original model and later enlargement diverge slightly. By the end of the decade, Egypt lifts her veil higher and has more pronounced breasts.[35]

Since it was erected in a busy square through which all those who came to Cairo by train had to pass—and train travel was a primary means of transport in those days—Mukhtar's *The Awakening of Egypt* had a captive audience. Even foreign travelers noticed the sculpture. "The visitor to Cairo is greeted on his arrival, as he passes out of the station, by a statue on the Station Square called *The Awakening of Egypt*," reported the American writer Ruth Woodsmall. "On his departure from Cairo this statue remains his last impression."[36] The statue became the preeminent symbol of the national struggle for Egyptians, evoking the revolution of 1919 and the optimism of the following decade. But it fell out of favor among Islamists who denounced "pagan" symbols in the 1930s.[37]

Nationalist celebrations of Egyptian peasants began in the 1890s, and by the 1920s, the peasant had come to be prized as the soul of Egypt.[38] That the monument to one of Egypt's earliest nationalists depicted the nation as a peasant and that one of the earliest sculptures by a contemporary Egyptian shows Egypt as a peasant woman is not surprising.[39] Many nationalisms celebrate male and female peasants as "culturally authentic," in opposition to urbanites, who are somewhat suspect in cultural terms, because they tend to be more cosmopolitan or westernized. Peasants have a concrete tie to the land, which is, after all, central to the claims of territorial nationalists.

The choice of imagery showed a transformation in elite attitudes. Whereas the old Ottoman-Egyptian aristocracy had disdained the peasantry, the new men on the rise, many of whom were landowners, took pride in their rural roots and tended to romanticize the tillers of the soil.[40] This imagery also made sense inasmuch as Egypt's sedentary population had always been significantly larger than her nomadic one. In contrast to Arabia and parts of the Fertile Crescent, peasants rather than tribesmen or nomads, popular elsewhere in the Arab world as symbols, became the embodiment of the nation. Depicting the nation as a peasant emphasized the agrarian basis of society and the source of the elite's wealth. Ennobling the peasant thus reinforced Egyptian identity over Ottoman or Arab alternatives without challenging the relationship between wealthy landowners and peasants. Juxtaposing the peasant with pharaonic symbols such as the Sphinx also distinguished Egypt from her neighbors and localized her claims.

## CARICATURES OF THE NATION

In sculpture, the *fallaha,* or peasant woman, emerged as the representation of the nation; but in the much more fluid medium of cartoons, peasants competed with pharaonic and Islamic women to represent Egypt in the interwar period. The 1920s witnessed the reemergence of the cartoon as an important medium for conveying political and social commentary.[41] By then, cartoonists could easily lampoon politicians whose photographs had appeared in the press. The caricatured figures were generally well known, and the captions in colloquial Arabic could have been read aloud to the illiterate. A number of weeklies, among them *al-Kashkul, al-Lata'if al-Musawwara,* and *Ruz al-Yusuf,* featured cartoons that played on familiar themes. They all chose to depict the nation as a woman, with images multiplying in the 1920s.

In the oldest of these papers, *al-Lata'if al-Musawwara,* cartoons generally appeared as black and white sketches on a page with other copy. They are interspersed with photographs, the main attraction of the paper (which will be discussed at greater length in chapter 4). The editor saw cartoons as a recent borrowing from Europe and initially felt it necessary to explain their political significance to viewers. Cartoonists such as Ihab Khulussi and Muhammad Hamdi sometimes signed their works or initialed them. While the creators varied, the cartoons reflected the pro-Wafd editorial policy of the paper. *Al-Lata'if al-Musawwara* competed intensively with *al-Kashkul,* which was backed by the palace and stridently anti-Wafdist, after it appeared in 1921.

Edited by Sulayman Bey Fawzi, *al-Kashkul* introduced a new sort of satirical political journalism into Egypt.[42] The paper had a format of four full-page color cartoons in each issue of sixteen or more pages in its first decade and ran until after World War II.[43] Cartoons were its specialty and probably were intended to be cut out, hung on walls, passed around, and saved. For the first decade, most seem to have been by the same hand. *Al-Kashkul* had a circulation estimated at ten thousand in 1927–28, compared to eight thousand for *al-Lata'if al-Musawwara*.[44] This figure placed it among the most popular weeklies in the interwar period and was considered sizeable at a time in which high illiteracy and the cost of ten *milliemes* per issue would have precluded mass distribution. Its broad circulation irritated those politicians who came under attack, and upon at least one occasion, the editor was arrested for insulting public officials in the pages of his paper.[45]

Together, these weeklies carried a range of cartoons that are fairly representative of production in this period. With very few exceptions, in cartoons in both weeklies, Egypt was depicted as a woman. A variety of "Egypts" ran in the interwar period, differing in age, size, and attributes. The first cartoons of the Egyptian nation appeared in *al-Lata'if al-Musawwara* in late 1919, probably after censorship had been lifted or modified. Images of pharaonic women were very popular in this period. (The cover of Balsam 'Abd al-Malik's journal *al-Mar'a al-Misriyya* carried the bust of a pharaonic queen in its center, with pharaonic motifs filling the page). Pharaonic images of the nation prevailed in *al-Lata'if al-Musawwara* for a few years and continued to run. Egypt appeared barefoot or in flat sandals, with jewelry adorning her arms. There was, however, little consistency in the style of her dress or headdress. By different hands, the cartoons seemed closer to "invented traditions" than "authentic" ones with any real historical validity.

An important shift took place in 1923, as the pharaonic images in *al-Lata'if al-Musawwara* were overshadowed by depictions of the nation as the "new woman." That was the most prevalent image from the start in *al-Kashkul*, which possibly because of its ties to the palace and the palace's links to Islamic groups never favored pharaonic images. In both periodicals, Egypt starts out modestly dressed, with a head scarf, a very light face veil, gloves, a cloak (underneath which she wears contemporary European dress), and high-heeled shoes. Her clothes change rapidly over the course of the decade: her cloak and dress become shorter; the gloves come off; the veil is removed. Egypt seems to be more up-scale in *al-Kashkul* than in its competitor: she sports a fur wrap, oversees the

Figure 7. "Awakening of the Muslim woman: A view of Egyptian Muslim ladies in an automobile transporting them last month to the harbor of Alexandria to a reception in honor of Liberal Party members of parliament while they are raising the banner of their groups." The banner reads "Society of Mothers of the Future." *Al-Lata'if al-Musawwara*, 10 October 1921, 4.

cook, travels, carries a clutch pocketbook, and drives a car. In either case, she is the "new woman" of the age, educated and sophisticated, the counterpart to *al-Kashkul*'s al-Misri Bey, who occasionally appeared representing the Egyptian elite.[46]

The "new woman" was decidedly urban, reflecting the realism and dynamism of contemporary Cairo, where politics were centered as the city experienced a tremendous growth.[47] Yet it also reflected the shifting realities of women during this period and their new political culture. A 1921 newspaper article showed a woman driving a car in Alexandria with companions holding flags and banners (of the Society of Mothers of the Future) during a celebration for the Liberal Constitutionalist Party (figure 7).[48] Two years later, a cartoon in *al-Kashkul* depicts Egypt as a "new woman" driving a car and navigating to avoid dangers on the road (figure 8).[49] In 1926, a woman's journal featured a photo and short article on a woman learning to drive, a novelty not unheard of by then.[50] Obviously, those who could afford cars came from the higher echelons, and driving was a feminist act only for the wealthy.

A third image shows a younger Egypt. She is an infant or a young girl with bows in her hair and on her dress, who looks weak and vulnerable:

Figure 8. Egypt tries to steer around dangers in the
road. *Al-Kashkul*, 14 December 1923, 20.

British warplanes and warships disturb her at play on a beach, and foreign men (John Bull and others) accost her. A cartoon on the cover of *al-
Kashkul* in August 1927 shows an Egyptian politician trying to bribe a
little girl "Egypt," who carries a doll and looks curiously at the box-bribe.
She represents innocence in the face of manipulating forces.[51] A fourth
image is that of a rural woman wearing a peasant scarf, ankle bracelets,
and no shoes. Less sophisticated than the "new woman," she is more sen-
sual and romanticized than the peasant woman captured in stone or bronze.
She is also more abused: she appears tied to a chair and gagged, in chains
and blindfolded, bolted to rocks in the desert. In addition, she conveys
more emotion: in one cartoon she wails at the side of a grave.[52] Cartoonists did not confine themselves to these sets of images but continuously
created new ones: a maternal Egypt giving birth to the constitution or
breastfeeding, and an elderly Egypt, emaciated with a walking stick.[53]

The political cartoons that appeared in the various papers were primarily concerned with criticizing British policy or Egyptian leaders. Yet they had other layers of meaning that reinforced the gender order. These cartoons conveyed their messages through caricatures based on widespread perceptions about gender and power, and they relied on sexual relations as metaphors for politics. A woman could easily suggest the attributes associated with colonial occupation because of her status in society: she was passive, prone, and weak. She also represented purity in the face of the corruption of Egyptian politicians. The sexual innuendo gave the artist almost unlimited opportunity for political critique. Egypt as a woman played opposite to England's John Bull (who was preferred to the female Britannia), as well as to Egypt's male politicians. The Egyptian nation was wooed and pursued, and occasionally provoked and punished. In this way, the cartoons provided an outlet for expressions of sexuality proscribed in other media.

The cartoons also contain explicit and implicit messages about race, class, and age. Irrespective of whether she is a pharaonic queen, a young girl, a "new woman," or a peasant, Egypt is almost always shown dressed modestly and with a light complexion, whereas the Sudan—depicted as a nearly naked woman, a baby, and in other guises—has dark skin and exaggerated facial and sexual features. One cartoon in *al-Lata'if al-Musawwara* in July 1932 lampooning the draining of Egyptian resources to invigorate the Sudan shows this contrast in race and respectability: Egypt and the Sudan lie juxtaposed on hospital beds while the Egyptian government and John Bull (England) facilitate a blood transfusion from Egypt to the Sudan (figure 9). Egypt is modestly covered with blankets, but the Sudan's blankets cover her middle only scantily, exposing her breasts and legs.[54] The Egypt of cartoons is clearly not akin to African territories to the south but closer in resemblance and style to the European north. Egypt is also, with some exceptions, depicted as a woman of means. This is not surprising, as elite Egyptians—lawyers and landowners—dominated nationalist politics in the 1920s and 1930s. Only elite women veiled themselves in the style shown for Egypt. Finally, Egypt is usually young. This makes sense, because nationalists were trying to mobilize the youth for their cause, and the young would most easily identify with images of the nation that mirrored their generation.

Political satire that attacked politicians in and out of the government as well as the British presence was possible during the decades in which Egypt experimented with parliamentary forms and an opposition press. Many of the images of the nation that appeared in cartoons were not

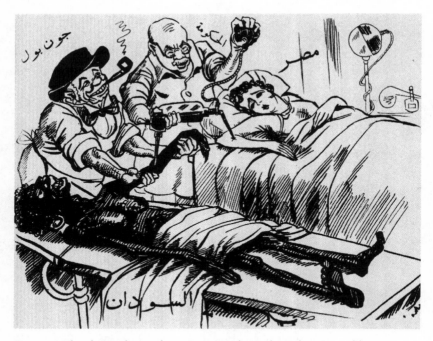

Figure 9. Blood transfusion from Egypt to the Sudan administered by
the Egyptian government, assisted by England's John Bull. *Al-Lata'if
al-Musawwara*, 11 July 1932, 24.

officially sponsored or sanctioned. It is interesting to compare these
images to iconography in a major medium that the state used to disseminate its views, postage stamps.

## POSTAGE STAMPS

Like coins and currency, postage stamps reveal a great deal about state
interests.[55] Generally designed by government officials in the postal
department, stamps were unsigned works (unlike cartoons, which were
sometimes signed), and we know little about stamp designers. The process by which certain images won approval over others is also hazy. The
designs had to be authorized at various levels, with directives coming
from the top. After nominal independence in 1922, the palace almost
certainly had a hand in the selection of images. If stamp designers
remained shadowy figures and the decision-making process a blur, the
site of production was more certain. Over the years, printing establish-
ments in London, Alexandria, and Cairo produced Egypt's stamps. From

the mid-1920s on, the Survey Department of Egypt, located in Giza, printed most Egyptian postal and revenue stamps.[56]

The first issue of Egyptian stamps in 1866 had Islamic-style geometric designs. Almost all subsequent stamps until 1914 showed the pyramids and Sphinx, and pharaonic themes dominated stamps until the early 1920s. After 1922 and the lifting of the British ban on royal and nationalist subjects on stamps, the Egyptian monarchy came to be the main subject. This followed the practice of featuring British royals on stamps.[57] The state clearly sought to promote the monarch as a national figure. King Fu'ad, his son Farouk, and their forebears dominate stamps in the period until 1952. This philatelic attention to the monarchy contrasted sharply with the absence of images of the king in cartoons probably as a result of state censorship.

Stamps from before the 1952 revolution occasionally feature ancient or contemporary royal women.[58] On the eve of World War I, Cleopatra appeared on a stamp, reinforcing the argument that Egyptian women should look to the past for models. Stamp designers employed images both of pharaonic women and of a Hellenistic ruler such as Cleopatra for this purpose, making them all Egyptian.[59] Yet women like Cleopatra and later Nefertiti were symbols of another sort than the iconography discussed here. They were not meant to represent the abstract collective but were considered part of the national heritage. On stamps and banknotes, they evoked an immediate association with Egypt's past glory and sometimes current political struggles. (Egyptians periodically sought to have the bust of Nefertiti that was on display in a museum in Berlin returned to Egypt.)[60] In the late 1930s, stamps bearing pictures of contemporary royal women made their debut. Queen Farida is shown with Farouk in a 1938 issue; an infant Princess Farial appears on a stamp to honor children in 1940; and the new Queen Narriman was featured with Farouk on the eve of the 1952 revolution.[61] The princesses also appeared on prerevolutionary fund-raising labels used as receipts for contributions to charities.[62] Stamps of ancient or contemporary royal women were meant to demonstrate royal authority and cement loyalty to the monarchy.

The Egyptian nation was represented as a peasant woman in stamps upon a couple of occasions. A special issue in 1937 commemorated the Montreux Agreement, signed in Switzerland, under which the powers agreed to abolish the privileges of foreigners in Egypt in 1949. The international treaty thereby removed an important obstacle to Egypt's complete sovereignty. The stamp features a medallion made for the conference

Figure 10. Postage stamp featuring a peasant
woman on the occasion of the Montreux Conference to abolish the Capitulations, 1937.

that shows a traditionally dressed peasant woman in profile (figure 10).
By finally eliminating foreign privileges, Egypt had, the stamp (and the
medallion) implied, regained her pride and honor.[63] And the stamps distributed for the 1938 and 1951 International Congress for Cotton also
show a peasant woman—a female cotton picker—emphasizing the agricultural roles of women.[64]

Stamp designers were slow to adopt the iconography of the nation
found in other media. Yet they faced certain constraints. The British

controlled the selection of stamps until the early 1920s, and then the palace influenced selection. The latter had its own agenda: promoting the monarchy as a national institution took priority over disseminating competing nationalist images. Stamp designers also followed their own conventions. In light of these considerations, the stamp commemorating the Montreux Agreement has a special importance, for it shows that the image of the nation as a peasant woman had infiltrated a tightly guarded trust by the 1930s.

The impact of stamps on viewers is hard to gauge. Although they may be read as records of state ideology and propaganda, they may have gone unnoticed by large segments of the population. Some stamps may have targeted a foreign audience rather than a domestic one. And a distinction should be made among different types of stamps. Postage stamps, for example, would have been viewed mostly by letter-writers and recipients, the literate. Revenue stamps would have been found affixed to any number of items (such as cigarettes) or on documents (such as those used for travel) and would have been more widespread, especially as the state found in them a useful way of generating income. In addition, special issue stamps also appeared, although these were generally short-lived. They appeared and then disappeared, preserved by cataloguers and treasured by collectors, but forgotten by most of the population. Yet pictures of stamps—new issues and special stamps commemorating congresses—appeared in the press as well, calling attention to their designs.[65]

## WOMEN ACTIVISTS AND IMAGES OF THE NATION

The sculptors, painters, cartoonists, and stamp designers who depicted the nation as a woman in official and unofficial media were mostly male. They were influenced by women's political activism and changes in their social situation. The "ladies' demonstrations," in particular, had an impact. Mukhtar and Naji both produced their works in the wake of the revolution of 1919. Naji included women in his procession, and Mukhtar had his peasant woman unveil (which was more acceptable at the time than having an urban upper-class woman do the same).

The earliest images of Egypt were of pharaonic or peasant women. Only when urban elite women lightened their veils or unveiled could they become the models for images, which multiplied in the 1920s with the spread of unveiling. Pharaonic women were partially pushed aside by the middle to late 1920s in favor of the "new woman." This image was based on a new breed of young elite women—educated, worldly, politically astute—who emerged in that decade. The female nationalists who appeared marching and protesting in photos throughout the decade provided artists with models.

In popular parlance, Egypt is *Umm al-Dunya* (Mother of the World), and some writers pointed out the assumed linguistic links of *umm* and *umma*, mother and nation. This was done in the context of a discourse on "Mothers of the Nation," which proved pervasive from the turn of the century. Yet, in general, Egyptians did not produce an allegorical or abstract "Mother Egypt" akin to Mother India in art and only sporadically showed a maternal or matronly Egypt. The absence of an abstract "Mother Egypt" may best be explained by the presence of a real "Mother of the Egyptians" (*Umm al-Misriyyin*), Safiyya Zaghlul. Pictures of her appeared widely in the national press in the interwar years, as we shall see in chapter 6.

Cartoonists may have found it convenient to depict Egypt as an abstract woman at a time when real women had not been elected to parliament or entered the cabinet. Egypt would not be confused, as a male figure might have been, with a living personality. But a few cartoons depicting the Egyptian nation as a woman bear likenesses to individual women activists. The woman portrayed in a series in 1923 in the pro-Wafd *al-Lata'if al-Musawwara* bears a close resemblance to Safiyya Zaghlul; the "Egyptian nation" criticizing the ministry's law of assembly appears maternal and authoritative, yet at the same time gentle (figure 11).[66] In the cartoon discussed above of Egypt in a hospital bed having blood taken from her arm for the Sudan, Egypt bears a striking resemblance to the actress-journalist Fatima ("Ruz") al-Yusuf (see the cartoon image of Ruz al-Yusuf in figure 28).[67]

The artists who produced nationalist iconography probably imagined their audience as mostly male. Representing the nation as a woman was meant to tap notions of honor and instill into male viewers the sense that they had a duty to support, protect, and defend it. Yet honor was not the only sentiment at stake. These images were also intended to generate a romantic attachment to the nation and encourage a fusion with it. By depicting Egypt as a woman, nationalists hoped to stimulate love for the nation and draw male youth to the cause. The man was the actor, the speaker, the lover; the woman was the acted upon, the listener, the beloved.

The audience for these images was imagined as male but differed in size and composition. The paintings and pictures had the most limited consumption, hung as they were in restricted quarters. The sculptures that appeared in public squares had a wider audience, yet one of limited

Figure 11. The Egyptian nation protests the new law of assembly to the government. *Al-Lata'if al-Musawwara*, 25 June 1923, 16.

circumference. Photographs of the paintings and sculptures circulated in the illustrated press, increasing the familiarity of certain images, as did cartoons. The latter could have been consumed by the illiterate, who often gathered around newspaper readers to hear sections of a paper read aloud and would have seen the pictures. By nature cartoons were much more timely, allowing a rapid response to a current political drama. They had a fluid nature, but were also quite ephemeral, because new cartoons appeared every week. Statues took much more time in the making and, as a result, proved to be more idealized.

Although a woman represented the nation, women were barred from seeing some of these images or restricted in their access. Audiences were particularly controlled at openings or unveilings. When the statue of Mustafa Kamil was unveiled in a school courtyard in 1921, a separate showing was designated for women.[68] Naji's painting decorated a wall in parliament, where a battle was fought in the mid-1920s to have special seats reserved for female spectators, who could not vote or be elected as members. Later in the decade, when the monumental version of *The Awakening of Egypt* was unveiled to an audience of thousands, Egyptian women were barred from the ceremony, as noted earlier.[69] Women of some means could, of course, buy periodicals, and they used stamps;

they were not, however, the targeted audience of many of these gendered images of the nation.

In short, women's inclusion in the nation was in question. Male Egyptians made the transition from subjects of a colonial state to citizens of a semi-independent nation-state with certain rights and responsibilities under the constitution of 1923, while women remained subjects with far fewer rights. The irony persists that although a woman symbolized the nation, women were pushed aside in national politics.[70] This situation was not particular to Egypt. In their revolution, the French replaced images of the toppled monarch with female allegories, but at the same time French women were excluded from republican politics.

Some female nationalists protested against their exclusion from Egyptian politics. But they did not protest the nationalist iconography representing the nation as a woman. Rather, they seemed to take pride in the images, as shown through their production and reproduction of them. The women's journal *al-Nahda al-Nisa'iyya* frequently carried a picture of the model of Mukhtar's sculpture on its cover from the time of its inauguration in 1921 (see figure 6).[71] The symbolism reinforced the argument of the founder, Labiba Ahmad, that national and women's progress were connected. The journal also featured a picture of Mustafa Kamil's statue on its cover.[72] Fatima al-Yusuf carried cartoons depicting the nation as a woman in her *Ruz al-Yusuf*. These women and their contemporaries did not see a causal connection between representing the nation as a woman and excluding her from political participation in the nation-state.

One of the most powerful ways of transmitting the idea of nationalism was through visual representations of the nation. From the 1870s on, the Egyptian nation was depicted in human form in cartoons, sculptures, paintings, and stamps. Any one of these visual images taken by itself could have been the whim of an artist or a state official commissioning art. Taken together, they form a consensus, even among opposing parties, on nationalist iconography: the nation should be represented as a woman (and was represented as a man on only few occasions). Depicting the nation as a woman was favored over showing it as a man for several reasons. Having a certain linguistic logic, the choice gave intellectuals and artists a rich field for political commentary through sexual innuendo and gendered metaphors. They found models and inspiration in the activities of contemporary Egyptian women and were also influenced by French examples. Those Egyptian intellectuals and artists who had spent time in France had certainly become acquainted with

Marianne as a symbol of the Republic. Yet there were important differences between Marianne—an ideal woman derived from ancient allegorical female figures—and the images of Egypt as a woman. Egyptian heritage—from pharaonic queens to Ottoman-Egyptian elites—had a significant impact on the production of images of the nation, making the indigenous imprint extremely important and giving the nationalist iconography of Egypt a unique trajectory.

Egypt came to be represented as a woman in a process that coincided with the unveiling of Egyptian women. This was not a self-evident or seamless process, but one that took time. Egypt could not effectively be represented as a woman until the debate on women's face covering had advanced. Unveiling then became a metaphor for national independence, although veiling also remained for many Muslims a metaphor for national purity.[73] Egypt as a woman was not then an importation of the French Marianne or of other European representations. The images of the Egyptian nation as a woman reflected something of the social situation of local women and of the Egyptian discourse on their place in society. Unlike the bare-breasted, allegorical Marianne, Egypt bared only her face, and in general, she respected local customs pertaining to modest dress.[74]

The spread of women as symbols of the nation corresponded with the effort of nationalists to broaden their movement. Not all images were disseminated widely or well received; some of them had broader circulation than others, and some were more easily understood than others. Moreover, not all nationalist iconography targeted the same audience or had the same meaning, for no one image of the Egyptian nation prevailed. While artists, intellectuals, and others came to agree that Egypt should be represented as a woman, they had different notions about what sort of woman she should be: young or old, healthy or ailing, urban or rural, pharaonic or Islamic. Symbolic women were set against backdrops that used other icons—the Nile, the Sphinx, pyramids—to emphasize territorial ties. The multiplicity of images reflects the struggle for power on behalf of different parties and their debates over Egyptian culture. The contrasting images of this period also show the fluidity of women's roles and blurring of gender boundaries rather than a timeless perception of Egyptian womanhood. The images were tied to debates by and about women on veiling and other topics from the 1890s. In short, if Egyptians agreed that the nation was to be represented as a woman, they disagreed as to which "woman" would be chosen and what being a "woman" meant.

CHAPTER FOUR

# Photography and the Press

A nation is made up of a multitude of people who have never seen the vast majority of their compatriots. "It is *imagined*," Benedict Anderson tells us, "because the members of even the smallest nation will never know most of their fellow-members, meet them, or even hear of them, yet in the minds of each lives the image of their communion." Anderson points to the importance of print culture and newspapers in building that "imagined political community."[1] Here we turn to a modern medium that suited the enterprise of nation-building and allowed members of the nation to see, if not meet, their compatriots—photography.

The rise and spread of Egyptian nationalism coincided neatly with certain innovations in photography, especially the ability of periodicals to reproduce numbers of photographs after the turn of the century. In contrast with the earlier landscapes and other images of foreign photographers, the pictures of local photographers reproduced in the Arabic press present a vivid human panorama. This trove of images circulated widely throughout Egypt in the first few decades of the twentieth century, helping to shape political identity. The new visual culture mapped the nation, familiarizing the viewer with its physical geography and human demography, and generating new nationalist symbols and leaders. The explosion of photographs of nationalist leaders strengthened the cult of the leader and loyalty to the party. Pictures of Egyptians of every class and region appeared in the illustrated press, not necessarily in equal numbers or in a similarly favorable light, but still in a sense of relatedness, of extended family. The proliferation of photographic images in Arabic illustrated periodicals and elsewhere generated a new visual mass culture that played a significant role in advancing a sense of national family.[2]

The camera, which served to solidify individual family memories, helped in the construction and maintenance of a collective national memory. Taking a picture became an integral part of a political event, and disseminating the photo helped broaden the boundaries of participation. The illustrated magazine, which presented the largest number of these images, became a collective photo album—a national scrapbook—and a central site of memory of the national family. This chapter sketches the early history of photography in Egypt as members of the collective increasingly appeared in the photographic images from the second half of the nineteenth century. It then focuses on the earliest Arabic illustrated newspaper, *al-Lata'if al-Musawwara*, which was founded in Cairo in 1915 and appeared for more than two decades. During its tenure, it carried tens of thousands of photographs, providing an important record for the period around the revolution of 1919, when it had no rival. Images from this periodical and others are analyzed here and in subsequent chapters to see how they shaped collective identity, instilled a sense of the nation as a family, and gendered national rituals.

A HISTORY OF PHOTOGRAPHY IN EGYPT

When, in 1839, the president of the French Academy of Sciences announced the invention of the daguerreotype, a system of metal-plate imaging, he immediately suggested its utility in accurately recording hieroglyphs. Within weeks, a team was dispatched to Egypt and the Levant to capture images of historical sites. Early photography was thus intimately linked with the Middle East and imperial efforts to decipher information about its past or to depict scenes that evoked its ancient splendor.[3] Nationalists, who drew on this same past to anchor their ideology and illustrate the longevity of the nation, also saw the appeal of photographic representations.

Scholars have shown a keen interest in photography in the Middle East, with most studies focusing on its first fifty or so years.[4] These studies have tended to emphasize the photographic oeuvres of foreign commercial photographers, whose images were produced mostly for Western consumption. Photographers with commercial interests established studios in Egypt as early as the 1860s. These men shot scenes that were carefully staged and, given the slow shutter speeds, took some time to shoot, and they marketed their postcards and loose prints to foreign residents and tourists. In an age before portable cameras, professional photographers shot pictures of landscapes and "natives" for the benefit of travelers, who selected images, placed them in photo albums, and carried the albums home.[5] Much of this photographic production has been labeled "Orientalist," for it propagated a fanciful vision of the region.[6] Commercial photographers often categorized local subjects by religion, ethnicity, vocation, and gender, and posed pictures of local "types," such as Bedouins, singers, and artisans.

Indigenous photographers of the nineteenth and twentieth centuries have received much less attention from historians than foreign photographers (and indigenous consumers hardly any). One of the earliest residents to try his hand at photography was the viceroy Mehmed Ali himself. In 1839, after receiving instructions from the Frenchman Horace Vernet, who had introduced him to the principles and techniques of photography, Mehmed Ali produced an excellent daguerreotype of the port of Alexandria and replicated his success from various angles. But his attempts to photograph the ladies of the royal household failed miserably, apparently because Vernet had sent his student off without having sensitized the plates, perhaps intentionally. The Frenchman then entered the harem to help him produce the desired daguerreotypes.[7] Mehmed Ali's own photographic career proved short-lived, and subsequent Egyptian viceroys and royals tended to be patrons rather than practitioners of photography, more preoccupied with having themselves portrayed and those images disseminated than with shooting images themselves. Their role in promoting photography contrasts sharply with that of sovereigns in Iran and the Ottoman Empire. Nasir al-Din Shah (r. 1848–96) introduced the Iranian court to photography, became adept at taking and developing pictures, and started a photography school within the palace. From these beginnings, photography trickled into Iranian society.[8] Sultan Abdul Hamid II (r. 1876–1909) also had a fascination with photography. Instead of touring his empire, he had photographers bring it to him. Scenes of hospitals, schools, ships, buildings, and so on were collected, collated, and placed in albums, which he presented as gifts to the British and American governments.[9]

Egyptian Muslims generally had no religious aversion to photography. Rather than viewing it as an artist's reproduction of human figures, which would have been proscribed, they considered it a scientific feat and called it *al-taswir al-shamsi* (drawing by the sun). Muhammad Sadiq Bey (ca. 1822–1902), a cartographer and colonel in the Egyptian army, produced some of the first photos of Mecca. In the early 1880s, he documented the hajj from Egypt to Mecca (an outpost of the Ottoman Empire), showing gatherings of pilgrims, encampment sites, and portraits of local personalities, and apparently taking photos of the Kaaba in stealth.[10] Other Egyptians followed in his footsteps: Ibrahim Rif'at Pasha (1857–1936), a general in the Egyptian army, recorded the hajj during three trips in the first decade of the twentieth century. His book *Mir'at al-Haramayn* (Mirror of the Twin Sanctuaries, 1925) included over three hundred and fifty photographs, the bulk of which he had taken himself.[11]

Religious and ethnic minorities played a prominent role in the early years of photography in Egypt, probably because of their greater contact with foreigners, who passed on the technical knowledge. Among the minorities, Armenians stood out: G. Lekegian took pictures from the 1860s through the 1890s, mainly of aspects of daily life in Egypt. He sold photos to foreign tourists and also aimed at the art market, particularly Orientalist painters seeking visual material. He signed his works in the 1880s as "Photographer to the British Army of Occupation."[12] The prints of another Armenian, Archak Fendian, appeared in the press in the first decades of the twentieth century in such women's journals as Labiba Ahmad's *al-Nahda al-Nisa'iyya* and in the illustrated press. Greeks also numbered among the early photographers: the Zangaki brothers produced images for travel albums.[13]

Photographic studios increasingly catered to an indigenous clientele, taking their portraits. There is ample literary and visual evidence that in the second half of the nineteenth century, the Egyptian elite commissioned photographs. Individual portraits of such male notables as Mustafa Kamil and Sa'd Zaghlul in their youth later appeared in the illustrated press.[14] These portraits were initially intended for private perusal, and this was especially true of photos of women. Most elite Muslim women veiled themselves in public until the early 1920s, and even in the early 1930s, they could still elect not to have their photographs affixed to passports if they were proceeding on the pilgrimage (although those traveling to Europe did not have that option).[15] Yet being veiled in public had not prevented them from having their photos taken in private for over half a century. The very wealthy brought the photographers to their homes, and the studio of Reiser and Binder even offered secluded women the services of a female photographer.[16] The camera caught Safiyya Zaghlul as an infant; and pictures show Huda Sha'rawi relaxing and playing as a young woman.[17]

Figure 12. Youthful portrait of Safiyya and Sa'd
Zaghlul. *Al-Lata'if al-Musawwara*, 5 September
1927, 13.

Studios also occasionally shot family portraits, although Muslim husbands and wives rarely appeared together in print. Safiyya and Sa'd Zaghlul, whose youthful photo frequently appeared in the press in the 1920s
and 1930s, proved a notable exception. In this photo (figure 12), Safiyya
stands in a gown with her hand on Sa'd's shoulder; he is seated and holds
papers in his hand. *Al-Lata'if al-Musawwara* identifies the photo in 1927
as taken in 1908, when Sa'd was minister of education; but Safiyya's
biographer identifies it as one taken the year of their marriage, which
was ten years earlier; and *al-Balagh al-Usbu'iyya* equivocates, saying it
is of the couple "in their youth."[18] Another notable exception are photos of elite Coptic families. Balsam 'Abd al-Malik, founder and editor of

*al-Mar'a al-Misriyya*, published "for the first and last time" a family portrait in response to a request from readers. She sits in middle-class attire,
her husband stands to her side, and two daughters frame them.[19] Huda
also posed with her husband, 'Ali Sha'rawi: in a photo from the early
1900s, the couple stand on either side of a chair, upon which their children sit, with their hands almost touching on the back of the chair.[20]
Curiously, in the photos just described, all of the figures appear bare-
headed, with the exception of 'Ali Sha'rawi, who wears a fez. The pictures all suggest a bourgeois family ideal, with the parties that made up
the conjugal couple balancing one another.

By the turn of the century, studios had already spread to the provincial towns of Egypt. Photographers advertised in the pages of the early
women's press, which was geared to middle-class readers, as that class
developed a taste for portraits. Women such as the educator Nabawiyya
Musa, the daughter of an army officer, had their pictures taken early in
the century. Nabawiyya posed in school robes in the studio of Muhammad Effendi Badr with her hand on a few books, probably on the occasion of her passing the secondary school exam in 1907, the first Egyptian
girl to do so. A book became a prop in photos of educated girls and
female intellectuals.[21] Malak Hifni Nasif, a woman of middle-class origin who wrote under the pen name "Bahithat al-Badiya" (Searcher in
the Desert), posed for a series of shots sometime before her premature
death in 1918, which show her in Bedouin dress sitting on a small divan
or standing. Labiba Ahmad (1870s–1951), daughter of a physician, sat
for a series of portraits throughout the interwar years that show her in
thoughtful poses (see figure 29).[22] And Munira Thabit (1902–1967),
writer, activist, and lawyer, also posed for portraits. In 1925, she is shown
in one, standing tall and confidently, reflecting the optimism of activists
in this period.[23]

Pictures commissioned by middle- or upper-class Egyptians for private purposes contrasted with those taken of the lower classes by commercial photographers for foreign consumption. The studio and
cameraman may have been the same, but the sense of purpose and control was altogether different, and the photographer was now at the service of the Egyptian patron. For example, Nabawiyya Musa, who fought
her family and officials at the ministry of education for the right to sit
for the secondary school exam, would hardly have been docile in the
hands of a photographer; the clenched fist in the photo shows her determination. Middle- and upper-class urban Egyptians became accustomed
to having their pictures taken and almost expected it, because they started

to pose for the camera. They chose to be represented in fine attire in their homes, if possible, with props such as books, flowers, and chairs, and sometimes with their children. Yet in spite of their ostensible control, they may have been unaware of many of the photographic conventions they unconsciously adopted.

Family photographs were displayed within homes and increasingly became part of domestic surroundings. In her household manual *Rabbat al-Dar* (Mistress of the House, 1915), the Coptic writer Malaka Sa'd tells her readers to hang a picture of the master and mistress of the house on a wall in the reception room.[24] Some went wild with photos, as the description by a British official of the interior of Princess Nazli Fazil's apartment shows: "Every table was loaded with photographs. . . . There must have been near a thousand photographs in the room. . . . Not only the numerous gilt screens, but every inch of the four walls of the vast apartment, were covered with pasted pages of the illustrated papers."[25] Although Nazli's presentation of photographs was by no means typical, photos increasingly appeared on walls in homes and offices, at memorial services, on tombs, in processions, and in the press.

Photography set off a revolution in ways of seeing, and Egyptian elites quickly learned how to "read" and interpret these multiplying images. An evolution in camera equipment soon transformed photography. As shutter speeds quickened, subjects no longer had to sit still for minutes. With the introduction of the first hand-held Kodak cameras in 1888, photographers became more mobile. Separating the processes of taking pictures and developing film opened the way to the wider marketing of cameras to consumers. The professional photographer no longer had a monopoly on picture taking, and the profession itself no longer remained a closed guild with secrets passed from masters to apprentices. Egyptians not only commissioned portraits, whose prices came down, giving the lower classes access to them, but also began to take photographs in numbers.

Technological advances in printing paralleled the evolution in camera equipment. The half-tone process, developed in the late nineteenth century, enabled newspaper editors to publish photos and inaugurated a new visual culture. Monthly literary journals such as *al-Hilal* included the occasional print, and women's journals such as *al-Jins al-Latif* sometimes carried photos of Christian women (although journals of an Islamist bent, such as *al-Manar*, remained committed to print rather than visual matter). Refinements in equipment after the turn of the century lowered the costs of reproduction and improved its quality. This set the stage for the establishment of illustrated Arabic periodicals.

## THE RISE OF THE ARABIC ILLUSTRATED PRESS

The first Arabic illustrated weekly, *al-Lata'if al-Musawwara*, appeared in Cairo in February 1915. Its founder, Iskandar Makariyus, came from a Greek Orthodox journalistic clan that had emigrated from Beirut to Cairo in the mid-1880s. His father, Shahin Makariyus (d. 1914) had worked with his uncle Faris Nimr and co-editor Ya'qub Sarruf to produce the highly successful literary journal *al-Muqtataf* (1876–1951), and the team had also launched the daily *al-Muqattam* (f. 1889).[26] His mother, Maryam Nimr (d. 1888), had written pieces on women's issues for his father's monthly journal *al-Lata'if* (1885–95). The latter journal provided the inspiration, name, and possibly the license for his own publishing venture.

At five piasters an issue, *al-Lata'if al-Musawwara* sought in its first few years to bring images of the war to the Egyptian public. Since European military authorities banned photography at the front, most of the images were artists' illustrations. Makariyus proved more successful at obtaining pictures closer to home, including columns of Ottoman prisoners on their way to an Egyptian prison camp, groups of Egyptian reserves protesting military conditions, and human and equine victims of German air attacks in Cairo.[27] The newspaper covered the disturbances in Egypt in 1919 in the wake of the war, depicting demonstrations, meetings, and leaders, all under the watchful eyes of the British military censor. More leeway seemed to be given to showing violence— corpses on battlefields and penal hangings—in Arab territories under French rule. The readers and viewers of *al-Lata'if al-Musawwara* quickly came to expect photos of all major local and regional political events. When no photos were available, such as of the attempted assassination of Sa'd Zaghlul in the Cairo railroad station in summer 1924, the journal published an artist's rendition of the scene.[28]

Pictures in *al-Lata'if al-Musawwara* covered a range of subjects: crime, charity, sports, ceremonies, celebrations, fairs, and funerals. The story of Egyptian nationalism as narrated by Wafdists provided the overarching frame for photos. The periodical began with an eight-page spread, and over two decades, its size quadrupled. Its staff also grew to include a director, an editor-in-chief, and an advertising agent, as well as typesetters, printers, and other workers. A picture taken in 1934 during the visit of the head of the Egyptian workers union to the paper shows a staff of nearly fifty.[29] The staff also produced an illustrated women's entertainment journal (*al-'Arusa*), a children's magazine (*al-Awlad*), and for a short time a daily.

Every issue of *al-Lata'if al-Musawwara* contained scores of pictures. The concentration of photos was the selling point of the illustrated weekly. Editors wrote captions that guided the viewers in reading and interpreting the photographs and usually gave the names of those depicted. Yet editors only occasionally credited the photographers who had taken the shots, and only a portion of the photos themselves carried the signatures of the photographers or stamps of the studios that had printed the photograph. Moreover, the number of signed photos in *al-Lata'if al-Musawwara* decreased after the weekly inaugurated its own developing room. The anonymity of most photojournalists should come as no surprise: photography was seen as a technical skill, a way of depicting reality with the aid of physics and chemistry, and deserved no special mention.

Makariyus frequently reported that photos were taken "especially for *al-Lata'if al-Musawwara*" and took pride in exclusive shots. From its first days, *al-Lata'if al-Musawwara* had photographers on staff who were sent on special assignments. Staff photographers covered ceremonies, traveled with the royal entourage or party leaders, and rushed to the scenes of fast-breaking stories. They are usually mentioned as "our special photographer" or just by surname, such as Sabunji.[30] Later staff photographers included Muhammad Yusuf, who moved from *al-Lata'if al-Musawwara* to the daily *al-Akhbar* of Dar al-Hilal.[31]

Makariyus, who was credited with a few photos himself, did not rely on staff photographers alone. To stock the pages of the periodical, he solicited original photos of people mentioned in the daily press and of current events from Egypt and the Arab world. Foreign and Egyptian commercial photographers provided a steady stream of photos. The war had cut off the trade to foreign tourists, who in any case increasingly traveled with their own cameras, and foreign photographers depended now more than ever on the local market. They shot pictures of the king (who had a series of official royal photographers), Sa'd and Safiyya Zaghlul, and leading personalities, and sold them to the press.[32] Other photos in *al-Lata'if al-Musawwara* from commercial photographers bear names (such as Archak Fendian and Muhammad Badr) that suggest local or regional origins. At a time when boycotting foreign goods and services proved popular, photographers increasingly identified themselves as "local." Riyad Shahata, an official photographer of the king, was called in captions "the famous local photographer." Egyptian effendis (educated men of the middle class) also sent in photos to the illustrated press, having taken up the hobby. Illustrated periodicals encouraged picture taking, both by example and through ads that marketed photo supplies and services. The growing middle class could now afford cameras, and advertisements for cameras came to outnumber those for the services of photographers. Photo stores could be found in numbers in Cairo and other cities at least from the teens on. Mitri's Photo Store marketed itself as a "local" photography shop and sought to attract the business of compatriots. Owners also acted as photojournalists: one Luxor shop owner sent photos taken upon the occasion of the visit of the Wafdist leader Mustafa al-Nahhas to the region to the press.[33]

The camera market was dominated to such an extent by Kodak that many stores offered "Kodaks and film," for Kodak was understood to mean "camera." Kodak seemed less concerned with competitors than with persuading Egyptians of the importance of taking pictures. Its advertising campaign emphasized time, memory, and simplicity, and targeted women. Time passed, ads suggested, and the only way to preserve memories was by taking pictures, made simple by Kodak cameras: "Preserve the memory of your excursion," read one ad. Others argued that the "days and years" sped by quickly, and the way to "preserve memories of your children's infancy and youth" was by means of the Kodak camera. Ads depicted women as the keepers of family memories and suggested that husbands surprise their wives with the gift of a camera.[34] One early ad shows a drawing of a lightly veiled woman with a camera in her hands but later ads adapted from American originals show little adaptation of illustrations or text for the Egyptian context.[35]

The extent to which Egyptian women actually took pictures is not clear. A couple of pictures that King Fu'ad's wife, Queen Nazli (not to be confused with the princess of the same name), took of her children were published in *al-Lata'if al-Musawwara*. But few other submissions by women were acknowledged. Women may have taken pictures for private viewing or published them elsewhere. Labiba Ahmad traveled with a camera, or at least had an eye for photographs, for her children and her trips are well documented in her interwar monthly, *al-Nahda al-Nisa'iyya*. The journal contains advertisements from photographers, a series on photography, and solicitations for photos, many of which were published. This was quite atypical for periodicals with an Islamic bent, and there were fewer photos in the 1930s as the religious orientation of the journal became more pronounced.[36]

Photography became increasingly popular among Egyptians, as evidenced by the establishment of local competitions, exhibitions, and photography clubs in schools.[37] Those interested in photography could now find instruction in Arabic on various aspects of the craft. Literary material included a pamphlet by Amin Hamdi of Benha on *Amateur Photography* (1922), a book by 'Abbas Effendi al-Harawi al-Khabir of 'Ain Shams on coloring photos (1924), and a sixteen-part series by Muhammad Effendi Zaghlul on photography in *al-Nahda al-Nisa'iyya* (1933–34).[38]

Although many photographers fought to have their visual products viewed as art rather than documents of reality, they in the meantime influenced the ways in which other artists worked. A subject no longer had to sit for a painter, who could now work from photos. *Al-Lata'if al-Musawwara* published a series of photographs of artists next to easels bearing portraits of Safiyya and Sa'd Zaghlul, Mustafa al-Nahhas, and others based on earlier photographs from the paper.[39] Sculptors too could work from photos, particularly in the making of memorials of nationalist leaders. Cartoonists also used photographs in the illustrated press to create caricatures of politicians and activists, and they relied on the public's familiarity with these frequently photographed figures. Without the illustrated press and the proliferation of photos, political cartoons could not have taken off the way they did in the 1920s.

The success of illustrated periodicals shows the extent to which the new visual culture caught the imagination of Egyptians. *Al-Lata'if al-Musawwara* was unrivaled in its first years, through the revolution of 1919, and shortly thereafter. The success is borne out by circulation figures. Makariyus reported in 1921 that he printed 30,000 copies of a special issue that covered Sa'd Zaghlul's return to Egypt.[40] In 1924, Makariyus boasted that *al-Lata'if al-Musawwara* had the largest print run—over 35,000—of any Arabic newspaper, and suggested that this translated into over one hundred thousand readers and viewers.[41] Multiplying circulation gives a better sense of real distribution, for papers were known to pass from hand to hand. But periodical owners were also known to inflate their circulation figures to attract advertisers. Makariyus's figures are consistent and close enough to estimates for the press in the 1920s that there may be an element of truth to them. In 1927–28, the dailies *al-Ahram* and *al-Muqattam* had approximate circulations of 30,000 and 25,000, respectively, and the weeklies *Ruz al-Yusuf* and *al-Musawwar*, which were only a few years old, already had circulations of 20,000. By then the latter two publications had probably cut into Makariyus's circulation, for the same report placed the circulation of *al-Lata'if al-Musawwara* at a more modest 8,000.[42]

A picture of readers of *al-Lata'if al-Musawwara* emerges from an analysis of entrants in competitions sponsored by the paper. Almost all of those who submitted photos and brief biographical descriptions at the end of the first year were young men from provincial towns and the larger cities of Egypt, who invariably wore the fez and Western dress. Among them was the young 'Abd al-Rahman al-Rafi'i, a member of the Watani Party, who went on to become one of Egypt's most prolific historians. These young professionals and government officials formed the core of the national movement in this period.[43] Entrants in a competition nearly twenty years later show a somewhat greater diversity. Roughly 10 percent of those photographed were women, and respondents came from throughout Egypt. Submissions also came from Damascus and Beirut, as well as Haifa and other Palestinian cities. Still, the profile of readers after twenty years of circulation shows a mostly young, male, educated middle-class Egyptian readership.[44]

The same sort of profile emerges from a series of photos published from 1930 to 1935 of some of *al-Lata'if al-Musawwara*'s most loyal readers. These photos, some ten in all, show subscribers standing or sitting next to a table on which are piled bound copies of *al-Lata'if al-Musawwara*. The men, who are traders in commodities, are dressed either in *gallabiyyas* (loose, long shirtlike garments) or in suits and ties; most wear fezzes.[45] The paper also claimed the famous among its readers: photos show Sa'd holding a copy in his hands; Nahhas poring over a page; the crown prince looking at pictures of his father in Europe; and sports heroes inspecting photos of themselves.[46]

In its first years, *al-Lata'if al-Musawwara* was unrivaled and served as a source of photos for other periodicals, but it soon faced competition from various quarters. Established daily newspapers eventually began to publish photographs and could do so in a more timely fashion than a weekly.[47] New weeklies soon competed more directly: *al-Kashkul* (1921) specialized in colored cartoons and carried photos, and *al-Musawwara* (1925) soon followed. Launched by Dar al-Hilal, the illustrated weekly *al-Musawwara* outlived the pioneer in its field (and probably purchased its photo archive). Another venture by the Hilal publishing group, the illustrated weekly *al-Ithnayn* (1934), was geared to a more popular audience and may have quickened the end of *al-Lata'if al-Musawwara*.[48] The editors of *al-Lata'if al-Musawwara* promised in late 1935 that the coming issue would be bigger and better, but the weekly did not survive for very long after that.[49]

## FACES OF THE NATION

Unlike earlier photos destined for Western audiences which highlighted landscapes and ruins with a few "natives" to give a sense of scale, photos in the Egyptian press focused on people. In short, the illustrated newspaper served as a scrapbook, a collection of images of the national family, which in turn sought to define the boundaries and strengthen the bonds of that family. The portrayal of the national community remained subjective, shaped by the mixture of pictures (with its inclusions and exclusions) and their content (how individuals and groups were presented). Certain sorts of images repeated over the years reinforced impressions of the composition of the nation and the stature of its leaders. Taken together, the pictures in the interwar period show a nation on the move.

Although nationalist ideologues often referred to the family as the building block of the nation, particularly in debates on the "Woman Question," photos of families configured around the mother and father rarely appeared in the nationalist press. (Photos of Coptic families such as that of the Wafdist Wisa Wasif or Balsam 'Abd al-Malik, mentioned earlier, proved an exception.)[50] Instead, other sorts of groups figured prominently. When professionals gathered to celebrate retirements, promotions, or transfers, cameramen documented the gathering. Government workers, police, students, journalists, and others repeatedly posed for the camera. A list of names of those depicted often accompanied these photos, suggesting that naming functioned to bring people into the communal circle. These were the new middle-class professionals who formed the core of the nationalist movement.

Youth appeared in a variety of photographic guises, representing future promise. Cameras were omnipresent at school functions: they captured scenes from school plays, outdoor activities, and graduation exercises. Photographs around the theme of education, formerly one of the most contested domains between British officials and Egyptian nationalists, suggested progress in this domain. The most photographed youth in his day was the "beloved" Prince Farouk. The palace released portraits and still shots of the young prince in multiple poses, sometimes with his sisters, in an attempt to build loyalty to the throne. Unlike his father or his heftier more mature self, the handsome boy won hearts. *Al-Lata'if al-Musawwara* even dedicated a special issue to him, featuring a picture of the prince in his scout uniform on the cover.[51]

Photos document the emergence and spread of the scouts, a nationalist youth movement that combined a number of virtues, notably, discipline, loyalty, and duty. The movement socialized young people for national service and contributed to the celebration of militarism. Young women also donned scout uniforms starting in the late 1920s. Under the leadership of Munira Sabri, an inspector of girls' physical training in the

Figure 13. Girl guides at the Giza pyramids. *Al-Lata'if al-Musawwara*, 29 July 1935, 13.

ministry of education, the number of Girl Guides grew. By 1936, it had surpassed six thousand, and Munira became one of the most visible women in the national press. Photos of outings carried multiple messages. One taken at the Giza pyramids in 1935 links ancient glory and future promise (figure 13). The fifty or so girls in their quasi-military uniforms convey a sense of solidarity and communal spirit. While most groups shown in the press were arranged in straight rows, reflecting a certain order, the young women on an outing sit or stand among the stones, conveying adventure, spontaneity, and strength.[52]

Scouts and other youth were photographed in numerous settings, but none fused images of the past and future as well as those of visits to pharaonic ruins. Pictures of Egyptian youth at ancient sites—"the temples of their ancestors"—showed the nation literally uncovering its past and helped define the historical parameters of Egypt. The photos enabled those who could not make the pilgrimage to the ancient sites to "learn about their country."[53]

Motion and action proved integral elements of nationalism, for a nation did not achieve independence sitting still. All sorts of photos showed the nation on the move, its citizens active. Travel, particularly by air, became a common theme of images of the interwar period, as photos celebrated aviation firsts: the first male and female Egyptian pilots, long-distance trips, and special planes. The fascination with flying suggests a supreme faith in science and technology. Sports photos also conveyed action extremely well, because they combined the elements of strength, agility, and pride. The sports page evolved early on in illustrated papers, featuring soccer teams, wrestlers, boxers, gymnasts, and swimmers. The seeds of the national obsession with soccer are apparent, and the Egyptian heroes of international competitions, such as the Olympics, became nationally recognized. An image of the glorified male body emerged in the 1930s, and some athletes were depicted nearly naked, with muscles bulging. The ideal male body had become a powerful one, the man of strength a model.[54]

The sorts of photos described above contain images mostly of the middle classes, the main engine of the nationalist movement in the interwar period. In contrast, photos of the poor usually depict them as passive and disordered: they sit on the ground awaiting handouts of clothes or food sent from the king; they are survivors of fires in villages or collapsed buildings in the cities; they are the perpetrators or victims of crimes.[55] These representations of the poor are in some ways similar to those taken by nineteenth-century foreign photographers in their manipulation of their subjects. Yet there is a notable development through this period, because poorer folk increasingly elected to have their portraits taken with props by professional photographers. These studio shots occasionally appeared in the press (e.g., when a child disappeared, a father and son were murdered, or a girl was hit by a car).[56] By having their portraits taken, the poor showed that they too wanted to participate in the new visual culture and wanted to be part of the national family.

The poor showed up on the nationalist stage as a crowd in photographic images. At outdoor political gatherings, a male crowd became a staple feature. Men gathered in front of the House of the Nation, ran alongside the train of the returning national leader Sa'd Zaghlul, and marched in demonstrations. The crowd presented evidence of strong support for the Wafd and represented the passion, enthusiasm, and unity of the nation. Visually, pictures of the crowd—the individual as part of something larger—came closest to capturing the notion of the nation.

The crowd is not without focus: it masses to hear or see a nationalist leader. Pictures of those leaders—Sa'd Zaghlul and his successor Mustafa al-Nahhas—dominated the pages of the illustrated press. Photos show Sa'd in many poses: a book or paper in hand, Safiyya at his side, the centerpiece of a group of Wafdists, on his way to negotiations. He always

appeared dignified, unifying the party and leading the nation. These photos convey a completely different feeling from those of King Fu'ad, whose
picture also appeared regularly. The king looks aloof and remote from
people, sitting on a throne on a deserted stage, walking alone in front of
a delegation. He is rarely physically near others and never smiling. With
his waxed, upturned mustache, he appears cold or bored. In contrast,
Zaghlul stands amid his colleagues and followers, who draw physically
close to him. Photos show respect for the king but love for Sa'd Zaghlul. After the latter's death, Nahhas (who had often stood by Sa'd's side
in photos) appears as the first among equals. He soon emerged as the
focus of the lens, the centerpiece of the political drama.

## PHOTOGRAPHY AND WOMEN'S POLITICAL CULTURE

The narrative of Egyptian nationalism weaves throughout the pages of
the illustrated press. Numerous photographs of female nationalists
appeared, showing women were an integral part of this story. Viewed
widely and often reprinted over the years, they helped to shape the
collective memory of Egyptians. Certain images stuck, especially ones
of demonstrating women in 1919 (discussed in chapter 5). These images
help in reconstructing the history of women's involvement in the nationalist movement. The camera places women in certain spots at specific
moments and catches details that writers may have missed. Just as with
written documents, these photographs must be assessed for reliability
and read critically for information. The photos and their captions thus
provide important documentary evidence that supplements the literary record.[57]

Photos also captured transformations in the gendering of public space
and political rituals, suggesting who belonged to the nation and who did
not, and what roles different groups could play. Photos of funeral processions, a distinctive genre in Egyptian photography, chart the changes
in this national ritual over time. Photographers followed leaders all the
way to the grave, allowing the public to share in the mourning. The funerals of nationalist leaders Mustafa Kamil, Muhammad Farid, and Sa'd
Zaghlul, as well as other "national martyrs," were great political events.
Flags draped coffins as students, workers, and professionals marched
with their associates, often carrying photos of the deceased. In comparison with royal funerals, which appear in photos to have been extremely
ordered affairs, funerals of nationalist leaders appear to have been more
spontaneous and emotional affairs.

Funerals showed a gendered division of labor. Typically, women watched and cried out as men marched in funerals, but national rites of mourning underwent a transformation in this period. Women observed Mustafa Kamil's funeral in 1907 from roofs and balconies, but when Muhammad Farid's body was returned to Egypt for burial in June 1920, elite women participated in the event. The procession included a broad array of students, workers, artists, and other mourners, who marched in groups arranged by profession, school, or class in delegations that carried flags, banners, and photos. A photo shows the order of the march, pointing out the gendered and class hierarchies through labels that identify the different groups participating in the ritual (figure 14). At the end of the procession, in the footsteps of the princes and notables, elite women rode in automobiles, one of which hoisted a banner with a flag and slogan embossed. This was one of the first times women had ridden in a national funeral procession.[58]

Female doctors paved the wave for girls and women to march on foot in funeral processions when they followed the coffin of a colleague in 1921.[59] A photo of the 1923 funeral of a notable shows a troop of young girls, protégés of one of the women's associations, carrying bouquets of flowers and marching parallel to those leading the coffin. Girls become incorporated, although off to the sides, into a public ritual that combined elements of order and chaos. (The photo also reveals the prominence of a Kodak store on one of Cairo's main boulevards.)[60] Photos of Sa'd's funeral in 1927 also show that schoolgirls joined the funeral procession.[61] Women still retained responsibility for publicly mourning: a photo taken on the doorstep of Sa'd's house as the procession sets off shows female mourners openly weeping when the coffin is carried down the steps.[62] Photographs of the nationalist ritual of funeral processions capture the ways in which women were included in, or excluded from, the nation, and the pace at which this took place. Young girls often led the way; but women remained underrepresented, giving the sense that they were a numerical minority and less significant part of the nation. Moreover, the gendering of public rituals did not follow a linear path toward desegregation, and women could find themselves once again excluded from such public ceremonies.

Visits to the graves of fallen fighters in the nationalist movement proved a recurrent ritual of Wafdist women, one loaded with significance. Committee members traveled to visit the "tombs of martyrs," recent victims of government violence, in Bilbays and Mansura in July 1930.[63] Again, in late 1935, in the wake of student protests, Sharifa Riyad led a delegation of the Sa'dist Committee to visit the "tombs of the martyrs."[64] In this, and

Figure 14. Muhammad Farid's funeral procession.
The writing and arrows indicate from bottom to top
the order of the march: the wreath, the bier, police,
the family of the deceased, princes and notables,
and, finally, the "ladies' automobiles." *Al-Lata'if
al-Musawwara*, 21 June 1920, 7.

in other ways, women took the traditional female role of public mourning and transformed it into a new political ritual.

Photos of the period also show the gradual removal of face veils.
There is an inherent irony in photographing women who wear face
veils, for the face is generally the focus of the camera, the feature that
most distinguishes the individual. Yet a veiled face may have been the

ultimate symbol of effacing the self for the sake of the nation, giving photos of veiled women their power. Two photos across a dozen years can be compared. The first shows women sitting in rows, listening to speeches in a tent erected in front of the House of the Nation on 13 November 1922. White veils cover all the faces except those of young girls. A second photo taken in another tent on the occasion of the Wafd's general meeting in 1935 showed rows of women, many of whom now look up directly at the camera, faces uncovered.[65]

The removal of the veil also meant the end of certain protections for nationalist women and elimination of taboos against arresting them. One interior shot shows women arrested in 1931 for protesting against the government; other shots from the same period show women looking out from the window of a building where they have been detained.[66] Photos in the 1920s show female students marching in orderly processions and carrying placards. Photos in the mid-1930s show female students confronting the police, and portraits of girls appear among the photos of the wounded in the press.

Photos of female demonstrators and activists appeared in the context of a growing body of photographs of educated women who became metaphors for modernity. Interwar monthly women's journals showed female doctors, lawyers, writers, and social welfare activists. The more popular illustrated women's weeklies, such as *al-Hisan* and *al-'Arusa*, helped to create nationally recognized female entertainers. Adoration for actresses such as Fatima (Ruz) al-Yusuf and singers such as Munira Mahdiyya and Umm Kulthum unified Egyptians around stars and enhanced national identity. Images in these entertainment periodicals contrasted with those in the more intellectual or socially edifying journals. While there was some degree of overlap and some sharing of portraits, the women's weeklies focused on entertainers. Rather than promote domestic virtues and give household instruction, they sought escape from the daily routine. The illustrated press was the first in a series of modern cultural products—records, radio, and film—to produce national icons.

Until 1919, photos of female nationalists rarely appeared. Thereafter, women allowed themselves to be the subjects of photojournalists and attempted to shape the making and initial publication of the images. But they could not then control how these images were copied, cut, cropped, and disseminated over time as the photographs memorialized political events and movements. Photos acted as a crucial link, documenting women nationalists in the midst of their activities and creating images— veiled and unveiled—that became symbols.

· · ·

The revolution in ways of seeing, and what one was permitted to see, proved most pronounced when photos of Egyptian Muslim women, who hitherto could not be seen, were increasingly published in the press. New attitudes and new technologies, which dovetailed neatly with the nationalist movement, made this possible. Nationalists could now disseminate images quickly and widely through the press. As a result, photography played a central role in Egyptian political culture in the interwar years and after, and launched a revolution in ways of collectively remembering and commemorating.

Photos became omnipresent—adorning walls, worn as medallions, carried as icons in marches, placed on tombs—and the cameraman was ubiquitous. Pictures even capture photographers as part of the scene, and at many official occasions, cameras can be seen perched on the sidelines, recording images.[67] An event was incomplete, indeed, it had not happened, if it had not been documented by the camera and presented to the public for viewing. Visual records triggered memories and shaped them both individually and collectively. In this way, photographic images in the press and elsewhere helped to shape the nationalist narrative and build a collective memory. Women were increasingly a part of this memory, but in specific ways, included in small numbers or symbolic roles.

Photographs proved crucial, and remained so, in creating a community of memory. This is illustrated by the format used in Dar al-Hilal's 1992 two-volume centennial collection of photos *Sijill al-Hilal al-Musawwar* (The Illustrated Record of al-Hilal). Drawing on its extensive archives, the editors created a national scrapbook that followed a standard narrative of national history. The book opens with an essay on photography and memory, and presents the historical photographs of Egypt as representations of past reality rather than artistic interpretation.[68] The editors divided the photographs into more than fifty categories, covering various institutions, rituals, quarters, groups, and aspects of life. The collection then ends with space for photos "from your private archive"—nine pages of blank rectangular frames of varying size for pasting in up to twenty-four photographs, "For it is impossible to end *Sijill al-Hilal al-Musawwar*, which documents the history of Egypt pictorially over the past one hundred years, without placing in it your picture and those of your forefathers."[69] By allotting space for individual and family memories to be integrated into the national story, *Hilal*'s scrapbook incorporates reader-viewers into the collective, their families into the national family.

# PART II

# The Politics of Women Nationalists

PART 2 TURNS TO THE POLITICS of women nationalists in the interwar years, focusing on the activities of a group of elite women who hoped to be remembered as important political actors. It opens with the story of the "ladies' demonstrations" of March 1919, or, rather, the way those events entered into collective memory. Subsequent chapters consider the career of the "Mother of the Egyptians," Safiyya Zaghlul; the politics of Wafdist women; and the Islamist path of Labiba Ahmad. These elite women alternated and mixed Wafdist, feminist, Islamist, and social politics, and saw their activism as an integral part of nationalism and nation-building. Together these stories show the vibrancy of women's political culture in this period, as well as its limitations. In foregrounding women nationalists, gendered images of the nation move to the background, but they do not disappear. Elite women proved adroit at manipulating family rhetoric and gendered symbols at the same time that they fought for a political space.

# CHAPTER FIVE

# The "Ladies' Demonstrations"

Elite Egyptian women entered the collective memory and political history of Egypt when, in March 1919, a week into the unrest that came to be known as the revolution of 1919, they staged their own demonstrations.[1] A mythology has grown up around the event, which has received attention in scores of Arabic and English texts and has achieved iconic stature. Memories of the "ladies' demonstration" were preserved and shaped through both literary vehicles and visual devices. The "ladies' demonstration" of March 1919 comes to be one of the most prominent symbols of revolution in the nationalist repertoire.

Collective memory helps to define a nation.[2] The parameters of the group are often drawn around those who share a past or, rather, a memory of the past, including triumphs and humiliations. Yet memories are not givens. They are selected, shaped, and preserved through visual records, texts, sites, and ceremonies. Photographs, as we have seen, serve as one of the major triggers of memory, preserving and filtering it in the process. Texts—oral and written—record attitudes to events and often become the scripts for rituals of remembering. Sites of memory, such as cemeteries, memorials, or museums, are visited to recall a person or event. Often, what are most remembered are wars and revolutions, which act as defining moments for a national community and subsequently form the core of the collective memory. Women's political culture has often been excluded from the collective memory or remembered only selectively at key moments when it served some symbolic purpose.

This chapter starts with an analysis of the women's demonstrations of March 1919 and argues that when they occurred, they conveyed different political messages from those subsequently attributed to them.[3] This first section combines U.S. and Egyptian archival, literary, and visual sources, giving greatest weight to those closest to the event, pointing out some of the contradictions in the data, and paying particular attention to the petitions penned by the demonstrators. The second section of the chapter traces the gendering of the collective memory of this event, revealing how Egyptians' memories changed over time and how the meanings men and women ascribed to these events diverged. The third section of the chapter examines a set of photos closely associated with the women's demonstrations of March 1919 that have acted as sites or triggers of memory. The chapter underscores the complex relationship between history and memory, activism and symbolism, and political and visual culture.

## DEMONSTRATING WOMEN

At the outset of World War I, the British severed Egypt's ties with the Ottoman Empire, deposed the Egyptian khedive, 'Abbas Hilmi II (who was in Istanbul at the time), and declared Egypt a protectorate. Egypt subsequently became a theater of war. The Ottomans, who twice attempted to cross the Suez Canal, were repulsed by the British, who used Egypt as a staging ground for military campaigns into Palestine and at Gallipoli. Egyptians were forced to provide labor and supplies for these and other campaigns. Male laborers were sent to assist the British war effort in Iraq, the Dardanelles, Salonika, France, and Italy, and elsewhere, while female laborers took to the fields.

Egyptians anticipated that cooperation during the war would lead to independence after it. Yet in spite of their sacrifices for the Allied cause, they were not invited to the peace talks in Paris. Eager to press for a renegotiation of Egypt's status, a delegation (Wafd) consisting of Sa'd Zaghlul, 'Abd al-'Aziz Fahmi Bey, and 'Ali Sha'rawi Pasha (Huda's husband) met with Sir Reginald Wingate, the British high commissioner, on 13 November 1918. The men, prominent members of the prorogued legislative assembly, asked for permission to go to Europe to press for Egyptian independence. After their request was denied, the Wafd launched a massive petition campaign to show that the group had the broad backing of the Egyptian population; Zaghlul emerged as the leading orator of the group during this phase. When Wingate was recalled to London, he left Sir Milne Cheetham in charge. Cheetham soon ordered the arrest and exile to Malta of four leading Wafdists on 8 March 1919. Protestors rallied for their release and right to present Egypt's claim for independence.

While the war had pushed peasant women out into the fields in greater numbers to replace male family members drafted into labor corps, it confined elite women to their homes. Prior to the war, middle- and upper-class women had been active in a range of educational, journalistic, and associational endeavors. These enterprises gave them a sense of national community and prepared them for political action. But the war forced a curtailing of these new activities: some schools were taken over to house refugees or hospitals, periodicals folded in the face of high production costs, and associations were disbanded. Urban elite women did not suffer physically during the war, but they faced inconveniences, shortages, and higher prices. Moreover, the war provided new lessons in colonial politics, increased hostility to the British occupation, and further familiarized elite women with the language of national determination.[4] While forced into quiescence during the war, elite women could not stand by afterward when other groups actively protested. Drawn into politics through their collective action, these women later became a symbol of the revolution.

The basic outlines of the story of the 1919 women's demonstrations in Egypt are well known, having been reconstructed from a number of British and Arabic sources, to which reports from the daily Arabic press and U.S. archives can be added. Yet the sources are rife with contradictions, making it almost impossible to produce a definitive detailed chronology and to disentangle the exact details of the March demonstrations, which have often been blurred in later accounts. The first demonstration occurred the morning of Sunday, 16 March, and was followed by another on Wednesday, 19 March, and/or Thursday, 20 March. *Al-Ahram* mentioned a "ladies' demonstration" on 16 March, in which women drove around in cars to consuls, and reported a gathering in Qasr al-'Ayni of 250 women who marched with flags on 20 March.[5] A petition from Egyptian women to the American consul-general dated 20 March speaks of a demonstration the previous day, with the elements of being stopped and surrounded that have become famous.[6] The London *Times* noted a demonstration of 400 women on 19 March.[7] It is quite possible that the events often associated with 16 March actually occurred on 19 or 20 March. It is also possible that the demonstrations followed similar scripts, for the symbolic components within and of the demonstrations were more or less the same.[8] As we shall see, these two or three demonstrations have often been conflated into one in collective memory.

The demonstrations of March 1919 are often depicted as being spontaneous. The marches of elite women were, however, planned in advance and well orchestrated. The circle around Huda Shaʻrawi, a leading organizer, sent a delegation to the authorities to obtain permission for a protest. They returned empty-handed but later read in the daily *al-Muqattam* that permission had been granted by colonial authorities. They then telephoned their friends to spread the word of the planned protest. Other advance preparations included the painting of banners and the penning of petitions. Although the Wafd reviewed at least one of these letters to give its stamp of approval, there is no evidence that the demonstrations themselves were planned by male nationalist leaders.

On the morning of the protest, women met at the home of ʻAtiyya Abu Isbaʻa, which was located in Garden City, near the central square of Maydan Ismaʻiliyya (later renamed Maydan al-Tahrir), government offices, and foreign legations. The women signed the petitions and discussed the route to be followed. The participants then marched in an orderly procession. Walking on foot created a different impact than demonstrating in a procession of cars. The urban street dress of these women—long black head scarves, white face veils, and black robes—revealed that they came from the elite. (A couple of Copts marched in hats.) Estimates of the number of participants ranged from 150 to 530, although later the figure was sometimes inflated. It was, in any case, a peaceful and ordered procession of finite size.

Those in front of the women's procession carried small flags and Arabic and French placards: "We protest the shedding of the blood of the innocent and the unarmed," "We demand complete independence," and so on.[9] As they walked, they shouted slogans similar to those on their placards: "Long live freedom and independence!" and "Down with the protectorate!" The procession moved along Qasr al-ʻAyni Street, the planned route, toward the foreign legations, where the organizers had originally intended to deliver written protests. But those in front diverted the march in the direction of Saʻd Zaghlul's house, a focal point for Wafdist meetings and political speeches, and the symbolic center of the "national family." It is here that the main drama of the day occurred.

"When we had arrived at the end of Rue Saad Zaghloul Pasha we were surrounded by British troops who leveled their weapons at us," the women related in their subsequent petition.[10] Huda (left unnamed in some accounts) then challenged the soldiers with the words: "We surrender to death, fire your rifle into my heart and make in Egypt a second Miss Cavell."[11] (Edith Cavell was a British nurse executed by the

Germans in Belgium in 1915 for helping Allied prisoners of war escape.) The choice of hero may seem paradoxical, for rather than draw from the pantheon of ancient Arab or Egyptian female heroes, Huda looked to the recent British past. Then again, the choice shows her ability to manipulate British symbols, and the words became a critical part of the memory of the event. A fellow marcher, who feared that any harm to Huda would inspire the unarmed students accompanying them to advance and lead to a bloodbath, restrained her. The officers then "kept us standing thus for two hours under a burning sun."[12] Sir Thomas Russell Pasha, British commander of the Cairo City Police, admitted to having decided to leave the women surrounded and alone to deplete their energies and enthusiasm. The standoff ended when Russell returned and called the women's carriages.[13] The American consul-general may have intervened toward that end as well.

The women later presented petitions to foreign legations and protested the treatment they had received. "We, the undersigned Egyptian ladies, have the honor to inform you that it was our intention yesterday to organize a pacific demonstration and to present ourselves at the various Diplomatic Agencies in order to present the written protest annexed to this letter," they wrote to the American consul-general. The list of signatories reads like a directory of the Egyptian elite and includes such female notables as Safiyya Zaghlul, Sharifa Riyad, Labiba Ahmad, Esther Fahmi Wisa, and the wife of the late Qasim Amin.[14] The petition lists confirm that the women came from the highest strata and were often the wives and daughters of pashas and beys, which is how they signed their names. The lists also show that women frequently protested in the company of female family members. About two-thirds of the women who signed the petitions linked to the protests were married, although some married women, like Hidiyya Barakat (who later headed the philanthropy Mabarrat Muhammad 'Ali), were still in their teens or early twenties. Huda Sha'rawi was about forty at the time and enjoyed a certain authority over more youthful protestors.

Delivering petitions to foreign legations became a central part of the ritual of elite women's protests. The texts reveal that these women conceptualized Egyptian women as a group and claimed to speak for the female half of the political community. "In the name of the women of Egypt," began one document. This one and others ended with such signatures as "The Ladies of Egypt" and "The Egyptian Women."[15] Women demonstrating in 1919 also deployed kinship idioms. They were, for example, "the mothers, sisters and wives of the victims massacred for the satisfaction of British ambitions."[16] By presenting themselves as "Mothers of the Nation," or other female relations, they strengthened the notion that the nation was a family, and they used their moral authority to dramatize Egypt's situation.

The petitions presented the case for Egyptian independence and protested the British military authorities' suppression of public demonstrations. The authors objected to the use of force against Egyptian demonstrators, "who have done nothing more than claim the liberty and independence of their country, in conformity with the principles proclaimed by Dr. [President Woodrow] Wilson and accepted by all belligerent and neutral nations." In particular they condemned the "shooting down with machine guns women and children, all absolutely unarmed; and this only because they had indulged in simple, pacific demonstrations of protest."[17] They addressed the international community: "We beg you to send our message to America and to President Wilson personally. Let them hear our call. We believe they will not suffer Liberty to be crushed in Egypt, that human Liberty for which you[r] brave and noble sons have died."[18] Over one hundred and eighteen women signed this particular petition.

In the demonstrations of March, elite women generally remained apart from women of other classes. One British account suggests that the veiled women came attended by their Nubian "handmaidens," but no other source substantiates this.[19] Just two years after the revolution broke out in Russia, elite Egyptian women took to the streets to become a new "political public," but theirs was no social revolution. They staged planned and orderly demonstrations in an effort to unseat the British colonial authority and shore up the power of their class. They wore the garb of privileged, secluded women who did not work in fields, factories, or other peoples' homes. They communicated over the phone to plan their march, arrived to protest in cars, and returned home that way. That Coptic and Muslim women from the same strata protested together further affirms the class alliance at work. The evidence belies the myth that the "lady demonstrators" expressed social solidarity and unity across class boundaries. Rather, their actions reinforced a hierarchical class vision for society.

The petitions used a feminine voice (as Egyptian women, or mothers, sisters, and wives of Egyptian men) to express nationalist concerns and appealed to an international audience. Although later many would characterize the March 1919 demonstrations as a feminist act, or claim that they had feminist content, the petitions and placards reveal that female demonstrators did not raise feminist concerns in the course of their marches. In 1919, elite Egyptian women did not explicitly mix causes. Working-class and peasant women occasionally mixed with men in the unrest, and actresses, who were already accustomed to working with men, sometimes joined men in their protests. But elite women remained apart from men in most demonstrations. As they entered a new public space, they remained segregated, reinforcing certain spatial gender boundaries.[20]

The event had inverted the usual gender order, although not in the ways that were often attributed to it later. Women took center stage on major thoroughfares, commanded public streets, and shouted slogans for a mostly male audience. As they carved out new political roles for themselves, elite women challenged the gender status quo. Herein lay the revolutionary potential of their demonstrations. These were women who would not walk in the streets alone for fear of being harassed, who had not engaged in collective public action such as funeral marches or other such ceremonies, and whose voices were often muted or controlled. Now they won admiration and respect when they marched for the nation. They submerged themselves in the collective, raised their voices to shout slogans, and emerged with a greater sense of solidarity. Participating in these demonstrations had a strong psychological impact on those involved. For in spite of the plans and the order, there was a certain spontaneity to the marches, a liberation in taking to the streets, an exhilaration in shouting. Recollections of those heady days of March 1919 stayed with this cohort, shaping their outlook, activism, and memories.[21]

## GENDERED RECOLLECTIONS

The women's demonstrations of March 1919 quickly became part of the collective national memory. Yet the collective memory of this "iconic moment" fractured along gender lines, converging at some points and diverging at others. The memories presented here are of Muslim and Coptic, male and female, mostly secular elites. This is not to say that gender provided the only fault line in collective memory. National memories also fractured along class, communal, secular-religious, and urban-rural lines.[22]

### Remembrances of Male Egyptians

The reaction of the male public to women's demonstrations proved overwhelmingly positive by most accounts. We are told that crowds came to cheer the women, and people watched from windows. Eight years earlier, when Egyptian women had tried to enter another public space—the

new national university—they had been heckled and blocked from holding segregated classes, even on a day when the university was officially
closed.[23] But this time the women had entered a public space to promote
the nationalist cause, not to advance their own educations, and no reports
appear of Egyptian onlookers heckling the demonstrators or blocking
their procession.

The event was quickly celebrated in verse. Hafiz Ibrahim's poem "The
Ladies' Demonstration" stands out as the single most important memorial
to the event. Hafiz came from a modest background and proved sensitive
to social issues. Known as the "Poet of the Nile," he was close to fifty and
headed the literary division at the Egyptian National Library at the time of
the revolution.[24] "The Ladies' Demonstration" was printed and circulated
anonymously, according to Huda Sha'rawi, and appeared thus in the journal *Lisan al-Umma*.[25] It was later published under Hafiz's name as part of
a collection of nationalist poems. It became a key trigger to remembering
the women's demonstration and shaped subsequent images of it.

> The fair ladies went out to protest,
> and I approached to see them gathering.
>
> Behold! from underneath the black
> of their clothes, their hair is shown free!
>
> They went up like shining stars
> that rise in the middle of darkness.
>
> They marched along the roads, and
> made for Sa'd's house, their goal;
>
> There they went in dignified demeanour,
> and their feelings were clearly demonstrated.
>
> Then, suddenly, an armed band came,
> and the horses were given free rein.
>
> Behold the soldiers! Their swords
> are drawn, and pointed at their breasts!
>
> And the guns, and the rifles!
> The sharpness of the swords, the teeth,
>
> All those horses, how they strike
> a cordon all around them!
>
> Roses and basil were on that day
> the only weapons on which they relied.
>
> The hours of struggle seemed so long
> that embryos might have become grey-haired.
>
> But then the women became feeble,
> for the fair sex has no physical strength.

They were defeated and fled,
dispersed, to their palaces.

What a glorious army indeed!
What a victory, to have defeated women!

Was it not as if the Germans
had dressed up in veils, and appeared

Among the women, having come secretly
to Egypt, with Hindenburg himself to lead them;

That would explain why they so much
feared their courage and their stratagem.[26]

Hafiz's "The Ladies' Demonstration" can be divided into three sections. In the first third, Hafiz celebrates the "ladies" who marched dignified and determined toward Sa'd's house. He twice contrasts darkness
("the black of their clothes" and "in the middle of darkness") with freedom and light ("their hair is shown free" and "like shining stars").
Women themselves become a light in the darkness. The middle third of
the poem turns to the central drama of the event: the confrontation with
soldiers. Here Hafiz contrasts the weaponry of the British (armed, swords,
pointed, guns, rifles, sharpness, teeth) against the frailty of the women
(roses, basil, feeble, defeated). Yet their defeat is transformed in the final
third. That the British needed such a show of force revealed their fear in
the face of women's moral courage.

The nationalists sensed that in the ladies' demonstration they had a
potent symbol in their hands. Ahmad Amin, a writer and teacher who
had been assigned the task of writing leaflets on important events by the
Wafd, penned a long pamphlet that was printed and distributed describ-
ing the women's demonstration. Amin recounted the basic outlines of
the event in his memoirs, published in 1950, and included, among other
things, the "Miss Cavell" line.[27]

In a short text published in Paris the year of the revolution, Muhammad Sabri, a graduate of the Sorbonne, presented Egypt's case to French
readers. In the context of remarks on the wide participation of all Egyptians in the revolution, he discussed women's "moving" demonstrations.
He recorded one line that seems to have struck him (in addition to the
oft-quoted "Miss Cavell" line): "I will not marry," a young woman delivering a speech outside Shepherd's Hotel reportedly declared, "so as not
to have an infant who will become the slave of the English."[28] Sabri's
book, and the second volume that followed two years later, contained
photographs taken during the unrest, including one of lower-class women
riding in a donkey cart during a demonstration, a second contrasting

image of an elite woman standing in a carriage, and a third that will be discussed below.[29] Demonstrations by elite women inspired Egyptian artists and sculptors such as Muhammad Naji and Mahmud Mukhtar, who were then working in Paris, the center of the art world (as discussed in chapter 3).

'Abd al-Rahman al-Rafi'i witnessed the revolution of 1919 as a young man of thirty and then chronicled it in his *Thawrat 1919*, which first appeared in 1946 and has gone through numerous reprintings. The prolific al-Rafi'i, who wrote over a dozen volumes on Egyptian history, drew on archival material, as well as his personal memories and links with political figures. Before the war, he was a member of the Watani Party and after it served as a member of the lower and upper houses of parliament.[30] His *Thawrat 1919* stands as one of the most detailed accounts of the revolution. In entries for 16 and 20 March, he describes the women's demonstrations and includes letters of protest, the names of those signing the letters, and the poem by Hafiz Ibrahim. Notable in his more lengthy account of the first demonstration is the reception given the demonstrators as "all of Cairo" poured out to cheer them on. He places the marches squarely in the context of the nationalist struggle and does not ascribe feminist meanings to them. He does, however, set the ladies' demonstrations apart, calling them exactly that.[31]

Salama Musa, a socialist from an elite Coptic family, recalled the women's demonstrations in his memoirs, published in Arabic a year after al-Rafi'i's book appeared. He also included Hafiz Ibrahim's poem in its entirety.[32] However, his interpretation of the events differed from that of the historian: "That even women went out to stage demonstrations was not only a revolt against the English, but even more so against a thousand years of veiled obscurity."[33] Musa, who had supported the women's rights movement ever since his student days in England, put the demonstrations in a feminist context.[34]

The "even the women" refrain is echoed in Naguib Mahfouz's novel *Bayna al-Qasrayn* (Between the Two Palaces, 1956). Mahfouz was only about eight in 1919, but he later researched the period in great depth, and he captures the collective memory of that year. "Even the women have organized a demonstration," Yasin, the eldest son in the 'Abd al-Jawad family, tells his brother Fahmi in the context of a conversation on the spread of the revolution. Fahmi responds by reciting the opening verses from Hafiz Ibrahim's poem, which the womanizer Yasin feels he ought to have memorized too. Like others, Mahfuz links the women's demonstration with Hafiz's poem in his evocation of the event.[35]

With the revisions of history in the wake of the revolution of 1952, the revolution of 1919 receded in importance in Egyptian historiography and was often seen as a missed opportunity. But the women's marches did not fade so quickly and completely in memory. In the historian 'Abd al-'Aziz Ramadan's account of the Egyptian nationalist movement, first published in 1968, the ladies' demonstrations remains a small but significant part of the story of 1919. Ramadan sets them in a dual context, both as a sign of the size of the nationalist struggle and as part of the struggle for women's rights. In discussing the latter, Ramadan mentions male champions of women's rights, such as Qasim Amin and 'Abd al-Hamid Hamdi, the publisher of *al-Sufur*, rather than female advocates. The latter had been forgotten, blocked from the national memory.[36]

A year later, upon the fiftieth anniversary of the 1919 revolution, the illustrated weekly *al-Musawwar* devoted a special issue to commemorating it. That issue shows a photograph of a veiled woman on the cover holding a flag aloft. The picture was originally framed, or has been cropped, to show a symmetry between the veiled woman and the flag, the woman as the nation. (I shall return to this photo below.) Although the editors sought to use the symbol of a veiled protestor to stir the national memory, they did not consider the women's demonstrations significant enough to place them early in the issue. Woman as a symbol was thought more important than women as historical actors. An article containing extracts from Huda Sha'rawi's memoirs and interviews of female participants appeared only toward the back of the issue, under the title "The Revolution of 1919 Raised the Veil on the Face of the Egyptian Woman!" Events of 1919 and the early 1920s are thus elided, and the feminist dimension of the demonstrations is stressed.[37]

In 1969, the government also issued a stamp commemorating the revolution of 1919 that prominently depicted veiled elite women alongside shaykhs and effendis in the crowd.[38] Veiled women also appeared in crowd scenes of the revolution of 1919 in film. In Hasan al-Imam's classic film version of *Bayna al-Qasrayn*, released in 1964, a ten-minute montage of revolutionary activities shows veiled elite women marching in demonstrations with men as well as cross-class and communal solidarity.[39] In both stamp and film, the nation is a fusion, with religious and secular, communal, class, and gender elements unified.

In short, the demonstrations by elite women in March 1919 inspired some of their male compatriots, who commemorated the event with oral recitations, written texts, and visual representations. The "ladies' demonstrations" of 1919 are initially presented by male Egyptians as proof of the breadth of the nationalist movement, as well as evidence of British suppression of free and peaceful expression. Later they also become a link in the struggle for women's rights, a struggle led and dominated by men in these accounts. Finally, demonstrating veiled women become key figures in the crowd and the quintessential symbol of patriotism.

*Women Recall 1919*

Women's memories of 1919 survived as oral traditions passed from one generation to the next, with some versions eventually written down. References to the "ladies' demonstration" also appeared early on in the women's press, where editors used the event both to inspire women and to castigate them for their current lack of activity. Labiba Hashim, editor of *Fatat al-Sharq*, reported the highlights of a speech in 1926 by Esther Fahmi Wisa, who had already elevated the number of women in the March demonstrations to one thousand.[40] Balsam 'Abd al-Malik, the editor of *al-Mar'a al-Misriyya*, printed Hafiz's poem in full in 1926 and wondered what had happened to the ladies of 1919.[41]

There are few memoirs by women covering this period, making Huda Sha'rawi's account a rare exception. Huda dictated her memoirs to her secretary sometime before her death in 1947. The last date mentioned in the text is 1935, and a journal in 1937 announced the imminent publication of the memoirs.[42] They did not appear then, however. *Al-Musawwar* published short selections only in 1969, and another decade passed before the women's magazine *al-Hawwa'* serialized them in 1980. They appeared in full the following year, when Dar al-Hilal published *Mudhakkirat Huda Sha'rawi*. An English translation of part of the memoir, *Harem Years: The Memoirs of an Egyptian Feminist*, based on a different version of the manuscript, appeared in 1986.[43]

The publishing history of the memoirs is complex, and it is difficult to determine when there are slips of memory or interventions by an editor or translator, especially when there are inconsistencies between the published versions. In remembering the events of March 1919, the founder of the Egyptian Feminist Union could not have drawn on al-Rafi'i's version (and he probably did not have her memoirs on hand as an aid either); but she had petitions and letters, some of which were reproduced in the text, to ground her memory. Still, that memory (like most memories) may not have been perfect. Huda mentioned only one March demonstration in the printed Arabic edition and set the date as 20 March. (The English translation gives the date as 16 March.) Another idiosyncrasy is the nationality of the soldiers surrounding the women. The translated version reads,

"The British also brought out Egyptian soldiers armed with sticks," which is consistent with Russell's report. But in the published Arabic version, Egyptian conscripts (who would be seen as collaborators) have been expunged by the editor or never existed in that text.[44]

Huda Sha'rawi's memoirs illuminate the emotional highs and lows of the event. After a decade or so had passed, she still remembered the internal tensions among the demonstrators. One incident involved misspellings of Arabic in the banners carried by marchers. Another involved a mutiny in the ranks over the route. Huda recalled that the young women in front had been informed of the planned route, which was to take them first to the foreign legations and then to the *Bayt al-Umma* (House of the Nation), the name by which Sa'd's house came to be known, but the girls in the lead attempted to reverse the order. The result: "We saw only a few people," and they learned only later that a crowd of foreigners had waited for them in front of the embassies with bouquets of flowers. (In the extracts in *al-Musawwar*, the internal discord that surfaced over the planning and execution of the march was toned down.) Huda was also disappointed in the number of women who marched; they had been unable to telephone more when they learned at the last minute that the protest had been approved.[45]

Huda more positively remembered her starring role and the "Miss Cavell" line in the encounter with the British troops. After the troops had encircled the demonstrators, she marched to the front, where a soldier quickly knelt and pointed a rifle at her chest. Huda was for advancing, but was cautioned against this, as the male students accompanying them would be harmed. "Those words returned me to my senses," she recalled. Huda ended this chapter of the published Arabic memoirs with reference to the poem that Hafiz Ibrahim had written "to encourage the women and record that historical event."[46]

Doria Shafiq, a liberal feminist of middle-class background and protégé of Huda Sha'rawi, included a chapter on "The Egyptian Woman in the Revolution of 1919" in her book *al-Mar'a al-Misriyya* (The Egyptian Woman, 1955) published three years after the Free Officers' revolution. Doria may not have been able to tap her own reminiscences of the women's demonstrations, for in 1919 she had been a ten-year-old living in the Egyptian provinces. She drew, instead, on documents Huda sent her for her doctoral thesis at the Sorbonne, as well as on 'Abd al-Rahman al-Rafi'i's account, and she also reprinted Hafiz's poem in full in her history. Yet the iconography that illustrates her chapter is distinct: a sketch shows a woman in the foreground with a flag in her right hand

and a torch in her left hand leading a group of veiled women marching with flags. Obviously, women in 1919 did not march with torches, which in Western iconography stand for enlightenment and reflect Doria's liberal philosophy.[47]

When Egyptians marked the fiftieth or "golden" anniversary of the revolution of 1919, several women's associations organized a joint committee to celebrate women's activities in the national movement. Some of the women who had marched or otherwise participated were still alive (including Jamila 'Atiyya, Ihsan Ahmad, and Esther Fahmi Wisa; Hidiyya Barakat died on the morning of the festivities). The jubilee celebration opened at the Opera House before an audience of international guests, government officials, and other dignitaries under the auspices of Gamal Abdel Nasser.[48] The press carried retrospectives: the special feature on women's roles in the revolution in *al-Musawwar*'s commemorative issue opened with selections from Huda Sha'rawi's memoirs, and interviews with ten participants then followed.

The women were all obviously young at the time (some had been students at the Saniyya Girls' School), and they looked up to such women as Huda Sha'rawi and Safiyya Zaghlul. Their involvement in the revolution varied: they marched, picketed, distributed literature, gave speeches, and wrote letters of protest. A few discussed their personal recollections of the demonstrations. 'Atiyya Abu Isba'a recalled that most of the women's marches started at her father's home. Ihsan Ahmad gave dates and names of female martyrs, distinguished between the different demonstrations, and spoke of the receptive crowds. Tahiyya Muhammad Isfahani remembered one breastfeeding mother: forced to choose between staying with the demonstration and leaving to feed her baby, the woman declared, "My country before my baby!" Esther Fahmi Wisa, who was about eighty at the time of the jubilee, remembered women of all classes joining the processions of women's marches.[49] The article moves from these generally elite women to lower-class martyrs in its closing section. One of the themes that emerged in memories of 1919 in the wake of the revolution of 1952 was the cooperation of women of all classes during the unrest.

Esther Fahmi Wisa delivered a speech at the jubilee on "the emancipation of Egyptian women and their freedom from the veil," which included reminiscences of the March demonstration. She recalled going with her aunt, Regina Khayyat, and a third woman to a house on Qasr al-'Ayni Street. "What, where are the hats?" they were asked, in a reference to Coptic women, who did not veil. Curiously, she does not ascribe the Nurse Cavell line to Huda, although Huda credits Esther's aunt with holding her back to prevent bloodshed. And Esther elides the March demonstrations with those held nine months later around the time of the founding of the Women's Wafd Central Committee (WWCC). This may explain her estimation of the number of participants as one thousand, a figure closer to that of the later demonstrations.[50]

An official history of the EFU on the occasion of its fiftieth anniversary appeared four years later in 1973. The small book echoes the populist themes that emerged in the jubilee interviews. Huda Sha'rawi headed a "demonstration made up of hundreds of women from all classes of the people," the authors wrote. Their list of slogans included feminist ones: "[T]hey demanded the exit of the English, complete freedom for Egypt, and equality with men in all rights and responsibilities."[51] The demonstrations of 1919 were linked directly to the formation of the EFU in 1923 and blurred with later protests.[52]

Scholarly works on twentieth-century Egyptian women's history with a special focus on the secular women's movement began appearing in Arabic in the 1970s and 1980s. Titles included Ijlal Khalifa's *al-Haraka al-Nisa'iyya al-Haditha: Qissat al-Mar'a al-'Arabiyya 'ala Ard Misr* (The Modern Women's Movement: The Story of the Arab Woman in the Land of Egypt [Cairo, 1973]); Latifa Muhammad Salim's *al-Mar'a al-Misriyya wa al-Taghyir al-Ijtima'i, 1919–1945* (The Egyptian Woman and Social Change [Cairo, 1984]); and Amal al-Subki's *al-Haraka al-Nisa'iyya fi Misr ma bayna al-Thawratayn 1919 wa-1952* (The Women's Movement in Egypt between the Two Revolutions, 1919 and 1952 [Cairo, 1986]). Khalifa, like Huda Sha'rawi forty years earlier, noted the importance of Hafiz's poem, "Many of those contemporary to the Egyptian Revolution of 1919 and children of the participants still recall Hafiz's poem and memorize it by heart."[53] Afaf Marsot's "The Revolutionary Gentlewomen in Egypt" appeared in English in this period as well (1978). Marsot drew on her conversations with Hidiyya Barakat before the latter's death, as well as on the memories of family and friends.[54]

These female historians agree, as their periodization alone makes clear, that 1919 marked the beginnings of women's public life in Egypt. "Thus it was a radical shock, like a nationalist uprising, which catapulted harem ladies into public life," wrote Marsot.[55] These historians also document the broad range of political nationalist activities in which women engaged—boycotts, pickets, distributing literature, marching—at the center of which they placed the demonstrations. They saw these activities as substantive and real contributions to the nationalist cause, which they argued proved women's nationalist credentials and gave them license to press their claims. "From then the idea of women's emancipation rid itself of its ancient chains and entered the stage of action," noted Latifa Salim.[56] These scholars credited the demonstrations with breaking down gender and other boundaries. They deemphasized the gender segregation that characterized much of elite women's activity at that time with references to the women who "agitated side by side with their men."[57] They tended to downplay or ignore the less visible sociopolitical activities of the previous decades on the part of elite women that had paved the way for their more visible roles after 1919.

These scholars also stressed the populist nature of the revolution and the participation of women of all classes in the struggle. Khalifa, for example, lists the names, places of residence, and dates of death of the "female martyrs." The female martyrs and veiled marchers were linked in collective action, although they may not have literally engaged in the same actions or had the same experiences. "It is said that the daughter of the wealthy or aristocratic class is the one who participated in the revolution and the adept political work after it," Khalifa writes; "and that the daughter of the middle and lower classes is the one who died as a martyr by the hand of colonialism, who felt its humiliation and oppression."[58] The feminist Nawal al-Sa'dawi, a physician by training, pushes this critique further, observing that "little has been said about the masses of poor women who rushed into the national struggle without counting the cost, and who lost their lives, whereas the lesser contributions of aristocratic women leaders have been noisily acclaimed and brought to the forefront."[59] Yet, rather than condemn the women's demonstrations and risk losing a potent symbol and point of reference, most accounts after the revolution of 1952 stress cross-class cooperation.

Seventy-five years after the event, official remembrances of 1919 had receded in importance. The celebration of 'Id al-Jihad al-Watani (the Day of National Struggle), commemorating the Wafd's visit on 13 November 1918 to the British high commissioner, had long since been abandoned.[60] Sa'd Zaghlul, once a towering figure in the Egyptian memory, had been reduced in stature. Yet the memory of women's demonstrations of March 1919 still resonated. When officials met in Cairo in June 1994 to promote a program for women's equality, they proclaimed the annual celebration of 16 March as "Egyptian Woman's Day."[61] The organizers of the event claimed the mantle of early women activists; and, as many women's advocates had done previously, they asserted that women deserved rights because of the contributions they had made to the national cause.

The "ladies' demonstration" quickly entered the collective memory, with visual records, texts, sites, and ceremonies shaping that memory. Hafiz's poem, 'Abd al-Rahman al-Rafi'i's chronicle, and women's memoirs and speeches were particularly instrumental in generating a mythology around it. Differences between male and female memories of a formative event in Egyptian history emerged, suggesting that collective national memory may be fractured along gendered as well as class, communal, and religious-secular lines. Egyptians came to agree that women's participation in the revolution of 1919 set the stage for the founding of the women's movement and gave it feminist content. Men and women disagreed, however, on the extent of women's contribution to the national cause. Male writers and artists stressed the inspirational value of veiled women marching. Their participation became a sign of the size of the uprising, with the phrase "even the women" echoing in male writings. Women writers acknowledged and manipulated female symbols, but they also emphasized women's solid contributions to the revolution and gave detailed descriptions of the events. These writers argued that in confronting the British, elite women helped to erode colonial control, attract international attention, and build national unity. Although elite women had marched segregated from working-class women, as well as men, after 1952, the event also came to have a populist dimension in recollections. The "ladies' demonstration" became central in middle- and upper-class women's memories of the past because women's and national history were fused at that moment, and elite women had a central role in the drama.

## THE PHOTOGRAPHIC RECORD

Visual material, and photographs in particular, played a crucial role in embedding the women's demonstrations of March 1919 in the collective memory. Photographs became a trigger for remembering the revolution and shaping the women's demonstrations as an iconic moment. In time, the veiled woman became the model militant, a major symbol of the national struggle, and an abstraction of the nation itself, while the details of the original events receded in importance. Both men and women used photos to illustrate their works and arguments, with men emphasizing women's symbolic importance in the struggle and women stressing the substantive contributions. Foreign scholars also found these images appealing.

I shall focus on a set of photos often associated with women in the revolution of 1919. My main purpose has been to examine the pictures that the Egyptian public viewed as they first appeared, rather than to find the original negative or prints. Grounding the photos in their original contexts challenges the purposes to which some of these photos were later put. Censorship was in effect during this period, delaying and sometimes preventing the publication of material. Because *al-Lata'if al-Musawwara* published the photos shortly after the events, it is presumed that the information given in its captions is more accurate than information published some time after the events. (*Al-Ahram*, a two-page daily at the time, reported on the women's demonstrations but did not carry photographs.) After dating the photos, situating them in their historical contexts, and suggesting who the cameramen may have been, I shall discuss the printed images.

The first photo (figure 15), published on 21 April 1919, shows four veiled women in a carriage.[62] Two sit and two stand: the one standing farthest forward holds a flag up; the other woman standing, whom the photographer has placed in the center of his frame, holds her right arm aloft. On the near side of the photo, men in turbans and tarbushes stand looking at the woman in the center, listening to her as men on the far side of the carriage march by. Servants in *gallabiyya*s sit on the front of the carriage, one carrying a tree branch (these were often carried in 1919 in lieu of flags by the lower classes). The photo appeared as part of a two-page spread of nine photos of celebrations held on 8 April upon news of the release of Sa'd Zaghlul and his colleagues from Malta. Next to the photo appears the banner "Long Live the Egyptian Ladies," and underneath the caption, "An Egyptian lady standing in her carriage raises her hand to greet the people and to acclaim the nation and Egypt." In the lower right corner of the photo, which is of better quality than others on the page, is inscribed R. Co. (Ramses Company).

This image has been frequently reprinted. The special issue of *al-Musawwar* published on the fiftieth anniversary of the 1919 revolution carried a cropped version, the middle slice with only three women. There, the woman standing was identified as Fikriyya Husni, a supporter of the Watani Party.[63] Since the journal *al-Musawwar*, which is part of the Hilal group, was not started until 1925, its photos of 1919 came from collections purchased over the years and probably from the photo archive of *al-Lata'if al-Musawwara*. A differently cropped version of the photo appears in al-Hilal's 1992 one-hundred-year anniversary album *Sijill al-Hilal al-Musawwar* (The Illustrated Record of al-Hilal).[64] Scholars have also reprinted this photograph from originals found in archives in New York and London, with one suggesting that these women were part of

Figure 15. "An Egyptian lady standing in her carriage raises her hand to greet the people and to acclaim the nation and Egypt." Photograph by the Ramses Company, 8 April 1919. *Al-Lata'if al-Musawwara*, 21 April 1919, 4.

"the women's demonstration."[65] Yet the carriage was not participating in the famous "ladies' demonstration" of March but rather in a celebration of the release of the detainees from Malta a few weeks later. In that April celebration, according to reports, women joined men in a procession organized by gender, profession, and rank. Cabinet members and legislators led off, followed by ulama (clerics), judges, lawyers, doctors, government employees, army officers, workers, and students. Elite women rode in cars in the rear, and after them came women of lesser means, sitting in donkey carts.[66] The organizers of the demonstration intended to present a show of national unity to the foreign powers, but the ceremony also reflected and reinforced gender and social divisions in Egyptian society.

A second image (figure 16) in the same issue of *al-Lata'if al-Musawwara* was from the same day of celebrations (8 April), according to the editor.[67] This photo shows a group of seven in a carriage: a driver, a young child, and a boy in front, and four women in the rear. Of the latter, two wear the dark face veil and nose pieces of lower-class women and are probably servants; the two others wear the white face veil of the elite. The woman in the middle holds a flag aloft, and the photographer (once again from the Ramses Company) has framed the picture around this flag. While the carriage in the first photo was part of a crowd, this

Figure 16. "A splendid scene took place that happy
day [8 April 1919]: the undertaking of Egyptian
ladies to cheer the people and the nation." Photograph by the Ramses Company, 8 April 1919.
*Al-Lata'if al-Musawwara*, 21 April 1919, 6.

vehicle appears solitary in a close-up showing long shadows. Several rid-
ers face the camera, posing for the photographer. Cropped versions cutting out the long shadows appear in contemporary books in Arabic and
English on Egyptian women.[68] By focusing in, the sense of the late hour
and isolation is gone. Other differences appear between the photo in *al-
Lata'if al-Musawwara* and these reprints. Most notably, in the versions
published in books, a cross and crescent appear on the flag, signaling
Muslim-Coptic unity. This is probably another frame in the same
sequence, cropped to give it greater drama.

The third photo, also bearing the stamp Ramses Co., appeared on 5 May (figure 17) and shows a horse-drawn carriage against the backdrop of a palatial building. A woman standing in the back of the carriage holds aloft an Egyptian flag, a child sitting on another woman's lap waves a small flag, a third woman peers at the camera, and two of the six males in the carriage are doffing their tarbushes (when, according to the editor, "they saw the photographer of al-Lata'if wanted to photograph them"). The caption explained that this was an Egyptian woman celebrating with her family on 8 April.[69] This particular photo appeared again on 13 November, the Day of National Struggle, and with the two photos discussed above in a spread in March 1933 showing scenes from celebrations following events in March 1919.[70] Al-Musawwar carried the photo on the cover of the special issue to commemorate the fiftieth anniversary of the revolution of 1919, or rather a portion of the photo (figure 18). Nearly everyone has been cut with the exception of the woman holding the flag and a young boy standing close behind her, who would be difficult to cut out, as well as part of the face of a veiled woman caught in the lower left of the frame.[71] A similarly cropped version also appeared in al-Hilal's golden anniversary album with the first photo mentioned and was meant to show that women "led demonstrations" and "jeered the English" in the revolution of 1919.[72] Viewing the cropped photo of the woman with the flag, one would never imagine the original family context of the photo or guess that it was taken amid the April celebrations and not the March demonstrations. It had become a quintessential symbol of women's political activism and the revolution of 1919.

The three photos discussed above, which have been among the most frequently associated with women and the revolution of 1919, were all taken on 8 April and bear the imprint of Ramses Company. This imprint appears only sporadically in 1919 in al-Lata'if al-Musawwara, and the name of the cameraman, who is identified only as a "staff photographer," remains unknown. He may have been on special assignment to cover the unrest and worked for several papers or news services. All three photos have been used by Egyptians and scholars of Egypt to evoke the "ladies' demonstrations" of March 1919, although they were all taken during the April celebrations and two show women in a family context. Ironically, a little-known book by 'Abd al-Fattah 'Abada published by al-Hilal in 1919 sets the photos from April 1919 (some of which he includes) in their proper context. 'Abada enumerates three demonstrations in which women participated in March and April 1919: the first

Figure 17. "An Egyptian lady goes out in her carriage with the members of her family the day of the big holiday—8 April—to participate in the manifestations of joy, and her sister has raised the beloved Egyptian flag." Photograph by Ramses Company. *Al-Lata'if al-Musawwara*, 5 May 1919, 6.

Figure 18. Enlargement of the woman holding the flag (figure 17). Cover of *al-Musawwar*, 7 March 1969.

of elite women in cars, the second of elite women on foot in which they were blocked by military force, and the third of women of different strata upon the release of the Wafd. He characterizes the latter as the "greatest of them" and describes it in detail, noting that this was the first time men rode with their wives and mothers in carriages.[73]

We now turn to three other photos, which were probably shot by three different photographers and whose relationship to the events of 1919 also needs clarification. The golden anniversary album of *al-Hilal* carried a photo of women marching right to left that the Arabic inscription says is of "Egyptian woman in the revolution of 1919," or more precisely, according to the printed text, the first women's demonstration of March 1919.[74] In the English translation of part of Huda Sha'rawi's memoirs, the same photo is labeled as one of a women's demonstration in Cairo during the revolution of 1919.[75] Yet the original photo is from a different time, place, and perspective. A dark and grainy picture, which is hard to reproduce, appeared in *al-Lata'if al-Musawwara* on 12 April 1921 as one of a series showing the decorations and processions in Alexandria when Sa'd Zaghlul returned to Egypt after his exile and attempt to negotiate Egypt's independence.[76] The women march from left to right, carrying a banner (illegible in later versions of the photo printed in reverse) of the Society of the Mothers of the Future, an Alexandrian organization that has been overshadowed by Cairene groups. That the men in the crowds on the sides of the street do not focus on the marching women reveals that by 1921, the presence of women in street demonstrations was not such a novelty. Other cameras caught the procession, and a photo that appeared in the *Illustrated London News* was later reprinted in *al-Lata'if al-Musawwara*.[77] Here the photograph from *Sijill al-Hilal al-Musawwar* is reversed (figure 19) and shown in the direction it originally appeared in *al-Lata'if al-Musawwara* on 12 April 1921. The important point is not so much the direction of marching as the correct setting and date.

Elite women who appeared or spoke in public in 1919 generally wore thin face veils. Thus the photo of an unveiled schoolgirl flanked by male students who spoke on the balcony of the House of the Nation in 1919, which also appeared in the English translation of Huda's memoirs, seems revolutionary in more ways than one.[78] But the image comes from 1928, not 1919, in the context of student protests against the efforts of a non-Wafdist Egyptian government to reach an agreement with the British. *Al-Lata'if al-Musawwara* carried a couple of photos of the protests, which were broken up by Egyptian police, including one on the balcony

Figure 19. "Egyptian ladies and girls parading for the leader and cheering him" in Alexandria, April 1921. Photo from *Sijill al-Hilal al-Musawwar* (Cairo, 1992), 2: 1014–15, reversed and shown as it originally appeared in *al-Lata'if al-Musawwara*, 12 April 1921, 7.

(figure 20) and one on the street (figure 21).[79] A female student speaking in public in 1928 surrounded by men after a decade of the blurring of boundaries was not nearly as shocking as it would have been a decade earlier. By then a few female students had entered the university, and elite women had become more seasoned veterans of urban protest. Elsewhere, the student was identified as Bahiyya Fahmi and the 1928 context of the photos given.[80]

Ironically, while photos shot weeks or years later were wrongly attributed to March 1919, one photo from that period has been post-dated to the 1928 protests following the closing of parliament.[81] Yet the photo, which originally appeared in *al-Lata'if al-Musawwara* on 27 April 1919, belongs with the cluster of photos shot on 8 April 1919 (figure 22).[82] It shows a crowd of men outside Sa'd Zaghlul's house looking up at the balcony, where his wife, Safiyya Zaghlul, who had signed the March petition, and who is the subject of chapter 6, is marked by an X. This photo was shot and/or printed by Sabunji.

Few photos of the women's demonstrations of March 1919 were published or actually seem to exist, in spite of claims to the contrary. A photo of an "Egyptian ladies' demonstration: the first ever staged in Cairo"

Figure 20. "Student protestors at the House of the Nation, standing in the balcony of the library listening to speeches." *Al-Lata'if al-Musawwara*, 19 March 1928, 4.

Figure 21. "Some of the male and female students standing in front of the House of the Nation when the police attacked them to break up their gathering." *Al-Lata'if al-Musawwara*, 19 March 1928, 4.

Figure 22. "A view of the house of His Excellency Sa'd Pasha Zaghlul the day of April 8th. His honorable wife came onto the balcony with the well-wishing visiting ladies (X [on upper left side of photo]) to greet members of the nation during their march as they cheered the nation and His Excellency Sa'd Pasha." Print by Sabunji. *Al-Lata'if al-Musawwara*, 28 April 1919, 4.

(figure 23) appears in a book by the American author Grace Thompson Seton, published in 1923.[83] The photo shows the tail end of a procession of veiled women in Garden City. The broad avenue dwarfs the size of the demonstration and large crowds are nowhere in evidence. Seton, who carried a camera and took snapshots, was in Cairo three years after the revolution, not during it. Whether the Egyptian women she met provided her with the print, and whether they and others in Egypt saw the photo, before or after publication, is, like the source of the print, unclear.

Sabri's *La Revolution égyptienne* contains a photograph of "[t]he demonstration of Egyptian ladies first authorized and later stopped by armed force." Yet one sees much more of the British officers in caps and Egyptian police in fezzes than the encircled group of women. The latter, and some of their banners, are barely visible.[84] The same photo appeared in a biography of Isma'il Sidqi, a politician who in 1919 was a member of the Wafd and whose wife was a signatory of the petition penned to protest the treatment of the ladies.[85] A photograph from a different angle and moment of the "ladies' demonstration" in which women, according to the caption, stood in the "rays of the sun for two hours" appeared in *al-Balagh al-Usbu'iyya* in 1927 shortly after the death of Sa'd Zaghul.

Figure 23. "Egyptian ladies' demonstration: The first ever staged in Cairo."
Grace Thompson Seton, *A Woman Tenderfoot in Egypt* (New York, 1923).

The police lines are now ordered neatly around a group in front of Sa'd's house. The women are not visible, but a banner rises above the heads of those forming the cordon.[86] None of the horses mentioned in Hafiz's poem are in evidence in either photo. One or the other of them may have been taken by the American consul-general, who, according to Huda Sha'rawi, took several photographs when he arrived on the scene to help negotiate the release of the women.[87]

The only photos that may well have been taken of the "ladies' demonstration" of March 1919 are much less dramatic than those ascribed to the event, with their flags, fists, crowds, and speakers. The latter lent themselves to enhancing the mythology of the first women's demonstration and transforming women into symbols. Male photo- and print journalists seem to have been particularly eager to do just that. In collective memory, the Cairene "ladies' demonstration" of March 1919—really a composite of several March protests—became a referent for women's political activism in Cairo and elsewhere throughout the decade. The "ladies' demonstrations" turn out to have been less dramatic visually and less radical politically than they have been mythologized as being. But probing the myth should force a reconsideration of that event and ones that have been elided into it on their own terms.

Women from the elite became a new "political public" in March 1919 when they staged their own demonstrations, marching in the streets of Cairo and delivering petitions to foreign legations. They entered a new public space amid general unrest, challenging the colonial authorities but not seriously undermining male authority or class hierarchy. Archival and literary records show that during the revolution, women spoke in a "feminine voice"—as mothers, sisters, wives, and representatives of the female half of the nation—making no special demands for women. Their action soon took on feminist and later populist meanings. The event proved malleable, because all sorts of meanings could be attributed to it, and all sorts of identities and ideologies—liberal, populist, feminist, socialist, and Islamist—became ascribed to marching veiled women.

As long as women veiled (and sometimes afterward) the illustrated press rarely gave the names of activists. The veil hid women's faces in the early years, and cameramen and editors, who were probably unfamiliar with most of the women activists in any case, made little effort to overcome their ignorance. Nameless women preserved the ideal of the patriotic Egyptian woman; particulars would have chipped at that ideal. As a result, multiple images of women activists who operated in numerous contexts were conflated into the powerful image of the female demonstrator, often with a flag, of March 1919. Getting the details right did not seem that important, for details only got in the way of the abstraction, as woman became a crucial site of the collective memory of the revolution of 1919. Women activists, whose own memories were often blurred and who frequently conflated the events of 1919, did not seem to mind being turned into symbols as long as the substantive parts of their contributions were also recorded and rewarded. But in time only the symbols remained. Veiled protestors became a crucial site of memory, as the "lady demonstrator" came to symbolize the true patriot, the revolution, and by implication, the nation.

CHAPTER SIX

# Mother of the Egyptians

Safiyya Zaghlul, wife of the Wafdist leader Sa'd Zaghlul, was on hand in March 1919 when her house was the focus of demonstrations, and she signed the women's petitions delivered to foreign consuls. After the revolution of 1919, she became widely known as "Mother of the Egyptians." Her title built on the nationalist role cast for elite women from the turn of the century as "Mothers of the Nation." First among the mothers, she became a popular nationalist symbol. At the same time, she wielded a great deal of power within Wafdist and nationalist politics and became a central force in Egyptian women's political culture.[1]

Women nationalists often spoke in a maternal voice and, like their male compatriots, adopted family metaphors and kinship idioms. This rhetoric reached its fullest flowering in Egypt in the interwar years with the creation of a national mother. The fiction generated a sense of solidarity and relatedness among people who were otherwise strangers or divided along class, race, ethnic, and religious lines. The "mothers" and "fathers" provided comfort, creating a sense of collective belonging and suggesting that the welfare of the people was in the right hands. Yet assertions that the nation was a family were also meant to insure obedience to the leaders and to silence dissent.

This chapter follows the life and career of Safiyya Zaghlul, "Mother of the Egyptians." Safiyya planned her public persona, carefully chose her words, weighed her actions, and controlled her image, particularly her photographic image. She manipulated maternal symbolism to carve out a political role for herself. In spite of opposition from the British and non-Wafdists, she took advantage of an opening and played her part well. As a result, she enjoyed political influence during her husband's lifetime and continued to exercise power long after his death.

## IMAGES AND MEMORIES

As the "Mother of the Egyptians," Safiyya Zaghlul became the keeper of Sa'd's memory when he was in exile and after his death, and a political actor in her own right. Although Safiyya was a major pillar of the national movement, historians of nationalism have generally ignored her. They have focused instead on male figures whose power was institutionalized through parties, parliament, and other formal structures. At the same time, scholars of women's history preferred to highlight feminists, intellectuals, radicals, and working-class women. Yet Safiyya embodied many of the paradoxes elite women faced in this period.

No woman appears in more photos in the national press in the interwar years than Safiyya. Her picture appeared regularly in periodicals, proof that she was one of the most visible and popular female figures of the period. While Sa'd and King Fu'ad competed as male leaders for press coverage, Safiyya encountered no competition from the palace. Queen Nazli did not appear unveiled before the Egyptian public through her husband's reign. Forced by convention and her husband's policy of catering to Islamic sentiments to stay out of sight, she almost never appeared in press photos.[2] Safiyya, on the other hand, manipulated politics to command a central role as a first lady of sorts. (How the queen felt about Safiyya's public visibility and usurpation of what she may have perceived as her role is not clear.) Safiyya's closest competitor in press photos, Huda Sha'rawi, appeared fairly frequently; but the total number of photos in the weekly *al-Lata'if al-Musawwara*, for example, adds up to about a fifth of those of Safiyya Zaghlul. In short, Safiyya enjoyed a prominence in the national press that was second to none. Her photos could be found on the front page or prominently inside numerous periodicals. *Al-Lata'if al-Musawwara* printed over one hundred photos of her, and women's weeklies and monthlies such as *al-Hisan* and *al-Mar'a al-Misriyya* showed her in various poses. The number of photos of Safiyya did not drop off after Sa'd's death, and indeed may have increased, showing her independent stature.

The many photos document Safiyya's movements and demonstrate her centrality in Wafdist politics. When she was depicted with Sa'd, she appeared at his side as a steady support. In other contexts, such as surrounded by Wafdist women, she became the focus of the photo. The editor even took care to guide the viewer to Safiyya if she was in a large crowd or in the distance by marking her with an X, such as in photos of her on the balcony of her home (see figure 22) or when she sat in the balcony at an opening of parliament.[3] The X was particularly important when Safiyya first appeared and was veiled, as in a visit to Damietta in the summer of 1921 that was captured by a local resident.[4] Once she had unveiled, her face became familiar to viewers.

Photos of Safiyya Zaghlul reveal a great deal about the woman and her political style. She maintained control of the image she projected over the years by allowing photographers to take her portrait at certain moments: at Sa'd's side, next to female companions, with male Wafdists. She moved cautiously, lowering her veil slowly, hoping to please with her pleasant looks and not offend conservative viewers. Elegant in her youth with fine gentle features, she matured gracefully, stepping back from the lens but never out of focus as her popularity grew over the years. She played a role that she helped to script and was very attentive to the public stage as theater. Photos in the contemporary press and periodical articles thus help recreate Safiyya's political career.

A biography by Fina Gued Vidal, Safiyya Zaghlul's close friend, provides another perspective.[5] Written in French shortly after Safiyya's death and published in the late 1940s, it blends discussions of family life with descriptions of nationalist and party politics. Fina witnessed much of what she writes about (she stayed with Safiyya during March and April 1919), traveled with her, probably kept a journal, and had access to Safiyya's papers (she at one time handled her correspondence). Safiyya, who was careful in crafting her image during her lifetime, no doubt authorized the work, which is a panegyric to her life and must be read critically and in combination with other sources.

Fahima Thabit, the young woman who accompanied Safiyya on her trip to Gibraltar in 1922 to join Sa'd in exile and stayed with the Zaghluls for the six months that they were there, kept a record of the experience. An unmarried schoolteacher of about thirty and member of the New Woman Society, Fahima was a likely candidate to accompany Safiyya. She was known in nationalist circles and did not have domestic responsibilities that tied her down. Her father, Husayn Thabit Bey, had been a deputy in the law court at Zaqaziq and was vaguely known to Sa'd. *Al-Za'im al-Khalid wa-Umm al-Misriyyin fi Manfan Jabal Tariq* (The Glorious Leader and Mother of the Egyptians in Exile in Gibraltar) documents how time was spent there and reads for the most part like a political diary. Fahima became a family intimate and shared walks, talks, hopes, and fears. This memoir, like the Vidal biography, was only published after Safiyya's death.[6]

Safiyya herself left little in the way of writing that is available, other than a few proclamations to her "sons," some letters, and correspondence with British officials, who kept a watchful eye on her, amassing thick files. They were not persuaded by her skillful use of rhetoric and public persona that she was above politics.

A DUTIFUL DAUGHTER

Cameras captured Safiyya as a child, a young married woman, and a dutiful daughter accompanying her father on cures in Europe, where she traveled without a veil.[7] Safiyya was born in a palace in Bab al-Luq, Cairo, 16 June 1876, into the Ottoman-Egyptian elite. Her father, Mustafa Pasha Fahmi, then governor of Cairo, was among those Ottoman officials the British enlisted after the 'Urabi revolt to help administer Egypt. He later served as prime minister under Khedive 'Abbas Hilmi II and enjoyed longevity in the post (with one stretch lasting from 1895 to 1908) precisely because Lord Cromer appreciated his cooperation. We know less about Safiyya's mother. Fina's biography has little to say about her but gives a photograph of a woman in European attire. Safiyya's mother was probably, like her husband, of Turkish origin. She bore a son who died at an early age and three girls who survived to adulthood, of whom Safiyya was the youngest.[8]

An elite household of this sort contained a number of retainers and blended European and Ottoman practices. A *dada* (nanny) helped raise Safiyya, and a German governess was charged with her private education, which included French and embroidery. After visiting an orphanage with her mother at age thirteen, Safiyya "adopted" a young girl. Adoption was technically illegal in Islam, but ways existed of creating fictive kinship and integrating orphans into a household.[9] "Rescuing" the girl seemed a commendable project for Safiyya; and in a pattern not dissimilar from the treatment of harem slaves in the past, she cared for her until her eighteenth birthday, at which time a suitable marriage was arranged. This sense of noblesse oblige continued throughout Safiyya's life. Fina reports that she provided daily meals to four poor Egyptians. But her personal generosity masks a lack of critique of the social and economic conditions that caused vast disparities in wealth among Egyptians. Her philanthropic impulse probably stemmed from her religiosity.

She kept a Qur'an above her bed, prayed regularly, made prayer tapestries, and never touched alcohol.[10]

At the age of eighteen, Safiyya was given the task of running the Fahmi household. Meanwhile, her father received numerous marital proposals for her. He finally accepted the offer of Sa'd Zaghlul, a politically ambitious judge on the court of appeals and a protégé of the Islamic reformer Muhammad 'Abduh. Born in 1857 or so in the Delta village of Ibyana, Sa'd was the son of a prosperous landowning *'umda* (village mayor). He attended the local Qur'an school, then went on to study at al-Azhar. After being briefly imprisoned for his role in the 'Urabi revolt, he studied law and eventually earned a degree in France. Upon his return to Egypt, he mingled with British officials and Egyptian ministers in, among other places, Princess Nazli Fazil's salon, where his marriage to Safiyya was rumored to have been arranged.[11]

Sa'd was nearly twenty years older than Safiyya and from an ethnic Egyptian rather than a Turkish background. Their marriage in 1896 linked him to a powerful minister, giving him political capital. On Mustafa Fahmi's side, the marriage helped to solidify the family's local ties and linked their fate to a rising star, one of the Western-educated professionals emerging from the ranks of the provincial notables. Marriages of the Turkish-speaking Ottoman-Egyptian elite to Egyptian professionals was an increasingly common strategy, giving one side financial security and the other higher social status.[12]

In spite of their attempts and desires, Safiyya and Sa'd had no children of their own. However, Safiyya raised the son and daughter—Sa'id and Ratiba—of Sa'd's deceased sister "as if they were her own."[13] Safiyya also had great affection for Wasif Ghali, whose father had been assassinated in 1911, and considered Wasif and his wife as her children as well.[14] Kinship proved so integral in Egyptian society that non-kin who were close to the family were often incorporated through fictive kinship relations. During her stay in Gibraltar in 1921, Safiyya revealed her despair at not having had children. "All Egyptians are your children," Fahima replied, adding that she loved the Zaghluls as parents, as well as "for their patriotism and goodness," and would not have loved them more even if she had been their daughter by blood.[15] The fact that Safiyya had no children of her own played in her favor politically, for she could become the mother of all Egyptians.

By most accounts Safiyya's and Sa'd's marriage was a harmonious union, and Fahima's account of their time in Gibraltar shows them as a loving couple.[16] In portraits of Safiyya and Sa'd, the latter is usually shown seated (he was a tall man) while Safiyya stands to his side or behind him with a hand on his shoulder (see figure 12).[17] In spite of the large gap in age, they were presented as a model for the sort of loving marriage increasingly advocated by intellectuals of the time. Qasim Amin noted that Sa'd, a fellow judge, had inspired him to write *al-Mar'a al-Jadida* (The New Woman, 1900), which he dedicated to him in friendship. Sa'd's union was a model for the companionate couple at the center of the bourgeois family, which would become the bedrock of the nationalist movement.[18]

The marriage helped Sa'd advance his career. With the blessing of Lord Cromer, he became minister of public instruction in 1906 in the last cabinet of Mustafa Fahmi. Cromer presumed that Sa'd's political sympathies resembled those of his father-in-law and foresaw a brilliant future for him. Sa'd received the title of pasha at this time and advanced to the even more powerful office of minister of justice in 1910. But two years later, he resigned to lead the opposition in the new legislative assembly, where he was elected vice president. There he honed his skills as a fiery orator. Along with other Egyptian nationalists, Sa'd increasingly yearned to oust the British from Egypt and would make his move after World War I. On the eve of the war, Safiyya nursed both her parents in their final illnesses. Her mother died in 1913 and her father a year later.

## SA'D'S "SECOND SELF"

Following the arrest and deportation of Sa'd Zaghlul and three companions in March 1919, demonstrations broke out all over Egypt. Members of the Wafd hurried to Zaghlul's house, where they had met since the Wafd's inception. The Wafdists wanted to collect their papers so that they could carry on meeting elsewhere, but Safiyya would not have it. She pledged her support "as a militant of the Wafd" and said that nothing could deter her from working and fighting in her husband's place.[19]

Safiyya astutely recognized the importance of continuing the meetings at her home in her husband's absence. This ensured his central position within the group and the focus of nationalist activity on the house, which became widely known as *Bayt al-Umma* (the House of the Nation), a name that helped to instill a sense of national family. This also gave Safiyya an opportunity to play a pivotal role in the movement. She had lived most of her life in the privilege of seclusion, aware of political events but out of the public eye, and her role now changed dramatically when she became a public figure. She met the delegations of men and women flocking to the house to pledge their support, signed the petitions of demonstrators who marched there in protest, and addressed the crowds that used the house as a rallying point. Safiyya joined the rebellion against British rule, while at the same time supporting gender divisions and social hierarchies.[20]

Safiyya's role as "Mother of the Egyptians" was shaped amid the unrest. After one particularly violent encounter between protesters and British soldiers, Fina says, a crowd brought a wounded protester to the house. Sensing his end was near, the young man lamented to Safiyya, "I am going to die far from my mother." Trying to comfort him, she asked, "My son, am I not also your mother?" "Yes," he responded, "but you are also the mother of all Egyptians."[21] According to another account, a group of women demonstrators from Tanta chanted at her door, "'Aisha was the Mother of the Believers (*Umm al-Mu'minin*); Safiyya is the Mother of the Egyptians (*Umm al-Misriyyin*)."[22] The name took hold in the popular imagination.

*Umm al-Misriyyin* (or *Masriyyin* in the colloquial) sounded similar to *Umm al-Mu'minin* (the name given to Muhammad's favorite wife), evoking associations with Islamic history. Egyptian nationalists—like nationalists elsewhere—borrowed with impunity from the religious past. The title *umm* also had contemporary and popular connotations. Among Arabic speakers, mothers often took their son's names and were literally called "Mother of Muhammad" or "Mother of Ahmad" or something similar rather than by their own name. Sons usually remained in close proximity to their natal families and their loyalty to their mothers proved strong. That Egyptians called Safiyya "Mother of the Egyptians" meant not only that they had "adopted" her as their mother and pledged loyalty to her, but that she derived her identity from them as well. Safiyya may well have cultivated the role precisely because it filled an emotional need as well as a political purpose for her.

With unrest growing in Egypt and the prestige of the Wafd on the rise, the British sent General (Field Marshal) Edmund Allenby, who had led the Palestine Campaign, to quell the protests. He advised the British government to release Sa'd and the other prisoners, who were subsequently set free. In a conversation with a British official shortly thereafter, Sultan (later King) Fu'ad acknowledged the "extraordinary influence of the women and particularly of Mme. Saad Zaghlul in exciting native hostility to the British."[23] Safiyya met up with Sa'd in Malta and proceeded with him to Paris, where negotiations over postwar arrangements were under way. By the time they arrived, however, the Americans had already endorsed Great Britain's protectorate over Egypt. The Wafd now understood that the international community would not support Egyptian demands and that they had to negotiate Egypt's political future directly with the British.

Leading members of the Wafd eventually proceeded to London for negotiations, but the dilemma of the Wafd soon became clear. Having built their mass appeal on demands for full independence, they could settle for nothing less. Yet the British were willing to offer only limited terms. When the first of many rounds of talks failed, Wafd members returned to Paris, where cracks began to appear in the Wafd façade. Opposition grew to the authoritarian role that Sa'd played within the group, with some suggesting that he put his own political ambitions before the interests of the country. Safiyya attempted to regroup the loyalists around her husband.

In spite of the failed talks and fissures within the Wafd, Sa'd and Safiyya returned home in April 1921 to an enthusiastic welcome. Safiyya sat in a closed car completely covered by flowers and saluted the cheering crowds, as women Wafdists followed in their cars and schoolgirls looked on.[24] "I was away two years and I could not believe the transformation in thought and action that I saw when I came back," commented Safiyya in reference to the dramatic changes she found in women's lives.[25] After their return, Safiyya continued to assist Sa'd in a role Fina characterizes as that of confidante, counselor, and right hand.[26] Huda Sha'rawi, who was head of the Women's Wafd at the time, noted Safiyya's influence over her husband. At one meeting when Sa'd thanked Huda for her help, Huda in turn asked him to greet Prime Minister 'Adli Yakan upon his return from London in the same way that 'Adli had welcomed Zaghlul earlier that year. Sa'd said he would do it if it were up to him personally, but he could not because others would not approve of it. As Huda wondered aloud who would oppose him if he wanted something, Safiyya interjected, "By God, Sa'd, if you place your hand in 'Adli's, I will not be your wife after what he has done."[27]

The Wafd continued to organize resistance to the British and the British-backed government. After Sa'd refused internal exile at his country estate in December 1921, the British decided to remove him and some of his colleagues from the scene in order to form a ministry that would negotiate more amicably. Safiyya immediately appealed for permission to join her husband. She was told that she would be permitted to do so only when his final destination was known. Safiyya subsequently decided to stay in Egypt. "Given the crisis which crosses the country," she wrote to Allenby, "I consider it my duty to remain here."[28] The Residency immediately instructed the commander of the Cairo City Police to have Safiyya Zaghlul "carefully watched," for it was soon apparent that she presented more of a danger in Egypt than with her husband in exile.[29]

Safiyya gave the reasons behind her decision to stay in an appeal to the nation (the collective "you") published in the press:

> When I saw the troops surrounding the house and filling the garden to take away Saad, my inclination at first was to follow him wherever this force took him. But when I saw you killed, all my affection and feeling went out to you, and I felt from the bottom of my heart that I could not abandon you at such a critical time, and that my duty was to share your fate.[30]

She then cautioned her "devoted sons" to be wise in the use of their energies, to hold fast to their strong ties of brotherhood, and to abstain from violence, to "protect our guests, and their houses and property." Egyptian elites feared anti-colonial unrest might take on social dimensions and threaten their economic interests. Safiyya ended by requesting that every Egyptian man and woman remember Sa'd and his colleagues and pray for their return.[31] Her appeals to her "devoted sons" worked to rhetorically exclude the "daughters" from the nation.

Safiyya received immediate messages of support from Egyptians at home and abroad. "We greet in your noble person the heroic representative of Egyptian womanhood and the devoted mother of the Egyptian people assuring you of the full support of your loyal sons," the members of the Edinburgh Egyptian Society cabled her. Similar messages came from other Egyptian societies in England.[32] The "national family" pulled together to face the crisis, and the "sons," however far away, rallied to the side of the "mother" who had picked up the mantle of leadership. The family unified to oust the outsiders, the British. The exiles were sent to Aden for two months and then on to the Seychelles, an island group in the Indian Ocean that was a British crown colony. Safiyya pushed for her husband's release, attempting to raise an international outcry and to keep his detention in the public eye.[33]

Safiyya continued to issue appeals in the press. With Wafdist leaders in prison or in exile and periodicals forbidden from publishing anything coming from the party, she took up the task of articulating her husband's positions and keeping the focus on his leadership. She warned her "dear sons" not to be deceived by politicians who allied themselves with the British and sought to form a new government in the absence of Sa'd and his colleagues. She spoke of the deportation of Sa'd and the others: "Why? And for what crime? Because they spoke loud in your name and called for your independence." She reiterated that support for Sa'd and the exiles equaled support for independence, and that this was the only legitimate nationalist position. She urged patience, for victory was at hand with "the help of God."[34] The British tried to block these communiqués, with some degree of success. "The press should be warned not to publish Madame Zaghloul's appeal," the oriental secretary instructed, "on account of its anti-British tone."[35]

Safiyya met with foreign visitors to present Egypt's case. She told the American writer Grace Thompson Seton, "Saad is a prisoner in Seychelles, but I keep myself here, his second self, his wife, and take his place."[36] Seton described meeting "a slim, middle-aged woman of fragile body, but dauntless spirit." Safiyya authorized her to publish a photo depicting her as an unveiled modern patriot, wearing high heels, a string of pearls, and a dress upon which was emblazoned the Egyptian flag of crescents and stars.[37] The flag at that time would have been red, not the green it subsequently became.

Delegations of rural notables once again came to the Zaghluls' home to pledge their support. Safiyya received them, as she informed her husband in a letter dated 5 February 1922 that was intercepted, and "talked to them from behind a screen, thanked them for their sympathy and encouraged them to go on demanding independence."[38] She reportedly received up to forty men at once, and often two hundred a day, and frequently delivered speeches to the delegations. As she described, she waited behind a screen until the group had assembled; then she emerged dressed in a white silk *gallabiyya* with a white gauze veil over her head and wrapped around her throat (not wanting to offend the sensibilities of the provincial men in the audience).[39] Her selection of a peasant style of dress (although most peasants did not wear silk) in addressing a rural audience shows her adroitness in manipulating symbols. She could be the determined village wife, the educated modern woman, the worldly aristocrat, quickly adjusting to the moment and playing the role to perfection.

In the letter to her husband intercepted by the British, Safiyya reported as well on her own role in trying to bring secessionists from the Wafd back into the party's fold. Safiyya welcomed some of the secessionists to the House of the Nation after an agreement had been reached. She spoke to the assembly "urging them to do their best for the cause of Egypt; to swear that they would sacrifice every personal interest for the common weal and to forget the past." Speakers cheered Safiyya, but the new union did not last, and the Wafd continued to show splits.[40]

Safiyya also spoke to the crowds that assembled in front of the house. Fina described one incident when a rather unruly group composed of workers, peasants, boatmen, and butchers arrived from the countryside. Safiyya attempted to pacify the crowd, which was armed with sticks and in an incendiary mood, by telling them that they were hurting the country, that Sa'd had many times repeated that he did not want revolution, that they would not win freedom through violence. "Your cause is just; right is with you; return to your work at home; and leave to your leaders the responsibility of winning the independence of the country." The crowd of over three hundred men then apparently set down their sticks, crying, "Long live Sa'd! Long live the Mother of the Egyptians!"[41]

Safiyya, like others of her class, sought to suppress social unrest and prevent economic damage by channeling peasant and worker grievances toward the anti-colonial struggle. In this she acted in concert with the Wafd leadership, which was made up mostly of landowners. Elite nationalists opposed violence that might threaten their own properties, and the specter of Russia's revolution could not have been far from their considerations. The family rhetoric that Safiyya Zaghlul utilized so skillfully thus had a dual function, creating a sense of solidarity and unity among the population while smoothing class and other antagonisms. Family, after all, was not an egalitarian institution, but rather a hierarchical one. Family rhetoric reinforced social and gender hierarchies, giving the sense that the elite had a natural right to lead in the same way that fathers and mothers had a natural right to raise their children, who owed them respect and obedience. In short, use of family rhetoric worked in this case to reinforce social inequalities.

With negotiations blocked, the British unilaterally issued a declaration of Egyptian independence on 28 February 1922. They ended the protectorate but reserved four points for future negotiations: the status of the Sudan, the protection of foreign interests and of minorities in Egypt, the security of British communications, and the defense of Egypt. Sultan Fu'ad subsequently took the title king, and members of the Liberal Constitutionalist Party, along with others, were assigned the task of writing a constitution. The Wafd opposed what its members considered a "false independence" and continued to agitate against those who cooperated with the British. The government cracked down on this opposition and imprisoned Safiyya Zaghlul in her house for four days in March. Safiyya was subsequently released from house arrest and, after pressuring the authorities, was allowed to visit members of the Wafd jailed nearby and to send them food on a daily basis.[42]

SHARING EXILE

Meanwhile, in the Seychelles, Sa'd's health deteriorated. A diabetic, he suffered from the climate and the food, and Safiyya petitioned the British in London yet again to release him.[43] She then sent envoys to Allenby requesting permission to join her husband in exile. The British replied that they had decided to move Sa'd to a new place, and told Safiyya that she could join him once he was settled there. In early September, Sa'd landed with two servants in Gibraltar, his new outpost in exile.[44] Negotiations then followed over who could accompany Safiyya. The British approved a traveling party consisting of her nephew Sa'id; Fahima Thabit; and two servants—Sakina Muhammad Tahir (an illiterate nineteen-year-old peasant from Sa'd Zaghlul's village whose mother had served the Zaghluls all her life), and Ibrahim Fadl Muhammad (a twenty-year-old Sudanese servant for Sa'd).[45]

Safiyya prepared for her departure. British officials and Egyptian security were well aware that the occasion might be used as an opportunity to stage demonstrations. They even debated moving the date up, for the ship's departure from Port Sa'id coincided with a public holiday honoring the king's accession, and it was feared the crowds might shout for Sa'd rather than for Fu'ad. Some Egyptian officials, having a good sense of Safiyya's popularity, argued that it would be better if Madame Zaghlul were made to leave quietly. But the British felt that altering the date would give her more attention than she was likely to attract.[46] The going-away ceremonies began the afternoon of Friday, 6 October, when the members of the New Woman Society threw Safiyya a party in her home. Delegations of women from Alexandria and Tanta joined the group from Cairo. Students from the society's workshop opened the party with a song, Ihsan Ahmad and other women delivered speeches, and guests recited poems.[47]

Huge crowds—"a wonderful send off"—turned out the afternoon of 8 October to escort Safiyya Zaghlul from her home to the Cairo train station. The dense crowd, according to the *Egyptian Mail*, numbered "many hundreds of thousands" and gave her as big a reception as that which had welcomed Sa'd upon his return to Cairo in April 1921. But it also had special features:

> There were ladies everywhere. There were black-robed ladies, lightly veiled, riding in luxurious motorcars—sixty cars were counted, but there were a great many more than that; there were middle class mothers and daughters on roofs and balconies and leaning from every window; there were women of the people, veiled in coarse black crepe-stuff, standing among the crowd in the streets.[48]

Students from al-Azhar kept order, clasping hands and forming a chain
to keep the crowds back as the cars streamed past toward the station.
Those assembled cheered and clapped, particularly when Safiyya rode
by in a closed car covered with students. They held up flags and banners
on which were inscribed a number of Arabic slogans, among them: "Good
bye, Mother of the Nation! Hope you will return under better conditions," and "Go with the blessing of God!" Others spoke of sacrifice and
love of the country: "We die that Egypt may live."[49]

Young schoolgirls had gathered at the train station. There Labiba
Ahmad, founder of the Society of Egyptian Ladies' Awakening, made a
presentation. Safiyya, in turn, issued a special appeal on the occasion of
her departure, once again invoking Sa'd's struggle. "It is for us that Saad
suffers all these pains," she declared. "His sacrifice, and that of his companions are water of life for the tree of independence so that it may grow
in our hearts." She urged her fellow countrymen not to lose courage, for
victory was at hand, and to stay focused on the House of the Nation.
"There are in the House of the Nation, successors and friends of Saad
who will raise your flag and support you." The "monster demonstration," as the *Egyptian Mail* called it, showed the appeal of the Wafd and
the power of Safiyya, who had become a central figure in the nationalist movement.[50]

The celebration of Safiyya on the eve of her departure did not end at
the Cairo station. A special train carried about fifty female notables (led
by Sharifa Riyad), fifteen members of the New Woman Society (headed
by Wajida Thabit), and a seventeen-woman delegation from Asyut
(presided over by Wajiha Tuhami Khashaba). In Port Said, the train was
met by a crowd, including a delegation from the local Women's Wafd
committee. The latter escorted Safiyya and the others to a reception.
Some hours later, they delivered Safiyya to her steamship, which left the
port at two in the morning.[51] In what a British official admitted was an
"overwhelming send-off," Egyptians had shown that Safiyya had a huge
following, including both men and women, Copts and Muslims, of different strata.[52]

Women nationalists venerated Safiyya for the leading role she had
played in the absence of her husband and as the focal point of their
activities. Labiba Ahmad praised her as "an honorable name in the history of our national renaissance, an eternal memory in the heart of every
Egyptian man and woman." She called her *Umm al-Misriyyin wa al-
Misriyyat* (Mother of Egyptian men and women) and *za'imat al-Misriyyat* (the leader of Egyptian women), a title that had historical

resonance. (Before the nineteenth century the *za'im Misr* was often the leading bey or other grandee.) In a play on her name, Labiba also spoke of Safiyya as *sifwat al-ummahat* (the best friend of the mothers), a reference to the women nationalists who often called themselves "Mothers of the Nation."[53]

Until the occasion of her departure to join Sa'd in exile, Safiyya had not unveiled before photojournalists in Egypt. In late 1921, her portrait had appeared on the cover of a French journal and was reprinted in *al-Lata'if al-Musawwara* in January 1922, giving the Egyptian public their first glimpse of Safiyya's face.[54] The day of her departure, Safiyya lowered her veil and smiled for the press as she stood in her garden next to an unnamed young woman (possibly Fahima Thabit). Safiyya, whose face was still unknown to most Egyptians, was marked by an X and identified as Mother of the Egyptians (figure 24).[55] She also released a portrait to the press, which appeared in the October issues of *al-Mar'a al-Misriyya* and *al-Nahda al-Nisa'iyya*, and in other periodicals throughout the decade. The studio shot shows Safiyya sitting sideways with a small book in her lap (possibly a Qur'an), looking past the camera.[56] The image reinforces the sense of her maternal aura and sanctity. Her face would quickly become familiar in countless other photos, her gaze at the camera more direct as her control over the images released to the press continued.

Safiyya joined Sa'd in Gibraltar after she had been carefully searched for hidden documents. British officials were relieved that no mention of "any indignities" was ever made public, for it might have had unpleasant repercussions. Sa'd dashed off a telegram addressed "to the nation" via the House of the Nation, which was published in *al-Afkar*, thanking his countrymen for giving his wife a "splendid send-off."[57]

Safiyya spent six months in Gibraltar with Sa'd and their companion Fahima Thabit, who ran the household and directed the staff. The three took short jaunts to town, sat in the garden, or read inside. They poured over newspapers, letters, and telegrams containing news from Egypt and analyzed political developments. Early in her stay, Safiyya received a supportive telegram from Irish women, who were sympathetic to the struggle against the British.[58] Sa'd, whose health was fragile, received frequent visits from his doctor. Safiyya and Sa'd celebrated their twenty-seventh anniversary in exile and waited.

Half a year later, the British released Sa'd, at which time Safiyya again received praise in the Egyptian press for her sacrifice and for sharing Sa'd's pain in exile.[59] Sa'd set out with Safiyya for Europe, where he was

Figure 24. "Mother of the Egyptians—the honorable wife of Sa'd Pasha Zaghlul (X) the day of her
departure to Gibraltar." *Al-Lata'if al-Musawwara*,
16 October 1922, 1.

met by Wafdists who filled him in on events in Egypt in his absence.
"Look at my pitiful state, my lack of strength," Sa'd told Fina. "Still,
in spite of my great need for the presence of my dear Safiyya, if I had
known how well she had replaced me [in Egypt], I would never have
called for her."[60] Although pictures could take weeks to arrive in the
era before wiring, *al-Lata'if al-Musawwara* obtained quite a few shots
of Sa'd and Safiyya in Europe. These show Safiyya with a hat or head
uncovered, with flowers or needlepoint in hand (symbols of femininity), composed and regal.[61] Sa'd's health remained fragile, and Safiyya

continued to stand in for him at certain events, including a reception in Lyon where she gave a speech.[62]

In Egypt, the new constitution had been promulgated and plans for elections were under way. Sa'd and other exiles were allowed to return home, and the Zaghluls sailed in September on the same boat as Huda Sha'rawi. Huda had publicly unveiled earlier that year and took to wearing a scarf over her head, leaving her face uncovered. Some discussion ensued on board the ship over whether Safiyya should appear veiled or unveiled upon her return from Europe.[63] Safiyya had not veiled in Europe and had already appeared unveiled in photographs in the Egyptian press, but in Egypt she had always covered her face in public. There are conflicting versions of what happened next.

According to Saiza Nabarawi, a feminist traveling with Huda, Sa'd Zaghlul asked Huda to help Safiyya fashion her scarf in a similar manner. Yet when members of the Wafd came on board to meet the party, they disapproved and told Safiyya that the people would never accept it.[64] Huda gave a slightly different account in her memoirs. After Sa'd had said how pleased he had been to see pictures of Huda unveiled, Safiyya promised to copy Huda. Yet when Huda prepared to disembark, she saw that Safiyya's face was covered and asked why. "I have more than one husband," Safiyya replied, explaining that Wasif Ghali (ironically, a Copt) thought it better not to unveil to avoid a bad impression among those people waiting for them.[65] Fina was also on board the ship, accompanying Safiyya. In her version, Huda Sha'rawi, who later split with Sa'd and for that reason may have been written out of the story, was not even mentioned (nor was she mentioned in Fahima Thabit's account of the return). Instead, Fina reported that the welcoming party asked Safiyya to unveil but she refused, insisting on maintaining the custom.[66]

All versions of the incident agree that Wafd officials cared whether or not Safiyya veiled. As the "Mother of the Egyptians," she had a certain stature to maintain. The different versions also agree that Safiyya remained conscious of her own public image and disembarked veiled. Safiyya had clearly become one of the most potent symbols of the nationalist movement. As Egyptians celebrated the couple's return to Egypt, the cameras caught more shots of the veiled Safiyya, and she proceeded to her home, where a reception awaited her.[67] The announcement of Sa'd's return in the press was coupled with praise for Safiyya, who, in the words of Balsam 'Abd al-Malik, was "at all times a model of sacrifice and pride . . . God bless her high aspiration and the aspiration of

the sincere ladies of this nation who put the honor of the nation above
every consideration."[68]


PARTNERS IN POLITICS

At home, Safiyya posed for Messieurs Zola and Charles, whose portraits
capture her looking relaxed and youthful. The photo appeared in *al-
Lata'if al-Musawwara* and on the cover of the first issue of the new ladies'
entertainment journal *al-Hisan*.[69] It is from this time as well that some
of the female cartoon images of the "Egyptian nation" bear a likeness
to Safiyya (see, e.g., figure 11).[70]

Sa'd had come home to stand for parliamentary elections, and the
Wafd, which had transformed itself into a political party, won an overwhelming victory. King Fu'ad then asked Sa'd to form a cabinet. Safiyya
received royal honors as well: the king presented her with the highest
decoration that a woman could receive, the Grand Sash of the Kamal
Order.[71] This suggests that the king may not have begrudged Safiyya her
title or at least thought it politically expedient to recognize her service.
(Huda Sha'rawi would receive the same honor from Fu'ad's son near the
end of her life.)[72]

A few months after his tenure as prime minister began, an attempt
was made on Sa'd's life. Security forces apprehended the assassin and
sought to connect him to a broader conspiracy involving Shaykh 'Abd
al-'Aziz Jawish, militant members of the Watani Party, and the ex-Khe-
dive 'Abbas Hilmi II. They also implicated Alexandra Avierino, the owner
of the turn-of-the-century women's journal *Anis al-Jalis*, and questioned
her at length. Sa'd, who was only slightly wounded, basked in the out-
pouring of sympathy from supporters. According to the editor of the
daily *al-Ahram*, this in turn made Safiyya, who was "very proud of her
position as mother of the Nation," pleased with the way her husband
had been glorified.[73]

After a quick recovery, Sa'd left with Safiyya for a new round of talks
in London. A photo of a reception of Wafdist women at the house of
Esther Fahmi Wisa on the eve of the departure of Safiyya and Sa'd for
Europe in 1924 shows her central place in women's political gatherings.[74]
In London, however, the talks failed. A photo of Safiyya with Sa'd at the
London train station in fall 1924 shows Sa'd waving to the crowds as
Safiyya stands next to him, smiling and looking in the opposite direc-
tion. The frame is balanced between the two figures, giving each equal
weight. Sa'd grins, but his face seems set and hardened, and he looks

fatigued; Safiyya, by contrast, looks rested and hopeful. In photos from this trip, Safiyya is a constant presence at Saʿd's side.[75]

Saʿd had tried to negotiate a settlement with the British to the outstanding questions in Anglo-Egyptian relations. At the same time, more militant nationalists argued that negotiations should not be held as long as the occupier's army remained on Egyptian soil, and they called for the use of force to achieve independence. That November, Sir Oliver Lee Stack, British commander (sirdar) of the Egyptian army and governor-general of the Sudan, was assassinated. The British ultimatum and claims for restitution forced Saʿd's resignation as prime minister a few days later. Shortly thereafter, a British official noted, "Madame Zaghlul has recovered from her emotion, and is inciting her husband to stir up open resistance."[76] Saʿd remained president of the chamber of deputies and head of the Wafd Party, and he continued to control things behind the scenes; but the British never again allowed him to form his own government.

When at about this time Huda Shaʿrawi resigned as head of the Women's Wafd, the Zaghlul loyalists rallied around Safiyya. As honorary president of the Saʿdist Ladies' Committee (heir to the Women's Wafd), she hosted monthly meetings at the House of the Nation and had a special room refurbished for them. Safiyya patronized charities, attended school festivals, and visited fund-raising fairs. The "Mother of the Nation" was omnipresent and photographed at numerous events. Her followers described themselves as "your daughters, the women of Egypt," demonstrating that the family metaphors had become widespread, and Safiyya received recognition from women's groups for her "sincere and wholehearted" dedication to the women's movement.[77] Yet she had her differences with Huda Shaʿrawi, the undisputed leader of that movement. In an interview reported to American authorities, Safiyya argued that "too much emphasis was being laid by the Egyptian feminists on the freedom and emancipation of woman, and not enough on the great need of women's education in all its forms."[78] Safiyya and Huda oscillated between cooperation and competition in their nationalist and feminist endeavors.

In a portrait from this period, Safiyya stands with a feather in hand, maternal and mature. The photo appeared in various journals in the following years, cropped and cut, sometimes with different studio imprints.[79] A portrait from that session also served as the model for an oil painting of Safiyya by an art teacher, who later gave it to her as a gift.[80] Another painting, by a Canadian artist, depicted Safiyya wearing her Kamal sash, and was entered in an art show in Paris.[81]

Photographs of Safiyya with Saʿd continued to depict their political partnership. In less spontaneous pictures with Saʿd, Safiyya generally repeats the pose of the photograph taken after their marriage, at his side or behind a seated Saʿd with a hand on his shoulder. The physical contact conveys Safiyya's constant support; her face reflects vitality while his shows exhaustion.[82] Saʿd died 23 August 1927 at about the age of seventy. Telegrams poured in and visitors came to the House of the Nation to offer their condolences. Wafdist women held a graveside memorial service: "I do not know to whom to present consolation upon the death of Saʿd except the Mother of the Egyptians, our mother," said Wajida Thabit. "Saʿd was not only one of us. Saʿd was the nation. Saʿd was Egypt."[83] Even in mourning, Safiyya found the right words to enhance her husband's mystique: "Saʿd was Egypt, her son, her leader, and her guardian. . . . The leader of the nation died, but the nation lives," she wrote in a letter to "my sons and sons of the homeland."[84]

In the decade that capped her husband's political career, Safiyya consolidated her own power. During his exiles, she took his place, issued public appeals, worked for his release, and kept the public focus on her home, the House of the Nation. By encouraging a cult of veneration around him and the spread of the myth that he embodied Egypt, she solidified her own position. When together, she acted as his confidante and partner, playing "Mother of the Egyptians" to his leader of the nationalist movement. Both worked through the Wafd, where their power was based, with Safiyya constantly trying to smooth ruptures but showing little patience with competing politicians. After Saʿd's death, she set out to shape the memory of Saʿd and once again inherited his mantle, emerging as a key player in partisan and nationalist politics.

## MEMORIALIZING THE DEAD

Saʿd Zaghlul was given a state funeral with full military honors. The ceremony started at the House of the Nation, where women mourners crowded the doorway as Safiyya bid farewell to her partner of thirty-one years.[85] The body was borne to the mosque for a short ceremony and then for burial in Imam al-Shafiʿi cemetery, a site where governors and grandees had long done obeisance. The crowds accompanying the coffin were estimated at 200,000 to 300,000, a large size considering that the funeral coincided with the summer holidays and took place at short notice.[86] For some, the funeral procession might have been reminiscent of that for Mustafa Kamil, the young nationalist leader who had been buried nearly twenty years earlier.[87] But much had changed in the interim. For one, the Egyptian state now sponsored the ceremonial funeral of a popular nationalist leader. For another, schoolgirls marched in the procession. They would also participate in a memorial service held forty days later in Giza, where prominent women nationalists addressed the gathering.[88]

After her husband's death, Safiyya donned black and wore it on almost all occasions until her own death, avoiding cinema, theater, weddings, and parties.[89] Through her own public acts of commemoration of Sa'd and her continued devotion to him, Safiyya became instrumental in shaping the way in which he was remembered. In death as in life, Sa'd was venerated, and the cult around him grew. Parents named their children Sa'd; shopkeepers hung his picture, and customers bought medallions engraved with his bust and scarves imprinted with his likeness. Photography continued to drive the propagation and manipulation of his image.

Sa'd's death transformed Safiyya's demeanor in photographs, and she became a perpetual mourner, her face draped in a dark veil. Photos show her crying at the forty-day memorial service, making frequent visits to Sa'd's tomb, and sitting at the annual commemorations of Sa'd's death and nationalist holidays.[90] These press photos continuously charted her movements. In them, she no longer smiles with twinkling eyes; instead, her face is pensive, her expression downcast, her bearing older. The camera pulled back to a respectful distance.

The Wafd was in and out of power in the decade following Sa'd's death, the crucial period for the construction of memorials to the leader of the revolution of 1919 and the head of the Wafd Party. The memorial plans moved ahead, with critical input from Safiyya. The cluster of memorials to Sa'd that she helped to create included a museum, a mausoleum, and public sculptures. She strove to turn the memorials into living monuments that engaged viewers and visitors.

Shortly after Sa'd's death, the coalition government of Wafdists and Liberal Constitutionalists purchased the House of the Nation, as well as the home where Sa'd had been born. The intention was to transform the House of the Nation into a national museum, with the understanding that Safiyya would live there until her death. Safiyya kept all of Sa'd's belongings in place, and at family gatherings she left his seat at the table empty. She also gave instructions that her German maid would be the caretaker of the museum when it opened, and that the domestic staff would stay on.[91]

The government purchased land adjacent to the House of the Nation as the site for the construction of a mausoleum for Sa'd, but later decided to buy land across the street that was considered better suited. Dissension arose over the tomb's design. Some argued that it should be pharaonic, reflecting the nationalist spirit of the decade in which Tutankhamen's tomb had been discovered, and Safiyya gave her full approval to the neopharaonic design that the department of works authorized. But some critics preferred an Arabo-Islamic style, condemning pharaonicism as paganistic.[92] Contention next arose over the cost of the structure—made of red granite from Aswan—and for nearly a year the Liberal Constitutionalist ministry halted construction. Work on the mausoleum finally resumed under a Wafd government in 1930 and was completed in 1931 under Isma'il Sidqi's premiership.

Debate then erupted over who should be interred in the tomb. Safiyya had approved the overall plan on the condition that she alone would be buried with Sa'd, and she refused Sidqi's proposal that nationalist leaders such as Mustafa Kamil should lie alongside her deceased husband. In response, Sidqi had mummies from the Egyptian national museum moved into the tomb.[93] Upon the Wafd's return to power in 1936, the mummies were removed. Safiyya gave her consent to Sa'd's interment in the mausoleum only after receiving a personal guarantee from the head of the Wafd that the government would pass a law declaring that only she and Sa'd would lie in the tomb.[94] In mid-June 1936, the government transferred Sa'd's body to the mausoleum with great ceremony. Safiyya subsequently visited the tomb daily to place flowers there. Politicians often assembled by the tomb to deliver speeches and then proceeded across the street to the House of the Nation to vow loyalty to Safiyya. Frequent visits by young and old Egyptians transformed the tomb into a living monument with new meanings.[95]

A set of monumental sculptures executed by the Egyptian sculptor Mahmud Mukhtar (who had sculpted *The Awakening of Egypt*) for squares in Alexandria and Cairo also memorialized Sa'd. In the towering piece designed for Alexandria, Sa'd stands erect, one foot in front of the other, arms at his sides, hands clenched, chest out, a fez atop his head. The stance gives the impression that the figure is marching forward with determination, while the size suggests the strength and power of the man. Safiyya visited the sculptor in his studio in Paris to view the completed piece in 1930. A photograph taken upon that occasion circulated widely in the press, showing Safiyya and Mukhtar dwarfed by the towering sculpture.[96] Mukhtar finished the second statue a year later; but this project, like other memorial projects to Sa'd, suffered from political squabbling. When Mukhtar died in 1934, he had still not received compensation from the Egyptian government for the works.[97]

The two statues were erected during the Wafd's tenure in office in 1936–37. But they were officially unveiled—again amid controversy— only in 1938 under Muhammad Mahmud's government. At the time of the ceremony, the head of the Wafd was out of the country, and for this and other reasons, Wafdists boycotted the unveiling. But the most glaring absence was that of Safiyya Zaghlul. She had apparently been led to believe that she would be seated next to King Farouk at the ceremony in Alexandria, but officials then informed her that women were not allowed to sit beside men, particularly the king, at official functions. Safiyya responded that she was an old lady and the "Mother of the Egyptians" and did not think that any traditions would be broken if she sat beside one of her "sons." But she was also angry that prominent women Wafdists were omitted from the list of those invited and declined to take up the seat in the special marquee that was built for her opposite the memorial. Instead, she listened to the speeches on the radio with a group of friends.[98]

## POWER OF THE LIVING

At the same time that Safiyya helped to create a complex of memorials to her deceased husband, she continued to play an active role in Wafd politics. Sa'd had not named a successor, and a competition for party leadership broke out shortly after his death. Safiyya's candidacy as honorary president was considered, as was the notion of an executive committee. But the leadership agreed that for practical reasons there must be a single head. According to British sources: "[t]he choice fell on [Mustafa al-]Nahas, largely owing to female influence. For one thing [Fathallah] Barakat was opposed to the proposal of Madame Zaghloul's honorary presidency and to allowing her any share in the responsible control of the Wafd organisation. He thereby alienated Madame Zaghloul. Nahas, on the other hand, was in favour of her co-operation, unofficial or otherwise."[99] Safiyya proved instrumental in having her candidate selected as the new leader of the Wafd. And it was agreed that she would be "consulted in all matters."[100]

Safiyya emerged in the post-Sa'd era as both a powerful political player and a potent national symbol around whom support for the Wafd could be rallied. When she returned from a summer trip in Europe a year after

Sa'd's death, the Wafd, then in opposition, planned a big demonstration to welcome her home. Large crowds composed of working-class Egyptians—"riff-raff" and "rabble" in the words of High Commissioner Lord Lloyd—waited alongside the docks for the landing of her party. Members of Safiyya's family came from Cairo along with a delegation of women, and Nahhas took out his own launch to meet the ship. But the government wanted to avoid a large demonstration of popular support for Sa'd's widow. Safiyya was removed from the ship and taken to another landing site. She was then sent on her way to Cairo by train without meeting the welcoming party.[101]

Two years later, when Safiyya again returned from abroad under similar circumstances—the Wafd was out of power and government troops and police were on hand to suppress disturbances—she was permitted to meet the waiting crowds. "The *sha'b* [folk] welcomed her in a manner suitable to her rank," reported *al-Nahda al-Nisa'iyya*.[102] She later issued a communiqué expressing her thanks to "my sons, the fellaheen," and to the "Senators and Deputies," for their enthusiastic welcome.[103] She had returned to participate in the commemoration of 13 November, the day Sa'd and his companions had first approached the British in 1918 with nationalist demands. At the close of the ceremony, which took place at Sa'd's tomb, she reportedly swore an oath to sacrifice all she possessed "in wealth and strength for the triumph of the homeland and the constitution." Safiyya's power within the Wafd derived from her status as Sa'd's widow, as well as her control over her husband's fortune and Wafd funds.[104]

Satirical cartoons suggest that not all Egyptians esteemed their "Mother." While *al-Lata'if al-Musawwara* occasionally took Safiyya as a model for the nation, cartoons in *al-Kashkul* lampooned her political influence, especially after Sa'd's death.[105] One of the most biting, a 1931 cartoon (figure 25), shows a domineering Safiyya Hanim Zaghlul yanking Nahhas's ear and scolding him. "How could you go to Hamid [al-Basil] and eat with Muhammad Mahmud, who snatched me away and attacked my home in the middle of the night?" she asks (referring to a raid on the Zaghluls' home in which Sa'd's papers, which Safiyya had guarded with the intention of publishing, were confiscated). A writhing Nahhas replies, "Have mercy on me. I'll repent and cut myself off [from their company]. If you ever see it happen again, kick me with your shoes."[106]

In April 1931, Safiyya joined with other prominent women in demonstrations against the Sidqi regime, forming a temporary alliance with Huda Sha'rawi. The latter also worked for the restoration of the

Figure 25. "In the House of the Nation": Safiyya
"Hanim" Zaghlul twists Nahhas Pasha's ear and
scolds him. *Al-Kashkul*, 30 January 1931, 32.

constitution, although not for the return of the Wafd to power.[107] Safiyya
remained in the public eye: she sponsored school celebrations, visited an
agricultural and industrial fair, and supported the opening of a sweet
shop. This was all in the name of encouraging indigenous industries and
nationalist enterprises.[108] At the same time, she continued to play her
role as "Mother of the Egyptians" to perfection and appeared as a maternal figure at funerals, on condolence calls, or in visits to the wounded—
"her sons"—in the hospital.[109]

The Wafd still met in a wing of the House of the Nation with Safiyya's
involvement. As a center of political activity, the house came under the
watchful eye of the government. In 1932, during a year in which Safiyya
had spoken out against the government at Sa'd's tomb, Sidqi placed a cordon of some forty police around the house and sent Safiyya a letter threat-
ening to close it. Safiyya replied indignantly, rejecting the attacks on the
House of the Nation—the cradle of the Egyptian nationalist movement—
and pointed out that even the British military authorities had not dared to
close it.[110] Huda Sha'rawi's journal *L'Egyptienne* published a statement

of support for the "Mother of the Nation," reflecting the common ground that Safiyya and Huda found in their enmity for Sidqi. But Sidqi made good on his threat, temporarily cutting off access to Safiyya's home.[111]

The Wafd rallied around Safiyya and built on her prestige. She promoted the party in its bid to return to power and remained visible in part because of her centrality in the party. Photos document the leadership breaking a Ramadan fast at her dining room table, visiting her at her summer house, and welcoming her back to Cairo.[112] Women Wafdists gathered to greet her when she returned from a summer break.[113] In the south with a group of politicians in 1934, she sat for a photo with members of local delegations, and photos of massive crowds of fellahin showed the large reception she received in the countryside.[114] The cover of *al-Lata'if al-Musawwara* also featured scenes of Safiyya and her companions on the balcony of the House of the Nation celebrating the return of constitutional rule in 1934: the first shows Safiyya leaning out a window and waving a handkerchief to the crowds below; the second shows her companions leaning on the window sill and looking down, as Safiyya smiles straight at the photographer, ever aware of her public persona.[115] These group photos convey the sense that Safiyya was figuratively surrounded with warmth, affection, and respect. Yet they also show that Safiyya wielded a great deal of power, that she was aware of this, and that leading male and female political figures flocked to her side. Both her allies and her enemies acknowledged her stature and influence.

From the founding of the Wafd, Safiyya had played the role of peacemaker to keep the factions together. (This did not mean, of course, that she harbored any particular sympathy for politicians who had cut their ties to the party.) One strategy she had used for mediating disputes was working through members of the Women's Wafd, urging them to pressure their husbands and sons to unify. In spite of her evident support and promotion of Nahhas after Sa'd's death, she professed neutrality and used her influence to placate feelings. She appealed to personal and family loyalties to prevent cracks in the party.[116] But as the rifts in the Wafd grew wider, she proved unable to bridge them. She could not in 1935 prevent the breach between party leaders and the newspaper *Ruz al-Yusuf*. According to American sources, Mahmud al-Nuqrashi supported the paper and had "the approval of intellectuals and of Madame Zaghlul."[117] By 1937, the tension between Nahhas and Nuqrashi led the latter to form the Sa'adist Party. At that point, Safiyya decided to retire from politics.

At the age of sixty or so, Safiyya closed the doors of the House of the Nation to Wafdist meetings and resigned her post as honorary head of the

Women's Wafd. Although still a public figure, she refrained from involvement in political affairs and refused to take sides in partisan disputes.[118] Safiyya nursed her two sisters, who died within six hours of one another in May 1938. After their deaths, she drew closer to their children, and when one niece was hospitalized, slept on a cot by her bedside for three weeks.[119] At home Safiyya still received visitors, among them women journalists such as Fatima Ni'mat Rashid, founder of the National Women's Party. In an interview published in *al-Ithnayn wa al-Dunya*, Fatima described her meeting with the silver-haired Safiyya in 1944: "Who would believe that this peaceful lady was herself at the head of the rebels, having replaced her husband in the course of his internment."[120] Safiyya, who had spent much of her life nurturing the memory of her husband in exile and in death, was now memorialized by a younger generation of Egyptian women.

Safiyya died unexpectedly on 12 January 1946 at the age of 69. The next morning the government announced the death of "the wife of the immortal leader Sa'd Zaghlul" and arrangements for the funeral that same afternoon. The king's grand chamberlain led the procession of ministers, diplomats, notables, and other dignitaries who followed the coffin, which was preceded by an Egyptian army detachment. Children from many schools marched together, while, along the route, an "immense crowd" watched the funeral cortege. After prayers were read in the mosque, Safiyya's body was taken to Sa'd's mausoleum, where the prime minister, together with other prominent political figures, laid the coffin to rest.[121] In death, as in life, she was Sa'd's partner.

Numerous obituaries of the "Mother of the Egyptians" appeared under that title in the press. *Al-Ahram* remembered her as "the example for Egyptian women fighting for their nation . . . the model for wives and of sacrifice in her assistance to her illustrious husband . . . the example of a tender mother towards the good people who had adopted her for their mother." *Le Bourse égyptienne* wrote that she had placed herself "in the front line of the patriotic movement, sharing the sufferings of Sa'd Zaghlul and participating in the battles of the people for which she had chosen to consecrate her life." *Le Journal d'Egypte* remarked that she was not just a heroic woman "facing dangers in the street at the moment of the riots, demonstrating at the head of Egyptian ladies, and brandishing the national flag," but was the adviser and confidante of a great man.[122] The obituaries reflected a nostalgia for an earlier era when the lines of the struggle between Egyptian nationalists and British colonialists were clearer and the Egyptian nation had been more unified.[123]

· · ·

Safiyya Zaghlul was one of the most visible symbols and most powerful women of her time. During her husband's exiles, she took up his mantle of leadership. Once she had tasted power, she did not easily give it up and instead became Sa'd's partner in politics. Safiyya crafted her own political persona, developing her own style, skills, and voice. As "Mother of the Egyptians," Safiyya represented a departure from less visible elite women of the past, whether they were concubines, co-wives, or secluded harem women. She was presented in the press and elsewhere as Sa'd's partner in life and in death, not just with words, but in numerous photographs documenting her movements. She used her power to advance a nationalist agenda centered on her husband, his party, and his legacy. Safiyya continued to wield a great deal of influence in party and national politics after his death, serving as the maker of party leaders and the keeper of Sa'd's memory. The British appreciated Safiyya's strengths and watched her closely; the palace recognized her unique position and rewarded her accordingly; non-Wafdist politicians tried to contain her; and Wafdists used Safiyya's stature as a national figure to gain popular support for their party.

Safiyya achieved an unparalleled position as a woman politician in the interwar years and served as a model. However, while acting as "Mother" of the nation allowed her and other women who used this rhetoric to carve out new political roles, these roles had limitations and no guarantees. The use of maternal language also reaffirmed women's reproductive and domestic roles as primary rather than their political roles. Moreover, in constantly speaking of her "sons," Safiyya implicitly excluded women from the nation in spite of her own close ties with female followers.

The title "Mother of the Egyptians" had a time and a place. At a critical moment in the struggle against the British, it served to give the Egyptian combatants a sense of relatedness, of belonging, of home, and of family. Nationalists, and Wafdists in particular, used family rhetoric, which glorified unity and harmony, because it helped to smooth over gender, class, religious, ethnic, and other divides in the population. The Zaghluls were the new conjugal couple, which in turn was the core of the bourgeois family that formed the base of the nationalist movement. Yet family rhetoric was a dual-edged sword. It condemned violence and stifled dissent from below, from the "devoted sons," and left decision-making in the hands of the elite. In this way, it worked to preserve social stratification and the primacy of landowners and the newly emerging bourgeoisie. In addition, by reinforcing domesticity, it ultimately circumscribed women's possibilities, and although it modified the gender order, it did not seriously challenge it.

CHAPTER SEVEN

# Partisans of the Wafd

The Wafd spearheaded the nationalist movement, and most Egyptian nationalists—male and female—fell in behind the "party of the nation." Elite women attempted to secure a political niche for themselves by founding an auxiliary party organization—the Women's Wafd—and by starting political periodicals that supported the Wafd. Yet these women wanted more than a symbolic role. In the wake of the revolution, the "lady demonstrators" of March 1919 sought to share the nationalist stage with male politicians. They wanted to be taken seriously as political actors and to push women's political culture in new directions.

This chapter cuts from a star player—Safiyya Zaghlul—to the circle of female nationalists involved in the Wafd in the interwar period. It pulls the lens back from Huda Sha'rawi, first president of the Women's Wafd, to look at her competitors and successors; from the center in Cairo to activities in other cities and towns; and from members of the auxiliary party to female political journalists. The female notables of the Women's Wafd and Wafdist female journalists used multiple strategies to make their voices heard in shaping government and making policy. They both demonstrated against the British and remonstrated with Egyptian politicians, waging a two-front battle. They did so on a shifting terrain as Egyptians moved from the fluidity of revolution to the rigidity of a structured politics of parties, parliament, and the palace.

Wafdist women tried to maintain unity yet proved unable to stay above the fray of partisan politics for long. They quickly learned that they could not be both a part of politics and apart from partisanship, a perhaps unrealistic ideal. Once they became entangled, they clashed with one another, as well as with the Wafd leadership. Male Wafdists attempted to push women from the playing field just when Egyptians had successfully wrested some control of the state from the British. The press was complicit in this process in that it gendered parliamentary and party politics as male, thereby excluding women from certain spheres. Women continued to chip away at this exclusion and simultaneously sought other paths to politics.

MEMORY AND MEMOIRS

The story of the Women's Wafd figures marginally in most accounts of Egyptian nationalism. Likewise, it flits in and out of the story of Egyptian feminism, prominent when Huda Sha'rawi presided, but receiving little coverage after Huda's break with Sa'd.[1] Yet this break did not spell the end of the Women's Wafd or of Wafdist women's endeavors in the field of journalism. We can tell the continuation of this story in part because three of the most active Wafdist women—Huda Sha'rawi (1879–1947), Munira Thabit (1902–67), and Fatima (Ruz) al-Yusuf (1898–1958)—left memoirs, and a fourth—Esther Fahmi Wisa (1895–1990)—was memorialized in a son's family history.[2] These four women are chosen as the focus of the story here not only because they were prominent players but because of the records they left. They sought to shape history and memory in an effort to have their lives and political activism remembered in specific ways. Their memoirs, and memories of them, reveal that they wanted to be considered important political actors who were at the center of the action in the interwar period and beyond. These memoirs remind us that memories can be fallible, particularly after a long lapse, but contemporary periodicals and archival records help sort out some of the confusion.

These political memoirs appeared in different decades and documented active lives, anticipating or reacting to one another. Munira's *Thawra fi . . . al-Burj al-'Aji* (Revolution in the Ivory Tower) came in the wake of World War II (1946) and recorded her struggle for women's political rights. Fatima al-Yusuf's *Dhikrayat* appeared a year after the 1952 revolution, covering her early life in theater and second career in journalism. Huda's *Mudhakkirat*, discussing her family life, feminism, and nationalist activism, were dictated to her secretary in the 1930s but did not appear in print in their entirety until 1981 (over thirty years after her death). Esther Fahmi Wisa's son, Hanna, brought out his English-language family memoir *Assiout: The Saga of an Egyptian Family* in 1994, four years after the death of his mother, whose role in nationalist politics is one of the main themes. He drew on clippings, correspondence, speeches, anecdotes, and Huda Sha'rawi's memoirs, which he contests on certain points.[3]

Family figures prominently in the memoirs. For the notable women—Huda and Esther—who came from wealthy families and were large landowners in their own right, family politics shaped their visions. Huda begins her memoir with an account of the life and career of her father, Muhammad Sultan Pasha, to vindicate his opposition to 'Urabi and to validate his nationalist credentials. In the absence of a male heir, she sought to claim her father's political mantle, as well as to clarify the historical record. Esther Fahmi Wisa also saw political power as an inheritance. Her father, Dr. Akhnukh Fanus, had been a famous lawyer and an orator in the Legislative Assembly; paralyzed in 1912, he died in 1918. According to her son, his place in Esther's life was taken by Sa'd Zaghlul, whom Esther saw as "a father figure, an idealist who was willing to sacrifice everything for his principles, and who could do no wrong in her eyes."[4]

British officials occasionally called these and other female notables the "feminine appendages" of politicians or "wives of notables."[5] Yet they were more than political wives supporting their husband's positions. To start, family politics proved complex: the women had loyalties both to their natal and conjugal families, sometimes with competing claims and stronger attachments to their father's kin (or memory) than to their husband. Some of them married cousins, as both Huda and Esther had done, and were bound as blood relations as much as spouses, but not all of them replicated their husbands' politics. Huda's husband was a founder of the Wafd but broke with it in 1921 and died in 1922; Huda chose to stay on, ostensibly above partisan politics, and broke with the Wafd only later. Some wives may have steered their husbands rather than the reverse. Esther's husband held a seat in parliament from 1924, but her son sees her as the more dominating force. Finally, female notables generally married older men and outlived them, enjoying political careers long after their husband's deaths. Sharifa Riyad (the widow of Mahmud Riyad), Safiyya Zaghlul, Huda Sha'rawi, and other women who demonstrated and signed petitions identifying themselves as widows followed this pattern. In short, the politics of the period were controlled by powerful families whose brothers and sons saw their entry into parliament as an inheritance and whose wives and daughters fought for some share. Elite women, like men, were not independent political actors but generally worked to support their family, class, and occasionally gender interests.

The female journalists came from a rising middle class that sought to break into this elite. Munira Thabit's father was a government employee, and when he died, Sa'd Zaghlul acted as a surrogate father. He took her under his political protection and encouraged her to speak out for women's political rights.[6] Yet her struggle to win the vote for women may well have been because she saw that the middle classes did not have the ready access to power of the female notables and considered the vote the best channel for political participation. Fatima al-Yusuf started out on the stage but then created the newspaper *Ruz al-Yusuf* to express her political views.

Wafdist women came from diverse ethnic and religious as well as class backgrounds. Huda's mother was Circassian, and Munira's was Turkish; Fatima's parents were Syrian, and Esther's were Copts. Their own family backgrounds and political trajectories show the transition from Ottoman households—with slaves and ex-slaves—to Egyptian families. Huda's mother was a concubine, and a Sudanese eunuch presided over the harem; Esther grew up in a household run by a Sudanese ex-slave, daughter of a chieftain. These women negotiated the dramatic social and political transformation from Ottomanism to Egyptian nationalism with finesse. The lives of these women also show the way in which provincial towns and cities were knit together by nationalism. Female nationalists came from different parts of Egypt and the Levant—Huda from Minya, Esther from Asyut, Munira from Alexandria, and Fatima from the port city of Tripoli, north of Beirut—and they often kept their local ties.

The memoirs capture the richness of women's political culture in the interwar years. At times they read like scrapbooks, with cuttings of articles, petitions, telegrams, letters, and other documents juxtaposed as the authors highlight their own or family member's pioneering roles and justify their positions. These women took their political missions seriously, saw themselves as major players in the Wafd, and considered their undertakings as crucial to the nationalist cause. The wealth of detail indicates that the women hoped to be remembered for their ardent political activities and sound judgments rather than condemned or forgotten. The works all reflect the personal dimension of politics in the interwar years, as access to power came through connections, and the texts are filled with stories of encounters and correspondence with prominent leaders. Yet struggles also emerge as a theme, as women were cut out of Wafdist politics, or chose to withdraw their support, and eventually channeled their energies into feminism, journalism, social welfare, law, and other activities.

## "IN THE HEART OF THE ACTION"

After the "ladies' demonstrations" of March 1919, elite women continued to protest, picketing ministries during strikes in April, joining street celebrations, publishing articles and poems in the press, and delivering petitions to foreign legations. Alexandrian women produced one such letter of protest in April 1919, using a feminine voice to testify to British injustices in Egypt. As "les dames Egyptiennes," they spoke on behalf of those imprisoned, deported, and killed—"their brothers"—and appealed to the hearts of European and American women. A few women gave their husbands' professions (engineer, judge, lawyer, doctor, general prosecutor, chief of finances, head of the postal service) and titles, which ranged from effendi to pasha (connoting middle and upper class), and one woman gave her own profession as school director. Many were related, and the mix included Copts as well as Muslims.[7]

Elite women also participated in the campaign against the Milner Mission, sent by the British in early December 1919 to evaluate the situation in Egypt in light of the unrest. Some two hundred women gathered inside St. Mark's Church in Cairo on 12 December, five days after the mission had arrived, to orchestrate a strategy of resistance. They had chosen the site because under martial law, large assemblies were banned in almost all other public places. The group composed an open letter of protest to the mission, then drove in a motorcade throughout the city to deliver their message: To find out about our nationalist expectations, speak to our designated leaders, the Wafd.[8]

The next month, in early January 1920, from five hundred to one thousand women gathered once again at St. Mark's Church to establish the Women's Wafd. In a secret ballot, they elected fifteen members to the Women's Wafd Central Committee (WWCC; Lajnat al-Wafd al-Markaziyya li al-Sayyidat). The committee members were all married—five to pashas, six to beys, two to effendis, and one to a doctor—and most to members of the Wafd. The exception was the unmarried Fikriyya Husni, a supporter of the Watani Party. Among the largest vote-getters were Huda Sha'rawi (who was at the time in Luxor, and whose husband was then vice president of the Wafd), Esther Fahmi Wisa (who steered the group in its first meetings as vice president), and Sharifa Riyad. The group declared its purpose to be "informing the Wafdist delegation of the loyalty of Egyptian women and their determination . . . to continue the demand for Egypt's complete independence . . . as long as the Wafd adhered to its proclaimed principles."[9]

The Wafd remained committed to legal and peaceful means to achieve complete independence. A party of mostly large landowners, it had no interest in encouraging social unrest. The WWCC issued circulars, wrote petitions, staged demonstrations, and organized boycotts. Through these actions, the Women's Wafd acted in unity with the Wafd leadership. Even as the ranks of men split in the first years, women stayed firm, considering themselves above partisan politics and capable of healing rifts.

Shortly after the large meeting in St. Mark's Church, the WWCC met in the palace of Huda Sha'rawi's sister-in-law and elected officers. (Huda herself was still in Luxor and did not return until after the WWCC had met some half dozen times.) The winning slate confirmed Huda as president, Esther Fahmi Wisa as vice president, her aunt Regina Khayyat as treasurer, and Fikriyya Husni as secretary.[10] With two Copts in prominent positions—Wisa and Khayyat—the WWCC mirrored the male Wafd in its religious balance. The women wrote an open letter and then took to the streets of central Cairo. Twice during the march, they confronted British soldiers, who on the second occasion confiscated the Egyptian flags that they carried.[11] At a subsequent meeting, the group invited Safiyya Zaghlul, who had sent a letter from abroad praising the committee, to be honorary president and their representative in Paris; Safiyya accepted the post.[12]

After the formation of the WWCC and a number of branch committees, the central group received petitions signed by female residents of Cairo and the provinces authorizing the committee to speak on their behalf. This petition campaign reenacted one conducted on behalf of the Wafd before its leadership was exiled in 1919. For example, women in Asyut sent in a petition stating: "We the undersigned declare that we have mandated the following ladies—Huda Sha'rawi, Esther Fahmi Wisa, Sharifa Riyad, Regina Khayyat . . . to establish a central Wafdist committee of Egyptian ladies, to carry out all the national functions which would lead to complete independence according to the principles of the Wafd, and to enable them to represent us before all institutions."[13] The head of the Society of Union and Progress of Egyptian Women in Tanta also sent a letter of support.[14] Petitions became a favorite tool of the Women's Wafd. 'Atiyya Abu Isba'a, the daughter of a member of the auxiliary at whose home women had gathered in March 1919, remembered going to private homes to collect signatures and subsequently delivering the documents to diplomatic representatives in Cairo.[15]

The WWCC pledged full support to the Wafd and imagined itself as the mirror image, or feminine half, of the central committee of the Wafd. They even called the latter the Men's Wafd Central Committee (Lajnat al-Wafd al-Markaziyya li al-Rijal). They considered themselves part advisory committee, part publicists for the Wafd, and strove to be "in the heart of the action."[16] The committee met regularly, weekly in its first months and more often if necessary, to discuss current affairs. They carefully read government reports, a variety of Wafdist and opposition periodicals, and the foreign press. They responded when provoked: after an article portraying Egyptian women in an unfavorable light appeared in the London *Times*, Esther Fahmi Wisa wrote a rebuttal for the WWCC.[17] The committee corresponded regularly with Sa'd Zaghlul and gave policy advice. Members, who felt they had earned the right to be consulted and taken seriously, did not like being ignored. When the Wafd circulated the Curzon plan in Egypt for reaction, the WWCC got hold of a copy and studied it in lengthy sessions. They published their rejection of it in the press and sent Sa'd a detailed critique, as well as a rebuke for not having sent them a copy of the plan directly.[18]

The Women's Wafd played a central role in the ritual of dispatching and receiving Wafdist leaders who went abroad. They were on hand in numbers, for example, to meet Sa'd and Safiyya Zaghlul when they returned from Paris in April 1921.[19] Sa'd appreciated this support, sensing that the Women's Wafd strengthened the position of the Wafd in general. He encouraged the WWCC but discouraged them from harboring any pretensions to power. "Your patriotism is pure," he was reported to have told them at a gathering in 1921 at the House of the Nation. "You search neither for honors nor for positions. And because you are the foundation stone of the family and your hearts are with us, the hearts of the fathers and sons will also be, thanks to you, with us."[20] Women were meant to be completely selfless in their political undertakings. That they, like men, had aspirations would eventually lead to clashes.

When British officials arrested and exiled Sa'd for the second time in late 1921, the WWCC protested and convened a large meeting. Gathering in January 1922, leaders of the Women's Wafd delivered speeches, young girls from charity workshops sang nationalist songs, and participants pledged themselves to a boycott in which Egyptians were encouraged to buy local rather than foreign products. The Women's Wafd organized committees in the main cities and provinces to orchestrate the action and also met with local shopkeepers to ensure their cooperation.[21] Public support for the boycott diminished with the unilateral British declaration of the end of the protectorate in February 1922, but Zaghlul later commended the Women's Wafd for the important role they had played in the boycott movement.[22]

The WWCC rejected British negotiations with non-Wafdists and the proposed conditions for independence. "These conditions are meant to sever the ties of the sacred union and bring us back to extremists and moderates," they argued. The press circulated the declaration under the signature of the acting secretary, Ihsan Ahmad. The British strove to prevent its publication, signaling their apprehension of the influence of the Women's Wafd.[23] Elite women in the provinces also added their voices to the February protests. The Society of Union and Progress of Egyptian Women in Tanta sent telegrams to British officials and newspapers, saying: "Ladies of [the province of] Gharbia protest against unlawful measures taken by English government against Egyptians. If Lord Allenby alleges he can solve Egyptian question in absence of our leader Zaghloul Pasha surely he shall be disproved." The president of the Asyut Feminine Union, Hayata Thabit, sent British officials a similar telegram, protesting "against present policy regarding Egypt." The Minya Women's Union Committee subsequently wrote directly to Sa'd, who was by then in exile in the Seychelles.[24]

The WWCC continued to stage protest marches and motorcade processions in the capital. In March 1922, approximately eighty cars carrying ladies protested against the second exile of Zaghlul, the program of the new ministry formed in Sa'd's absence, and the "false independence" declared unilaterally by the British. In a procession lasting two hours, the demonstrators raised placards with French and Arabic writing and delivered written protests to foreign diplomats.[25] In October 1922, when Safiyya left to join Sa'd in exile in Gibraltar as mentioned in the previous chapter, a motorcade of more than sixty cars escorted her to the train station, and a smaller contingent traveled with her to Port Said to see her safely onto the boat.[26] The Women's Wafd also participated in Wafdist commemorations. On 13 November 1922 (the fourth anniversary of the Wafd's first visit to the British high commissioner), a large number gathered in the women's section of tents outside the House of the Nation to hear speeches.[27]

Although the Wafd was based in Cairo, Alexandria played an important role as a center of Wafdist activism. Members of the Society of Mothers of the Future were generally on hand to greet traveling Wafdist dignitaries. They marched in the streets of Alexandria upon Sa'd's return in April 1921 (see figure 19), and later that year, they staged further protests. They planned in October 1922 to open the "Society of Mothers of the Future School and Zaghlul's Workshop," which the Egyptian Wafd had placed under its patronage. The group, presided over by Anisa Rashid, with the writer Zaynab 'Abd al-Hamid as secretary, coordinated their activities with the WWCC.[28]

## HUDA SHA'RAWI: "MOTHER-IN-LAW OF THE NATION"

The Women's Wafd under Huda Sha'rawi's presidency worked hard for the release of Sa'd and the other exiles, as well as of Wafdists imprisoned in Egypt. At the same time, Huda's own interests seemed to be shifting toward international feminism. Arguing that women ought to present Egypt's case abroad, she invited members from the WWCC to her home on 16 March 1923 to found the Egyptian Feminist Union (EFU) and to form a delegation for a conference in Rome. The delegation to Rome in May 1923 included Esther Fahmi Wisa and Regina Khayyat.[29] The following September, when Huda returned from Europe on the same boat as the Zaghluls, she conversed amicably with Sa'd. A large contingent of Wafdist women met Safiyya in Alexandria, and sixty escorted her back to Cairo.[30] But beneath the surface, a rift between Huda and Sa'd had emerged. The sources of the rift were multiple: Huda's husband 'Ali Sha'rawi had split with Sa'd early on, as mentioned previously; Huda and other women Wafdists had hoped that Sa'd would treat Egyptian politicians who had been active in his absence with greater respect; and the WWCC had been slighted when it had not been consulted. There were other policy differences as well.

When Sa'd became prime minister in 1924, following the electoral victory of the Wafd, the tensions between Huda and Sa'd were exacerbated. To start with, the Women's Wafd was excluded from ceremonies in March 1924 at the opening of the Egyptian parliament. This was a big affront to those female notables who had prided themselves on their contributions to the national cause and their access to power. Excluded from the ceremony, the WWCC staged protests in concert with the EFU (whose membership overlapped with its own). Huda sent girls from the New Woman Society, a philanthropy under her charge, to hold up placards outside parliament. These signs, unlike those from 1919, articulated both feminist and nationalist demands. These included women's right to vote, which had been denied in the new constitution. It was increasingly clear to the more feminist-minded nationalists that women's progress was being sacrificed in the name of national solidarity.[31]

The final split between Huda and Sa'd came over the issue of the Sudan. There is a certain irony to this as support for unity of the Nile Valley, a rallying cry of Egyptian nationalists through much of this period, looks in hindsight more like colonialism than radical nationalism, although the two are obviously related.[32] Huda does not give her motives for so strongly clinging to the Sudan, and in the absence of hard evidence, we can only speculate. As part of a large landowning family, she may have felt threatened by the potential diversion of Nile waters for the Sudan and may also have feared that the resultant competition would lower cotton prices. Such views would have been consistent with those of other Egyptians who perceived British plans to develop agricultural projects in the Sudan as detrimental to their interests. Huda's husband had earlier criticized the Milner-Zaghlul agreement specifically because it had omitted mention of the Sudan, and on this Huda agreed with him.[33]

Huda may also have felt a strong emotional bond to the Sudan. Having grown up under the watchful eye of a Sudanese eunuch, who remained a retainer in her household, she may have seen Egypt and the Sudan as intimately connected, part of the same "national family."[34] The Sudan was a litmus test for a particular brand of nationalism. Other female notables, such as Esther Fahmi Wisa, repeatedly defended Egyptian interests in the Sudan and opposed British designs to wrest ultimate control of the territory from their hands. Ihsan Ahmad pressed for the "complete independence of Egypt and her Sudan."[35] Some nationalists were ready to compromise on this issue; Huda was not.

Huda quarreled with Zaghlul over statements he made in parliament in late May 1924 regarding the Sudan and expressed the fear that Sa'd was backing down on Egypt's claims. She published her criticism in *al-Siyasa*, the newspaper of the Liberal Constitutionalist Party, which had been founded by some of the first secessionists from the Wafd. Field Marshal Viscount Edmund Allenby reported, "the publication of her manifesto caused Zaghlul Pasha both annoyance and concern. Mme. Sharawi Pasha, as the leader of the feminist movement in this country, has undoubted influence both in the harems and among the women teachers of the Government schools."[36]

Zaghlul unleashed the Wafdist press on Sha'rawi in a counteroffensive. Wafdist writers highlighted Huda's family interests to undermine her credibility. They accused her of being motivated by personal animosity—her son-in-law had just been dismissed from government service—

and advised her to give up her bid for political leadership. The Wafdist newspaper *al-Balagh* pointedly suggested that Huda was not the mother-in-law of all Egyptians, and that mothers-in-law on the stage and in real life were in any case always ridiculous. (The implicit comparison with Safiyya Zaghlul, "Mother of the Egyptians," showed that maternal metaphors could be used to denigrate as well as elevate women.) Bitter articles elsewhere charged Huda with having assumed a leadership role in Egypt due to her husband's position but argued that this gave her no special authority.[37]

The anti-Wafdist *al-Kashkul* defended her in a cartoon that showed her pouring water on a procession marching under her window, in which Sa'd was depicted as an organ grinder. "What is the good of making all that noise and saying you are serving the nation," Huda says. "We have done nothing but make noise since 1919, and all we have gotten out of it is a bad headache." In short, the cartoon suggested that female nationalists had worked hard and had not been rewarded by the Wafd, whose leaders were no better than street performers. With the Wafd still in power, the publisher of *al-Kashkul* landed in jail for showing Sa'd as an organ grinder, and *al-Siyasa* faced legal proceedings for a number of articles it had published against the Wafd.[38] In the meantime, *al-Lata'if al-Musawwara* had countered with a cartoon of Huda on a "scale of truth" (figure 26). As a paper flies from her hand, she stares at the results in horror. Sa'd looks on, laughing and punning on her name ("right way") by suggesting that she has not taken the right path. The cartoon also lampoons Sulayman Bey Fawzi's *al-Kashkul*, the rival of *al-Lata'if al-Musawwara,* depicting it as a rather ugly dog.[39] Fawzi's office was attacked later that year by Wafd supporters, and copies of *al-Kashkul* were strewn about the street.[40]

The jousting between Huda and Sa'd had wide repercussions, as women Wafdists were forced to take sides. Some women's committees in Tanta and Cairo—Labiba Ahmad's Society of Egyptian Ladies' Awakening, for example—immediately came to Sa'd's support and published manifestos in the press.[41] Cracks in the WWCC widened: Sharifa Riyad sent Huda a letter of resignation in mid-June when her attempts to broker an agreement among the members of the WWCC failed.[42] And the ruptures among these women became public knowledge: "There has arisen among some of the ladies working in the women's awakening some differences in opinion leading to schism and partisanship," Balsam 'Abd al-Malik, the editor of *al-Mar'a al-Misriyya*, reported in September.[43]

Figure 26. Sa'd Zaghlul laughs at Huda Sha'rawi
when she is alarmed by the verdict of a "scale of
truth." *Al-Lata'if al-Musawwara*, 9 June 1924, 16.

Huda's resignation as head of the WWCC was a foregone conclusion,
although exactly when it came is not clear. In the fall, she helped organize renewed boycotts of English goods to protest British actions in the
Sudan that included using Egyptian laborers to help build dams, closing
Khartoum College, and detaining political prisoners. She urged the Egyptian government to press its right to administer the Sudan and to raise
the Egyptian flag over all government buildings there. But she spoke now
in the name of "Egyptian Ladies" or the "Ladies Assembly" rather than
as president of the WWCC.[44]

The assassination of Sir Oliver Lee Stack, British commander of the
Egyptian army and governor-general of the Sudan, in late November, and
Sa'd's response to the resulting British ultimatum, brought the conflict
between Huda and Sa'd to its peak. Speaking in the name of "Egyptian
women" rather than the WWCC, Huda protested against the British policy of holding the Egyptian nation collectively responsible for the crime
of an individual and advised Zaghlul to refuse the British demands. She
subsequently condemned his capitulation and called for his resignation

as prime minister. Huda later made a last attempt to patch up her differences with Sa'd and unite the feuding political parties but met with little success.[45]

As president of the WWCC, Sha'rawi had supported the Wafd but maintained the autonomy of her group, and she had used the position to articulate her own political views. An authoritarian leader herself, she proved unafraid to clash with the head of the Wafd, who felt threatened enough by her influence to orchestrate an attack on her in the press. After her resignation as president, she continued to speak out on a variety of issues. But she no longer spoke with the weight of the Women's Wafd behind her.[46] Nor did she feel weighed down by a vision of the Wafd as "the nation" or of Sa'd as an unassailable leader. She joined the opposition and focused her energies on building the EFU, through which she pushed for social reforms.

ESTHER FAHMI WISA: "THE RIGHT SPIRIT"

Contrary to some expectations, after Huda Sha'rawi and her supporters left the WWCC in 1924, the committee did not disintegrate. Instead, it was reconfigured by, among others, Esther Fahmi Wisa and renamed the Sa'dist Ladies' Committee. A product of an English nanny and American Presbyterian schooling in Asyut, Esther had also come under the iron fist of the liberated Sudanese slave Bahr al-Nil, who ran the household of her mother, Balsam Wisa Boctor Wisa. After graduating from the American College in Asyut, she married her cousin Fahmi Bey Wisa (she was eighteen; he was thirty). Together they had six children, one of whom died at a young age.

When Sa'd and his colleagues were arrested in March 1919, Esther rushed from a family visit in Asyut to Cairo to pledge her support to Safiyya Zaghlul. She participated with her aunt in the March "ladies' demonstrations," protested against the Milner Mission in December 1919, and helped to found the WWCC in January 1920, leading it in its first meetings.[47] Esther subsequently became one of the preeminent speakers and propagandists for the Women's Wafd. She wrote articles (signing some as "Daughter of the Nile") and correspondence for the committee.[48] When Sa'd was exiled with other Wafdists in 1922 and another group was sentenced to life imprisonment in Egypt, Esther urged Allenby to free the prisoners or alleviate their conditions. Her correspondence with Allenby ranged over three years, touched on numerous issues, and was imbued with a moral voice. He replied to her personally and

met with her upon occasion.[49] As a Coptic notable and from a family
that had converted to Protestantism, Esther had a degree of mobility,
excellent English language skills, and access to officials, which made her
eminently suited to represent the Wafd.

After Sha'rawi resigned, Esther emerged from her shadow. The Sa'dist
Ladies' Committee campaigned for the Wafd in the elections of 1925,
protesting seizure of the party's election pamphlets. In an appeal to the
"sons of Egypt," Esther criticized the tyranny of the non-Wafdist government. Sharifa Riyad, who had earlier tried to iron out differences
among women Wafdists, condemned Egyptian women's rush into partisan politics. Esther's reply legitimized the Sa'dist women's current policies and implicitly criticized her predecessor:

> [W]hen we entered the political field, there were no women parties in
> Egypt, we were all solidly behind the principles of the Egyptian Delegation
> (Wafd) calling for complete independence of Egypt and the Sudan.
>     But when some members split from the Wafd, we did not follow suit as
> they did, but stood steadfast. So I don't think that this could be called par-
> tisanship. If we had maintained our original stand, supporting our original
> cause, and rejecting any deviation or incursion by external influences, our
> first women's society would have remained above party politics.[50]

Esther argued that the differences had started even before Zaghlul
returned from exile. These differences had essentially paralyzed the committee, which she was trying to rejuvenate, and she appealed to Sharifa
Riyad to work with her.[51] Sharifa later rejoined the group, adding her
prestige and resources.

With Huda out of the picture, a constellation of other women now
shared the stage. Twenty-two members of the reconstituted Women's
Wafd appeared on the cover of the new illustrated weekly *al-Musawwar*
in March 1925.[52] The executive committee over the next few years
included Esther, Ulfat Ratib, Ra'ifa Musa, Regina Khayyat, Ihsan Ahmad,
and Wajida Thabit.[53] The latter, no relation to Munira, was one of four
sisters whom Sa'd's secretary described as "the backbone" of the Women's
Wafd. (Her sister Fahima had accompanied Safiyya Zaghlul to Gibraltar.)[54] Farida Fawzi, head of the women's section in the journal *al-Hisan*
and a member of the Women's Wafd, publicized their call for new members and reported on their meetings. Among other activities, they built
a public institute for female students and sent telegrams of protest to
British officials.[55]

The Sa'dist Ladies' Committee called for the restoration of the constitution in the late 1920s to pave the way for the return to power of the

Wafd. "Since the overthrow of constitutional regime in Egypt, British Government has concluded agreements with dictatorial Ministry affecting destiny of Egypt," Esther telegrammed top British officials in 1929, "We protest strongly against conclusion of agreement which affects vital interests of future generations of the Egyptian people." Such protests did not engender sympathy for Wafdist women on the part of the Egyptian government, which occasionally prevented the committee from meeting.[56]

Women Wafdists and ex-Wafdists drew together in May 1931 to protest against the Sidqi regime and the elections that it planned to hold in the absence of the constitution. Esther was probably out of the country at the time, because her name does not appear on petition lists. Sharifa Riyad, who emerged as the leader of the Women's Wafd in the 1930s, took on the role of chief spokeswoman for the Sa'dist Ladies' Committee. The events of 1931 were a reprisal of 1919 but on a smaller scale and with different goals. The chief target was an authoritarian Egyptian government supported by the British and opposed by Wafdists, Liberal Constitutionalists, and others.[57] In the wake of the 1931 protests, a movement to boycott British goods was resumed. The British high commissioner reported that the boycott was supported by "Egyptian ladies of the higher classes."[58] Boycotts were balanced by fund-raisers, as the power of female notables stemmed in great part from their collective purse: the Sa'dist committee, for example, raised funds for workers shot by the police during Sidqi's tenure.[59]

Women Wafdists continued to maneuver to improve the party's chances of returning to power. In 1932, when Esther requested a meeting with the minister of foreign affairs in London, an official wrote, "She has possibly been put forward by the Wafd as a feeler, in the hope that we shall be impressed by the novelty of a female emissary." Although they were not impressed and denied the request, British officials recognized that Esther "enjoys a lot of publicity."[60] Undeterred by the rejection, she addressed a large crowd in London, speaking on the political situation in Egypt. She emphasized Anglo–Egyptian rivalry over the Sudan and control of water: "When Egypt hesitated to give the English another key to the Nile, she was accused of being an enemy to England."[61]

Esther emerged in the 1920s and 1930s as one of the key female speakers of the Wafd at home and abroad, and worked as an unofficial representative.[62] "Madame Esther Fahmi Wisa, a prominent Wafdist lady, much interested in charitable works, called on me," Miles Lampson, British high commissioner, wrote from Egypt in 1934. Esther admitted in the meeting that the Wafd's methods were occasionally mistaken and condemned the recent splits. Yet she argued that the Wafd was the only hope for Egypt and that with them lay "the ultimate salvation of the country."[63] Lampson later described her as "a well-meaning enthusiast, much given to good works. Her Wafdism is sincere and idealistic."[64]

Capping her speaking career, Esther addressed a "monster meeting" of Wafdists in Cairo in early 1935. The Wafd had been prevented from holding any public assembly for over four years, but when the ban was lifted, organizers sent invitations to Wafdists throughout the country. Between twenty and twenty-five thousand loyalists converged on gigantic marquees set up in Ramsis City, with four hundred women sitting in a special section reserved for them. Esther and Nur al-Hassan, a young woman of Bedouin origin, addressed the crowd, speaking on the past roles and future possibilities of Egyptian women in the national movement. The two were considered "excellent speakers" who made a "great impression."[65] The following year, Esther lectured in the United States, where she also made a favorable impression upon Eleanor Roosevelt, the wife of President Franklin D. Roosevelt.[66]

The Wafd's fortunes continued to oscillate. When King Farouk dismissed the Wafd government in 1937, Mustafa al-Nahhas asked Esther to push for the return of the party to power by reviving the Women's Wafd.[67] But Esther—like Huda before her—had grown increasingly disillusioned by the policies and practices of the Wafd. She had thought that Nahhas would continue Sa'd's support for women's participation in the struggle for complete independence. "Nahas did not want women poking their noses into politics," Esther's son writes, "and he told them so clearly. He did not mind them discarding their veils, or improving their education, but he had no intention of helping them to obtain their political rights."[68] By 1937, Esther had concluded that male politicians had abandoned their principles and were striving instead to advance their own ambitions and pockets.[69] Esther declined to revive the Women's Wafd and continued to devote most of her energies to social welfare, women's progress, and religious advocacy.[70]

## MUNIRA THABIT: "AN AMUSING INFANT"

Huda Sha'rawi's defection in 1924 dealt a blow to the Wafd. As the founder of the EFU, she was often identified as the head of the "women's awakening" in Egypt. Now that the Wafd could no longer count her among its loyalists, it faced a predicament. Male nationalists had striven from their earliest days to depict themselves as supporters of women's progress. They mostly did this to demonstrate the modernity of their nationalist movement, which meant that this had a greater impact on the nationalist discourse than on legislative reforms.[71] Sa'd in particular had been close to Qasim Amin, who had dedicated his *al-Mar'a al-Jadida* (The New Woman, 1900) to him.[72] Not wanting to give the edge to his adversaries, Sa'd encouraged Munira Thabit as a counterweight to Huda Sha'rawi and the EFU.

Munira (again, not one of the Thabit sisters mentioned earlier) began her writing career in 1920 by sending articles to the daily *al-Ahram*, the weekly *al-Sufur*, and French periodicals. A student at the time, she usually signed her name as "al-Misriyya" (the Egyptian woman) or "al-Tha'ira" (the revolutionary) or simply gave her initials. She called for political rights for women—to vote and to be elected to parliament—before a parliament even existed in Egypt.[73] On the eve of the opening of parliament, Munira noted that no seats had been set aside for female visitors to legislative sessions. She protested, as did the EFU and WWCC, when the legislature opened in mid-March 1924 and the only women invited to the celebration were spouses of government officials and foreign dignitaries. Munira continued to press for special seating for women, writing letters to the head of the assembly and appealing directly to Zaghlul, and eventually special seating was set aside for them in the balcony. Munira crusaded to have women enter parliament not only as visitors but as members. Her voice remained a solitary one for years, as the EFU set different priorities and many feminists opposed her.[74]

Munira became a frequent visitor to the House of the Nation from 1924, when Huda Sha'rawi's visits would have tapered off. Sa'd applauded her efforts and assured her that he would give women political rights when the political situation in Egypt had stabilized. But Zaghlul enjoyed only a brief tenure as prime minister. The Wafd then watched as the new government closed its publications one by one and denied applications for new permits. In light of these circumstances, Munira proved something of a maverick; she walked the "tightrope" between the opposition and the government and returned with permits for two periodicals in hand—the French *L'Espoir* and the Arabic *al-Amal*—both meaning "Hope." The coup earned her the epithet "the Amazon of the Egyptian press." Munira admitted that her late father's close ties with Sidqi, then minister of interior, proved helpful.[75]

Munira launched the Arabic weekly *al-Amal* in early November 1925, printing it on the press of the Wafdist *al-Balagh*. It operated more independently than *L'Espoir*, which had a Wafdist board of directors and funding.[76] *Al-Amal* promoted itself as "the journal defending women's rights," and differed from preceding and competing women's journals in its explicit interest in party affairs. Munira coupled her demands for freedom and independence in Egypt with support for women's political and social rights. The first issue included a letter from Makram 'Ubayd, who was high in the Wafd leadership, and subsequent ones carried letters from Sa'd and interviews of Wafdist leaders.[77] Contributions came from women such as the actress Fatima Rushdi and the educator Nabawiyya Musa, as well as from women in Lebanon, who were probably most responsive among contemporary Arab women to calls for political rights.[78]

Munira continued to style herself a "revolutionary" and felt strongly about the struggle for women's political rights. Yet she found little support in the 1920s for her positions, even among members of the EFU. She clashed with them and had little compunction about criticizing them in *al-Amal*.[79] They rebutted that the timing was premature to push for women's right to vote and to be elected. In addition, they condemned her personal decision to become the second wife of the journalist 'Abd al-Qadir Hamza.[80] EFU members called Munira, according to the latter, "an amusing infant" and labeled her demands foolish and childish. She, in turn, found them old and reactionary. Munira also encountered resistance from conservative quarters and the Islamic press.[81]

Munira's attack on the government landed her in trouble. A former deputy minister brought a case against her in 1926, accusing her of undermining his honor and demanding reparations for articles she had published. Although Hamza offered to answer the charges, the young journalist took responsibility and appeared in court herself.[82] After publishing *al-Amal* for three years, Munira decided to dedicate herself to her legal studies. In 1925 she had become the first woman to enroll in the French Law School in Cairo, and she continued her legal training in Paris. In 1934, when invited to join a celebration for the first female university graduates, Munira became reconciled with the EFU. The group subsequently took up the call for female suffrage.[83]

Munira completed her political memoir, which was published in 1946, when she was in her forties. In it she equated the illegal expropriation of Egypt's rights with the illegal appropriation of women's political rights. Egypt would never win its rights, including sovereignty over the Sudan, until women had achieved theirs. By 1946, she was no longer alone in her call for women's right to vote or to be elected. She would find a fellow-struggler in the writer-activist Doria Shafiq, whom she joined in a hunger strike in 1954.[84] But by 1946, she was also no longer the ardent

Wafdist that she had been in her youth. She now found the Wafdist government characterized by "a lot of words, little action and productivity." Among other things, "the Wafd Party did not acknowledge the principle of equality between the sexes or even among one sex!"[85]

Munira continued to contribute a regular column to *al-Ahram* until 1948. She revived her own journal weeks before the Free Officers seized power in July 1952 and ran it until her death fifteen years after that. Whereas earlier periodicals had often styled themselves as *majallat nisa'iyya* (women's journals), she explicitly called her revitalized review a *majallat niswiyya siyasiyya* or, in French, a *revue feministe politique* (a feminist political journal). This early usage of *niswiyya* for feminism rather than *nisa'iyya*, which depending on context can mean "women's" or "feminist," has been forgotten by activists and overlooked by historians.[86] In short, Munira seems to have been ahead of her time in linguistic usage, as well as in championing suffrage.

## FATIMA AL-YUSUF AND "THE PARTY OF RUZ AL-YUSUF"

Political wars were often fought in the press, where one of the principal papers backing the Wafd from the late 1920s was Fatima al-Yusuf's *Ruz al-Yusuf*. Fatima began acting at an early age with different theatrical troops in Alexandria and rose to become a star of Egyptian theater, where she was known as Ruz (Rose) al-Yusuf. During the war, she watched British troops suspend theatrical performances, and after it, she participated in anti-British protests, carrying a banner at the front of an actors' demonstration in 1919.[87]

Fatima founded *Ruz al-Yusuf* as a literary and cultural weekly in 1925. Yet she soon realized the limited audience of such a journal and transformed it into a political paper. The story of running a weekly, as she tells it, is a story of determination in the face of obstacles, not the least of which was being a woman in a man's profession. Fatima, who vied with Munira Thabit for the honor of being Egypt's first female political journalist, received encouragement from Huda Sha'rawi, with whom Munira had her differences.[88] Fatima began her career as a political journalist by covering the trial of Ahmad Mahir and Mahmud al-Nuqrashi, Wafdists accused of conspiracy in the murder of Sir Oliver Lee Stack and other British officials. The courts eventually acquitted the two, who both ironically later died at the hands of assassins.[89]

*Ruz al-Yusuf* increasingly moved in orientation toward the Wafd Party, although initially it received no financial support from the party. Rather,

Fatima's support for the Wafd meant that the paper was occasionally subjected to confiscations. In one year alone (1928–29), more papers were confiscated (sixty-two) than appeared (forty-two). The following year, Fatima frequently published her paper under borrowed names, a not uncommon practice in the Egyptian press. The relationship between the party and the paper became so strong that the Wafd was sometimes called "the Party of *Ruz al-Yusuf*," and Fatima developed close ties to Nahhas. By 1933, when courts fined her and sent her editor to jail, she had become one of the most famous journalists in Egypt. Her picture appeared frequently in the press, and her paper had become one of the best selling and most popular weeklies. With a circulation of approximately 20,000, *Ruz al-Yusuf* offered a steady stream of political analysis and satirical cartoons.[90]

Based on the success of her weekly, Fatima al-Yusuf decided to launch a daily in 1935.[91] But by then Fatima had begun to have differences with Wafd leaders. She traced her difficulties to 'Ubayd, who protested against the independent stands she sometimes took. Fatima felt obligated to voice her opinion, while 'Ubayd expected her to stick to the party line. That line in 1935 was support for the government of Tawfiq Nissim, with whom the Wafd worked for reconciliation. Yet Fatima opposed Nissim's government and fought instead for the return of the constitution. The breach between the Wafd and Fatima widened, according to the latter, when 'Ubayd convinced Nahhas of her disloyalty. Safiyya Zaghlul tried to avert a break between the paper and the party, but in late September, the Wafd executive decided that the paper no longer represented its views.[92]

Massive student protests against the government erupted in November 1935. The size and composition of the demonstrations, which were "reinforced by girl students," according to American sources, pushed the equivocating political parties to unify in a coalition, forced the resignation of Nissim, and brought a return of the constitution.[93] This paved the way for elections and the Wafd's return to power in 1936. The sequence of events vindicated Fatima's position, but the Wafd proved vengeful. It suspended the license of the daily *Ruz al-Yusuf* and cancelled government advertising in the weekly. The harassment of the former Wafd supporter did not stop there. The guarantor of the paper withdrew his support under directives from the party, and Fatima al-Yusuf had twenty-four hours to raise a substantial sum of money to retain her license. The censor then applied pressure, and his complaints landed her in jail for a night.[94] But Fatima persevered, and in spite of the Wafd's opposition, *Ruz al-Yusuf* continued to thrive long after the Wafd had languished.

The Wafd negotiated a treaty with the British in 1936, which Huda Sha'rawi, Munira Thabit, and some of the other women nationalists opposed. This treaty signaled the Wafd's shift in posture from opposition to cooperation with the British. In 1937, the Wafd split when Nuqrashi and Mahir broke ranks with Nahhas and 'Ubayd and started the Sa'dist Party. In 1943, 'Ubayd, who for so long had shielded Nahhas, also left, publishing a "Black Book" that disclosed tales of corruption within the government. By then the Wafd had been tainted in the eyes of many Egyptians by its ties to the British, who had returned the party to power by force in 1942. Fatima al-Yusuf, Huda Sha'rawi, Zaynab al-Ghazali, and scores of "wives of notables"—female notables in their own right—sent a petition to the British Embassy protesting British interference in the Egyptian government. The former women Wafdists now found common cause in opposing the party. They used a feminine voice, speaking not as the WWCC or Ladies' Sa'dist Committee but rather as "mothers of the present and coming generation," to articulate their concerns.[95] They relied on maternal authority and appealed to morality precisely because they had few options for making themselves heard. In spite of two decades of attempting to break into the political system, they had not yet obtained the right to vote, to run for parliament, or to hold office. Writing remained one of their few political weapons.

## IMAGES OF POLITICAL WOMEN AND MALE POLITICIANS

Elite women took their politics seriously and sought to have an impact on decision-making. Thick British files on the activities of the Women's Wafd and attempts to censor them show respect for their power. Yet representations in the Egyptian press—photographs and cartoons—increasingly indicate that politics was a masculine domain, and that women could only participate if they played the role of supporting characters.

Photos show groups of women going in launches to meet Wafd delegations, waiting on wharves, carrying placards in motorcades, comforting the families of martyrs, and visiting the tombs of the fallen. Photos also show them rallying around the "first family"—seeing Safiyya Zaghlul off in Cairo, accompanying her to Port Said, and riding in boats to meet her upon her return to Alexandria. Cameramen catch women rushing to the hospital after the attempted assassination of Sa'd and a few years later sitting at Safiyya's side during memorial services. Little effort is made to identify the individual women within the photos either while they were veiled or later when they unveiled. Captions call these veiled and unveiled women the "nationalist ladies," the "Egyptian ladies," the "women Wafdist demonstrators," or members of the "Sa'dist committee."[96] Not naming individuals suggested that all the women played the same supporting role, and that leadership came from the men.

The general labels obscured the roles of individuals as well as of different female associations, which tended to be elided into one. Banners of such organizations as the Society of Mothers of the Future and the Society of Egyptian Ladies' Awakening appear in photos, documenting the variety of women's groups that took to the streets in demonstrations in the 1920s and 1930s. These groups had their own leadership, political platforms, and agendas, as well as their own bases. Not distinguishing among the groups in captions and treating them as all the same generated the impression that female nationalists acted together as a patriotic chorus and shared political perspectives. Individual women who headed different groups do not emerge from the shadow of the center as leaders or politicians in their own right.

Photos of Huda Sha'rawi, Esther Fahmi Wisa, Munira Thabit, and Fatima al-Yusuf also appeared in the press. Female political activists attempted to control their images by providing the press with portraits, and these photos remained in archives ready for republication. When Huda unveiled in 1923, several papers carried a picture of a youthful looking Huda with her new style of head covering. That picture or a similar one (probably from the same photo session) appeared over the years.[97] Esther gave a photograph of herself in a maternal pose (sitting with one of her babies on her lap) to *al-Mar'a al-Misriyya* in 1923 and an intellectual shot (her hand supports her chin) to *al-'Arusa* in 1925.[98] Munira's portrait, standing behind an ornate chair with hands clasped, appeared in *al-Hisan* and *al-'Arusa* when she "entered the field of men" and started her daily paper in 1925.[99] Fatima al-Yusuf, whose picture was already familiar to Egyptian audiences from her days in theater, also sought to control her image. A shot dated 1925 showing her in outdoor dress, and with her head covered, holding a flag aloft appeared on the cover of *al-Hisan*. A subsequent portrait taken from the shoulders up that recasts Fatima in her new profession was reprinted in the press. In some group shots with male journalists, Fatima appears with her daughter at her side.[100]

These women tried to project youthful, feminine, maternal, or intellectual images in portraits. The journalists Fatima and Munira could control their images within their own periodicals. Huda, too, could control self-representation in the several publications that she oversaw as president of the EFU. Other female activists tried to document their activities

Figure 27. Huda "Hanim" Sha'rawi and Safiyya "Hanim" Zaghlul chased by Egyptian policemen. *Al-Kashkul*, 22 May 1931, 16.

and publicize them. When Esther Fahmi Wisa hosted a reception for Safiyya, a photographer recorded the gathering. The group poses on the front steps of the house, with small girls in front with flowers and Safiyya in the middle, flanked by friends, relatives, and supporters. Esther stands prominently with one of her sons at the bottom right of the frame, where the eye is drawn, because the group is arranged in a triangle.[101] In a similar way, the Sa'dist Ladies' Committee had its portrait taken in an indoor shot.[102] Yet female political activists eventually lost the tight control of their images in the press, with some photographs portraying them in less than flattering poses.[103]

These activists also had little control over how cartoonists turned photographic images into satire and current events into parodies. Depictions

Figure 28. "The Party of Ruz al-Yusuf": Mustafa
al-Nahhas and Muhammad Mahmud hide behind
Fatima (Ruz) al-Yusuf. *Al-Kashkul*, 15 May 1931, 1.

of veiled women engaged in politics in the early 1920s showed them
behind the scenes, strolling or sipping tea, discussing developments.[104]
Women who engaged more directly in politics were often shown as
matronly, manly, or defeminized, even in *Ruz al-Yusuf*, which reflected
the political norms.[105] When Huda and Safiyya joined forces in 1931 in
opposition to the Sidqi regime and staged a protest, they were satirized
in a cartoon in *al-Kashkul* (figure 27). The picture shows two aged ladies
being chased in the street by Egyptian policemen with bats. Huda
"Hanim" Sha'rawi addresses Safiyya as "My Mother," but Safiyya
"Hanim" Zaghlul replies that she is not her mother and not even of the
generation of her children.[106] The cartoon satirizes the use of maternal
rhetoric by male and female nationalists, and at the same time depicts
women engaged in politics as uncomely and masculine. (The protestors
in that event actually rode in motorcars and carried signs calling for the
return of the constitution and boycott of elections.)

Rather than trying to defeminize Fatima al-Yusuf, who was a famous
actress and icon, cartoonists chose another tack. In cartoon imagery,

she never escapes from her theatrical past and usually appears scantily clad in high heels, feminized but not sexualized. In a cartoon on the cover of *al-Kashkul* in 1931, Fatima stands on stage in a flimsy dress with arms outstretched, hiding Nahhas and Muhammad Mahmud, who cower behind her (figure 28). The image was meant to show that the journalist was more manly than the male leaders of the Wafd.[107] In a cartoon that appeared in *al-Lata'if al-Musawwara* after *Ruz al-Yusuf*'s break with the Wafd in 1935, "Ruz al-Yusuf" is dressed in similar manner, but this time she performs a customary female role, following a coffin and mourning the fate of one of her writers.[108] Moreover, Fatima herself became upon occasion a model for the cartoon image of Egypt (see figure 9).

To be a powerful politician was to be masculine; weak politicians were emasculated and feminized. A cartoon in *al-Kashkul* in 1927 shows Huda standing with one arm on her waist and the other outstretched in a position of defiance, speaking with "al-Bash Agha," the eunuch who had been part of her household from childhood. "Ya Hanim Effendi," he asks, "if there is no independence, what are those men doing?" suggesting that male politicians are not doing enough. Huda Hanim Sha'rawi replies, "Listen, ya Bash Agha, . . . you're more of a man than all of them."[109] The satire is biting as a eunuch—a castrated man—is presented as more masculine than the male nationalists Huda is criticizing. Both *Ruz al-Yusuf* and *al-Kashkul* carried images of male politicians dressed as women, depictions meant to show them as weak and caught up in subterfuge.[110]

Cartoons represented politics as a masculine preserve, with weak politicians feminized and female political activists parodied and defeminized. Moreover, cartoons of the nation as a woman vastly outnumbered those of real women activists. According to the conventions of Egyptian political culture, women could not be politicians or seriously engage in "peacetime" politics. This contrasts with the favorable image of women in the 1919 revolution. As in other countries, women's political mobilization was tolerated and even encouraged in crisis—war and revolution—but discouraged when the crisis had receded. Women's political activities were suppressed in accounts of the period and memories repressed.

The memoirs of female nationalists sought to challenge this perspective, to prove that elite women were "in the heart of the action," and to vindicate their political positions. The publication of most of these memoirs, however, had to await a more auspicious moment. Fatima's critique of the Wafd came in 1953, after its fall. Huda's waited even longer. During the Nasser years (1952–70), stories of female notables were simply not in vogue. The state's memorializing of Huda came only under Anwar al-Sadat (1970–81), with the issuing of a stamp in 1973 upon the fiftieth anniversary of the founding of the EFU and the one hundredth anniversary of state education for girls.[111] The full publication of Huda's memoirs, which highlight her nationalist and feminist endeavors, came in 1981. Esther's family story waited another decade, when nostalgia for the "liberal experiment" of the interwar years had begun to take root.

In the wake of the 1919 revolution, elite women attempted to capitalize on their forays into the public sphere and maintain their momentum. Since they could not join the Wafd, they created an auxiliary, the Women's Wafd. Politics became partisan, and it proved difficult for elite women allied with different factions and positions to maintain their unity. Although women combined maternal and moral voices in their political expression, they got drawn into the divisions between the Wafd and other parties, and within the Wafd itself. Some, like Huda Sha'rawi, chose to break ranks, and others, like Esther Fahmi Wisa, to stay put. The splits inevitably led to rifts and rivalries within the ranks of elite women.

The real push for women's citizenship rights came from the middle classes, where women did not have the same access to power as those notable women who commanded great wealth or whose male relatives held high government posts. The middle class used the press as a tool for participating in political culture. Having run their own women's journals or contributed to those of others for decades, middle-class women entered into political journalism, and party politics, for the first time in the 1920s. Munira Thabit's experiment proved short-lived in its first incarnation; Fatima al-Yusuf's endured and thrived. Both women grew impatient with the Wafd, which proved to be an authoritarian organization that treated dissenters with disdain. The story of women's engagement with the Wafd highlights some of the inherent weaknesses of the party, as well as the strategies of trying to gain power by forming a female auxiliary or party organ.

The discourse of the nation as a family and the emphasis on domesticity knit abstract women into the nation,[112] and the nation itself was represented as a woman, but when real women made bids for greater power to contribute to policy-formation and decision-making, they were excluded. The exclusion was reinforced through representations that gendered politics as male. The attempts by Huda Sha'rawi, Esther Fahmi

Wisa, Munira Thabit, Fatima al-Yusuf, and others to enter the political field threatened cultural definitions of masculinity and femininity, as well as the political dominance of elite men. Male nationalists tried to harness the energies of female nationalists, particularly at moments of crisis, and control them. When they could not, they were not averse to using all sorts of tactics to undermine them, including satirizing them in the press. The rough and tumble of politics could be cruel, and women were given no special dispensation. Yet politics was not a game of winner takes all as far as elite women were concerned. They quickly adapted to their exclusion from party and parliamentary politics and turned their attention to social, feminist, and Islamist politics, which they saw as critical aspects of nation-building.

# CHAPTER EIGHT

# The Path of an Islamic Activist

The politics of Labiba Ahmad (1870s–1951) diverged from those of many of her female contemporaries. Most endorsed the secularism of the Wafd, the Liberal Constitutionalists, and other like-minded parties, although the attempts of these parties to divorce religion from politics was never complete, and their support for women's participation in the public domain was often more rhetorical than real. Labiba, by contrast, favored the Islamic bent of the Watani Party, with its stress on Muslim brotherhood and gender segregation. She spearheaded a movement that conceptualized women's rights in Islamic terms and pushed for a fusion of Islam and nationalism, helping to strengthen an Egyptian Islamic nationalism.[1]

Islamist currents such as the one Labiba espoused have generally been ignored in the historiography of Egypt. This is partially a result of theorizing about nationalism based on western European models that characterize nationalism as a secular phenomenon. In the building of nation-states in the modern period, civil religion, secular rituals, and territorial ties were meant to replace older religious traditions and loyalties. Yet nationalisms often borrowed, built upon, or incorporated religious practices and symbols in the Middle East and elsewhere, giving rise to religious-nationalist fusions.

This chapter examines the political activism of Labiba Ahmad, following the trajectory of her family and party ties, social welfare and journalistic endeavors, and religious travels and affiliations. It argues that she helped to create an alternative to secular nationalism by celebrating

Watani Party leaders, nurturing the revival movement, and paving the way for a new cadre of Islamic activists. In this way, she bridged generations, linking the *Salafi*s (Islamic reformers who looked to the first generation of Muslims as a model) and later Islamic radicals. Although she used conservative language and urged a return to traditions, her perspective and practices were embedded in modernity and contemporary women's political culture. She founded an association—the Society of Egyptian Ladies' Awakening (Jamʿiyyat Nahdat al-Sayyidat al-Misriyyat)—and started a journal—*al-Nahda al-Nisaʾiyya* (The Women's Awakening)—to propagate her views. She used social welfare to enact local change and win adherents. And she sought to introduce the image of the "new Islamic woman" as a credible alternative to the "new (secular) woman" as a cultural ideal.

## LOOKING FOR LABIBA AHMAD

Until recently Labiba Ahmad had been nearly forgotten, displaced from nationalist, feminist, and Islamist narratives. Retrieving her life story presents certain challenges, partly because she was more interested in promoting her cause than herself and maintained a modest public demeanor. Like the secular women nationalists discussed earlier who left memoirs, Labiba wrote a memoir, or rather, assembled her correspondence for publication, but the work did not seem to circulate widely.[2] One daughter, interviewed in the 1960s, gave oral testimony on some of her mother's activities.[3] And Labiba's name occasionally surfaces in state archives, specifically in clippings on Egyptian nationalism and files on the Muslim Brothers. The contemporary illustrated press, particularly *al-Lataʾif al-Musawwara*, provides some further clues.

The best historical record of Labiba's life in the interwar period is her own monthly, *al-Nahda al-Nisaʾiyya*, which was shaped by multiple hands and contains a trove of material from over two decades. From the start, *al-Nahda al-Nisaʾiyya* was a cooperative venture. A staff helped the founder, and younger colleagues eventually took over directing, editing, and producing the periodical. Letters from readers, advertisements, photographs, announcements, and news stories, as well as Labiba's own essays, reveal pieces of the puzzle of her life. The journal presents a sympathetic portrait, but, as with any source, can be probed for biases and silences, and can be read critically.[4]

Labiba also left a photographic trail. Like other women nationalists who sought to disseminate their images in the press but at the same time

Figure 29. Portrait of Labiba Ahmad on the
occasion of her making the hajj on the cover of
*al-Nahda al-Nisa'iyya*, March 1933.

control them, Labiba used her own publication to regularly publish her
picture. She sat for portraits on at least five occasions in the interwar
years. These were featured repeatedly on the cover or prominently inside
*al-Nahda al-Nisa'iyya* or in such papers as *al-Lata'if al-Musawwara*, particularly on the occasion of her making the pilgrimage. The photos show
a maturing Labiba: she appears with wire-framed glasses and in conservative dress, wearing a black head covering and dark robe. In the earlier
shots from the 1920s, she looks off into the distance. In the later poses,
from the 1930s, she looks straight at the camera. Her determination,
confidence, and seriousness show in a shot carried on the cover of *al-
Nahda al-Nisa'iyya* in 1933 (figure 29). She looks directly at the camera in a pose clearly set for an intellectual. Labiba seems intent on
presenting a counterimage to the secular nationalists and feminists featured prominently in the press in the interwar years: a conservative but
active Muslim woman.[5]

## A DOCTOR'S DAUGHTER, A JUDGE'S WIFE

By the time Labiba Ahmad entered public life, she had already passed
through the child-bearing and child-rearing years. She was born in
the Cairene middle class. Her father, Ahmad 'Abd al-Nabi Bey, was

a physician, and two of her brothers and two of her children also became doctors.[6] Labiba was tutored at home; she had an excellent command of Arabic, a good knowledge of the Qur'an, and learned to play the piano.[7]

Labiba was married to 'Uthman Bey Murtada, who rose through the judiciary, eventually attaining the post of judge in the Alexandria Mixed Court of Appeals and the rank of pasha. (He sat as a secretary at the Dinshaway trial.) Murtada cultivated close relations with Khedive 'Abbas Hilmi II and was named chief of the khedivial council in January 1914, an honor that was short-lived, because 'Abbas was exiled later that year. The Watani Party leader Muhammad Farid described 'Uthman in his notebooks in not very flattering terms as "a man of corrupt morals, bisexual (up to now), from a very base origin," but admitted, "he has a solid education."[8] Labiba never mentions her husband in her journal, and it may well be that the couple were estranged.

Labiba had five daughters and a son, whose pictures occasionally appear in her journal. Her son, Dr. Isma'il Bey Murtada, contributed articles and sometimes helped out with her social welfare ventures.[9] One daughter was the wife of 'Abd al-Sattar Bey al-Basil, a tribal shaykh from al-Fayyum and a Wafdist, who had earlier been married to the writer Malak Hifni Nasif (1886–1918). This unnamed daughter died in the "spring of youth," causing her mother much grief, and Labiba's grandchildren were subsequently raised alongside the children of Labiba's second daughter, Hayat Murtada.[10] A third daughter, Malak Muhammad, was noted for her Sufi attributes: night-time praying and daytime fasts.[11] The last two daughters, Zaynab and Qamar, were twins and the "babies" of the family. Zaynab attended the Saniyya Girls' School, a state institution popular with nationalists whose curriculum included Arabic and Islamic instruction, and in 1925 joined a group of female students sent by the government to England, where after three years of study, she was awarded a teacher-artist certificate by the Royal Drawing Society. While Zaynab "nurtured the spirit," Qamar "treated the body" and studied medicine on the same mission.[12]

## MEMORIALIZING MUSTAFA KAMIL

Little is known of Labiba Ahmad's political activities prior to 1919. According to one observer, she had participated in associations, given speeches, and written in newspapers and journals.[13] She may have been among those supporters of Mustafa Kamil's Watani Party who formed

Figure 30. Memorial gathering at the tomb of Mustafa Kamil on the anniversary of his death; seated third from right in the front row, Labiba Ahmad. Photo by Nasif Ayyub. Print by Sabunji. *Al-Lata'if al-Musawwara*, 1 March 1920, 5.

a women's auxiliary.[14] Labiba had close ties with members of Mustafa Kamil's family, including his brother 'Ali Fahmi Kamil and his nieces, and probably had contacts with him as well.[15] From 1919 on, we can better document Labiba's activities. That March, she participated in the "ladies' demonstrations" and affixed her signature—"Madame Osman Pacha Mortada"—above those of her daughters on the petitions submitted to foreign legations.[16] According to her daughter Zaynab and other contemporaries interviewed by the Egyptian historian Ijlal Khalifa, Labiba worked during this period to mobilize women from working-class neighborhoods such as Sayyida Zaynab against the British occupation.[17]

Labiba emerged as a preeminent patron in rituals of remembering Watani Party leaders. She presided in February 1920 over a sizeable gathering of "nationalist ladies" commemorating the anniversary of Mustafa Kamil's death. The women gathered at his tomb, where Labiba "Hanim" among others gave speeches and read poems. A photo that appeared in March 1920 shows a group of nearly fifty women clustered around the tomb of Mustafa Kamil (figure 30). The "famous photographer" Nasif Effendi Ayyub (who advertised in Labiba's journal) recorded the event, and Sabunji's studio made the print exclusively for *al-Lata'if al-Musawwara*. The photo of the nationalist leader hanging on the tomb serves as the focal point, and women sit, kneel on the floor, or stand, gazing at the camera. Most of those on the left side of the frame have donned their face veils before the male photographer; those on the right side (including one or two foreign or Coptic women) remain unveiled. The veiled Labiba Ahmad is third from the right, identified by her signature wire-framed glasses. Although she is identified in the caption, she is not marked in the picture, and she remains part of the unnamed collective of women nationalists. The meeting precipitated a demonstration, and the women left shouting slogans for independence, the nation, and the memory of the recently deceased Muhammad Farid.[18]

Sometime in late 1920 or early 1921, Labiba founded the Society of Egyptian Ladies' Awakening. A delegation from the group, including orphaned girls that the society had undertaken to raise, marched in a women's demonstration on 22 March 1921 in support of 'Adli Yakan's ministry, which the Wafd opposed. They carried banners with their name and that of their president under the sign of three stars, a cross, and crescent that were used to show Egyptian national unity in this period. The group also marched in April upon Sa'd's return from negotiations.[19] In her capacity as the president of the society, Labiba "Hanim" Ahmad served as a patron for graduation ceremonies in girls' schools, which invariably included patriotic songs, nationalist speeches, and student plays.[20]

In September 1921, Labiba traveled to Alexandria to deliver a farewell address in honor of 'Ali Fahmi Kamil, who as a Watani Party deputy had been forced into exile. A photograph taken upon that occasion (but published a half dozen years later) shows a veiled Labiba standing with a girl of five or six (one of the orphans in her care) and 'Ali Fahmi.[21] The latter subsequently sent Labiba a letter from exile and an article entitled "The Future of the Egyptian Woman" for publication in the periodical that she had just launched.[22]

Labiba took center stage in the demonstrations marking the departure of Safiyya Zaghlul for Gibraltar to join Sa'd in exile in October 1922. At the Cairo train station, Labiba presented Safiyya with a Qur'an, an Arabic almanac, a book of blessings (*Dala'il al-Khayrat*), and a list of women and girls who had pledged on the Qur'an to support the principle of complete independence for Egypt and the Sudan.[23] Labiba consciously infused her participation in the ritual send-off with Islamic symbolism. Shortly thereafter, she received a note from Sa'd Zaghlul confirming his support for her society and journal.[24]

Labiba continued to support the Wafd and receive its blessings. She celebrated the release of the political prisoners from the Seychelles and the subsequent return of Sa'd in October 1923.[25] "The world has learned unequivocally that there are none in the nation except Sa'dists," she wrote after the electorate endorsed Sa'd in February 1924. The Society of Ladies' Awakening later gave the Wafd a vote of confidence.[26] Labiba and the Zaghluls enjoyed close relations: she had intended to go to their summer residence in 1926 to inquire after their health, but her own weak condition prevented her from traveling, and she exchanged notes with Safiyya instead.[27] The next year, she mourned Sa'd's death, printing and reprinting the letter he had sent from Gibraltar in commemoration of him and as testimony of his support for her activities.[28]

Although Labiba loyally supported the Wafd, she continued to cherish the memory of Mustafa Kamil. She printed Kamil's photo repeatedly in her journal and published extracts from his speeches and poems in his honor, including one by the educator Nabawiyya Musa.[29] She featured the bronze sculpture commissioned after his death on a cover, showed photos of his French patron Juliette Adam, and castigated those officials who allowed the anniversary of his death to pass unnoticed.[30] Labiba also remained faithful to 'Ali Fahmi Kamil, trumpeting his return to Egypt in the fall of 1923.[31] When he died in 1927, she delivered a eulogy: "You died, 'Ali, on the political battlefront, not in smoothed sheets on your bed." Shortly thereafter, she prepared a volume in his memory, including photographs, a biography, extracts from his writings and speeches, and remarks on the occasion of his death.[32] Her own bookshelves contained 'Ali Fahmi Kamil's writings, as well as works in memory of Mustafa Kamil.[33]

Labiba's political activities paralleled those of the other female notables into whose ranks she had risen. She participated in demonstrations, signed petitions, patronized schools, gave speeches, and presided over memorial services. While supporting the Wafd, she continued to cherish the memory of the Watanists, who had preferred immediate independence to westernizing reforms and Islamic to secular culture. By injecting Islamic content into nationalist rituals and writings, she increasingly set herself apart from the secular nationalists.

## THE SOCIETY OF EGYPTIAN LADIES' AWAKENING

Labiba chose not to join the women who formed the Women's Wafd after the 1919 revolution. Instead, she committed herself to a course of

moral action and founded her own Islamic social welfare society—the
Society of Egyptian Ladies' Awakening. The rise of women's philanthropic associations coincided with the emergence of nationalism in
Egypt. Organizations with similar names had been established in previous decades, and members had often spoken of their work as a contribution to the national cause.[34] Initially, these groups sought to counter
the activities of foreign missionaries and diplomatic wives or to add to
them. Women's societies were an acceptable way for affluent women to
contribute to the national cause and at the same time provide services
to the poor, in the absence of state social welfare programs. Labiba wrote
that in founding her society, she had been inspired by God and motivated by the desire to help the nation. The goal of the society was "to
raise the girl" and "to teach her the commandments of her religion."[35]
A society was thus a way to disseminate a founder's ideology and to win
adherents for a political position.

Members of Labiba's society swore an oath: "I swear that modesty
will be my crown, and virtue my light, and I shall live purely: a useful
and devout wife, whose hand in child-raising is superior. I shall fulfill
my rightful and correct duty, toward God, the homeland, the family."[36]
They set a code of behavior that every Egyptian woman should follow:
to strive for the happiness of her household; to maintain proper modesty in the street; to wear traditional Egyptian dress and to cover her
face, hands, and other body parts stipulated by Islamic law; to avoid the-
aters and comedy houses; and to leave behind corrupt ancient customs.[37]
This was the Salafi line, particularly as it developed after the death of
Muhammad 'Abduh (1849–1905), an early reformist thinker. The Salafis
opposed folk customs (such as the *zar*, a ceremony to exorcise spirits)
that deviated from Islamic injunctions, as well as the blind adoption of
Western practices by Egyptian Muslims. Reformers such as Labiba Ahmad
echoed the calls for modesty made by members of the Society of Woman's
Progress (Jam'iyyat Tarqiyat al-Mar'a, 1908) and contributors to the
conservative press in the first two decades of the century.[38] In spite of
her conservative language and the evocation of the past, her message was
grounded in recently launched debates and her means of spreading it was
essentially modern.

Labiba balanced words with action, organizing and spreading her
message to ever wider circles in Egyptian society. She had a broad mission of inculcating Islamic values and a specific project: she gathered
together 170 girls who had been orphaned or abandoned by their parents (which, she pointed out, occasionally happened in cases of divorce)

and vowed to raise, protect, and provide for them.[39] When fathers of
orphans were unknown, the children were presumed to be the offspring
of illegitimate encounters and carried the stigma of the crime. Labiba
not only wanted to "save" these girls but to shape them: to inculcate into
them Islamic values, nationalist ideals, and proper notions of social and
gender relations. They were to be ready, moreover, to march in nationalist demonstrations.

Labiba was the guiding force behind the group and the prime admin-
istrator of its affairs. Although little is known of the identity of the other
officers of the association—its deputy, secretary, and secretary's assis-
tant—or the composition of the membership, Labiba's own daughters
and nieces were probably involved.[40] Delegations from the society conducted official business: visiting schools, calling on ministers, and writing letters.

The enterprise was legitimized on nationalist grounds. "The Egyptian
Ladies' Awakening saw that uplifting nations is by uplifting the mothers in them," she wrote when announcing the founding of a workshop
in July 1921 in which poor girls would be taught sewing and other skills
so that they might later support themselves.[41] The office of the workshop stood ready to accept volunteers willing to render "holy national
service" by lecturing on morality and teaching the principles of house-
keeping and handiwork. Labiba also appealed for donations of clothes
and money for the girls, twenty of whom were shown in a photograph.[42]
A hymn she wrote for them began:

> We are daughters of the homeland
> Time has prepared us for service
> Our spirit takes precedence over the body
> We are willing to give all for the sake of the homeland[43]

Labiba resolved to broaden her educational program in 1923 in the
wake of the discovery of an Egyptian gang that apparently "debauched"
young native girls, kidnapping and raping them and keeping them in
brothels in Cairo. "We all felt sorrow in our souls, a wound in our hearts,
and pain in our core from that distressing affair," Labiba wrote. "It
made an impression on me as it made an impression on many others. I
resolved to dedicate the remainder of my life in service to Egypt, and to
sacrifice every valuable and dear thing for the sake of rescuing the Egyptian girl from the hands of those devils who abuse her." She decided to
expand beyond the orphanage and workshop and open a facility to train
girls so that they could make an honorable living and would not be
forced into prostitution.[44]

After searching for an appropriate site for the new institute, Labiba reported, "God gave us success." The society rented the palace of the late 'Abd al-Qadir Pasha Hilmi in the neighborhood of Sayyida Zaynab. "The Institute and Workshop of the Women's Awakening" opened in late 1923 with close to fifty girls.[45] Labiba made an emotional appeal to "the sons of my country" to support the school in whatever way possible. To raise funds, she offered a book for sale, which inspectors distributed in Egyptian schools.[46] Her actions won her praise. "She does not limit herself to literary activity alone," wrote Ruz Haddad, a fellow journalist, "but she also endeavors to promote social welfare in the country."[47] Other observers lauded the group for its focus on national problems rather than international forums, an implicit critique of Huda Sha'rawi's Egyptian Feminist Union (EFU).[48] In helping these girls, Labiba propagated Islamic values and styles. This is very clear in before-and-after shots of the girls entering the institute. In a shot taken of the institute at its opening, Labiba sat (still veiled) with women assistants surrounded by a ragged group of girls.[49] In a subsequent shot, they appear neatly dressed in white uniforms with white headscarves, arrayed in neatly ordered rows.[50]

The Society of Egyptian Ladies' Awakening operated the orphanage, workshop, and institute on one track, a track of benevolent enterprises dedicated to poor women and children. It disseminated its ideology to elite women on a second track. Members gathered for the first large assembly in late 1921 and met throughout the years to hear lectures on scientific and religious topics. The core members also continued to monitor and spread their message about Islamic reform.[51] The society distinguished its message from that of Huda Sha'rawi's EFU, which was founded a few years after it. Labiba was an honorary charter member of the EFU and applauded some of Huda's nationalist and social welfare activities. She was well aware of feminist debates and had Qasim Amin's *Tahrir al-Mar'a* (The Liberation of Woman, 1899) on her shelf. But the two associations clearly diverged in their priorities and goals. The feminists sought to reform Islamic family law rather than spread the word about its merits and strengthen Egyptians' religious identity. In short, the EFU based their vision for women's progress on liberal ideas, whereas the Society of Ladies' Awakening opted for a religious framework.[52]

Islamic nationalists placed religious morality at the center of their program. Labiba argued, for example, that the Egyptian state should curb vices such as drinking, consumption of narcotics, and dancing, and her group closely monitored state actions. When the head of the Cairo City

Police issued regulations that prevented dancers from sitting with crowds in large halls, the society immediately sent a letter of commendation.[53] Their interest in morality intensified in the 1930s, and the society issued a call for new members in 1934. Preparing for "a war against innovation, immorality, and corruption," it asked women to embark with it on this bold step "in service of religion and humanity."[54] The principal way that the society and its president propagated its message of Islamic reform and nationalism over two decades was through its journal.

## DISSEMINATION THROUGH PRINT

The first issue of *al-Nahda al-Nisa'iyya* appeared in July 1921. Its title reiterated the phrase "the women's awakening," which in recent decades had come to stand for the sense of dramatic transformation in Egyptian women's lives.[55] Labiba envisioned a women's awakening tied to religious revival. The mottoes that appeared on the journal's front page projected her philosophy that women's awakening and national renaissance went hand in hand: "A people will not die so long as both sexes work together energetically toward a goal." And on the top and sides, in smaller type, the sayings, "Awaken your women; your nations will thrive," and "Men make nations; mothers make men."

For the cover of her journal, Labiba chose a picture of Mahmud Mukhtar's award-winning sculpture *Nahdat Misr (The Awakening of Egypt)*, discussed earlier (see figure 6), which had become a key symbol of Egyptian national aspirations. It appeared repeatedly on the cover of Labiba's journal for a dozen years, linking Egypt's awakening to women's progress. That the peasant woman drew aside her face veil did not seem to bother Labiba, who herself veiled until the mid-1920s. In the 1930s, however, when the pharaonic style came under attack by Islamists for its celebration of the pagan past, the picture of Mukhtar's sculpture was removed from the cover. In its stead, Arabic calligraphy, floral paintings, and "more Islamic" designs appeared. But its presence on the front of the journal for over a decade affirms that the secular and religious nationalists shared symbols before their paths significantly diverged in the 1930s.

*Al-Nahda al-Nisa'iyya* faced competition from other women's journals. Labiba Hashim's *Fatat al-Sharq* (Girl of the East, 1906–39) had already been running for over fifteen years and would run up until World War II; Ruz Haddad revived her Alexandrian monthly *al-Sayyidat wa al-Banat* (Women and Girls, 1903–6) in 1921 and published it under similar titles until the end of the decade. These Syrian Christian editors attracted a somewhat different audience (including Syrians in Egypt and abroad) than Labiba did, pushed an Eastern or Arab identity rather than Egyptian nationalism, and had a Western orientation. A second set of Arabic women's monthlies started by Coptic women—Malaka Sa'd's *al-Jins al-Latif* (The Gentle Sex, 1908–25) and Balsam 'Abd al-Malik's *al-Mar'a al-Misriyya* (The Egyptian Woman, 1920–39)—advocated a secular Egyptian nationalist line.[56] Other women's Arabic monthlies arose on the scene in the interwar years, but few had long runs. The EFU's *al-Misriyya*, for example, lasted only from 1937 to 1940. A number of more popular women's illustrated weeklies were also introduced in this period, including *al-'Arusa* and *al-Hisan*. These featured photos of actresses, singers, and other famous men and women and did not concern themselves with heavier intellectual fare and social criticism.[57]

Labiba Ahmad sought to carve out a special niche for *al-Nahda al-Nisa'iyya*, claiming that it was "the first Egyptian women's journal" to research "social and religious affairs."[58] In fact, the Islamic thrust of the journal had precedents in earlier monthlies, such as Fatima Rashid's *Tarqiyat al-Mar'a* (Woman's Progress, 1908–9) and Sarah al-Mihiyya's *Fatat al-Nil* (Daughter of the Nile, 1913–15) as well as the weekly *al-'Afaf* (Virtue, 1910–22), which ceased publication at about the time that Labiba's journal took off.[59] Labiba appealed to those critical of the secularizing tendencies in Egyptian culture, who were receptive to the idea of Islamic reform as the path to national revival and women's progress. *Al-Nahda al-Nisa'iyya* aimed at instructing rather than entertaining and presented itself as the "desired remedy to many of our feminine social diseases."[60]

An essay by Labiba opened nearly every issue and set the tone for the journal. These essays dealt with society, morality, culture, and political economy. They were rarely about women's issues per se (such as veiling or domesticity) and neither were they exclusively or even mostly for women. Rather, they constituted a basic call to Egyptian men and women to reform society and work for its complete independence. The essays were often written in response to contemporary events, debates, or issues, and they generally called for action.

The tone that these essays set was further reinforced in notices and selections. Labiba saw economic independence as integral to Egyptian independence, and numerous essays dealt with economic issues. During the boycott of British goods in 1922, she called upon Egyptian women to sew their own dresses from Egyptian cloth and sponsored a contest to this end.[61] She praised Talat Harb, who conceived of a plan to found an Egyptian bank and companies, and urged her compatriots to buy shares in the new Bank of Egypt and support native products.[62] She later decried "economic enslavement" and the fact that "the wealth of the country is not in the pockets of its sons." And she condemned those who spent money abroad on summer vacations in Europe, labeling it a crime against the nation.[63]

Labiba criticized social practices whose very existence she found problematic in an Islamic country. These included legalized prostitution, alcohol consumption, use of narcotics, and gambling, issues her society also took up. She attacked mixed bathing at the beach and called on "morals police" to enforce separate swimming hours for men and women. She even opposed the building of a sports complex for girls: "Isn't the woman capable of exercising while she is in her home . . . for in prayer and its movements are the greatest exercise." Instead, she called for the formation of new Islamic societies to confront Egypt's moral dilemmas and praised charitable works.[64]

In a pattern common among women's advocates, Labiba focused on education. She appealed for increasing time spent on studying the Qur'an, strengthening Arabic instruction, boycotting foreign schools, and building more schools for the poor. She demanded equal fees for girls and boys, but at the same time criticized a curriculum that trained boys and girls identically, preparing them for the same exams, because she saw them as destined for different roles in life.[65] Some of these suggestions were presented to the minister of education by a delegation from the Society of Ladies' Awakening headed by Labiba, who corresponded regularly with education ministers.[66] Higher education for Egyptian women expanded in the 1920s and early 1930s, but Labiba felt that women should enter fields such as medicine and teaching (as her daughters had), rather than law or literature. "When will the people understand that the duty of a girl is to be a mother?" she asked.[67] She valued the role of teachers highly, commended some by name, and called for the opening of a school like Dar al-'Ulum (a higher teacher-training school) for women, which would prepare women teachers of Arabic.[68]

Labiba's essays on marriage followed arguments set out in her discussions of education. Girls needed more training in household management and preparation for child-raising, their true vocations, as well as greater religious education to guide the family. Labiba applauded the "influence of the virtuous mother in shaping the nation," and asked, "what is the nation if not a collection of families?"[69] Labiba was troubled by easy divorce, the emphasis on money in selecting spouses, and Egyptian men's marriage to foreign women. That the domestic roles laid out for women in Labiba's Islamic ideology upheld the ideals of a modern bourgeois family rather than some "traditional" or "authentic" Islamic ideal is further proof of the modernity of her message.[70]

Like other Islamic nationalists, Labiba supported King Fu'ad and his young son and successor Farouk, who were both lauded in essays. She also demanded the restoration of the constitution and celebrated the return of the Wafd to power in 1936.[71] In the 1930s, her nationalist impulse broadened. She called for financial aid to Palestinians during the 1936 Arab revolt and advocated a more unified curriculum across the Arab world—"one curriculum for one nation."[72]

Labiba opened the pages of *al-Nahda al-Nisa'iyya* to other writers, providing an outlet for Islamist thinkers in the early and mid-1920s when few such forums existed. (*Al-Manar* was a notable exception, but its editor, Muhammad Rashid Rida, had earlier fought with Egyptian nationalists.) Labiba's journal published contributions from seasoned writers such as Muhammad Farid Wajdi, a prominent Salafi writer who later edited al-Azhar's journal *Nur al-Islam* (Light of Islam) in the mid-1930s (and whose wife Fatima Rashid had founded the Islamically oriented Society of Woman's Progress.)[73] At the same time, Labiba nurtured younger male and female writers. These included 'Aisha 'Abd al-Rahman, a native of Damietta, who sent in articles and poems under the pen name Bint al-Shati' (Daughter of the Coast). She subsequently became famous for her Qur'anic exegesis and biographies of female relatives of the Prophet.[74] Biographies in *al-Nahda al-Nisa'iyya* featured notable Muslim women rather than the Western women who were often profiled in other women's journals. Labiba's journal also contained *hijri* dates based on the Islamic calendar, timetables for fasting, and space for hadith and Qur'anic commentary. Over time, the Islamic orientation of *al-Nahda al-Nisa'iyya* became more pronounced.

The journal's office shifted between Labiba's home (where male and female readers were invited to visit her on separate days), her institute, and the shops of the various presses that printed the journal.[75] The masthead identified Labiba as the president-founder of the Society of Ladies' Awakening and presented her alternately as the founder, owner, director, and editor of the journal. Others who shared in the running of the journal included her daughter Malak, who helped in Labiba's absence and served as an editorial secretary; the schoolteacher Muhammad Sadiq 'Abd al-Rahman, who edited the journal from the outset; and the Salafi thinker and Syrian émigré Muhibb al-Din al-Khatib, who took on this task starting in 1935.[76] A picture of the men and women involved in the production of *al-Nahda al-Nisa'iyya* appeared in the journal in 1930 upon the occasion of the convening of a women's congress in Damascus.[77]

Labiba's association with al-Khatib, whose books she promoted, illuminates her network.[78] He was among the founders of the Association of Muslim Youth (*Jam'iyyat al-Shubban al-Muslimin*, or the Young Men's Muslim Association, YMMA), which was begun in 1927 as a sort of "alumni society" for Watanists.[79] Al-Khatib edited *al-Fath* (f. 1926), a journal of Islamic outlook, and directed the Muslim Brothers' weekly *Majallat al-Ikhwan al-Muslimin* in the mid-1930s. Like others, he linked the fate of women and the nation, which he articulated in an article on "Woman's Progress as the Model for National Progress" in Labiba's journal. When he took over the editing of *al-Nahda al-Nisa'iyya*, he moved the offices of the journal to the Salafiyya Press, which he owned. He also directed the Salafiyya bookstore, where reform-minded religious activists and thinkers gathered.[80]

*Al-Nahda al-Nisa'iyya* appeared regularly throughout the year, including the summer months, when more secularly oriented women's monthlies tended to take a break. Publication of the journal was interrupted only on rare occasions: once in the mid-1920s when Labiba fell ill and once in the early 1930s when the government issued a new press law mandating security payments that raised obstacles to swift publication.[81] Labiba appointed Yusuf Effendi Ahmad, a former inspector of Arab antiquities and a frequent contributor to the journal, as director at one point and authorized him to represent her interests in court.[82]

Many Arabic periodicals were run on a modest budget, which explains the proliferation of newspapers and journals that appeared and disappeared within a short span of time. Labiba probably dipped into her own resources in the initial period, but *al-Nahda al-Nisa'iyya* quickly seemed to find firm financial footing. Using well-established strategies to raise funds and to broaden its base of readers, the journal pressured subscribers to pay their annual subscriptions and offered discounts to students. "The journal *al-Nahda al-Nisa'iyya* was founded as a service to elevate the state of affairs of the Egyptian nation and we consider the esteemed subscribers united in solidarity with us in undertaking this honorable goal . . . and the management of the journal does not expect profit from this work."[83] Agents were appointed to handle the journal's affairs outside of Egypt: subscribers and potential advertisers in Iraq, southern Iran, and the Persian Gulf region could, for example, contact the agent in Basra.[84]

In a development that virtually guaranteed the financial security of her journal, Labiba received contracts from various Arab governments. The Egyptian and Sudanese ministries of education and waqfs, as well as the provincial councils, officially authorized the distribution of *al-Nahda al-Nisa'iyya* in their schools; the Iraqi ministry of education assigned the journal as a text; the Syrian government purchased block subscriptions; and the Saudis subscribed to a "large number" on the instructions of King 'Abd al-'Aziz Ibn Sa'ud.[85] Moreover, the journal received support from royal and wealthy donors, among them the kings of Egypt, Saudi Arabia, and Iraq.[86] Such backing was unprecedented for an Egyptian women's magazine, and rare for any periodical. It showed that people in high places liked Labiba's message, which dovetailed with their conservative policies and upheld the social order. Her influential backers probably saw this Islamist journal and the modern but modest ideal Islamic woman it championed as a good counterweight to feminist and other secular literature.

Labiba had tapped a sizeable and wide market: she had a captive audience of teachers and schoolgirls in Egypt and other parts of the Arab world. While no distribution figures are available for the journal, earlier women's journals claimed circulation in the hundreds to thousands, and later Islamic ones (such as *al-Risala*) had circulations in the tens of thousands. (Circulation should be multiplied several times to yield approximate readership, for journals were frequently passed from hand to hand.)[87] *Al-Nahda al-Nisa'iyya* probably enjoyed a circulation in the thousands.

Contributors cannot be equated with readers, most of whom never wrote for the journal. Yet looking at them is one way to get a profile of the journal's readership. In its fifth year, the journal published a list of contributors—forty-two men and twenty-seven women (including the educator Nabawiyya Musa)—of articles to date. The men included researchers, doctors, journalists, clerics, poets, and lawyers. Their titles indicate that some were men of religious education (*shaykh*), high social rank (*bey*), or descent from the prophet (*sayyid*), but most were middle-rank government employees (*effendi* and *ustaz*). Thus while a notice to advertisers described the journal's readership as coming from the "highest classes," its contributors came mostly from the middle strata.[88]

Contributions took a variety of forms: letters in praise of the paper and its founder; brief inquiries to the advice column; and essays, of which there was no shortage. These came both from nearby (e.g., Damietta, Tanta, and Alexandria) and far away (e.g., Beirut, Mecca, and

Baghdad). The journal published contributions from individuals such as the head of the National Library, a photographer in the Egyptian museum, and students at al-Azhar and various other schools, as well as women teachers and journalists and women who gave no profession, such as Anisa A. A., Na'ima, and Fatima Husayn Badawi. In short, a journal with an Islamist outlook attracted a broad public response. It touched a chord mostly with the middle strata and professional classes, and with those with both Western-style and religious educations. These were the segments of the population who proved most responsive to an Islamist appeal and formed the rank and file of the earliest Islamist groups in Egypt. Among the contributors were also a few future leaders of that movement, notably Shaykh Tantawi Jawhari, who edited the Muslim Brothers' *Jaridat al-Ikhwan al-Muslimin* (1933–38); Mustafa Salih 'Ashmawi, an editor of another Muslim Brother's weekly; and Shaykh 'Abd Allah 'Afifi.[89]

Reprinted letters from readers and reviews by journalists in such papers as *al-Istiqlal* and *Sawt al-Hijaz* present the most telling testimony of the positive reception of *al-Nahda al-Nisa'iyya* in certain quarters in Egypt and the Arab world (although the journal may not have printed negative letters).[90] "I am unable to thank you, my dear lady, and cannot describe in words the central position you have come to occupy in the hearts of Egyptian women," noted Jalila Shawqi al-Bahrawi.[91] "You often gave speeches at meetings, wrote in newspapers and journals, and advised mothers, but all this did not satisfy you," commented the student Safiyya Rami. "You founded the journal *al-Nahda al-Nisa'iyya*, and look how it has spread throughout Egypt, from the Sudan to Alexandria, shouting encouragement to its readers, male and female."[92] One male reader wrote, "My family and I are among the readers of the journal *al-Nahda al-Nisa'iyya*, and it is our shared opinion that it has rendered a great service to the women's moral movement by guarding highly valued ethical and religious principles."[93] Each found in the journal something special. "It is a mirror that reflects the efforts of the Egyptian woman in the nationalist movement, and it is the guide for the girl at all stages of her life," wrote Safiyya Hasan Surur of Shubra.[94]

These responses came from men and women, indicating that the journal attracted a loyal male readership in addition to a female one. That the journal recognized that it served a mixed audience is apparent in its editorial notices and the voice of essays aimed at male and female readers. *Al-Nahda al-Nisa'iyya* debated national progress, social reform, women's roles, and Islamic revival for nearly two decades, an impressive record by any standard. This longevity shows that Labiba Ahmad created a successful vehicle to disseminate her vision of women's progress and Islamic revival in a fully independent Egypt. That vision had broad appeal.


## A VETERAN OF THE HAJJ

The combination of running a journal and directing social welfare operations exhausted Labiba Ahmad, who fell ill in the fall of 1924, and she suspended publication of *al-Nahda al-Nisa'iyya* for over a year.[95] After her recovery, she resolved to go on hajj (pilgrimage) to Mecca for the sixth time. Two years later, Labiba traveled on a seventh hajj, and she went thereafter almost every year. By 1938, she had made sixteen pilgrimages, equaling the number of years she had published her journal.[96] A journey incumbent upon Muslims once in their lifetime became an annual ritual for Labiba, who was drawn repeatedly to Arabia in an "attempt to satisfy the spirit."[97] While there Labiba, who had reached that stage in her life when she could hold discussions with unrelated men without raising eyebrows, forged personal contacts with Islamic leaders. These contacts helped firmly establish *al-Nahda al-Nisa'iyya* and her role as one of the preeminent women in the Islamic revival.

Labiba traveled with other pilgrims from Egypt, sometimes accompanied by family members.[98] But the trips were not always trouble-free: in the early years, when a few tribes in the Hijaz had not yet been subdued, there was still some violence; in later years, Labiba faced her own physical frailties. Security improved as King Ibn Sa'ud solidified his rule, and after completing their duties in Mecca, many pilgrims proceeded on a lesser pilgrimage to Medina to visit the tomb of the Prophet Muhammad. Labiba also enjoyed at least a summer or two in the mountain resort of Ta'if near Mecca.[99]

While Huda Sha'rawi and her friends made "pilgrimages" to London, Paris, Geneva, or Rome, Labiba returned year after year to Mecca, expanding her circle of contacts. She nurtured ties with the Saudi king, who extended his hospitality and gave her journal a generous subvention. She met with shaykhs, government officials, professionals, and other pilgrims, and was in turn honored at receptions. She mingled with Muslims from other countries and developed a wide circle of correspondents in the Arab world, in India (where leaders of a movement to revive the caliphate were based), and beyond.[100]

Her pilgrimages took on a familiar pattern over the years. Friends came to bid her farewell at home or at the train station; she sent in essays from abroad; and she received telegrams and letters of congratulations from as far away as Singapore upon her return. She subsequently thanked those who had assisted her in her travels.[101] Each trip in turn enhanced Labiba's prestige. Supporters praised her in poems and letters, increasingly calling her "al-Hajja." But, as one wrote, she was missed and urged to return "to your homeland to shine your light on the Nile Valley, which awaits your guiding hand, and to your children, who await your sympathy and affection."[102]

Labiba also made a visitation to the third sacred city of Islam—Jerusalem—in the fall of 1930. The previous year had been marked by widespread violence in Palestine triggered by a dispute over ownership and control of the wall adjacent to the mosque complex. Having completed the pilgrimage to Mecca earlier in 1930, Labiba traveled to Jerusalem in the company of another "hajja" and her sons. A shot that appeared in al-Nahda al-Nisa'iyya shows an unveiled Labiba with her travel companions in front of al-Aqsa (the Dome of the Rock).[103] While in Jerusalem, she met dignitaries such as al-Sayyid Muhammad Amin al-Ansari, custodian of the Mosque of 'Umar and of al-Aqsa and director of the Khalidiyya Library. A picture of al-Sayyid Amin al-Husayni, the mufti of Jerusalem and president of the Supreme Muslim Council, subsequently appeared on the cover of al-Nahda al-Nisa'iyya.[104]

## ISLAMIST NETWORKS

On the occasion of Labiba's pilgrimage in 1933, 'Aisha 'Abd al-Rahman noted: "She barely stops or rests! She is all movement and activity and sanctifies work, dedicating her life to it. She doesn't understand the meaning of living if it is not for the sake of work. These long years that have passed with sorrow and suffering [a reference to her daughter's death] were unable to harm her love for work or to cause in her any amount of despair or resignation."[105]

Labiba's activism took a new form when in the summer of 1933, after returning from the hajj, she took to the airwaves. Radios were new to Egypt and probably existed mostly in the homes of the urban well-to-do or in coffee shops; they spread quickly into towns and villages, becoming a popular form of entertainment. Once a week, Labiba went to the recording studio to deliver a regularly scheduled address on Royal Egyptian radio. Readers "who loved her and showered her with their affection and their encouragement" tuned in to listen. Labiba would not have addressed a live male Egyptian audience, but as a disembodied voice—

she was heard but not seen—she could speak on the radio, using the new technology to disseminate her views. Labiba's talks treated moral, religious, and social themes, resembling her monthly column in content.[106] Her access to the airwaves and a national radio audience suggests that the Sidqi government, which had dissolved parliament and abrogated the 1923 constitution, thought her message might be of some service. Labiba joined those conservative Muslim forces mobilized by Sidqi and his allies at the palace to counterbalance the secularism of the Wafd and help suppress it. She, on the other hand, used the opportunity to advance her agenda.

Through her travels, writings, and radio addresses, Labiba disseminated a brand of Islamic nationalism that increasingly countered the secular variety of the Wafd. She was particularly interested in fostering new Islamic associations and claimed credit for the blossoming of such organizations in the late 1920s and early 1930s. She pointed to the Association of Muslim Youth as "one of the results of our cries on the pages (of *al-Nahda*)," in addition to the Societies of Islamic Guidance, Memorizing the Noble Qur'an, and others.[107] Labiba became a respected patron of the new associations. At the opening of a charity bazaar run by the Society for Memorizing the Noble Qur'an to raise funds for a school for orphans and the poor, Fatima Amin thanked "al-Hajja Labiba Ahmad" for her support.[108]

Labiba had particularly close ties to the Association of Muslim Youth, which strove to teach Islamic morality, to disseminate knowledge adapted to modernity, to unify Muslims, and to take the best of Eastern and Western cultures.[109] Officers included the president, Dr. 'Abd al-Hamid Bey Sa'id; vice president, Shaykh 'Abd al-'Aziz Jawish; secretary-general Muhibb al-Din al-Khatib; and editor of the group's review, Ahmad Yahya al-Dardiri (who contributed to *al-Nahda al-Nisa'iyya*). Labiba's journal reported on speeches given at the Association's club, sometimes to female audiences.[110] In May 1932, the photo of a bearded man wearing a fez, suit, and tie appeared in the upper right corner of the picture of the sculpture *The Awakening of Egypt* on the cover of *al-Nahda al-Nisa'iyya*. The likeness, which appeared several times thereafter, seems to be that of Dr. Sa'id.[111] Labiba was invited to address a congress on education held at the hall of the association in 1936 and delegated Ustaz 'Abd al-Mun'im Khalaf to deliver her talk to the over four thousand participants.[112]

Labiba also had ties to the Society of the Muslim Brothers, which eventually emerged as the most important of the Islamist groups, as well as links with Hasan al-Banna (1906–49), its founder. She had covered his speeches in Cairo in the early 1930s in her journal, including one at the club of the Association of Muslim Youth.[113] Al-Banna had studied in Cairo at Dar al-'Ulum in the mid-1920s, seeking out the counsel of prominent Salifi thinkers such as Muhammad Farid Wajdi and Muhibb al-Din al-Khatib.[114] He subsequently moved to the Suez Canal town of Isma'iliyya to take up a teaching post and there founded the Muslim Brothers in March 1928. After building a base and branches in other provincial towns, he received a post in the capital, where he continued to organize.[115] The Salafi thinkers he so admired had focused on disseminating their messages primarily through their writings, but al-Banna chose the medium of preaching and spoke to groups of Muslims in their homes, coffee shops, mosques, and streets. The new organization aimed to counter the secularizing trends evident in Egyptian society and to spread Islamic teaching. In this it shared the goals of the Society of Ladies' Awakening, the Association of Muslim Youth, and similar such groups. Yet the Muslim Brothers became distinguished by their ability to recruit large numbers of followers and came to rival the Wafd in popularity. Their success was due to al-Banna's magnetism, rhetorical skills, and organizational abilities as well as the readiness of young, urban Egyptians to respond to such a message.

Labiba identified al-Banna early on as a charismatic figure capable of rallying the Islamist movement and guiding Egypt's religious revival. Hasan al-Banna had likewise early on recognized the centrality of women to the reform movement. In Isma'iliyya, he created a school to teach girls—"future mothers" who would shape the character of their children—about their religion. The "Institute for Mothers of the Believers" developed around 1932 into the first branch of the Muslim Sisters (al-Akhwat al-Muslimat), which was composed mostly of female relatives of Brothers.[116] A larger branch with the same name was subsequently founded in Cairo, and headed, according to some accounts, by Labiba Ahmad.[117] In 1934, Labiba helped launch another related Islamic enterprise, the League of Islamic Awakening (Rabitat al-Nahda al-Islamiyya). A delegation from the league met with al-Banna, who delivered Labiba Ahmad's recommendations for moral revival—encouraging noble traits of character, virtuous actions, and devotion to the true religion—at one of its first functions. The league gathered every Friday evening to hear lectures on a variety of topics.[118] Al-Banna and Labiba had close ties, for they shared a mission.

The Muslim Sisters initially faced resistance from male members of the Brotherhood in recruiting and building up a women's section. Their

venture took off in 1944 when a group of women determined to organize anew. They formed a central leadership made up of twelve members renewed annually under the directorship of Hasan al-Banna, who
named a liaison between his office and the women, and they established
their headquarters in Cairo. The Muslim Sisters adopted as their sign a
white head scarf (similar to the one worn by students in Labiba Ahmad's
schools), instead of the black one, often associated with grief and mourning. Members taught at special schools for "mothers of the believers,"
worked in medical facilities, helped the society develop their ideas about
women and the family, and propagated their message wherever they
could. To these Sisters, true emancipation for women would come only
with knowledge of their religion. Branches quickly spread throughout
Egypt, and within four years, they numbered fifty and total membership
reached five thousand.[119] Considering that this reflected less than four
years of organizing, and that Egyptian women simply did not mobilize
in mass for any party or organization in the 1940s, these numbers were
significant. They should be compared with the modest membership figures for women in secular organizations such as the EFU or the Com-
munist Party.

Labiba Ahmad's own role in the Muslim Sisters remains unclear. When
the first branches were founded in the 1930s, she was probably a woman
in her late fifties or early sixties. Her presidency of the Cairo branch may
have been an honorary title in acknowledgment of her pioneering work
over the years, her commitment to the Islamist cause, and her seniority.
When the Muslim Sisters became more active in the 1940s, she would
have been in her seventies. By then the keeper of the flame, who had
stoked the fire when it had grown faint in the 1920s, had passed the
torch to a new generation.

Among this new generation was Zaynab al-Ghazali (b. 1917), whose
new Muslim Ladies' Association (Jam'iyyat al-Sayyidat al Muslimat),
founded in 1937, was announced in the pages of *al-Nahda al-Nisa'iyya*.[120]
Membership lists of the organization reveal a preponderance of younger
women, such as Widad Sadiq 'Anbar, the group's secretary and a contributor to *al-Nahda al-Nisa'iyya*, and Na'ima Murtada, Labiba's grand-
daughter.[121] These women were figuratively and sometimes literally the
heirs of Labiba Ahmad, and the Muslim Ladies' Association continued
the work of the Society of Ladies' Awakening. Members sought to famil-
iarize Muslim women with their religion, through which, it was con-
tended, they would find emancipation. Their goal was to "purify society
in general and Muslim women in particular from the filth shaking their

convictions and to fight passion and disgraceful abominations."[122] The association also maintained an orphanage, helped poor families, and led groups of women on the hajj. When Hasan al-Banna asked Zaynab to fold her association into his, she politely refused (although she later pledged her allegiance to him), and in time the Muslim Ladies' Association had 118 or 119 branches.[123] This generation of Islamic activists—Labiba Ahmad's children and grandchildren—pushed the movement in a radical direction.

When Labiba returned to Cairo from the hajj in 1937, she went through her papers and resolved to prepare her memoirs for publication. "Life is made of memory and hope: memory of the past and hope for the future," she wrote in the introduction to the memoirs. "It was among my greatest hopes that I would serve my homeland *[watani]*, my people *[ummati]*, and the daughters of my sex by producing the journal *al-Nahda al-Nisa'iyya*, which I founded over sixteen years ago and persisted in publishing all this time without interruption, praise God." As a result of working on the journal, she explained, she corresponded with kings, ministers, politicians, and clerics. She arranged the materials in the book chronologically and by region. The earliest letters came from King Ibn Sa'ud, and with these she placed other correspondence from the Hijaz. Next followed a letter from Mustafa Kemal Ataturk, the nationalist hero and first president of Turkey; notes and telegrams from the staff of the Egyptian royal family; and letters from Sa'd Zaghlul and other Egyptian politicians. Finally, she ended with letters from "the dear ones and people of virtue." With her typical modesty, she presented the collection as a testimony of the sympathy of those people for her "small service." She placed and dated the memoirs Cairo, 15 Dhu al-Qi'da 1356, and identified herself, as she had throughout the years, as the founder of the Society of Ladies' Awakening. She thus brought her life as an activist to an end.[124]

The last issue of *al-Nahda al-Nisa'iyya* appeared in 1939. By then Labiba, who had recently undergone surgery, was ready to retire.[125] She could see the rootedness of Islamic nationalism in Egypt in the late 1930s and take pride in her contribution to the cause. Other long-running women's journals also folded on the eve of the war, signaling the end of an era in the Arabic women's press and the passing of a generation of female notables.[126] The 1940s, in contrast to the interwar period, were characterized by the spread of radical politics. In her final years, Labiba withdrew into ritual and prayer. She probably heard about the detention of Islamists during World War II and the troubles of the Muslim Brothers after it, including the assassination of Prime Minister Mahmud al-Nuqrashi by a Brother in 1948, the subsequent banning of the organization, the murder of Hasan al-Banna in 1949 by government agents, and the struggles faced by the Muslim Sisters in sustaining the families of those Brothers imprisoned from 1948 to 1950.[127] She may even have heard that the Muslim Brothers expected a lifting of the ban after the Wafd swept elections in early January 1951. "Al-Hajja" Labiba Ahmad died later that month at the age of nearly eighty. She left behind four children, six grandchildren, and numerous nieces and nephews.[128]

Labiba's politics were those of a gentlewoman and a gentler time, when different rules had prevailed. She came out of the same context—the 1919 revolution—as other women nationalists active in the interwar years, and like many of them, she mingled with nationalist leaders, ministers, and kings. She shared common conceptions with other notables about the duty of the daughter of a bey and the wife of a pasha to work for national reform and social welfare. The views she initially propagated overlapped with those of the secular nationalists, and they shared symbols and rhetoric. Yet their paths increasingly diverged as Labiba pushed for Islamization of society. Her political trajectory is captured by the shift in the titles of the organizations with which she was affiliated—from the Society of Ladies' Awakening to the Muslim Sisters—and in the shift in her own title—from Labiba "Hanim" Ahmad, an honorific ("lady") evoking the Ottoman-Egyptian past, to "al-Hajja" Labiba Ahmad, commemorating her journeys to Mecca and stressing her Islamic worldview.

Labiba looked to Islam, not Europe, for solutions to Egypt's social ills. She propagated her message widely in Egypt and abroad by founding associations, publishing a periodical in Arabic, traveling throughout the region, and speaking on the radio and to gatherings. As such, she was thoroughly modern in her methods and developed a wide following among the professional classes. She played a pivotal role in the political culture of the 1920s, a period of perceived Islamist inactivity, propagating reformist ideas and nurturing a generation of religious thinkers and activists. Her activism bore fruit in the 1930s, a decade of greater Islamist identity in Egypt. Labiba provided a crucial link in the chain from the Salifis to the Muslim Brothers, from the Watanists to later Islamic nationalists, from Fatima Rashid's Society of Woman's Progress to Zaynab al-Ghazali's Muslim Ladies' Association. Her story affirms that Islam, in different manifestations and with diverse meanings, was part of Egyptian political culture through this period and did not emerge full-grown in the 1930s as a sort of wrong turn.

   Labiba Ahmad's story also illuminates the creativity and diversity of women's political culture in this period. At a time when women lacked the right to vote, her social welfare and journalistic endeavors provided them with a political platform. She showed that women were not just objects of the Islamist discourse but activists in their own right, and her vision promoted an image—that of a modern Islamist woman—that competed with the secular "new woman" ideal. However, while Islamist politics provided some new images and outlets for women's activism, it ultimately narrowed their options and restricted political participation. The Islamist ideology of Labiba and her allies, some of the most conservative forces in the region, also helped to shore up the position of landowning elites and the new bourgeoisie. By stressing the Islamic cultural component as integral to nationalism, she limited the possibility of rewriting social relations along more egalitarian lines.

# Conclusion

This book opens with the unveiling of the monumental version of Mahmud Mukhtar's *The Awakening of Egypt*. Even though Mukhtar's sculpture depicts a peasant girl unveiling, contemporary unveiled Egyptian women could not attend the ceremony, suggesting that they were favored as symbols rather than as political actors, and seemingly confirming that the more women appeared in visual culture as representations of the nation, the less they appeared in the public arena. As I have sought to show, however, the relationship of the gendering of the nation to women nationalists was more complex—as was the story of *The Awakening of Egypt*. Many women were attracted to the sculpture and appreciated the sculptor. Labiba Ahmad consciously selected this image when it was still a model and not yet a public monument (or anathema to Islamists) and ran a picture of it on the cover of her journal for over a decade. Safiyya Zaghlul visited Mukhtar in his atelier, and Huda Sha'rawi gave funds to open a museum to showcase his work. In spite of their exclusion from the public ceremony, women appropriated the monument for their own use and celebrated the artist. Over time, *The Awakening of Egypt* became a symbol of women's rights as well as of Egyptian nationalism.[1]

Part 1 of this study looked at images of the nation. It started with the ethnic origins of the nation, mapping inclusions and exclusions in the national family. The end of slavery, it was argued, contributed to the unraveling of the large multi-ethnic households of the Ottoman-Egyptian elite in the nineteenth century. This generated a crisis that led to debates about the family and paved the way for a nationalist rhetoric that deployed familial terms and concepts. Nationalists used maternal, fraternal, and paternal rhetoric to render the collective as a family, and characterized the particular sort of family they had in mind as a bourgeois one. This model was presented as the best alternative for transformed elite families and the most suitable one for newly emerging middle-class families in a modern, capitalist-oriented nation-state.

Nationalists appropriated the concept of family honor, elevating it to the national plane to produce a discourse of national honor. The nation not only had to defend and avenge honor, but honor defined the collective and was at the core of its identity. Those who shared honor belonged to the community; those who did not could be excluded. The notion of national honor, never static, was used for different purposes by various groups, who all claimed to be protecting it. Women writers tried to steer the concept of honor away from female purity, but never challenged the concept of honor itself, or making women its repositories.

Part I then turned from family discourses and their sociopolitical contexts to visual culture, specifically iconography and photography. Egypt came to be depicted as a woman in nationalist iconography, whether it took the form of cartoons, paintings, monuments, or postage stamps. Rather than one model, multiple images of "Egypt" or the "Egyptian nation" emerged. These images reflected the social situation of Egyptian women and the obstacles that had to be overcome in depicting the nation as a woman when real women still veiled themselves. Initially, pharaonic and peasant women proved most viable as representations. In the early 1920s, and under the inspiration of women's new public visibility, the "new woman" became the model. That she was fair-skinned and modestly cloaked in contrast to a dark, sexualized Sudan epitomized the asymmetry of the relationship between Egypt and the Sudan, as well as the persistence of Ottoman influence and ideals in Egypt. Cartoonists occasionally took individual women activists such as Safiyya Zaghlul or Fatima al-Yusuf as models for Egypt. They were also inspired by women's political actions and new activities in sketching settings for the nation.

Photography helped to create and disseminate nationalist iconography and the sense of the nation as a family. Over the years, the illustrated press disseminated thousands of pictures of national leaders, symbols, and rituals. The collage of photographic images showed an active, modern nation on the move. Photography became a critical part of visual culture, crucial to documenting events and packaging them for public consumption. Sharing images helped incorporate the viewer into the national community, while at the same time the images showed the proper gendering of public space and political roles. In time, some of these images became symbols and a core component of collective memory.

Literary discourses and visual images of women and the family helped to propagate nationalism, making it at once familiar, stirring, and appealing. Elite women were themselves engaged in this process of familializing nationalist rhetoric and feminizing the nation. They could have chosen other words or selected different symbols, but family discourses and female images seemed to suit them. They used their authority as "Mothers of the Nation" or "Mother of the Egyptians" to address British and other foreign officials, Egyptian politicians, and their compatriots. Motherhood, patterned on bourgeois ideals, gave them the license to speak out and the rank to impose their will on their "sons," or at least try. The role complemented that of the "father" of the nation (Sa'd Zaghlul) and party leaders, although male politicians, whose legitimacy on the public stage was not contested, used paternal language less. Women specifically used maternal rhetoric because they were contesting public space, seeking to carve out new political roles, and sought legitimization for the process. Women writers and activists also propagated a rhetoric of national honor. They might have avoided this rhetoric altogether as the concept was grounded in ideals of female purity. Instead, they attempted to desexualize the notion by choosing certain words over others.

Elite women did not seem averse, as well, to having the nation represented as a woman, and saw no inherent danger in this sort of symbolism. They appropriated Mukhtar's sculpture (as discussed above), among other imagery, as a sign of women's progress. Their periodicals also replicated images of the nation as a woman: Fatima al-Yusuf's *Ruz al-Yusuf* carried cartoons similar to those in the male-owned and edited periodicals *al-Lata'if al-Musawwara* and *al-Kashkul*. Women were attuned to the power of photography, attempting to use the new visual culture to craft favorable public images.

This study has focused on feminine discourses, especially maternal ones, and female images, seeking to link them to women's political culture. Future research might pay more attention to paternal and fraternal discourses and the role of masculinity in shaping the nation and, conversely, the role of nationalism in constructing masculinity. Ideals of masculinity prove crucial in preparing soldiers to kill and die for the nation, come to the fore in times of revolution and war, and form the basis for codes of honor. This is implicit but needs to be made explicit.[2]

Part 2 of this book examined the politics of elite women nationalists, who found themselves caught between the horns of being transformed into political symbols or excluded as political actors. The stories told here show how they confronted this dilemma, seizing the opportunities presented and looking for new openings. Elite women took politics seriously and saw themselves as major actors in the national drama. The contemporary press and public regarded them as important players as well, documenting meetings, recording movements, and giving them good but sometimes critical coverage. Women nationalists sought avenues where they could have influence and an impact, and expanded women's political culture to fill the vacuum left by men's political culture. They set up auxiliaries to influence the new parties; built up social welfare associations and power bases; sought to shape public opinion in periodicals; and acted as liaisons and representatives.

Women nationalists started out together with the common goal of ending the British occupation, and whether their roots were in the Umma or Watani Parties, they had unified at the critical moment in 1919 around the Wafd. Yet they came to take different paths, as the trajectories of their careers increasingly diverged. Safiyya Zaghlul stayed the course with the Wafd, surrounded by a core of loyalists, working at returning or keeping the Wafd in power and enhancing her husband's prestige. Huda Sha'rawi broke with the leaders of the Wafd, who had disappointed her, and championed feminist politics. Esther Fahmi Wisa regrouped the Women's Wafd under a new name when Huda left and remained active through the 1930s, combining this with her commitment to social welfare. Labiba Ahmad parted with the secularists early on, dedicating herself to Islamist politics as the key to national and women's progress.

Most of the elite women discussed here took to the public stage in the interwar period and exited that stage in the late 1930s or 1940s. Safiyya withdrew from politics in 1937, Labiba retired from journalism in 1939, and Huda remained active through the war but died in 1947. The younger activists of the interwar period, including Fatima al-Yusuf, Munira Thabit, and Esther Fahmi Wisa, continued their journalistic or social welfare work, but were eventually eclipsed by a younger generation. In the 1940s, women's political culture shifted away from a politics of female notables or gentlewomen. This was part a radicalization of Egyptian politics, as the middle classes challenged the politics of pashas and criticized their hold on power, and part a result of greater gender desegregation in Egyptian society. Activist women joined Islamist, socialist, and other organizations and started new feminist endeavors.

While making history, women nationalists had not been so preoccupied with writing it, and only a few left memoirs. Historical accounts tended to marginalize their activities, and elite women became better known as sites of memory or as nationalist symbols than as political actors. Thus, women protestors—veiled and with flags—became prominent reminders of the 1919 revolution, Safiyya gained stature as the "Mother of the Egyptians," and the Women's Wafd along with other nationalist groups, including that of Labiba Ahmad, served as a nameless nationalist chorus. Until recently, it appears, women were often better at observing and serving history than preserving, shaping, and commemorating it. The lesson seems to be that it is not enough to participate in a nationalist movement; female actors must also preserve memories and propagate them.

Public commemoration of elite women nationalists and their cohort was not consistent or constant. After the 1952 revolution, they were among those targeted in the reaction against the old regime and upper classes. Safiyya Zaghlul was remembered, or forgotten, alongside her husband in the House of the Nation Museum, whose doors remained closed for many years. Esther Fahmi Wisa witnessed the appropriation of the facility that had housed the Work for Egypt Society that she headed for almost forty years but was subsequently honored among other veterans of the 1919 revolution upon its fiftieth anniversary. Huda Sha'rawi did not live to see the state appropriate and destroy her home, the site of Egyptian Feminist Union meetings for many decades, or, in a turnaround, issue a stamp in 1973 to commemorate the fiftieth anniversary of the founding of the EFU.[3] Labiba Ahmad remained little known, although the Islamic revival of the 1990s created an interest in earlier Islamists. In spite of the occasional recognition of female nationalists on stamps and in street names, museums, and commemorations, these women were ultimately marginalized. Women nationalists were thus marginalized twice, blocked from contemporary party and parliamentary politics and later erased from the collective memory.

Some scholars claim that nationalist discourses and symbols knit women into the nation. They did, on a certain level, as this study shows. But real women were cut out of access to the state at the critical moment when the nationalists seized power. Other scholars suggest that women's involvement in a nationalist movement or anti-colonial struggle must be separated from later exclusions by male nationalists. This work has reiterated that the nation-state must be pried apart and women's relationship to the nation and to the state seen separately. Nationalist movements (and discourses) both provided opportunities for women's participation and circumscribed roles, both mobilized women and marginalized them, both engaged and disappointed. In short, the nationalist movement may have eventually ended the British occupation, but it did not make women full citizens of the state. Yet that is not the whole story.

Nationalist politics must be conceived broadly, not just as party or parliamentary politics, from which women were often excluded, but as incorporating a range of "nation-building" activities in diverse spheres, including education, journalism, feminism, and social welfare. This is more than a sleight of hand to rescue women nationalists from oblivion and rewrite the ending to the narrative of women and the nationalist struggle. Almost everywhere the pattern was the same, one of exclusion (and women were not the only group excluded). Yet elite Egyptian women overcame the limitations and pushed in new directions. When men's political culture seemed paralyzed by British interference, palace intractability, and party wrangling, women stepped into the breach to address daunting socioeconomic problems. They built social welfare organizations, pushed for legislative reform, met with politicians and policy makers, agitated for education programs, and worked at the grassroots level to provide medical and other services. They had neither the resources nor the tools to make a large dent in Egypt's urban and rural poverty, yet they left an imprint. But the attempt of women to promote social welfare is another story.

# Notes

ABBREVIATIONS

*Arabic Periodicals*

| | |
|---|---|
| *AF* | *al-'Afaf* |
| *AH* | *al-Ahram* |
| *AJ* | *Anis al-Jalis* |
| *AL* | *al-'Aila* |
| *AM* | *al-Amal* |
| *AN* | *Abu Naddara* |
| *AR* | *al-'Arusa* |
| *BU* | *al-Balagh al-Usbu'iyya* |
| *FS* | *Fatat al-Sharq* |
| *HL* | *al-Hilal* |
| *HN* | *al-Hisan* |
| *IM* | *al-Ikhwan al-Muslimun* |
| *JL* | *al-Jins al-Latif* |
| *KK* | *al-Kashkul* |
| *LM* | *al-Lata'if al-Musawwara* |
| *MF* | *Misr al-Fatat* |
| *MHJ* | *al-Mihrajan* |

MM      *al-Mar'a al-Misriyya*

MQ      *al-Muqtataf*

MSR     *al-Musawwar*

NN      *al-Nahda al-Nisa'iyya*

RY      *Ruz al-Yusuf*

SF      *al-Sufur*

SR      *al-Sayyidat wa al-Rijal*

TM      *Tarqiyat al-Mar'a*

*English Periodicals*

IJMES   *International Journal of Middle East Studies*

*Books*

SHM     *Sijill al-Hilal al-Musawwar, 1892–1992* [The Illustrated Record of
        al-Hilal, 1892–1992], 2 vols. (Cairo, 1992)

*State Archives*

FO      Foreign Office, United Kingdom, Public Record Office, London

SD      State Department, United States, National Archives, Washington, D.C.

## INTRODUCTION

1. Badr al-Din Abu Ghazi, *Maththal Mukhtar* (Cairo, 1964); Israel Gershoni and James P. Jankowski, *Egypt, Islam, and the Arabs: The Search for Egyptian Nationhood, 1900–1930* (Oxford, 1986), 186–88; Liliane Karnouk, *Modern Egyptian Art: The Emergence of a National Style* (Cairo, 1988), 14–17; Daisy Griggs Philips, "The Awakening of Egypt's Womanhood," *Moslem World* 18 (1928): 402. Officials later moved the statue to the road leading to the main entrance of Cairo University in Giza.

2. Ruth Roach Pierson, "Nations: Gendered, Racialized, Crossed with Empire," in *Gendered Nations: Nationalisms and Gender Order in the Long Nineteenth Century*, ed. Ida Blom, Karen Hagemann, and Catherine Hall (London, 2000), 44.

3. See works by Karen Hagemann, e.g., " 'A Valourous *Volk* Family': The Nation, the Military, and the Gender Order in Prussia in the Time of the Anti-Napoleonic Wars, 1806–15," in *Gendered Nations,* ed. Blom et al., 179–205.

4. For an excellent overview, see Alon Confino, "Collective Memory and Cultural History: Problems of Method," *American Historical Review* 102 (1997): 1386–1403.

5. For a general appraisal of the literature on gender and nationalism, see *Gendered Nations,* ed. Blom et al. For samplings of the vast literature on nationalism, see John Hutchinson and Anthony D. Smith, eds., *Nationalism* (Oxford, 1994), and Geoff Eley and Ronald Grigor Suny, eds., *Becoming National: A Reader* (New York, 1996).

6. See Katherine Kish Sklar, "The Historical Foundations of Women's Power in the Creation of the American Welfare State, 1830–1930," in *Mothers of a New World: Maternalist Politics and the Origins of Welfare States*, ed. Seth Koven and Sonya Michel (New York, 1993), 43–93, esp. 79–80 n. 4.

7. See Ehud R. Toledano, "Forgetting Egypt's Ottoman Past," *Cultural Horizons: A Festschrift in Honor of Talat S. Halman*, ed. Jayne L. Warner (Syracuse, N.Y., 2001), 150–67.

8. On the shaping of this narrative, see Gabriel Piterberg, "The Tropes of Stagnation and Awakening in Nationalist Historical Consciousness: The Egyptian Case," in *Rethinking Nationalism in the Arab World*, ed. James Jankowski and Israel Gershoni (New York, 1997), 42–61; Yoram Meital, "Revolutionizing the Past: Historical Representation during Egypt's Revolutionary Experience, 1952–62," *Mediterranean Historical Review* 12 (1997): 60–77.

9. See, e.g., Ehud R. Toledano, *State and Society in Mid-Nineteenth-Century Egypt* (Cambridge, 1990); Khaled Fahmy, *All the Pasha's Men: Mehmed Ali, His Army and the Making of Modern Egypt* (Cambridge, 1997).

10. See, e.g., Juan R. I. Cole, *Colonialism and Revolution in the Middle East: Social and Cultural Origins of Egypt's 'Urabi Movement* (Princeton, N.J., 1993).

11. See, e.g., Gershoni and Jankowski, *Egypt, Islam, and the Arabs*; id., *Redefining the Egyptian Nation, 1930–1945* (Cambridge, 1995); Donald Reid, *Whose Pharaohs? Archaeology, Museums, and Egyptian National Identity from Napoleon to World War I* (Berkeley, Calif., 2002).

12. Eve M. Troutt Powell, *A Different Shade of Colonialism: Egypt, Great Britain and the Mastery of the Sudan* (Berkeley, Calif., 2003).

13. Margot Badran, *Feminists, Islam, and Nation: Gender and the Making of Modern Egypt* (Princeton, N.J., 1995).

14. See Lila Abu-Lughod, ed., *Remaking Women: Feminism and Modernity in the Middle East* (Princeton, N.J., 1998); Leila Ahmed, *Women and Gender in Islam* (New Haven, Conn., 1992); Marilyn Booth, *May Her Likes Be Multiplied: Biography and Gender Politics in Egypt* (Berkeley, Calif., 2001); Selma Botman, *Engendering Citizenship in Egypt* (New York, 1999); Mervat Hatem, "Egyptian Upper- and Middle-Class Women's Early Nationalist Discourses on National Liberation and Peace in Palestine (1922–1944)," *Women and Politics* 9 (1989): 49–70; Lisa Pollard, "The Family Politics of Colonizing and Liberating Egypt, 1882–1919," *Social Politics* 7 (2000): 47–79; Mona L. Russell, "Creating the New Woman: Consumerism, Education, and National Identity in Egypt, 1863–1922" (Ph.D. diss., Georgetown University, 1997); Beth Baron, *The Women's Awakening in Egypt: Culture, Society, and the Press* (New Haven, Conn., 1994).

15. Nadir Özbek, "Imperial Gifts and Sultanic Legitimation during the Late Ottoman Empire, 1876–1909," in *Poverty and Charity in Middle Eastern Contexts,* ed. Michael Bonner, Mine Ener, and Amy Singer (Albany, N.Y., 2003), 203–20.

16. See, e.g., Beth Baron, "Mothers, Morality, and Nationalism in Pre-1919 Egypt," in *The Origins of Arab Nationalism*, ed. Rashid Khalidi et al. (New York, 1991), 271–88; Wendy Bracewell, "Women, Motherhood, and Contemporary Serbian Nationalism," *Women's Studies International Forum* 19 (1996): 25–33; Deborah Gaitskell and Elaine Unterhalter, "Mothers of the Nation: a Comparative Analysis of Nation, Race and Motherhood in Afrikaner Nationalism and the African National Congress," in *Woman–Nation–State*, ed. Nira Yuval-Davis and Floya Anthias (London, 1989), 58–78; Afsaneh Najmabadi, "*Zanha-y millat*: Women or Wives of the Nation?" *Iranian Studies* 26 (1993): 51–71.

17. Pranay Gupte, *Mother India: A Political Biography of Indira Gandhi* (New York, 1992); Anne McClintock, "Family Feuds: Gender, Nationalism and the Family," *Feminist Review* (Summer 1993): 61–80.

18. On maternalism, see Koven and Michel, *Mothers of a New World*, intro. Sklar argues that "maternalism" covers only a part of women reformers' agendas and prefers the concept of women's political culture. (See her "Historical Foundations of Women's Power," 43–93.) "Maternalist" in this study refers to a nationalist rhetoric rather than a specific political agenda.

19. See Nikki R. Keddie, *Women in the Middle East since the Rise of Islam* (Washington, D.C., forthcoming).

20. Baron, *The Women's Awakening in Egypt*.

21. Russell, "Creating the New Woman."

22. Clarissa Lee Pollard, "Nurturing the Nation: The Family Politics of the 1919 Egyptian Revolution" (Ph.D. diss., University of California, Berkeley, 1997); Lisa Pollard, "Family Politics," 49–50.

23. Lila Abu-Lughod, "The Marriage of Feminism and Islamism in Egypt: Selective Repudiation as a Dynamic of Postcolonial Cultural Politics," in *Remaking Women*, 255–61; on women's ties to their natal families, see Iris Agmon, "Women, Class, and Gender: Muslim Jaffa and Haifa at the Turn of the Twentieth Century," *IJMES* 30 (1998): 477–500.

24. Judith Tucker has sketched shifts in peasants' and workers' families in the nineteenth century; Mona Russell looks at the emergence of new middle-class families; and Ken Cuno has written about transformations in elite households and, with Michael Reimer, the promise that census data can tell us much more. See Judith E. Tucker, *Women in Nineteenth-Century Egypt* (Cambridge, 1985); Russell, "Creating the New Woman"; Kenneth M. Cuno, "Joint Family Households and Rural Notables in Nineteenth-Century Egypt," *IJMES* 27 (1995): 485–502; Kenneth M. Cuno and Michael J. Reimer, "The Census Registers of Nineteenth-Century Egypt: A New Source for Social Historians," *British Journal of Middle Eastern Studies* 24 (1997): 193–216. Egypt lacks a quantitative study comparable to Alan Duben and Cem Behar, *Istanbul Households: Marriage, Family, and Fertility, 1880–1940* (Cambridge, 1991).

25. Baron, *Women's Awakening*, 81–84.

26. Akram Fouad Khater, *Inventing Home: Emigration, Gender, and the Middle Class in Lebanon, 1870–1920* (Berkeley, Calif., 2001).

27. Cuno explains this shift as a new pattern of princes marrying women of the Muhammadi (dynastic) family; these marriages by definition had to be

monogamous. See Kenneth M. Cuno, "Ambiguous Modernization: The Transition to Monogamy in the Khedival House of Egypt," in *Family History in the Middle East: Household, Property, and Gender*, ed. Beshara Doumani (Albany, N.Y., 2003), 247–70.

28. See Michael Meeker, "Meaning and Society in the Near East: Examples from the Black Sea Turks and the Levantine Arabs," *IJMES* 7 (1976): 243–70.

29. See, e.g., David Koester, "Gender Ideology and Nationalism in the Culture and Politics of Iceland," *American Ethnologist* 22 (1995): 572–88, esp. 574–75.

30. Dominic David Alessio, "Domesticating 'the Heart of the Wild': Female Personifications of the Colonies, 1886–1940," *Women's History Review* 6 (1997): 239–69.

31. On the evolution of these terms in the nineteenth century, see Ami Ayalon, *Language and Change in the Arab Middle East* (Oxford, 1987).

32. On film and nationalism, see, e.g., Walter Armbrust, *Mass Culture and Modernism in Egypt* (Cambridge, 1996).

33. Marnia Lazreg, *The Eloquence of Silence: Algerian Women in Question* (New York, 1994), 118–19.

34. See Elizabeth Thompson, *Colonial Citizens: Republican Rights, Paternal Privilege, and Gender in French Syrian and Lebanon* (New York, 2000); Ellen L. Fleischmann, *The Nation and Its "New" Women: The Palestinian Women's Movement, 1920–1948.* (Berkeley, Calif., 2003). For an excellent overview of the literature, see Fleischmann, "The Other 'Awakening': The Emergence of Women's Movements in the Modern Middle East, 1900–1940," in *Social History of Women and Gender in the Modern Middle East*, ed. Margaret L. Meriwether and Judith E. Tucker (Boulder, Colo., 1999), 89–139.

35. Jane Hathaway, *The Politics of Households in Ottoman Egypt: The Rise of the Qazdaglis* (Cambridge, 1997), 106–24, quotation from 116. See also Afaf Lutfi al-Sayyid-Marsot, *Women and Men in Late Eighteenth-Century Egypt* (Austin, Tex., 1995); Mary Ann Fay, "Women and Waqf: Toward a Reconsideration of Women's Place in the Mamluk Household," *IJMES* 29 (1997): 33–51.

36. For one account, see Nada Tomiche, "The Situation of Egyptian Women in the First Half of the Nineteenth Century," in *Beginnings of Modernization in the Middle East: The Nineteenth Century*, ed. William R. Polk and Richard L. Chambers (Chicago, 1968), 171–84.

37. Baron, *Women's Awakening*, chap. 8; id., "Mothers, Morality, and Nationalism."

38. Geoff Eley, "Culture, Nation and Gender," in *Gendered Nations*, 37.

39. In an earlier article, I conceptualized the initiatives of these women as a "politics of female notables." My intent was to gender "notable politics," a widespread paradigm in Middle Eastern history first advanced by Albert Hourani. That concept has lately come under attack from different quarters for a variety of reasons. Viewing elite women's initiatives as part of a broader women's political culture that included middle- as well as upper-class women and had no specific ethnic or rural-urban connotations seems more useful here. See Beth Baron, "The Politics of Female Notables in Postwar Egypt," in *Borderlines: Genders and Identities in War and Peace, 1870–1930*, ed. Billie Melman (New York,

1998), 329–50; Albert Hourani, "Ottoman Reform and the Politics of Notables," in *The Emergence of the Modern Middle East* (London, 1981), 36–66, repr. in *The Modern Middle East: A Reader*, ed. Albert Hourani, Philip S. Khoury, and Mary C. Wilson (Berkeley, Calif., 1993), 83–109.

40. For a study of one pivotal figure, see Cynthia Nelson, *Doria Shafik, Egyptian Feminist: A Woman Apart* (Gainesville, Fla., 1996).

## CHAPTER ONE. SLAVERY, ETHNICITY, AND FAMILY

1. The writers on nationalism most frequently cited by historians include Benedict Anderson, *Imagined Communities: Reflections on the Origin and Spread of Nationalism*, rev. ed. (New York, 1991); Ernest Gellner, *Nations and Nationalism* (Ithaca, N.Y., 1983); E. J. Hobsbawn, *Nations and Nationalism since 1780: Programme, Myth, Reality* (Cambridge, 1990); and Anthony D. Smith, *The Ethnic Origins of Nations* (Oxford, 1986). See also Geoff Eley and Ronald Grigor Suny, eds., *Becoming National: A Reader* (New York, 1996), and John Hutchinson and Anthony D. Smith, eds., *Nationalism* (Oxford, 1994).

2. On ethnicity and nationalism, see Anthony D. Smith, "The Origins of Nations," *Ethnic and Racial Studies* 12 (1989), repr. in *Becoming National*, ed. Hutchinson and Smith, 106–30; id., "The Nation: Invented, Imagined, Reconstructed?" *Millennium* 20 (1991): 353–68; id., *Ethnic Origins*.

3. Some historians of Egypt have argued that 1798 should not be taken as a rupture, pointing to the many continuities between the eighteenth and nineteenth centuries. They have also challenged the narrative of progress and modernization that used to be associated with 1798 as a point of departure. I am mostly concerned with changes that accelerated in the second half of the nineteenth century and that followed in part from the change in power inaugurated by Mehmed Ali.

4. See works by Gabriel Baer, Juan Cole, Ken Cuno, Khaled Fahmy, Afaf Lutfi al-Sayyid-Marsot, Robert Tignor, Ehud Toledano, and Judith Tucker.

5. Ehud R. Toledano, *State and Society in Mid-Nineteenth-Century Egypt* (Cambridge, 1990), intro; Khaled Fahmy, *All the Pasha's Men: Mehmed Ali, His Army and the Making of Modern Egypt* (Cambridge, 1997).

6. Ehud R. Toledano, "Social and Economic Change in the 'Long Nineteenth Century,'" in *The Cambridge History of Egypt*, vol. 2: *Modern Egypt, from 1517 to the End of the Twentieth Century*, ed. M. W. Daly (Cambridge, 1998), 263–64; id., *State and Society*; F. Robert Hunter, *Egypt under the Khedives, 1805–1879: From Household Government to Modern Bureaucracy* (Pittsburgh, 1984).

7. Dror Ze'evi, "*Kul* and Getting Cooler: The Dissolution of Elite Collective Identity and the Formation of Official Nationalism in the Ottoman Empire," *Mediterranean Historical Review* 11 (1996): 177–95; Toledano, *State and Society*, 58; id., *Slavery and Abolition in the Ottoman Middle East* (Seattle, 1998), chap. 1; Jane Hathaway, *The Politics of Households in Ottoman Egypt: The Rise of the Qazdaglis* (Cambridge, 1997), intro.

8. Alexander Schölch, *Egypt for the Egyptians! The Socio-political Crisis in Egypt, 1878–1882* (Oxford, 1981), 24, 67; Gabriel Baer, *Studies in the Social*

*History of Modern Egypt* (Chicago, 1969), chap. 10; Ehud R. Toledano, *The Ottoman Slave Trade and Its Suppression: 1840–1890* (Princeton, N.J., 1982); id., *Slavery and Abolition*, chap. 1. In her *The Imperial Harem: Women and Sovereignty in the Ottoman Empire* (New York, 1993), Leslie Peirce discusses how such arranged marriages were meant to cement bonds of loyalty to the Ottoman sultan in an earlier period.

9. Kenneth M. Cuno, *The Pasha's Peasants* (Cambridge, 1992); id., "Joint Family Households and Rural Notables in Nineteenth-Century Egypt," *IJMES* 27 (1995): 485–502.

10. Huda Sha'rawi, *Mudhakkirat Huda Sha'rawi* (Cairo, 1981), 10–31; F. Robert Hunter, "The Making of a Notable Politician: Muhammad Sultan Pasha (1825–1884)," *IJMES* 15 (1983): 537–44.

11. Sha'rawi, *Mudhakkirat*, 32–40; Huda Shaarawi, *Harem Years: The Memoirs of an Egyptian Feminist (1879–1924)*, trans. and intro. Margot Badran (London, 1986), 23–26.

12. Sha'rawi, *Mudhakkirat*; Emine Foat Tugay, *Three Centuries: Family Chronicles of Turkey and Egypt* (London, 1963); Ehud R. Toledano, "Slave Dealers, Women, Pregnancy, and Abortion: The Story of a Circassian Slave-girl in Mid-Nineteenth Century Cairo," *Slavery and Abolition* 2 (1981): 53–68; Ron Shaham, "Masters, Their Freed Slaves, and the *Waqf* in Egypt (Eighteenth–Twentieth Centuries)," *Journal of the Economic and Social History of the Orient* 43 (2000): 162–88; Judith E. Tucker, *Women in Nineteenth-Century Egypt* (Cambridge, 1985), 164–93.

13. Ehud R. Toledano, "Forgetting Egypt's Ottoman Past," in *Cultural Horizons: A Festschrift in Honor of Talat S. Halman*, ed. Jayne L. Warner (Syracuse, N.Y., 2001): 150–67.

14. Toledano, *State and Society*; id., "Social and Economic Change," 252–84; F. Robert Hunter, "Egypt's High Officials in Transition from a Turkish to a Modern Administrative Elite, 1849–1879," *Middle Eastern Studies* 19 (1983): 277–91.

15. Baer, *Studies in the Social History of Modern Egypt*, 176–89; Ehud R. Toledano, "Late Ottoman Concepts of Slavery (1830s-1880s)," *Poetics Today* 14 (1993): 477–506; id., *Slavery and Abolition*, 24–41; id., *Ottoman Slave Trade*; Y. Hakan Erdem, *Slavery in the Ottoman Empire and Its Demise, 1800–1909* (New York, 1996).

16. Ze'evi, "*Kul* and Getting Cooler," 193–94.

17. For more on the history of sexuality, including homosexuality, in Egypt, see Bruce W. Dunne, "Sexuality and the 'Civilizing Process' in Modern Egypt" (Ph.D. diss., Georgetown University, 1996).

18. Hathaway, *Politics of Households in Ottoman Egypt*.

19. Juan Cole characterizes the movement as a social revolution that sought to overthrow a dual elite of Ottoman-Egyptians and Europeans. He argues that "a nativist discourse temporarily helps subsume the class differences among the challengers under a broad proto-nationalism" (Juan R. I. Cole, *Colonialism and Revolution in the Middle East: Social and Cultural Origins of Egypt's 'Urabi Movement* [Princeton, N.J., 1993], 283). Schölch does not see social and political revolution as driving forces but rather points to a reforming impulse that had no intention of setting up a secular Egyptian national state (Schölch, *Egypt*

*for the Egyptians!* 313). For an analysis of the debates, see Toledano, "Social and Economic Change," 267–70.

20. Ahmad 'Urabi, *The Defense Statement of Ahmad 'Urabi the Egyptian,* trans. Trevor le Gassick (Cairo, 1982), 18. For the split between Arabic-speaking soldiers and Turkish-speaking officers in the Egyptian army in the first half of the century, see Khaled Fahmy, *All the Pasha's Men,* chap. 6.

21. Schölch, *Egypt for the Egyptians!* 221, 341 n. 8.

22. British and Foreign Anti-Slavery Society Papers, Rhodes House, Oxford, C22/G30, Blunt to Allen, Suez, 17 Mar. 1882.

23. FO 141/128, Borg to Vivian, Cairo, 3 Feb. 1879.

24. A. M. Broadley, *How We Defended Arabi and His Friends* (London, 1884; rep. Cairo, 1980), 373–76.

25. Quote from 'Urabi, *Kashif al-Sitar,* trans. in *Defense Statement,* 42; Wilfrid Scawen Blunt, *Secret History of the English Occupation of Egypt: Being a Personal Narrative of Events* (1907; repr. New York, 1967), app. 1; Schölch, *Egypt for the Egyptians!* 283–84, 288.

26. For more on Sanu'a, see chapter 3.

27. Selim Deringil, "The Ottoman Response to the Egyptian Crisis of 1881–82," *Middle Eastern Studies* 24 (1988): 3–24.

28. On Cromer, see Afaf Lutfi al-Sayyid, *Egypt and Cromer: A Study in Anglo-Egyptian Relations* (New York, 1969).

29. Eve Marie Troutt Powell, "Colonized Colonizers: Egyptian Nationalists and the Issue of the Sudan, 1875–1919" (Ph.D. diss., Harvard University, 1995), 98–99, rev. as id., *A Different Shade of Colonialism: Egypt, Great Britain and the Mastery of the Sudan* (Berkeley, Calif., 2003); Yitzhak Nakash, "Reflections on a Subsistence Economy: Production and Trade of the Mahdist Sudan, 1881–1898," in *Essays on the Economic History of the Middle East,* ed. Elie Kedourie and Sylvia G. Haim (London, 1988), 51–69.

30. Quote from Powell, "Colonized Colonizers," 151; see intro., chap. 3; see also FO 407/127, No. 91, Rodd to Kimberley, Cairo, 31 Aug. 1894, pp. 56–58; FO 407/127, No. 98, Rodd to Kimberley, Alexandria, 14 Sept. 1894, p. 62; FO 407/127, No. 121, Rodd to Kimberley, Cairo, 16 Sept. 1894, pp. 72–73.

31. Powell, "Colonized Colonizers," 180–81.

32. See, e.g., cartoons in *KK,* no. 92 (1923): 1; no. 132 (1923): 11; 4, no. 162 (1924): 20; 3, no. 153 (1924): 1; and *LM,* 11 July 1932, 24. See also Beth Baron, "Nationalist Iconography: Egypt as a Woman," in *Rethinking Nationalism in the Arab Middle East,* ed. James Jankowski and Israel Gershoni (New York, 1997), 105–24; Powell, *Different Shade of Colonialism,* 217–20.

33. Baer, *Studies in the Social History of Modern Egypt,* 3–16, quotation from p. 3.

34. Alexander Schölch, "The Egyptian Bedouins and the 'Urabiyun (1882)," *Die Welt des Islams* 17 (1976–77): 44–57.

35. Ibid., 44–45.

36. Thomas Russell Pasha, *Egyptian Service, 1902–1946* (London, 1949), 54–78.

37. Beth Baron, *The Women's Awakening in Egypt: Culture, Society, and the Press* (New Haven, Conn., 1994), 183–86; *MM* 10 (Nov. 1929): 389–90.

38. Ami Ayalon, *The Press in the Arab Middle East: A History* (New York, 1995); Baron, *Women's Awakening*, chap. 1.

39. FO 407/100, No. 26, Baring (Cromer) to Salisbury, Cairo, 25 Apr. 1890, p. 33.

40. Ibid., pp. 31–35; FO 407/100, No. 53, Baring (Cromer) to Salisbury, Cairo, 8 June 1890, p. 61.

41. Zachary Lockman, "The Egyptian Nationalist Movement and the Syrians in Egypt," *Immigrants and Minorities* 3 (1984): 233–51.

42. Baron, *Women's Awakening*, 26–27.

43. Religious minorities occasionally elected to go to the Islamic shariʿa courts. See Ron Shaham, "Jews and the Shariʿa Courts in Modern Egypt," *Studia Islamica* 82 (1995): 113–36.

44. Smith, "Origins of Nations," 123.

45. For background on the Copts in modern Egypt, see Doris Behrens-Abouseif, "The Political Situation of the Copts, 1798–1923," in *Christians and Jews in the Ottoman Empire*, ed. Benjamin Braude and Bernard Lewis (New York, 1982), 1: 185–205; Airi Tamura, "Ethnic Consciousness and Its Transformation in the Course of Nation-Building: The Muslim and the Copt in Egypt, 1906–1919," *Muslim World* 75 (1985): 102–14; Donald Malcolm Reid, "Archeology, Social Reform, and Modern Identity among the Copts (1854–1952)," in *Entre reforme sociale et mouvement national: Identité et modernisation en Egypte (1882–1962)*, ed. A. Rousillon (Cairo, 1995), 311–35; Subhi Labib, "The Copts in Egyptian Society and Politics, 1882–1919," in *Islam, Nationalism, and Radicalism in Egypt and the Sudan*, ed. Gabriel R. Warburg and Uri M. Kupferschmidt (New York, 1983); Thomas Philipp, "Nation State and Religious Community in Egypt—The Continuing Debate," *Die Welt des Islams* 28 (1988): 379–91.

46. Faruq Abu Zayd, *Azmat al-Fikr al-Qawmi fi al-Sihafa al-Misriyya* (Cairo, 1982), 58–59, cited in Israel Gershoni and James P. Jankowski, *Egypt, Islam, and the Arabs: The Search for Egyptian Nationhood, 1900–1930* (Oxford, 1986), 12.

47. See, e.g., *AN* 7, no. 9 (1883): 100; 8, no. 3 (1884): 142; *LM*, 29 Mar. 1920, 4; 11 July 1921, 7; Baron, "Iconography."

48. Malaka Saʿd, "al-Marʾa fi Misr," *JL* 1 (1908): 38–39.

49. Walid Kazziha, "The Jaridah-Ummah Group and Egyptian Politics," *Middle Eastern Studies* 13 (1977): 373–85; Arthur Goldschmidt Jr., "The Egyptian Nationalist Party: 1892–1919," in *Political and Social Change in Modern Egypt*, ed. P. M. Holt (London, 1968), 308–33; id., "The National Party from Spotlight to Shadow," *Asian and African Studies* 16 (1982): 11–30; Zachary Lockman, "The Social Roots of Nationalism: Workers and the National Movement in Egypt, 1908–19," *Middle Eastern Studies* 24 (1988): 445–59; Gershoni and Jankowski, *Egypt, Islam, and the Arabs*, 4–10.

50. Leila Ahmed, *Women and Gender in Islam: Historical Roots of a Modern Debate* (New Haven, Conn., 1992), 163.

51. Lila Abu-Lughod, "The Marriage of Islamism and Feminism in Egypt: Selective Repudiation as a Dynamic of Postcolonial Cultural Politics," in *Remaking Women: Feminism and Modernity in the Middle East*, ed. id. (Princeton, N.J., 1998), 243–69.

52. Clarissa Lee Pollard, "Nurturing the Nation: The Family Politics of the 1919 Egyptian Revolution" (Ph.D. diss., University of California, Berkeley, 1997).

53. For comparison, see Deniz Kandiyoti, "Some Awkward Questions on Women and Modernity in Turkey," in *Remaking Women*, 270–87; id., "End of Empire: Islam, Nationalism and Women in Turkey," in *Women, Islam and the State* (Philadelphia, 1991), 22–47; id., "Slave Girls, Temptresses, and Comrades: Images of Women in the Turkish Novel," *Feminist Issues* 8 (1988): 35–49.

54. See Baron, *Women's Awakening*.

55. Albert Hourani, *Arabic Thought in the Liberal Age, 1798–1939* (Cambridge, 1983), 164–70; Juan Ricardo Cole, "Feminism, Class, and Islam in Turn-of-the-Century Egypt," *IJMES* 13 (1981): 387–401; Arthur Goldschmidt Jr., *Biographical Dictionary of Modern Egypt* (Boulder, Colo., 2000), 22–23.

56. Qasim Amin, *Tahrir al-Mar'a* (Cairo, 1899); id., *al-Mar'a al-Jadida* (Cairo, 1900).

57. See Beth Baron, "The Making and Breaking of Marital Bonds in Modern Egypt," in *Women in Middle Eastern History*, ed. Nikki R. Keddie and Beth Baron (New Haven, Conn., 1991), 275–91.

58. Esther Moyal, "al-Sayyid 'Abd al-Khaliq al-Sadat wa-Karimatuhu," *AL*, 1 Aug. 1904, 83–84; Ahmad Baha' al-Din, *Ayyam Laha Ta'rikh* (Cairo, 1954), 1: 47–61; Abbas Kelidar, "Shaykh 'Ali Yusuf: Egyptian Journalist and Islamic Nationalist," in *Intellectual Life in the Arab East, 1890–1939*, ed. Marwan R. Buheiry (Beirut, 1981), 10–20; Yunan Labib Rizk, "Al-Ahram: A Diwan of Contemporary Life," *AH*, 6–12 Feb. 1997, 9.

59. Muhammad Farid, *The Memoirs and Diaries of Muhammad Farid, an Egyptian Nationalist Leader (1868–1919)*, trans. Arthur Goldschmidt Jr. (San Francisco, 1992), 19. The saga also inspired fiction, becoming the basis for Out El Kouloub's novel *Ramza*, trans. Nayra Atiya (Syracuse, N.Y., 1994), which was crafted out of stories Kouloub had heard in the harem as a child.

60. Fatima Rashid, "Kalima 'an al-Hal al-Hadira," *TM* 1 (1908): 76.

61. *AF*, 12 May 1911, cover; 29 May 1911, 4; 29 June 1911, cover.

62. 'Abd al-Hamid Hamdi, "al-Sufur," *SF*, 21 May 1915, 1; 22 May 1919, 1. See Beth Baron, "Unveiling in Early Twentieth-Century Egypt: Practical and Symbolic Considerations," *Middle Eastern Studies* 25 (1989): 370–86.

63. Baron, "Unveiling in Early Twentieth Century Egypt."

64. Fatima Rashid, "al-Wataniyya wa al-Mar'a," *TM* 1 (1908): 28.

65. F. J., "Kalima 'an Khutbat al-Anisa Victoria Sa'd," *JL* 9 (1916): 139.

66. Beth Baron, "Mothers, Morality, and Nationalism in Pre-1919 Egypt," in *The Origins of Arab Nationalism*, ed. Rashid Khalidi et al. (New York, 1991), 271–88.

67. FO 371/2355/4307, "Note from the Adviser of the Interior on the General Situation in Egypt," Cairo, 27 Dec. 1914, p. 9.

68. *AF*, 13 Oct. 1911, 6; see Baron, *Women's Awakening*, ch. 8.

69. *MSR*, 7 Mar. 1969, 44.

70. Correspondence from Arthur Goldschmidt Jr., who interviewed Farid's daughter (22 Feb. 1996).

71. Baron, *Women's Awakening*, 183–86.

72. Baron, "Mothers, Morality, and Nationalism in Pre-1919 Egypt."

73. FO 371/2355/4307, "Note from the Adviser," p. 9.

74. See Toledano, "Forgetting Egypt's Ottoman Past," 163–80.

75. Toledano, "Social and Economic Change," 264.

## CHAPTER TWO. CONSTRUCTING EGYPTIAN HONOR

1. This chapter elaborates some of the ideas presented in Beth Baron, "The Construction of National Honour in Egypt," *Gender and History* 5 (1993): 244–55. For comparison with other areas of the Middle East, see Afsaneh Najmabadi, "*Zanha-yi millat*: Women or Wives of the Nation?" *Iranian Studies* 26 (1993): 51–71; id., "The Erotic *Vatan* (Homeland) as Beloved and Mother: To Love, to Possess, and to Protect," *Comparative Studies in Society and History* 39 (1997): 442–67; Sheila Hannah Katz, "*Adam* and *Adama*, '*Ird* and *Ard*: En-gendering Political Conflict and Identity in Early Jewish and Palestinian Nationalisms," in *Gendering the Middle East: Emerging Perspectives*, ed. Deniz Kandiyoti (Syracuse, N.Y., 1996), 85–105.

2. Michael Herzfeld, "Honour and Shame: Problems in the Comparative Analysis of Moral Systems," *Man* 15 (1980): 339–51.

3. Hans Wehr, *A Dictionary of Modern Written Arabic*, 3d ed. (Ithaca, N.Y., 1976), 467, 604, 822.

4. See Michael E. Meeker, "Meaning and Society in the Near East: Examples from the Black Sea Turks and the Levantine Arabs," *IJMES* 7 (1976): 243–70.

5. See, e.g., Lama Abu-Odeh, "Crimes of Honour and the Construction of Gender in Arab Societies," in *Feminism and Islam: Legal and Literary Perspectives*, ed. Mai Yamani (London, 1996), 141–96; Richard T. Antoun, "On the Modesty of Women in Arab Muslim Villages: A Study in the Accommodation of Traditions," *American Anthropologist* 70 (1968): 671–97; and Gideon M. Kressel, "Sororicide/Filiacide: Homicide for Family Honor," *Current Anthropology* 22 (1981): 141–58.

6. Frank Henderson Stewart, *Honor* (Chicago, 1994).

7. For more on the relationship of honor and the state, see Beth Baron, "Women, Honor, and the State: The Evidence from Egypt," *Middle Eastern Studies* 42 (fothcoming). Nathan Brown argues that there was little resistance to the adoption of French law in place of the shari'a for criminal matters. See Nathan J. Brown, "Shari'a and State in the Modern Muslim Middle East," *IJMES* 29 (1997): 359–76.

8. Alexander Schölch, *Egypt for the Egyptians! The Socio-political Crisis in Egypt 178–1882* (London, 1981), 269, 288.

9. Ahmad 'Urabi, *Hatha Taqriri* (Cairo, 1981), 51; id., *The Defense Statement of Ahmad 'Urabi the Egyptian*, trans. Trevor Le Gassick (Cairo, 1982), 42.

10. For transformations of this term, see Ami Ayalon, *Language and Change in the Arab Middle East* (Oxford, 1987), 51–53.

11. 'Abd Allah al-Nadim, *Sulafat al-Nadim fi Muntakhabat* (Cairo, 1995), 218–53; Naffusa Zakariyya Sa'id, *'Abd Allah al-Nadim bayna al-Fusha wa al-'Amiyya* (Alexandria, 1966), 107–19.

12. Moustafa Kamel Pasha, *What the National Party Wants* (Cairo, 1907), 7.

13. Ibid., 12.

14. Ibid., 14, 23, 27, 28.

15. Ibid., 19.

16. P. J. Vatikiotis, *The History of Modern Egypt*, 4th ed. (Baltimore, 1991), 205.

17. Kamel, *What the National Party Wants*, 23.

18. Pierre Cachia, *Popular Narrative Ballads of Modern Egypt* (Oxford, 1989), 255–57. The ballad was recorded in 1959 by the staff of the Cairo Folk Arts Center, and the balladeer ascribed authorship to Mustafa Ibrahim Ajaj, who had died in 1936 (p. 247).

19. Ibrahim Hafiz, *Diwan Ibrahim Hafiz* (1937; 2d ed., Cairo, 1980), 2: 21, trans. in Mounah A. Khouri, *Poetry and the Making of Modern Egypt (1882–1922)* (Leiden, 1971), 86.

20. Khouri, *Poetry and the Making of Modern Egypt*, 88.

21. Quotation from ibid., 85.

22. Mahmud Tahir Haqqi's novel *'Adhra' Dinshaway* appeared in 1906; for a translation of what was, according to the translator, "a best-seller in its own day" (p. 5), see *Three Pioneering Egyptian Novels*, trans. Saad El-Gabalawy (Fredericton, N.B., 1986), 17–48. Hasan al-Mar'i's play *Hadithat Dinshaway* was censored and not performed on stage until the 1950s. A movie version also appeared. See Jacob M. Landau, *Studies in the Arab Theater and Cinema* (Philadelphia, 1958), 120–21, 202; and Ilhami Hasan, *Dirasa Mukhtasara 'an Ta'rikh al-Sinima al-Misriyya, 1896–1976* (Cairo, 1976).

23. Muhammad Farid, quoted in Khouri, *Poetry and the Making of Modern Egypt*, 89–90.

24. Khouri, *Poetry and the Making of Modern Egypt*, 94.

25. Ibid., 96.

26. FO 371/2357/195078, McMahon to Grey, Cairo, 7 Dec. 1915, translation of documents taken from prisoners after the Bir Mahdat Patrol Action.

27. Islamists also used the honor of Muslim women as a central motif in asserting the dangers that the West presented.

28. FO 141/189, Police Report, Cairo, 20 Apr. 1919.

29. FO 141/825/1132, procès-verbal, 27–28 Mar. 1919 at Azizia and Badrashein.

30. FO 371/3722/167843, Proceedings of the Court of Enquiry, Naslet El Shobak Incident, 12 June 1919, p. 24.

31. Ibid., 22–23.

32. Ibid., 59.

33. Ibid., quotation from 245, 246–48.

34. Ibid., quotation from 4, 246–48.

35. SD 883.00/158, Hampson to secretary of state, 9 Apr. 1919.

36. FO 141/684/9419, Circular: To the Bride-groom; see FO 371/376/77762, Allenby to Foreign Office, Cairo, 22 May 1919. The Arabic original is not in the file.

37. Marilyn Booth, *Bayram al-Tunisi's Egypt: Social Criticism and Narrative Strategies* (Oxford, 1990), 56–59.

38. FO 141/753/8955–4, pamphlet: "The Faith of Goodness Is in the Nation," Cairo, June 1919. *Zina'* (illicit sex) refers to adultery and rape; the latter term

would have been the better choice for translation. The original Arabic document was not preserved in the file.

39. FO 141/680/9527–2, Mohamed Badr El Din, report, "Waez Printing Press," Cairo, 25 July 1919. These circulars were sometimes transported by young girls: When one twelve-year-old daughter of the owner of a printing press who carried a basket on her head was arrested for carrying seditious literature, she claimed not to know the contents.

40. FO 371/3721/155070, *The Egyptian Circular*, ed. Kyriakos Mikhail, London, 15 Nov. 1919; FO 371/3721/159718, Tilley to Troup, London, 12 Dec. 1919.

41. FO 141/825/1132, Sherwen to Congreve, Cairo, 3 Jan. 1922.

42. For a discussion of the historicity of the novel, see Israel Gershoni, "Between Ottomanism and Egyptianism: The Evolution of 'National Sentiment' in the Cairene Middle Class as Reflected in Najib Mahfuz's *Bayn al-Qasrayn*," in *Studies in Islamic Society*, ed. Gabriel R. Warburg and Gad G. Gilbar (Haifa, 1984), 227–63, esp. 233–36.

43. Najib Mahfuz, *Bayna al-Qasrayn* (1956; repr., Cairo, 1979), 446–47; Naguib Mahfouz, *Palace Walk*, trans. William Maynard Hutchins and Olive E. Kenny (New York, 1990), 467–69.

44. For dramatists, see, e.g., Muhammad Mustafa Badawi, *Early Arabic Drama* (Cambridge, 1988), 85–101; Ibrahim Ramzi, *Abtal Mansura* (Cairo, 1915).

45. Cachia, *Popular Narrative Ballads*, 30. See the two versions, pp. 269–322, recorded in 1941 and 1971 respectively.

46. Ibid., 283–85.

47. Ibid., 291.

48. See, e.g., *LM*, 24 Feb. 1930, 1; 20 Oct. 1930, 29.

49. On prostitution in Egypt, see Bruce W. Dunne, "Sexuality and the 'Civilizing Process' in Modern Egypt" (Ph.D. diss., Georgetown University, 1996), 298.

50. Judith E. Tucker, *Women in Nineteenth-Century Egypt* (Cambridge, 1985), 150–55; Margot Badran, *Feminists, Islam, and Nation: Gender and the Making of Modern Egypt* (Princeton, N.J., 1995), chap. 10; SD 883.1151/2–2549, "Military Proclamation Abolishing Prostitution in Egypt," Cairo, 25 Feb. 1949; Dunne, "Sexuality," p. 298, n. 116, citing Law No. 68 of 1951. For comparison with prostitution in French Algeria, see Marnia Lazreg, *The Eloquence of Silence: Algerian Women in Question* (New York, 1994).

51. Ellis Goldberg noted the importance of debates on prostitution (and Christian proselytization) in the Egyptian press of the 1930s. See his "al-Bigha' wa al-Tabshir wa al-Kiyan al-Siyasi al-Misri" (Prostitution, Missionary Activity and the Egyptian Polity), *Abwab* 12 (Spring 1997): 64–73.

52. *HN*, 28 Aug. 1926, 3.

53. *NN* 3 (Dec. 1923): 145–46; 8 (April 1930): 109–10, 122; 9 (June 1931): 183–84; 10 (June 1932): 181–83.

54. Hasan al-Banna, *Five Tracts of Hasan Al-Banna' (1906–1949)*, trans. Charles Wendell (Berkeley, Calif., 1970), 127; Richard P. Mitchell, *The Society of the Muslim Brothers* (London, 1969), 27, 292.

55. Mustafa Muhammad al-Hadidi, "Mushkilat al-Bigha' al-Rasmi," *IM* 2 (Sifr 1353): 18.
56. FO 371/23305/1980, British Embassy to Halifax, Cairo, 5 May 1939.
57. FO 141/466/1429–1, Maxwell to McMahon, Cairo, 29 Sept. 1915.
58. Naguib Mahfouz, *Midaq Alley*, trans. Trevor Le Gassick, 2d ed. (Washington, D.C., 1989), 241–42.
59. See, e.g., *LM*, 4 Nov. 1935, 32; *KK* 5, no. 233 (1925): 20.
60. *LM*, 20 June 1927, 19. See also *LM*, 30 Apr. 1924, 32; *KK* 4, no. 185 (1924): 1; *KK* 11, no. 525 (29 May 1931): 32.
61. *RY*, 26 Nov. 1929, 7.
62. 'Ali Fahmi Kamil, "Mustaqbil al-Mar'a al-Misriyya," *NN* 2 (Oct. 1922): 62.
63. Fatima Rashid, "al-Wataniyya wa al-Mar'a," *TM* 1 (1908): 28.
64. Labiba Ahmad, "Karamat Misr," *NN* 6 (Nov. 1928): 362. See also *NN* 6 (July 1928): 217–18; 6 (Dec. 1928): 397–98; 11 (Mar. 1933): 63–65.
65. *AM*, 20 Feb. 1926, 1.
66. Huda Sha'rawi, *Mudhakkirat Huda Sha'rawi* (Cairo, 1981), 314–15.
67. FO 371/35533/1969, enclosure: Huda Sha'rawi, etc., to Churchill, 18 Apr. 1943.
68. FO 371/80601/1941–18, Campbell, Cairo, 15 May 1950; FO 371/80601/1941–24, Stevenson to Younger, Alexandria, 24 June 1950; FO 371/80601–29, Stevenson to Bevin, Alexandria, 5 Aug. 1950.

CHAPTER THREE. NATIONALIST ICONOGRAPHY

1. Here I take the "imagined" in Benedict Anderson's "imagined community" quite literally. Benedict Anderson, *Imagined Communities: Reflections on the Origin and Spread of Nationalism*, rev. ed. (London, 1991).
2. Robin Ostle examines general motifs and themes in the iconography of Egyptian nationalism in his "Modern Egyptian Renaissance Man," *Bulletin of the School of Oriental and African Studies* 57 (1994): 184–92. Here I focus on gendered representations of the nation.
3. See Maurice Agulhon, *Marianne into Battle: Republican Imagery and Symbolism in France, 1789–1880*, trans. Janet Lloyd (Cambridge, 1981).
4. One of the earliest representations of a modern nation was that of John Bull, who first appeared as a character representing the English nation in the early 1700s. He is considered a "personification of the English nation; Englishmen collectively, or the typical Englishman" (*Oxford English Dictionary* [1933; repr. Oxford, 1978], 5: 593). By the late 1890s, he had come to symbolize English imperialism.
5. See Irene L. Gendzier, *The Practical Visions of Ya'qub Sanu'* (Cambridge, Mass., 1966).
6. Blanchard Jerrold, *Egypt under Ismail Pacha* (London, 1879), 218–19, 222, 107.
7. Gendzier, *Practical Visions*, 70.
8. Ibid., 64; Irene L. Gendzier, "James Sanua and Egyptian Nationalism," *Middle East Journal* 15 (1961): 25.

9. On readers of the Arabic press, see Beth Baron, "Readers and the Women's Press in Egypt," *Poetics Today* 15 (1994): 217–40; Ami Ayalon, *The Press in the Arab Middle East* (Oxford, 1995), chap. 6.

10. 'Abd al-Latif Hamza claims that the paper *Abu Zayd* carried the first caricatures in the Egyptian press. I have been unable to trace this paper. See Hamza, *Adab al-Maqala al-Suhuf fi Misr* (Cairo, n.d.), 3: 69. For a brief history of the cartoon in Egypt, see Afaf Lutfi al-Sayyid Marsot, "The Cartoon in Egypt," *Comparative Studies in Society and History* 13 (1971): 2–15; Zahda, "al-Maistro," *RY,* 29 Oct. 1984, 34–37. For some related studies, see *Images d'Egypte: De la fresque à la bande dessinée* (Cairo, 1991); Allen Douglas and Fedwa Malti-Douglas, *Arab Comic Strips: Politics of an Emerging Mass Culture* (Bloomington, Ind., 1994). On the problems that contemporary Middle Eastern cartoonists have faced, see Garry Trudeau, "Drawing, Dangerously," *New York Times,* Sunday, 10 July 1994, Week in Review, 19.

11. See, e.g., *AN* 5, no. 11 (1881): 191; *al-Watani al-Misri* 1, no. 2 (1883): 127. I have used the copies of *Abu Naddara* and related journals reprinted in black and white in a multivolume set issued by Dar Sadir (Beirut, n.d.)

12. *Al-Nizarat al-Misriyya* 1, no. 7 (1880): 112; 19, no. 1 (1895): 6; 21, no. 3 (1897): 14; 26, no. 4 (1902): 42; 30, no. 10 (1906): 42.

13. *Abu Naddara Zarqa'* 7, no. 10 (1883): 101.

14. Ibid., no. 9 (1883): 100.

15. *AN* 8, no. 3 (1884): 142.

16. *AN* 18, no. 12 (1894): 50. France and Russia have been mislabeled in the cartoon.

17. For an interesting comparison, see Palmira Brummett, "Dogs, Women, Cholera, and Other Menaces in the Streets: Cartoon Satire in the Ottoman Revolutionary Press, 1908–11," *IJMES* 27 (1995): 433–60.

18. Marsot, "Cartoon in Egypt."

19. On the challenges contemporary Egyptian illustrators face in reaching viewers, see Nagwa Farag, "Illustrations: To Whom Is It Addressed?" in *Images d'Egypte,* 285–90. When cartoons first appeared in *al-Lata'if al-Musawwara,* the editor carefully explained the meaning he intended them to have.

20. Cartoons appeared in Salim Sarkis's *al-Mushir* in the mid-1890s.

21. 'Ali Fahmi Kamil, *Mustafa Kamil Basha fi 34 Rabi'an,* 9 vols. (Cairo, 1908–11), 3: 70–73; 'Abd al-Rahman al-Rafi'i, *Mustafa Kamil: Ba'ith al-Haraka al-Wataniyya, 1892–1908,* 5th ed. (Cairo, 1984), 61–63; Arthur Goldschmidt Jr., "The Egyptian Nationalist Party: 1892–1919," in *Political and Social Change in Modern Egypt,* ed. P. M. Holt (London, 1968), 313 n. 4.

22. A. F. Kamil, *Mustafa Kamil,* 3: 71.

23. Ibid., 3: 70; Rafi'i, *Mustafa Kamil,* 62.

24. *SHM,* 1: 454–55.

25. Liliane Karnouk, *Modern Egyptian Art: The Emergence of a National Style* (Cairo, 1988), 25–27; Iffat Naji et al., *Muhammad Naji (1888–1956)* (Cairo, n.d.), 53; Hamed Said, *Contemporary Art in Egypt* (Cairo, 1964), 120; Ostle, "Modern Egyptian Renaissance Man," 187.

26. See, e.g., *LM,* 1 Jan. 1923, 9; 30 Mar. 1925, 12.

27. *HN,* 8 Jan. 1927, 14; *SHM,* 1: 176, 178.

28. *LM*, 21 Feb. 1921, 5, 11; Rafiʻi, *Mustafa Kamil*, 296–98; Goldschmidt, "Egyptian Nationalist Party," 324, n. 6.

29. Rafiʻi, *Mustafa Kamil*, 297.

30. Beth Baron, "Unveiling in Early Twentieth Century Egypt: Practical and Symbolic Considerations," *Middle Eastern Studies* 25 (1989): 370–86.

31. *LM*, 21 Feb. 1921, 5, 11; *SHM*, 2: 1085; Rafiʻi, *Mustafa Kamil*, 298; Goldschmidt, "Egyptian Nationalist Party."

32. *NN* 6 (Apr. 1928), cover. The model of Mukhtar's sculpture appeared on the cover of the journal, usually in profile, from the time of its founding in 1921. For more on *al-Nahda al-Nisa'iyya*, see chapter 8.

33. *LM*, 24 May 1920, 8; 21 June 1920, 12; 28 June 1920, 1–8; 28 May 1928, 4, 9, 12–13; 27 Aug. 1934, 2; *RY*, 31 July 1928, 7; *KK*, no. 57 (1922): 16; 4, no. 165 (1924): 10; 4, no. 185 (1924): 1; 5, no. 216 (1925): 11; 6, no. 297 (1927): 1; 7, no. 353 (1928): 11. Badr al-Din Abu Ghazi, *Maththal Mukhtar* (Cairo, 1964); Karnouk, *Modern Egyptian Art*, 14–17; Israel Gershoni and James P. Jankowski, *Egypt, Islam, and the Arabs: The Search for Egyptian Nationhood, 1900–1930* (Oxford, 1986), 186–88; Daisy Griggs Philips, "The Awakening of Egypt's Womanhood," *Moslem World* 18 (1928): 402.

34. Karnouk, *Modern Egyptian Art*, 15.

35. See the model on the cover of *al-Nahda al-Nisa'iyya*.

36. Ruth Frances Woodsmall, *Moslem Women Enter a New World* (New York, 1936), 174, photo f. 168.

37. See, e.g., *NN* 6 (June 1928): 209.

38. Correspondence from Zachary Lockman, 7 Dec. 1992; Gershoni and Jankowski, *Egypt, Islam, and the Arabs*, 205.

39. Egypt has a long tradition of female statuettes, which served principally as fertility symbols and took the form of *ʻarusat al-mawlid* (brides of the birthday, specifically for the anniversary of the Prophet's birth). See Saphinaz Amalnaguib, "'Arusa: Doll, Bride or Fertility Symbol?" *Araby* 1 (1986): 3–10.

40. Muhammad Husayn Haykal's novel *Zaynab* (Cairo, 1914) presents a good example of this trend. The novel became the subject of one of the first Egyptian films.

41. For comparison with late Ottoman cartoons, see Brummett, "Dogs, Women, Cholera," and Fatma Müge Göçek, "From Empire to Nation: Images of Women and War in Ottoman Political Cartoons, 1908–1923," in *Borderlines: Genders and Identities in War and Peace, 1870–1930*, ed. Billie Melman (New York, 1998), 47–72.

42. P. J. Vatikiotis, *The History of Modern Egypt*, 4th ed. (Baltimore, 1991), 485.

43. Ayalon, *Press*, 78. I have not seen issues of *al-Kashkul* beyond May 1932.

44. FO 371/13880/8570, Annual Report for 1927–1928, Cairo, 26 Aug. 1929; Ayalon, *Press*, 149.

45. FO 371/10021/5233, Allenby to MacDonald, Cairo, 8 June 1924; see *al-Kashkul* (June 1924).

46. See, e.g., *KK* no. 77 (1922): 16; no. 78 (1922): 16; no. 86 (1923): 1; no. 88 (1923): 1; 3, no. 140 (1924): 11; 5, no. 233 (1925): 20; 5, no. 250 (1926): 1; 6, no. 301 (1927): 10; 10, no. 500 (1930): 32.

47. Janet L. Abu-Lughod, *Cairo: 1001 Years of the City Victorious* (Princeton, N.J., 1971), 125.

48. *LM,* 10 Oct. 1921, 4

49. *KK,* no. 135 (1923): 20.

50. *HN,* 13 Mar. 1926, 4

51. See, e.g., *LM,* 19 Jan. 1920, 3; *KK* 5, no. 241 (1925): 1; 6, no. 265 (1926): 1; 6, no. 275 (1926): 1; 6, no. 314 (1927): 1; 7, no. 328 (1927): 1; 8, no. 369 (1928): 1; 8, no. 371 (1928): 1.

52. See, e.g., *KK* no. 34 (1922): 16; 3, no. 140 (1924): 20; 6, no. 295 (1927): 1; *LM,* 16 July 1923, 16; 23 July 1923, 8; 10 June 1935, 32.

53. See, e.g., *KK* no. 51 (1922): 1; 10, no. 490 (1930): 1.

54. *LM,* 11 July 1932, 24. See also *KK,* no. 90 (1923): 9; 7, no. 350 (1928): 11; Eve M. Troutt Powell, *A Different Shade of Colonialism: Egypt, Great Britain, and the Mastery of the Sudan* (Berkeley, Calif., 2003), 217–20.

55. On postage stamps as a vehicle of iconographic propaganda, see Emmanuel Sivan, "The Arab Nation-State: In Search of a Usable Past," *Middle East Review* 19, no. 3 (1987): 21–30; and see also Donald M. Reid, "The Symbolism of Postage Stamps: A Source for the Historian," *Journal of Contemporary History* 19 (1984): 223–49.

56. Peter R. Feltus, *Catalogue of Egyptian Revenue Stamps* (Southfield, Mich., 1982): xviii–xix; *LM,* 21 Sept. 1925, 16 shows a picture of a new printer for producing stamps.

57. Donald M. Reid, "Egyptian History Through Stamps," *Muslim World* 62 (1972): 210–13; *Scott's Standard Postage Stamp Catalogue (1994),* 150th ed. (Sidney, Ohio, 1993), 3: 117–65.

58. Reid, "Egyptian History," 223; *Scott's Standard Postage Stamp Catalogue (1994),* 3: 117–22.

59. Yvert and Tellier-Champion, *Catalogue de timbres-poste,* 50th ed. (Amiens, 1946), 474. Cleopatra, a Ptolemy of Macedonian Greek descent, ruled Egypt from 51 to 30 B.C.

60. FO 371/13878/1666, clipping, "Battle for Bust of a Queen," *Daily Express,* 13 June 1929; FO 13878/1828, Chancery to Egyptian Dept., Berlin, 26 June 1929; Sir F. K. to Murray, 4 July 1929. *LM,* 1 July 1929, 15. The matter of the bust came up again in the wake of World War II when U.S. forces occupied the sector of Berlin that contained the museum in which it was displayed. Nefertiti appeared on an Egyptian postage stamp after the 1952 revolution.

61. Yvert and Tellier-Champion, *Catalogue,* 477–78.

62. Feltus, *Egyptian Revenue Stamps,* 200–201.

63. Yvert and Tellier-Champion, *Catalogue,* 477; *Scott's Standard Postage Stamp Catalogue (1994),* 3: 120.

64. Yvert and Tellier-Champion, *Catalogue,* 478; *Scott's Standard Postage Stamp Catalogue (1994),* 3: 121.

65. See, e.g., *LM,* 13 Apr. 1925, 4; 20 Dec. 1926, 8; 9 Dec. 1929, 13; 5 Feb. 1934, 17.

66. *LM,* 17 Sept. 1923, 16; see also *LM,* 25 June 1923, 16; 23 July 1923, 9; 27 Aug. 1923, 16.

67. See, e.g., *LM,* 4 Apr. 1932, 24, and 11 July 1932, 24.

68. *LM,* 21 Feb. 1921, 5.
69. Daisy Griggs Philips, "The Awakening of Egypt's Womanhood," *Moslem World* 18 (1928): 402.
70. See Selma Botman, *Engendering Citizenship in Egypt* (New York, 1999).
71. See *NN* 1 (Jan. 1921): cover, and following volumes.
72. *NN* 5 (Mar. 1927): cover.
73. See Baron, "Unveiling in Early Twentieth Century Egypt."
74. Ironically, when Egyptians began representing the nation as a woman, French and other European iconography of insurgency began to shift from female to male figures. Eric Hobsbawm, "Man and Woman in Socialist Iconography," *History Workshop* no. 6 (Autumn 1978): 124.

CHAPTER FOUR. PHOTOGRAPHY AND THE PRESS

1. Benedict Anderson, *Imagined Communities: Reflections on the Origin and Spread of Nationalism,* rev. ed. (London, 1991), 6.
2. For a comparative view of photography and nationalism, see, e.g., Donald E. English, *Political Uses of Photography in the Third French Republic, 1871–1914* (Ann Arbor, Mich., 1981); Ruth Oren, "Zionist Photography, 1920–41: Constructing a Landscape," *History of Photography* 19 (1995): 201–9. For interesting suggestions about femininity, photography, and nationalist representations, see Annelies Moors, "Embodying the Nation: Maha Saca's Post-Intifada Postcards," *Ethnic and Racial Studies* 23 (2000): 871–87.
3. Carney Gavin, "Photography and Social Sciences—in Light from Ancient Lands," in *The Invention of Photography and Its Impact on Learning* (Cambridge, Mass., 1989), 49; Nissan N. Perez, *Focus East: Early Photography in the Near East (1839–1885)* (New York, 1988), 15. For background on the history of photography, see Alma Davenport, *The History of Photography: An Overview* (Boston, 1991); Naomi Rosenblum, *A World History of Photography* (New York, 1981); and the essay by Susan Sontag, *On Photography* (New York, 1977).
4. Engin Çizgen, *Photography in the Ottoman Empire: 1839–1919* (Istanbul, 1987); Perez, *Focus East;* Filippo Zevi and Sergio Bosticco, *Photographers and Egypt in the Nineteenth Century* (Florence, 1984); Nazan Ölçer et al., *Images d'empire: Aux origines de la photographie en Turquie* (Istanbul, n.d.)
5. Many of the prints that survive are of good quality. Harvard University's Fine Arts Library houses an excellent collection of photography of the Middle East that was built around the Semitic Museum Photographic Archives. I thank Jeff Spurr and Andras Reidlmayer for sharing their knowledge of Middle Eastern photography.
6. See Sarah Graham-Brown, *Images of Women: The Portrayal of Women in Photography of the Middle East, 1860–1950* (New York, 1988); Irvin Cemil Schick, "Review Essay: Representing Middle Eastern Women: Feminism and Colonial Discourse," *Feminist Studies* 16 (1990): 345–80.
7. Perez, *Focus East,* 196. None of Mehmed Ali's daguerreotypes seem to have survived.
8. Lecture by Reza Shaikh on the "History of Photography in Iran" at Harvard University, 18 Apr. 1997.

9. Allen Williams, "The Abdul Hamid II Collection," *History of Photography* 3 (1984): 119–45; Carney Gavin, "Imperial Self-Portrait: The Ottoman Empire as Revealed in the Sultan Abdul-Hamid II's Photographic Albums Presented as Gifts to the Library of Congress (1893) and the British Museum (1894)," *Journal of Turkish Studies* 12 (1988); Elizabeth Brown Frierson, "Unimagined Communities: State, Press, and Gender in the Hamidian Era" (Ph.D. diss., Princeton University, 1996).

10. Gavin, "Photography and Social Sciences," 57; Perez, *Focus East,* 52–52, 214.

11. Gavin, "Photography and Social Sciences," 52–53, 59; Ibrahim Rif'at Pasha, *Mir'at al-Haramayn,* vol. 1 (Cairo, 1925).

12. Perez, *Focus East,* 191; Barry Iverson, "The Pictures of Garo Balian's Work: Photography in Egypt at the Turn of the Century," in *Garo Balian: An Ottoman Court Architect in Modern Egypt* (Cairo, 1994), 2–3.

13. Perez, *Focus East,* 233.

14. See, e.g., *MF,* 7 Mar. 1909, 1; *LM,* 5 Sept. 1927, 8–9.

15. SD 883.0128, Howell to secretary of state, Cairo, 22 Dec. 1922; FO 371/15290/3764, Graves, Cairo, 4 July 1931.

16. *AJ* 4 (1901): p. 9 of ads.

17. Huda Shaarawi, *Harem Years: The Memoirs of an Egyptian Feminist (1879–1924),* trans. and intro. Margot Badran (London, 1986), 38, 47; Fina Gued Vidal, *Safia Zaghloul* (Cairo, 1946), facing p. 12.

18. *LM,* 5 Sept. 1927, 13; *BU,* 2 Sept. 1927, 29; Gued Vidal, *Safia Zaghloul,* after title page. On family photographs, see Julia Hirsch, *Family Photographs: Content, Meaning, and Effect* (New York, 1981).

19. *MM* 7 (Apr. 1926): facing p. 184.

20. *SHM,* 2: 994.

21. *SHM,* 2: 999. Frierson notes that Ottoman girls and women often appeared in photographs carrying books or were shown reading (Frierson, "Unimagined Communities," 141).

22. For Malak Hifni Nasif, see *MM* 2 (Jan. 1921): 31; *HN,* 26 Nov. 1925, 3; 2 Dec. 1925, 4; *MM* 15 (Nov.–Dec. 1934): 397. For Labiba Ahmad, see *NN* 3 (July 1924): cover, and again 10 (Apr. 1932): 126; 4 (June 1926): 227; 6 (June 1928): 202; 8 (May 1930): cover, and again 8 (July 1930): cover; 11 (Mar. 1933): cover, and again 14 (Mar. 1936): 86; 12 (Mar. 1934): cover; and *LM,* 20 Mar. 1933, 25.

23. *HN,* 14 Oct. 1925, enclosure; see also *AR,* 2 Sept. 1925, 1.

24. Malaka Sa'd, *Rabbat al-Dar* (Cairo, 1915), 28.

25. Ronald Storrs, *The Memoirs of Sir Ronald Storrs* (New York, 1937), 98.

26. Byron D. Cannon, "Nineteenth-Century Arabic Writings on Women and Society: The Interim Role of the Masonic Press in Cairo—(al-Lata'if, 1885–1895)," *IJMES* 17 (1985): 463–84; Ami Ayalon, *The Press in the Arab Middle East: A History* (New York, 1995), 53–54.

27. *LM,* 14 Feb. 1916, 5; 14 Aug. 1916, 6; 4 Dec. 1916, 6.

28. *LM,* 21 July 1924, 1.

29. *LM,* 3 Dec. 1928, 9; 24 Dec. 1934, 13.

30. On the Sabunji brothers, see Perez, *Focus East,* 214; Çizgen, *Photography in the Ottoman Empire,* 114–18.

31. *SHM,* 1: 656–57, 667; *LM,* 29 July 1929, 31.

32. Iverson, "Photography," 3; *LM,* 18 Feb. 1934, 3.

33. *LM,* 12 Feb. 1917, 13; 4 Feb. 1918, 7; 22 May 1922, 13; 28 May 1928, 16; 27 Jan. 1930, 14.

34. *LM,* 23 May 1921, 3; 29 Nov. 1926, 6; 17 Apr. 1933, 20.

35. *LM,* 12 Dec. 1920, 7.

36. *LM,* 28 Feb. 1927, 1; on Labiba Ahmad, see chapter 8.

37. *SHM,* 1: 662–63; *LM,* 28 Dec. 1931, 2.

38. *LM,* 21 Aug. 1922, 2; 17 Mar. 1924, 7; *NN* 11 (Apr. 1933): 130–32 through 12 (Sept. 1934): 313–14.

39. *LM,* 28 May 1923, 5; 28 Nov. 1932, 4

40. *LM,* 12 Apr. 1921, 2.

41. *LM,* 13 Feb. 1924, 5.

42. FO 371/13880, Annual Report for 1927–28, Cairo, 26 Aug. 1929, p. 97; Ayalon, *Press,* 148–49.

43. *LM,* 31 Jan. 1916, 2; 27 Mar. 1916, 2, 7.

44. *LM,* 12 June 1933, 27; 26 Mar. 1934, 18, or 7 Jan. 1935, 31; 14 Jan. 1935, 31.

45. See, e.g., *LM,* 17 Feb. 1930, 30; 2 Nov. 1931, 23.

46. *LM,* 12 Apr. 1921, 2; 12 Dec. 1932, 2; 15 July 1929, 1; 1 Dec. 1930, 2.

47. For a cartoon of this competition, see *LM,* 1 Nov. 1920, 3.

48. Gershoni and Jankowski, *Redefining the Egyptian Nation,* 64. These authors give *al-Ithnayn*'s circulation in the mid-1940s as 90,000, compared to *al-Musawwar*'s 60,000.

49. *LM,* 30 Dec. 1935, 12.

50. *LM,* 8 June 1931, 13; *MM* 7 (Apr. 1926): facing 184.

51. *LM,* 9 Mar. 1934, 1.

52. *LM,* 22 July 1935, 29; 29 July 1935, 13; Munira Sabri, "The Girl Guide Movement," trans. A. Khaki in *The Bulletin* 29 (Oct. 1948): 4–5.

53. See, e.g., *LM,* 10 Apr. 1922, 8–9; 1 Mar. 1926, 12.

54. See, e.g., *LM,* 30 Sept. 1935, 30.

55. See, e.g., *LM,* 29 Sept. 1924, 8–9; 9 Mar. 1925, 8–9, 12; 1 Sept. 1930, 29; 11 Mar. 1929, 29; 31 Aug. 1925, 1.

56. See, e.g., *LM,* 26 Jan. 1931, 30; 1 Nov. 1926, 13; 1 Sept. 1930, 29.

57. On reading photographs, see Eric Margolis, "Mining Photographs: Unearthing the Meanings of Historical Photos," *Radical History Review* 40 (1988): 33–48; Allan Sekula, "On the Invention of Photographic Meaning," in *Photography in Print: Writings from 1816 to the Present,* ed. Vicki Goldberg (New York, 1981), 452–73.

58. *LM,* 21 June 1920, 1–7.

59. *LM,* 6 June 1921, 5.

60. *LM,* 13 Aug. 1923, 8.

61. *HN,* 20 Sept. 1927.

62. *LM,* 5 Sept. 1927, 16, reprinted 22 Aug. 1932, 12.

63. *LM,* 28 July 1930, 16–17.

64. See photos of Sharifa Riyad with Nahhas in *LM,* 20 May 1935, 2, and 25 Nov. 1935, 20; 2 Dec. 1935, 16–17.

65. *LM*, 4 Dec. 1922, 8; 14 Jan. 1935, 16–17.

66. See *LM*, 25 May 1931, 32.

67. See, e.g., *LM*, 5 Nov. 1923, 12; *HN*, 20 Sept. 1927.

68. *SHM*, 1: 2–5.

69. *SHM*, 2: 1419–27, quotation from 1419.

## CHAPTER FIVE. THE "LADIES' DEMONSTRATIONS"

1. Elite Egyptian women participated in nationalist demonstrations for the first time in 1919. Judith Tucker has discussed women's participation in revolts and uprisings in the nineteenth century. Judith E. Tucker, *Women in Nineteenth-Century Egypt* (Cambridge, 1985), 139–43.

2. The rich literature on collective memory is too lengthy to cite here. For an overview of the debates, see Alon Confino, "Collective Memory and Cultural History: Problems of Method," *American Historical Review* 102 (1997): 1386–1403.

3. James Gelvin argues that demonstrations are collective ceremonies that contain symbols and act, in their entirety, as a symbol. Borrowing from Clifford Geertz and others, he elaborates a methodology by which ceremonies might either be a "model of" reality ("a symbolic representation of social solidarity") or a "model for" reality ("the means by which hegemonic groups in society impose their values on subordinate groups"), or some combination thereof. James L. Gelvin, "Demonstrating Communities in Post-Ottoman Syria," *Journal of Interdisciplinary History* 25 (1994): 23–44, esp. 24, 29–31. See also Beth Baron, "The Meanings of Women's Demonstrations in the 1919 Egyptian Revolution" (in Arabic), *al-Nahj* 11, no. 41 (1995): 235–43.

4. For more on women's experiences of the war, see Beth Baron, "The Politics of Female Notables in Postwar Egypt," in *Borderlines: Genders and Identities in War and Peace, 1870–1930*, ed. Billie Melman (New York, 1998), 330–34.

5. *AH*, 17 Mar. 1919, 2; 21 Mar. 1919, 2.

6. SD 883.00/135, enclosure: petition dated 20 Mar. 1919.

7. *The Times* (London), 11 Apr. 1919, 11.

8. The most detailed attempt to sort out the events is John D. McIntyre Jr., *The Boycott of the Milner Mission: A Study in Egyptian Nationalism* (New York, 1985), 127–55. The section that follows is drawn from his chapter; the archives of the U.S. State Department; St. Antony's College, Oxford, Private Papers; *al-Ahram* and *The Times* (London); as well as (in order of publication): Thomas Russell, *Egyptian Service, 1902–1946* (London, 1949), 207–9; 'Abd al-Rahman al-Rafi'i, *Thawrat Sanat 1919: Ta'rikh Misr al-Qawmi min 1914 ila 1921* (1949; 3d ed., Cairo, 1968) 1: 126–30, 141–42; *Musawwar*, no. 237 (7 Mar. 1969): 42–47; Ijlal Khalifa, *al-Haraka al-Nisa'iyya al-Haditha: Qissat al-Mar'a al-'Arabiyya 'ala Ard Misr* (Cairo, 1973), 151–60; Afaf Lutfi al-Sayyid Marsot, "The Revolutionary Gentlewomen in Egypt," in *Women in the Muslim World*, ed. Lois Beck and Nikki Keddie (Cambridge, Mass., 1978), 261–76; Thomas Philipp, "Feminism and Nationalist Politics in Egypt," in *Women in the Muslim World*, 277–94; Huda Sha'rawi, *Mudhakkirat Huda Sha'rawi* (Cairo, 1981); Hanna F. Wissa, *Assiout—The Saga of an Egyptian Family* (Lewes, Sussex, 1994), 190–94,

206; Margot Badran, *Feminists, Islam, and Nation: Gender and the Making of Modern Egypt* (Princeton, N.J., 1995), 74–78.

9. The flag of the protectorate, like that of the Ottoman Empire, was red. Egypt adopted a green flag with one white crescent and three white stars in 1923. SD 883.015, Hampson to secretary of state, Cairo, 30 Apr. 1919; SD 883.015/4, Ives to secretary of state, Alexandria, 1 Sept. 1924; SD 883.015/12, Patterson to secretary of state, Cairo, 18 Dec. 1948.

10. SD 883.00/135, enclosure: petition dated 20 Mar. 1919.

11. The texts of this line vary, for they are translated from English (or French) into Arabic and back, and remembered differently.

12. SD 883.00/135, enclosure: petition dated 20 Mar. 1919.

13. St. Antony's College, Oxford, Private Papers, Thomas Russell Pasha, about 1 Apr. 1919; Thomas Russell, *Egyptian Service* (London, 1949), 208.

14. SD 883.00/135, enclosure: petition dated 20 Mar. 1919.

15. SD 883.00/130, enclosure: "The Egyptian Women to the American Diplomatic Agent and Consul-General, Cairo," 18 Mar. 1919; SD 883.00/135, enclosure: petition dated 20 Mar. 1919; SD 883.00/135, enclosure: "To the U.S. Diplomatic Agent in Egypt, Cairo," 24 Mar. 1919.

16. SD 883.00/130, enclosure: "The Egyptian Women to the American Diplomatic Agent and Consul-General, Cairo," 18 Mar. 1919.

17. Ibid.

18. SD 883.00/135, enclosure: "To the U.S. Diplomatic Agent in Egypt, Cairo," 24 Mar. 1919.

19. *The Times* (London), 11 Apr. 1919, 11.

20. See Badran, *Feminists*, 76–77.

21. The sociologists Howard Schuman and Jacqueline Scott have argued the general hypothesis "that memories of important political events and social changes are structured by age," and the more specific hypothesis "that adolescence and early adulthood is the primary period for generational imprinting in the sense of political memories." Howard Schuman and Jacqueline Scott "Generations and Collective Memories," *American Sociological Review* 54 (1989): 377.

22. Other fractures in collective memory have been explored in literature on the Middle East. Ted Swedenburg looks at differences between elite and nonelite as well as urban and rural memories in his *Memories of Revolt: The 1936–1939 Rebellion and the Palestinian National Past* (Minneapolis, 1995); Yael Zerubavel explores the ways the Left and Right have used collective memories to support their positions in her *Recovered Roots: Collective Memory and the Making of Israeli National Tradition* (Chicago, 1995). Nationalists and imperialists had distinctly different memories of the "ladies' demonstrations," but space does not permit exploration of changing British perspectives here.

23. Beth Baron, *The Women's Awakening in Egypt* (New Haven, Conn., 1994), 185.

24. Mounah A. Khouri, *Poetry and the Making of Modern Egypt (1882–1922)* (Leiden, 1971), 77–79.

25. Sha'rawi, *Mudhakkirat*, 191; *MSR*, 7 Mar. 1969, 44.

26. Hafiz Ibrahim, *Diwan Hafiz Ibrahim* (Cairo, 1980), 2: 87–88. I have used the English translation in Salama Musa, *The Education of Salama Musa,* trans. L. O. Schuman (Leiden, 1961), 106–7, with one minor modification.

27. Ahmad Amin, *Hayati* (Cairo, 1950), 189–90; id., *My Life,* trans. Issa J. Boullata (Leiden, 1978), 132.

28. Muhammad Sabry, *La Revolution égyptienne,* vol. 1 (Paris, 1919), quotation from p. 43; see also p. 42.

29. Ibid., 39, 67; Muhammad Sabry, *La Revolution égyptienne,* vol. 2 (Paris, 1921), facing p. 112.

30. See Afaf Lutfi al-Sayyid-Marsot, "Egyptian Historical Research and Writing on Egypt in the Twentieth Century," *Middle East Studies Association Bulletin* 7, no. 2 (1973): 6–7.

31. Rafi'i, *Thawrat 1919,* 1: 126–30, 141–42.

32. Salama Musa, *Tarbiyat Salama Musa* (Cairo, 1947), 150–51; id., *Education,* 105–6.

33. Ibid., 150.

34. See Baron, *Women's Awakening,* 109.

35. Najib Mahfuz, *Bayna al-Qasrayn* (1956; repr. Cairo, 1979), 341–42; Naguib Mahfouz, *Palace Walk,* trans. William Maynard Hutchins and Olive E. Kenny (New York, 1990), 374.

36. 'Abd al-'Azim Ramadan, *Tatawwur al-Haraka al-Wataniyya fi Misr min Sanat 1918 ila Sanat 1936,* 2d ed. (Cairo, 1983), 132–34.

37. *MSR,* 7 Mar. 1969, cover and 42–47.

38. *Scott's Standard Postage Stamp Catalogue (1994),* 150th ed. (Sidney, Ohio, 1993), 3: 134.

39. Joel Gordon, "Film, Fame, and Public Memory: Egyptian Biopics from *Mustafa Kamil* to *Nasser 56,*" *IJMES* 31 (Feb. 1999), 72.

40. *FS* 20 (June 1926): 454.

41. *MM* 7 (Feb. 1926): 83.

42. *MHR,* 15 Dec. 1937, 74–75; Huda Shaarawi, *Harem Years: The Memoirs of an Egyptian Feminist,* trans. and intro. Margot Badran (London, 1986), preface; the British edition is used here throughout.

43. For an account of the publishing history of the Arabic and English memoirs, see Margot Badran, "To the Editor," *Women's Review of Books* 5 (Feb. 1988): 5; Shaarawi, *Harem Years,* preface.

44. Sha'rawi, *Mudhakkirat,* 188–91; Shaarawi, *Harem Years,* 112–14; Russell, *Egyptian Service,* 208. Badran mentions in the preface to the English translation that she intervened in the text to preserve the narrative flow (p. 3). Leila Ahmed criticized Badran for her handling of a text so central to "our mothers' memories." Shaarawi, *Harem Years,* 2–3; Leila Ahmed, "Women of Egypt," *Women's Review of Books* 5 (Nov. 1987): 8; and Badran's reply, "To the Editor." An American edition of the translation published by the Feminist Press also exists in a slightly different format.

45. Sha'rawi, *Mudhakkirat,* 188–89; *MSR,* 7 Mar. 1969, 43.

46. Sha'rawi, *Mudhakkirat,* 190–91.

47. Duriyya Shafiq, *al-Mar'a al-Misriyya* (Cairo, 1955); 118–27; Cynthia Nelson, *Doria Shafik, Egyptian Feminist: A Woman Apart* (Gainesville, Fla., 1996), 85–86.

48. Bahija Sidqi Rashid, Tahiyya Muhammad Isfahani, and Samiyya Sidqi Murad, *al-Ittihad al-Nisa'i al-Misri* (Cairo, 1973), 27–29; Wissa, *Assiout*, 190–94, 197.

49. *MSR*, 7 Mar. 1969, 44–47.

50. Wissa, *Assiout*, 190–94, 206, quotation from p. 192; Sha'rawi, *Mudhakkirat*, 190.

51. Rashid, *al-Ittihad al-Nisa'i al-Misri*, 28.

52. Ibid., 7.

53. Khalifa, *al-Haraka al-Nisa'iyya al-Haditha*, 156.

54. Marsot, "Revolutionary Gentlewomen," 275–76 n. 10.

55. Ibid., 269.

56. Salim, *Taghyir*, 29.

57. Marsot, "Revolutionary Gentlewomen, 269.

58. Khalifa, *al-Haraka al-Nisa'iyya al-Haditha*, 158.

59. Nawal El Saadawi, *The Hidden Face of Eve: Women in the Arab World*, trans. Sherif Hetata (London, 1980), 176.

60. SD 883.407/1, Fish to secretary of state, "List of Official Egyptian Holidays," Cairo, 11 Jan. 1937; SD 883.407/2, Merriam to secretary of state, "Egyptian National Holidays," Ramleh, 13 Sept. 1938; Emmanuel Sivan, "The Arab Nation-State: In Search of a Usable Past," *Middle East Review* 19, no. 3 (1987): 26.

61. Rania Khallaf, "Women Rally for Equality," *al-Ahram Weekly*, 9–15 June 1994, 1.

62. *LM*, 21 Apr. 1919, 4.

63. *MSR*, 7 Mar. 1969, 43.

64. *SHM*, 1: 94.

65. Shaarawi, *Harem Years*, 21; Huda discusses the April demonstration on p. 118; Sarah Graham-Brown, *Images of Women: The Portrayal of Women in Photography of the Middle East, 1860–1950* (New York, ), 225.

66. See Ahmad Shafiq, *Hawliyyat Misr al-Siyasiyya* (Cairo, 1926), 1: 314–16.

67. *LM*, 21 Apr. 1919, 6.

68. Khalifa, *al-Haraka al-Nisa'iyya al-Haditha*, 153; Shaarawi, *Harem Years*, 117. The photo in *Harem Years* came from the private collection of Hawa Idris, cousin and confidante of Huda Sha'rawi (*Harem Years*, vii, 3). A highly stylized version appears on the jacket of Badran's *Feminists, Islam, and Nation* with women on the front and men on the back.

69. *LM*, 5 May 1919, 6.

70. *LM*, 13 Nov. 1919, 8; 20 Mar. 1933, 14–15.

71. *MSR*, 7 Mar. 1969, cover.

72. *SHM*, 1: 94. Two other photos in this set are purportedly from 1919 (1: 95). One shows Safiyya Zaghlul and friends in street dress and was taken upon the occasion of Safiyya's departure for Gibraltar in October 1922. The other shows female students carrying the banner of the Saniyya School and a photo of Sa'd Zaghlul; that one woman carries a wreath suggests that they might be laying it on a tomb, possibly Sa'd's, which would date the photo to 1927.

73. 'Abd al-Fattah 'Abada, *Nahdat al-Mar'a al-Misriyya wa al-Mar'a al-'Arabiyya fi al-Ta'rikh* (Cairo, 1919), 22–27.

74. *SHM*, 2: 1014–15.

75. Shaarawi, *Harem Years*, 116.

76. *LM*, 12 Apr. 1921, 7.

77. *LM*, 9 May 1921, 11.

78. Shaarawi, *Harem Years*, 115.

79. *LM*, 19 Mar. 1928, 4.

80. Khalifa, *al-Haraka al-Nisa'iyya*, 166.

81. *SHM*, 1: 192.

82. *LM*, 28 Apr. 1919, 4.

83. Grace Thompson Seton, *A Woman Tenderfoot in Egypt* (New York, 1923), facing p. 30.

84. Sabry, *Revolution égyptienne*, vol. 2, facing p. 112.

85. Malak Badrawi, *Isma'il Sidqi (1875–1950)* (Curzon, 1996), 82c; SD 883.00/135, enclosure: petition dated 20 Mar. 1919.

86. *BU*, 16 Sept. 1927, 33.

87. Sha'rawi, *Mudhakkirat*, 190–91.

CHAPTER SIX. MOTHER OF THE EGYPTIANS

1. SD 883.00/135, enclosure: petition dated 20 Mar. 1919; Fahima Thabit, *al-Za'im al-Khalid wa-Umm al-Misriyyin fi Manfan Jabal Tariq* (Cairo, 1948), 15; Beth Baron, "Mothers, Morality, and Nationalism in Pre-1919 Egypt," in *The Origins of Arab Nationalism*, ed. Rashid Khalidi et al. (New York, 1991), 271–88.

2. One exception is a reprint of a photo of Queen Nazli with her face covered that first appeared in the English press and was reprinted in *LM*, 30 May 1927, 16, and *HN*, 4 June 1927, cover. There was a scandal in 1937 when, after the king's death, the queen appeared in photos in *al-Ahram* and elsewhere taken on a visit to England that showed her unveiled and walking in front of, rather than behind, her son, King Farouk. FO 371/20883/1341, Lampson to Oliphant, Cairo, 10 Mar. 1937.

3. *LM*, 20 Jan. 1930, 16–17.

4. *LM*, 20 June 1921, 5.

5. Fina Gued Vidal, *Safia Zaghloul* (Cairo, 1946).

6. Thabit, *Fi Manfan Jabal Tariq*.

7. See photos in *Safia Zaghloul*, after title page, facing pp. 12 and 49.

8. Ibid., 15, picture facing p. 48.

9. Amira al-Azhary Sonbol, "Adoption in Islamic Society: A Historical Survey," in *Children in the Muslim Middle East*, ed. Elizabeth Warnock Fernea (Austin, Tex., 1995), 45–67.

10. Gued Vidal, *Safia Zaghloul*, 16–17, 81–82, 92.

11. Ibid., 19–20; *MQ*, June 1928, 687, cited in Mary Flounders Arnett, "Qasim Amin and the Beginnings of the Feminist Movement in Egypt" (Ph.D. diss., Dropsie College, Philadelphia, 1965), 78. On Sa'd Zaghlul, see Afaf Lutfi al-Sayyid-Marsot, *Egypt's Liberal Experiment, 1922–1936* (Berkeley, Calif.,

1977), chaps. 2–3; Elie Kedourie, "Sa'd Zaghlul and the British," in *The Chatham House Version and Other Middle-Eastern Studies* (London, 1970), 82–159; 'Abbas Mahmud 'Aqqad, *Sa'd Zaghlul: Sira wa-Tahiyya*.

12. For more on the localizing of Ottoman-Egyptians, see chapter 1.

13. Gued Vidal, *Safia Zaghloul*, 21–22.

14. Ibid., 54.

15. Thabit, *Fi Manfan Jabal Tariq*, 77–78.

16. See ibid.

17. See, e.g., *HN*, 4 Nov. 1925, insert; 1 Oct. 1926, cover; *LM*, 5 Sept. 1927, 13; *MM* 8 (Sept. 1927): 293.

18. Qasim Amin, *al-Mar'a al-Jadida* (Cairo, 1900), preface; on debates over marriage, see Beth Baron, "The Making and Breaking of Marital Bonds in Modern Egypt," in *Women in Middle Eastern History*, ed. Nikki R. Keddie and Beth Baron (New Haven, Conn., 1991), 275–91.

19. Gued Vidal, *Safia Zaghloul*, 34–35.

20. SD 883.00/135, "To the Diplomatic Agent and Consul General of the U.S., Cairo," 20 Mar. 1919; Gued Vidal, *Safia Zaghloul*, 32–33.

21. Gued Vidal, *Safia Zaghloul*, 33–34. Use of the title "Mother of the Egyptians" became particularly widespread from 1922: see the article from *al-Balagh* reprinted in *NN* 5 (Oct. 1927): 348–49.

22. Arthur Goldschmidt Jr., *Biographical Dictionary of Egypt* (Boulder, Colo., 2000), 235.

23. FO 407/184/286, Allenby to Curzon, 20 Apr. 1919, enclosure: "Colonel Symes' Note on Interview with the Sultan, Apr. 17, 1919," quoted in John D. McIntyre Jr., *The Boycott of the Milner Mission: A Study in Egyptian Nationalism* (New York, 1985), 136.

24. *LM*, 12 Apr. 1921, 1–12; "A Record Ovation for Lord Zaghlul," *Egyptian Mail* (6 Apr. 1921), in Grace Thompson Seton, *A Woman Tenderfoot in Egypt* (New York, 1923), 22.

25. Seton, *Woman Tenderfoot*, 32.

26. Gued Vidal, *Safia Zaghloul*, 38–39.

27. Huda Sha'rawi, *Mudhakkirat Huda Sha'rawi* (Cairo, 1981), 234; see Huda Shaarawi, *Harem Years: The Memoirs of an Egyptian Feminist*, trans. and intro. Margot Badran (London, 1986), 124–25.

28. FO 141/511/14086–3, Saphia Zaghloul [Safiyya Zaghlul] to Allenby, Cairo, 25 Dec. 1921.

29. FO 141/511/14086–1, "Minute, Cairo Residency," 25 Dec. 1921; FO 141/511/14086–4, Ryder, Cairo, 25 Dec. 1921. See also Gued Vidal, *Safia Zaghloul*, 39–40, and Seton, *Woman Tenderfoot*, 25–26.

30. *BU*, 31 Dec. 1921, reprinted 2 Sept. 1927, 27; "Mme. Zaghlul's Appeal," in Seton, *Woman Tenderfoot*, 28. This is not the English translation of the Arabic appeal on p. 27, as Seton suggests.

31. Ibid.

32. FO 141/511/14086–7, "Telegram from Members of Edinburgh Egyptian Society to Madame Zaghloul in Cairo," 1 Jan. 1922.

33. FO 141/511/14086–8, Saphia Zaghloul to Mrs. Barnes in London, 1 Jan. 1922; FO 141/511/14086–10, Saphia Zaghloul to Olagnier in Paris, 15 Jan. 1922.

34. FO 141/511/14086–11, Safia Zaghloul, "The Appeal of the Leader's Wife," Cairo, 4 Feb. 1922; the Arabic original of this appeal can be found in Seton, *Woman Tenderfoot*, 27.

35. FO 141/511/14086–12, oriental secretary to Monteith-Smith, 4 Feb. 1922.

36. Seton, *Woman Tenderfoot*, 25.

37. Ibid., 24, 45, facing p. 20. Other women also made dresses with a flag affixed; see *LM*, 27 Apr. 1931, 29.

38. FO 141/511/14086–11, letter from Mme Zaghloul Pasha to her husband, Cairo, 5 Feb. 1922 (translated from the Arabic), 1. On the censoring of this and other letters, see FO 141/511/14086–13, 14, and 16.

39. Ibid.; Seton, *Woman Tenderfoot*, 34–35.

40. FO 141/511/14086–11, letter from Mme Zaghloul Pasha to her husband, Cairo, 5 Feb. 1922, 1–3.

41. Gued Vidal, *Safia Zaghloul*, 41–42; Seton, *Woman Tenderfoot*, 25.

42. FO 141/511/14086–15, House of Commons, parliamentary question, London, 12 Apr. 1922; Gued Vidal, *Safia Zaghloul*, 45.

43. FO 371/7735/7203, Saphia Zaghloul to colonial secretary, 8 July 1922.

44. FO 141/511/14086–18, Kamal to Allenby, 9 Aug. 1922; FO 141/511/14086–19, first secretary to Saphia Zaghlul, Ramleh, 10 Aug. 1922; FO 141/511/14086–20, Allenby's private secretary to Madam Abdel Salam Bey Fahmy, Ramleh, 24 Aug. 1922; FO 141/511/14086–21, Allenby's secretary to Saphia Zaghlul, Ramleh, 3 Sept. 1922; FO 371/7735/7132, Foreign Office telegram to Allenby in Ramleh, 20 July 1922.

45. FO 141/411/14086–22, telegram from Saphia Zaghloul to Allenby, Cairo, 22 Sept. 1922; FO 141/411/14086–26, telegram from Madame Zaghlul to high commissioner, Cairo, 24 Sept. 1922; FO 141/411/14086–47, Mackintosh to the residency, Cairo, 8 Oct. 1922; Thabit, *Fi Manfan Jabal Tariq*.

46. FO 141/511/14086–34, Badr El Din to the residency, Cairo, 28 Sept. 1922; FO 141/511/14086–36, residency to Badr el Din, Ramleh, 30 Sept. 1922; FO 141/511/14086–37, minute, 2 Oct. 1922; FO 141/511/14086–42, minute, 6 Oct. 1922.

47. *MM* 3 (Oct. 1922): 351.

48. SD 883.00/431, enclosure: "Cairo's Goodbye to Madame Zaghlul," *Egyptian Mail*, 9 Oct. 1922.

49. Ibid.; SD 883.00/431, Howell to secretary of state, Cairo, 16 Oct. 1922; FO 141/511/14086–39, Mackintosh to the residency, Cairo, 4 Oct. 1922; FO 141/511/14086–43, minute, 10 Oct. 1922; see also Thabit, *Fi Manfan Jabal Tariq*, 21.

50. "Cairo's Goodbye," *Egyptian Mail*, 9 Oct. 1922; *LM*, 16 Oct. 1922: 8–9.

51. *MM* 3 (Oct. 1922): 349–50; FO 141/511/14086–39, Mackintosh to the residency, Cairo, 4 Oct. 1922; *LM*, 16 Oct. 1922, 8–9.

52. FO 141/511/14086–43, minute, 10 Oct. 1922.

53. *NN* 2 (Oct. 1922): facing p. 58; see picture *MM* 3 (Oct. 1922): 347.

54. *LM*, 16 Jan. 1922, 5.

55. *LM*, 16 Oct. 1922, 1. The photo was reprinted a decade later in *LM*, 7 Nov. 1932, 11.

56. *NN* 2 (Oct. 1922): facing p. 58; *MM* 3 (Oct. 1922): 347; *FS* 22 (Nov. 1927): 81; *LM*, 17 Sept. 1923, 1; *NN* 8 (Dec. 1930): 422.

57. FO 141/511/14086–54, "Thanks from the President to the Nation," Gibraltar, 16 Oct. 1922.

58. Thabit, *Fi Manfan Jabal Tariq*, 21, 77.

59. See, e.g., *MM* 4 (Apr. 1923): 222.

60. Gued Vidal, *Safia Zaghloul*, 49.

61. *LM*, 7 May 1923, 1; 14 May 1923, 1; 4 June 1923, 1; 9 July 1923, 1; 6 Aug. 1923, 9.

62. Thabit, *Fi Manfan Jabal Tariq*, 114.

63. Debates about unveiling had flourished in the women's press and other publications for a few decades. See Beth Baron, "Unveiling in Early Twentieth Century Egypt: Practical and Symbolic Considerations," *Middle Eastern Studies* 25 (1989): 370–86.

64. Personal communication from Saiza Nabarawi to Margot Badran, cited in Shaarawi, *Harem Years*, 129–30, 147 n. 21.

65. Sha'rawi, *Mudhakkirat*, 291–92.

66. Gued Vidal, *Safia Zaghloul*, 52; Thabit, *Fi Manfan Jabal Tariq*, 121–25.

67. *LM*, 24 Sept. 1923, 4; *NN* 3 (Oct. 1923): 85; Gued Vidal, *Safia Zaghloul*, 52–53.

68. *MM* 4 (Sept. 1923): 382; see also *SR* 5 (15 Nov. 1923): 36–39, where Safiyya's photo appears on the occasion of their return.

69. *LM*, 1 Oct. 1923, 9; *HN*, 23 Sept. 1925, 1. A third print from the photo session appears in *AR*, 4 Feb. 1925, 1, and *SHM*, 1: 86.

70. *LM*, 17 Sept. 1923, 16; 25 June 1923, 16; 30 July 1923, 16; see chapter 3.

71. *MM* 5 (15 Apr. 1924): 220; Gued Vidal, *Safia Zaghloul*, 54–55.

72. SD 883.43/12–1747, Tuck to secretary of state, Cairo, 17 Dec. 1947; Shaarawi, *Harem Years*, 136–37.

73. FO 371/10021/6467, Allenby to MacDonald, Ramleh, 21 July 1924, enclosure 2, p. 3, enclosure 3, pp. 4–5. On Avierino, see Beth Baron, *The Women's Awakening in Egypt* (New Haven, Conn., 1994), 17–20.

74. *LM*, 4 Aug. 1924, 8–9.

75. *LM*, 12 Oct. 1924, 1, reprinted in *BU*, 7 Oct. 1927, 4; *LM*, 3 Nov. 1924, 8; 10 Nov. 1924, 4.

76. FO 141/511/14086–61, Elgood to Furness, Cairo, 27 Nov. 1924.

77. Quotation from *FS* 22 (Nov. 1927): 81; *HN*, 23 Sept. 1925, cover; 30 Sept. 1925, enclosure; 14 Oct. 1925, 6; 21 Oct. 1925, enclosure; 11 Nov. 1925, enclosure; 3 July 1926, 8–9. The enclosed pictures were "presents" from the journal to subscribers.

78. SD 883.0131/4, Gunther, "Memorandum on the Outstanding Characteristics of the Feminist Movement in Egypt," Alexandria, 12 Sept. 1930, p. 7.

79. *BU*, 2 Sept. 1927, 27; *HN*, 20 Sept. 1927, 1; *L'Egyptienne* 8 (Oct. 1932); *LM*, 7 Nov. 1932, 1; *MHJ* 1 (Dec. 1937): insert.

80. *LM*, 19 Oct. 1931, 1, 16.

81. *AR*, 18 Feb. 1925, 1, 8.

82. *HN*, 4 Nov. 1925, enclosure; 1 Oct. 1926, cover.

83. *HN,* 5 Oct. 1927, 2.

84. *MM* 8 (Sept. 1927): 315–16; Gued Vidal, *Safia Zaghloul,* 64.

85. See photos in *HN,* 20 Sept. 1927; *LM,* 5 Sept. 1927, 16.

86. FO 371/12359/2450, Henderson to Chamberlain, Ramleh, 27 Aug. 1927; FO 371/12359/2470, Henderson to Murray, Ramleh, 27 Aug. 1927; Gued Vidal, *Safia Zaghloul,* 65.

87. 'Abd al-Rahman al-Rafi'i, *Mustafa Kamil: Ba'ith al-Haraka al-Wataniyya, 1892–1908,* 5th ed. (Cairo, 1984), 274–80.

88. *HN,* 12 Oct. 1927, 12–13.

89. Gued Vidal, *Safia Zaghloul,* 69–72, 80.

90. See, e.g., *LM,* 12 Sept. 1927, 4, 13; 19 Sept. 1927, 1; 10 Oct. 1927, 1; 14 Nov. 1927, 13; 19 Nov. 1928, 4; 4 Nov. 1929, 1.

91. FO 371/13880/2420, Lloyd to Henderson, Cairo, 9 July 1929, "Egypt: Report for 1927 and 1928"; *MM* 8 (Sept. 1927): 308; *LM,* 7 Dec. 1931, 4; Gued Vidal, *Safia Zaghloul,* 105, 116; Veronica Seton-Williams and Peter Stocks, *Blue Guide Egypt* (New York, 1984), 181: tomb of Sa'd Zaghlul and the Bayt al-Ummah Museum.

92. *MSR,* 20 Jan. 1928, 2–3, cited in Ralph M. Coury, "The Politics of the Funereal: The Tomb of Saad Zaghlul," *Journal of the American Research Center in Egypt* 29 (1992): 192 n. 6; on the debate over the pharaonic characteristics of the mausoleum, see Israel Gershoni and James P. Jankowski, *Egypt, Islam and the Arabs: The Search for Egyptian Nationhood, 1900–1930* (New York, 1986), 188–89.

93. Coury, "Politics of the Funereal," 191–200; Gued Vidal, *Safia Zaghloul,* 72–73; *NN* 5 (Dec. 1927): 412; *LM,* 23 May 1932, 4, for a picture of a worker transporting mummies by cart, and 19 Aug. 1935, 32, for a cartoon satirizing the struggle.

94. Coury, "Politics of the Funereal," 191–200; Gued Vidal, *Safia Zaghloul,* 72–73.

95. *NN* 14 (July 1936): 219; Gued Vidal, *Safia Zaghloul,* 73–74, 92.

96. *LM,* 8 Dec. 1930, 1; *HL* 39 (Jan. 1931): 327; *LM,* 20 Feb. 1933, 17, and 4 June 1934, 8; Gued Vidal, *Safia Zaghloul,* facing p. 96.

97. Gershoni and Jankowski, *Egypt, Islam and the Arabs,* 189–90; Badr al-Din Abu Ghazi, *Maththal Mukhtar* (Cairo, 1964).

98. SD 883.413, Fish to secretary of state, "Unveiling of Statues of Zaghloul Pasha in Alexandria and Cairo," Ramleh, 7 Sept. 1938; Gued Vidal, *Safia Zaghloul,* 83–84, 93–96, 136.

99. FO 371/12359/2730, Henderson to Patrick, Ramleh, 24 Sept. 1927.

100. FO 371/12359/2730, Henderson to Patrick, Ramleh, 24 Sept. 1927. See also SD 883.00/620, Winship to secretary of state, Ramleh, 20 Sept. 1927; *HN,* 5 Oct. 1927, 15.

101. FO 141/511/14086–62, Lloyd to Chamberlain, 23 July 1928; *LM,* 30 July 1928, 16; Gued Vidal, *Safia Zaghloul,* 74–76.

102. Quotation from *NN* 8 (Dec. 1930): 422. For photos from the trip, see *LM,* 23 June 1930, 4, and 17 Nov. 1930, 1, 4.

103. FO 371/14622/3799, Loraine to Henderson, Cairo, 13 Nov. 1930.

104. FO 371/14622/3810, Loraine to Henderson, Cairo, 15 Nov. 1930; FO 371/15405/1611, Diller, minutes, 21 May 1931.

105. See, e.g., *KK*, 18 Aug. 1928, 11; 15 Feb. 1929, 1.

106. *KK* 10 (30 Jan. 1931): 32. See Gued Vidal, *Safia Zaghloul*, 77–78; FO 371/12359/2450, Henderson to Chamberlain, Ramleh, 27 Aug. 1927.

107. FO 371/15405/1611, Stevenson to Henderson, Cairo, 8 May 1931; Sha'rawi, *Mudhakkirat*, 438; *KK*, 12 May 1931, 16.

108. See, e.g., *LM*, 5 Jan. 1931, 1; 9 Mar. 1931, 4; 5 Oct. 1931, 12–13.

109. See, e.g., *LM*, 22 June 1931, 13; 6 July 1931, 17. See also *LM*, 26 Nov. 1934, 20, and 9 Dec. 1935, 1.

110. *LM*, 25 Apr. 1932, 1; FO 371/16110/3068, Campbell to Simon, Cairo, 4 Nov. 1932; FO 371/16110/3074, "The Quarrel in the Wafd," *The Times* (London), 16 Nov. 1932; FO 371/16110/3197, Loraine to Simon, Cairo, 19 Nov. 1932.

111. *L'Egyptienne* 8 (Oct. 1932): plate.

112. *LM*, 8 Feb. 1932, 1; 9 Oct. 1933, 1; 27 Aug. 1934, 1.

113. *LM*, 15 Oct. 1934, 4.

114. *LM*, 26 Feb. 1934, 16–17.

115. *LM*, 26 Nov. 1934, 1, 13; 10 Dec. 1934, 1.

116. Gued Vidal, *Safia Zaghloul*, 78–81.

117. SD 883.00/854, Merriam to secretary of state, Cairo, 2 Oct. 1935; Fatima al-Yusuf, *Dhikrayat* (1953; repr. Cairo, 1976), 195.

118. Gued Vidal, *Safia Zaghloul*, 85–87. Munira Thabit recounted a humorous occasion when Safiyya received female delegations from the Nahhasites and the Sa'dists and treated both with the utmost respect (*AM*, 15 Jan. 1952, 18–20).

119. *HN*, Sept. 1927, 13, for a picture of Safiyya with her sister Fahima Sarhank; Gued Vidal, *Safia Zaghloul*, 107.

120. *Al-Ithnayn wa al-Dunya*, 13 Mar. 1944, in *Safia Zaghloul*, 119–125, quotations from pp. 120–21.

121. *Du journal d'Egypte*, 14 Jan. 1946, in *Safia Zaghloul*, 137–38.

122. *AH*, 13 Jan. 1946, *De la bourse égyptienne*, 14 Jan. 1946, *Du journal d'Egypte*, 13 Jan. 1946, in *Safia Zaghloul*, 126–44.

123. Safiyya presented a contrast to Zaynab al-Wakil, Nahhas's wife, who was about thirty years younger than her husband; the latter was considered a corrupting influence on party members and accumulated a large fortune using her connections (al-Sayyid-Marsot, *Egypt's Liberal Experiment*, 124).

CHAPTER SEVEN. PARTISANS OF THE WAFD

1. See Margot Badran, *Feminists, Islam, and Nation: Gender and the Making of Modern Egypt* (Princeton, N.J., 1995), 80–88.

2. Huda Sha'rawi, *Mudhakkirat Huda Sha'rawi* (Cairo, 1981); Munira Thabit, *Thawra fi . . . al-Burj al-'Aji* (Cairo, 1946); Fatima al-Yusuf, *Dhikrayat* (1953; repr. Cairo, 1976); Hanna F. Wissa, *Assiout: The Saga of an Egyptian Family* (Lewes, Sussex, 1994).

3. See, e.g., Wissa, *Assiout*, 206, 214–16.

4. Ibid., quotation from 197–98, 179.

5. FO 371/15405/1611, Stevenson to Henderson, Cairo, 8 May 1931; FO 371/35533/1969, British Embassy to Eden, Cairo, 23 Apr. 1943.

6. Thabit, *Thawra,* 17–19; Muhammad Ibrahim al-Jaziri, *Sa'd Zaghlul* (Cairo, n.d.), 211.

7. SD 883.oo/165, "Protestation des Dames Egyptiennes d'Alexandrie A Monsieur le Consul d'Amérique," Apr. 1919.

8. 'Abd al-Rahman al-Rafi'i, *Thawrat Sanat 1919: Ta'rikh Misr al-Qawmi min 1914 ila 1921* (1949; 3d ed., Cairo, 1968), 2: 75; Muhammad Ahmad Anis, *Dirasat fi Watha'iq Thawrat 1919* (Cairo, 1963), 1: 164: letter from Fahmi to Sa'd Zaghlul dated 23 Dec. 1919; John D. McIntyre Jr. *The Boycott of the Milner Mission: A Study in Egyptian Nationalism* (New York, 1985), 138–45; Wissa, *Assiout,* 215–16.

9. Quotation from Sha'rawi, *Mudhakkirat,* 203. Fahmi Wissa suggests that the clause was inserted later to justify subsequent events (Wissa, *Assiout,* 215). Anis, *Thawrat 1919,* 1: 180, letter from Fahmi to Sa'd Zaghlul dated 14 Jan. 1920; Ijlal Khalifa, *al-Haraka al-Nisa'iyya al-Haditha* (Cairo, 1973), 160–61. Khalifa, who interviewed participants and had access to archival materials, gives the figure of those present at the founding of the Women's Wafd as five hundred.

10. Sha'rawi, *Mudhakkirat,* 209.

11. McIntyre, *Boycott,* 146–47; Rafi'i, *Thawrat Sanat 1919,* 2: 75.

12. Sha'rawi, *Mudhakkirat,* 211–12; al-Jaziri, *Sa'd Zaghlul,* 208.

13. Wissa, *Assiout,* 204–5.

14. Sha'rawi, *Mudhakkirat,* 204; al-Jaziri, *Sa'd Zaghlul,* 208.

15. *MSR,* 7 Mar. 1969, 46.

16. Sha'rawi, *Mudhakkirat,* 239.

17. Wissa, *Assiout,* 227–29.

18. Sha'rawi, *Mudhakkirat,* 221–24.

19. *LM,* 12 Apr. 1921, 7; Sha'rawi, *Mudhakkirat,* 230–31.

20. Quotation from Fina Gued Vidal, *Safia Zaghloul* (Cairo, 1946), 79.

21. Marius Deeb, *Party Politics in Egypt: The Wafd and Its Rivals, 1919–1939* (London, 1979), 68; Sha'rawi, *Mudhakkirat,* 278; Grace Thompson Seton, *A Woman Tenderfoot in Egypt* (New York, 1923), 29–31; Badran, *Feminists,* 83–84; *MSR,* 7 Mar. 1969, 44; Afaf Lutfi al-Sayyid Marsot, "The Revolutionary Gentlewoman in Egypt," in *Women in the Muslim World,* ed. Lois Beck and Nikki Keddie (Cambridge, Mass., 1978), 271–72. For the connection of the boycott to consumerism, see Mona L. Russell, "Creating the New Woman: Consumerism, Education, and National Identity in Egypt, 1863–1922" (Ph.D. diss., Georgetown University, 1997), pp. 179–81.

22. Sha'rawi, *Mudhakkirat,* 233; Seton, *Woman Tenderfoot,* 30; Deeb, *Party Politics,* 68; Badran, *Feminists,* 84.

23. FO 141/511/14083–3, Ihsan Ahmed, "Decision of the Women's Central Committee of the Delegation," Cairo, Feb. 1922; FO 141/511/14083–4, oriental secretary to Smith, Cairo, 7 Feb. 1922.

24. FO 141/511/14083–5, telegram, 9 Feb. 1922; FO 141/511/14083–6, telegram, 21 Feb. 1922; FO 141/511/14083–10, telegram, 23 May 1922.

25. Seton, *Woman Tenderfoot,* 31; *LM,* 20 Mar. 1922, 1.

26. *LM,* 16 Oct. 1922, 8–9.

27. *LM,* 4 Dec. 1922, 8.

28. *LM,* 12 Apr. 1921, 7; 10 Oct. 1921, 4; 21 Nov. 1921, 13; 4 Aug. 1924, 12 (reprinted in *SHM,* 1: 96); SD 883.00/427, Maynard to secretary of state, Alexandria, 19 Sept. 1922, enclosure: "Future-mother's salutation to the Kemalist troops"; SD 883.00/429, Maynard to secretary of state, 2 Oct. 1922, enclosure: "The Egyptian Delegation at Alexandria."

29. Badran, *Feminists,* 86; Wissa, *Assiout,* 231.

30. *LM,* 24 Sept. 1923, 12; Sha'rawi, *Mudhakkirat,* 288–91.

31. Sha'rawi, *Mudhakkirat,* 296–97; *LM,* 21 Apr. 1924, 4.

32. See Eve Marie Troutt Powell, "Colonized Colonizers: Egyptian Nationalists and the Issue of the Sudan, 1875–1919" (Ph.D. diss., Harvard University, 1995).

33. Wissa, *Assiout,* 218.

34. I thank Eve Trout Powell for helping me to see this possibility.

35. FO 141/511/14083–3, Ihsan Ahmed, "Decision of the Women's Central Committee of the Delegation," Cairo, Feb. 1922.

36. FO 371/10021/5059, Allenby to MacDonald, Cairo, 1 June 1924.

37. Ibid.

38. *KK* 4, no. 160 (6 June 1924): 10–11; FO 371/10021/5059, Allenby to MacDonald, Cairo, 1 June 1924; FO 371/10021/5233, Allenby to MacDonald, Cairo, 8 June 1924.

39. *LM,* 9 June 1924, 16. In 1921, *al-Lata'if al-Musawwara* published a *zajal* (colloquial poem) selected from many letters of support in favor of their defense of Sa'd Zaghlul when al-Kashkul attacked him. Marilyn Booth, "Colloquial Arabic Poetry, Politics, and the Press in Modern Egypt," *IJMES* 24 (1992): 430.

40. See *KK* 4 (June 1924); *LM,* 24 Nov. 1924, 5.

41. FO 371/10021/5059, Allenby to MacDonald, Cairo, 1 June 1924; *NN* 3 (June 1924): 387.

42. Sha'rawi, *Mudhakkirat,* 301–2.

43. *MM* 5 (Sept. 1924): 385.

44. Sha'rawi, *Mudhakkirat,* 309–10; FO 141/511/14083–19, "Resolutions Agreed Upon by Egyptian Ladies, 30 Oct. 1924"; FO 141/511/14083–21, telegram, 10 Nov. 1924, from Charaoui [Huda Sha'rawi].

45. SD 883.00/510, Charaoui to under secretary of state for foreign affairs, Cairo, 28 Nov. 1924, and Charaoui, "Appel à l'opinion publique mondiale," 26 Nov. 1924; Sha'rawi, *Mudhakkirat,* 316–18, 333–42.

46. Huda chose to use her title as head of the WWCC rather than as president of the EFU in a protest that was sent to the press in the fall of 1923, indicating that she thought the former carried more clout than the latter or was more appropriate. See *MM* 4 (Oct. 1923): 425.

47. Wissa, *Assiout,* 170–216; *LM,* 14 May 1928, 2; *al-Taliba* 6 (July 1943): 2–3; Daisy Griggs Philips, "The Growth of the Feminist Movement in Egypt," *Moslem World* 16 (1926): 278.

48. Wissa, *Assiout,* 227–30; *LM,* 4 Aug. 1924, 8–9; *MSR,* 7 Mar. 1969, 47.

49. See letters in Wissa, *Assiout,* 363–412; *LM,* 14 May 1928, 2.

50. Esther Fahmy Wissa to Sherifa Riad, n.d., in Wissa, *Assiout,* 426.

51. Ibid., 426–27.

52. Wissa, *Assiout*, 428–35; *MSR*, 13 Mar. 1925, cover; also in Sarah Graham-Brown, *Images of Women: The Portrayal of Women in Photography of the Middle East 1860–1950* (New York, 1988), 226.

53. FO 141/511/14083–26, telegram from Mousa to Lloyd, Cairo, 7 Jan. 1926; FO 141/511/14083–28, telegram from Women's Executive Committee to the minister of Great Britain, Alexandria, 14 Aug. 1928; FO 141/511/14083–30, telegram from Weisa [Esther Wisa] to Chamberlain, Cairo, 8 May 1929.

54. Al-Jaziri, *Sa'd Zaghlul*, 209; Fahima Thabit, *al-Za'im al-Khalid wa-Umm al-Misriyyin fi Manfan Jabal Tariq* (Cairo, 1948); *HN*, 1 Oct. 1926, 17.

55. *HN*, 15 Jan. 1926, 10; 1 May 1926, 6; 1 Oct. 1926, 17; 30 Oct. 1926, 16–17; 1 Jan. 1927, 8; 25 June 1927, cover, 23; *LM*, 27 Oct. 1924, 4, 8, 9; Gued Vidal, *Safia Zaghloul*, 78–79, 88; al-Jaziri, *Sa'd Zaghlul*, 208–9; FO 141/511/14083–26, Moussa to Lord Lloyd, Cairo, 1 Jan. 1926.

56. Quotation from FO 141/511/14083–30, telegram from Weisa [Esther Wisa] to Chamberlain, Cairo, 8 May 1929; see also FO 141/511/14083–28, telegram from Women's Executive Committee to the minister of Great Britain, Alexandria, 14 Aug. 1928; Gued Vidal, *Safia Zaghloul*, 72, 75–76, 88.

57. FO 371/15404/1358, "Message from Egyptian Women," *Manchester Guardian*, 4 May 1931; FO 371/15405/1611, Stevenson to Henderson, Cairo, 8 May 1931; Sha'rawi, *Mudhakkirat*, 438–39; Badran, *Feminists*, 210–12.

58. FO 371/15406/2084, Loraine to Henderson, Cairo, 18 June 1931.

59. Badran, *Feminists*, 308 n. 21.

60. FO 371/16109/1930, Esther Wissa to secretary of state, 7 July 1932, and "Minutes: Request for interview with Secretary of State to discuss Egyptian question."

61. FO 371/16109/1930, extract from *Egyptian Gazette*, 22 July 1932.

62. *LM*, 25 July 1932, 1; *HN*, 15 Jan. 1926, 10; *MM* 7 (Nov. and Dec. 1926): 486–89.

63. FO 371/17978/1382, Lampson to Oliphant, Cairo, 25 May 1934.

64. FO 141/539/598, Lampson to Campbell, Ramleh, 2 Aug. 1935.

65. SD 883.00/837, Fish, Egypt, 9 Mar. 1935; *LM*, 14 Jan. 1935, 16–17, and 21 Jan. 1935, 28.

66. Wissa, *Assiout*, 169.

67. Ibid., 262–63.

68. Ibid., 250.

69. Ibid., 256.

70. Goldschmidt, *Modern Egypt*, 226–27; see also Istir [Esther] Fahmi Wisa, *al-Qalb al-Tahir* (Alexandria, 1979).

71. Clarissa Lee Pollard, "Nurturing the Nation: The Family Politics of the 1919 Egyptian Revolution" (Ph.D. diss., University of California, Berkeley, 1997).

72. Qasim Amin, *al-Mar'a al-Jadida* (Cairo, 1900; reprint, 1984), dedication page.

73. Thabit, *Thawra*, 17–19.

74. Ibid., 20–23; al-Jaziri, *Sa'd Zaghlul*, 210.

75. Thabit, *Thawra*, 17–19, 24–26; al-Jaziri, *Sa'd Zaghlul*, 211–12.

76. Al-Jaziri, *Sa'd Zaghlul*, 212–13.

77. Thabit, *Thawra*, 26–29; *AM*, 28 Nov. 1925, 7. For more background, see Khalifa, *al-Haraka*, 65–70; al-Subki, *al-Haraka al-Nisa'iyya*, 110–12; Anwar al-Jundi, *Adab al-Mar'a al-'Arabiyya* (Cairo, n.d.), 63–65.

78. *AM*, 28 Nov. 1925, 4; 3 Apr. 1926, 15; 10 July 1926, 8.

79. See, e.g., *AM*, 24 Apr. 1926, 1–2; 8 May 1926, 1–2; 9 Oct. 1926, 9.

80. Badran, *Feminists*, 130, 208–12.

81. Thabit, *Thawra*, 13, 38–41. See, e.g., *NN* 4 (July 1926): 277, and (Sept. 1926): 336; *AM*, 9 Oct. 1926, 7.

82. Khalifa, *al-Haraka*, 169–70; Salim, *al-Mar'a al-Misriyya*, 123; *AM*, 2 Oct. 1926.

83. Thabit, *Thawra*, 41–45; *NN* 6 (Feb. 1928): 49; *LM*, 26 Nov. 1928, 3; 18 Dec. 1933, 13; Badran, *Feminists*, 149–53; Goldschmidt, *Modern Egypt*, 212–13.

84. Nelson, *Doria Shafik*, 197, 298 n. 8; Goldschmidt, *Modern Egypt*, 212–13; Ilse Lichtenstadter, "The 'New Woman' in Modern Egypt: Observations and Impressions," *Moslem World* 38 (1948): 166–67.

85. Thabit, *Thawra*, 136, 168.

86. See the cover of *al-Amal* from 6 May 1952.

87. Al-Yusuf, *Dhikrayat;* M. Perlmann, "Memoirs of Rose Fatima Al-Yusuf," *Middle Eastern Affairs* 7 (1956): 20–27, esp. 21; Ibrahim 'Abduh, *Ruz al-Yusuf* (Cairo, 1961); Joseph T. Zeidan, *Arab Women Novelists* (Albany, N.Y., 1995), 316 n. 8.

88. Al-Yusuf, *Dhikrayat*, 113–17, 120.

89. Ibid., 118–20, 129–30, 143.

90. Al-Yusuf, *Dhikrayat*, 138–48; Ami Ayalon, *The Press in the Arab Middle East* (New York, 1995), 78, 148–49; *LM*, 5 June 1933, 11; 17 July 1933, 15; 7 Aug. 1933, 11; 6 Nov. 1933, 27; 12 Mar. 1934, 4.

91. Ayalon, *Press*, 78; see photo in *LM*, 11 Mar. 1935, 20.

92. Al-Yusuf, *Dhikrayat*, 189–98; SD 883.00/854, Merriam to secretary of state, Cairo, 2 Oct. 1935.

93. SD 883.42, Fish to secretary of state, Cairo, 12 Dec. 1935; *LM*, 16 Dec. 1935, 16–17, 20.

94. Al-Yusuf, *Dhikrayat*, 220–22.

95. FO 371/35533/1969, Sha'rawi to Churchill, Cairo, 18 Apr. 1943.

96. *LM*, 20 Sept. 1920, 2; 13 Dec. 1920, 8; 20 Mar. 1922, 1; 28 July 1930, 16–17; 16 Oct. 1922, 8–9; 24 Sept. 1923, 12; 21 July 1924, 5, 9; 4 Aug. 1924, 12.

97. See, e.g., *LM*, 28 May 1923, 1; *AR*, 11 Feb. 1925, 1; *NN* 9 (June 1931): 211.

98. *MM* 4 (May 1923): 247; *AR*, 28 Jan. 1925, 12.

99. *AR*, 2 Sept. 1925, 1; *HN*, 14 Oct. 1925, insert.

100. *HN*, 30 Mar. 1926, 1; *LM*, 3 Mar. 1930, 17; 6 Nov. 1933, 27; 7 Aug. 1933, 11; 17 July 1933, 15; 20 Oct. 1933, 15.

101. *LM*, 4 Aug. 1924, 8–9.

102. *MSR*, 13 Mar. 1925, cover; Graham-Brown, *Images of Women*, 226.

103. See, e.g., a very tired Fatima al-Yusuf in *LM*, 21 Mar. 1935, 20.

104. *KK*, no. 92 (1923): 16; no. 110 (1923): 1; 4 (10 Apr. 1925): 11.

105. This was especially true of Nabawiyya Musa, who worked for the ministry of education and was satirized in numerous cartoons. See *KK* 5 (12 Mar. 1926): 11; 6 (18 June 1926): 11; 6 (1 Oct. 1926): 11; 11 (14 Aug. 1931): 32; *RY*, 18 Feb. 1930, 13.

106. *KK* 10 (22 May 1931): 16. On the women's protests of 1931, see FO 371/15404/1358, "Message from Egyptian Women," *Manchester Guardian*, 4 May 1931; FO 371/15405/1611, Stevenson to Henderson, Cairo, 8 May 1931; Sha'rawi, *Mudhakkirat*, 438–39; Badran, *Feminists*, 210–12.

107. *KK* 10 (15 May 1931): 1.

108. *LM*, 14 Oct. 1935, 32. See also *KK* 10 (15 Aug. 1930): 15; *LM*, 18 June 1934, 32.

109. *KK* 6, no. 297 (1927): 11. The Sudan is generally depicted in the press in the 1920s as a highly sexualized woman but is occasionally presented as a feminized man or eunuch. See, e.g., *KK*, no. 78 (1922): 16.

110. *RY*, 19 Nov. 1929, cover; *KK* 10 (7 Nov. 1930): 32.

111. *Scott's Standard Postage Stamp Catalogue (1994)*, 150th ed. (Sidney, Ohio, 1993), 3: 137.

112. Clarissa Lee Pollard, "Nurturing the Nation."

CHAPTER EIGHT. THE PATH OF AN ISLAMIC ACTIVIST

1. On Islamic nationalism, see Israel Gershoni and James P. Jankowski, *Redefining the Egyptian Nation, 1930–1945* (Cambridge, 1995), chap. 4.

2. Labiba Ahmad, *Mudhakkirat Labiba Ahmad* (Cairo, 1938). I have only read descriptions of the book, which seems to resemble a collection of papers more than an autobiography, not the book itself. See description in *NN* 16 (Feb. 1938): 65.

3. Ijlal Khalifa, *al-Haraka al-Nisa'iyya al-Haditha* (Cairo, 1973), 60.

4. Important work has been done on the production and reception of the press, which sets the foundation for using the press as a historical source.

5. *NN* 3 (July 1924): cover, and again 10 (Apr. 1932): 126; (June 1926): 227; 6 (June 1928): 202; 8 (May 1930): cover, and again 8 (July 1930): cover; 11 (Mar. 1933): cover, and again 14 (Mar. 1936): 86; 12 (Mar. 1934): cover. See also *LM*, 20 Mar. 1933, 25.

6. Khayr al-Din al-Zirikli, *al-A'lam: Qamus Tarajim*, 7th ed. (Beirut, 1986), 5: 240; *al-Ahram*, 31 Jan. 1951, 7.

7. *NN* 1 (Jan. 1922): 159.

8. Muhammad Farid, *The Memoirs and Diaries of Muhammad Farid, an Egyptian Nationalist Leader (1868–1919)*, trans. Arthur Goldschmidt Jr. (San Francisco, 1992), 121; Mahmud Tahir Haqqi, "The Maiden of Dinshway," in *Three Pioneering Egyptian Novels*, trans. Saad El-Gabalawy (Fredericton, N.B., 1986), 35; Maged M. Farag, *1952, The Last Protocol: Royal Albums of Egypt* (Cairo, 1996), 39.

9. *NN* 1 (July 1922): 371; 9 (Jan. 1931): 31; 9 (Apr. 1931): 118.

10. See eulogy in *MM* 10 (Nov. 1929): 389–90; *NN* 7 (Nov. 1929): 387.

11. *NN* 8 (May 1930): 145–46; 14 (Mar. 1936): 83–85, 96; 14 (Apr. 1936): 111; 14 (Sept. 1936): 390.

12. *NN* 4 (May 1926): 187; 6 (Feb. 1928): 56; 6 (Sept. 1928): 308; 6 (Nov. 1928): 390; 7 (June 1929): 181–83; advice to the departing students reprinted, 16 (Feb. 1938): 55.

13. *NN* 3 (June 1924): 386.

14. Arthur Goldschmidt Jr. interviewed Muhammad Farid's daughter, Farida, who suggested that such a group existed. Correspondence from Goldschmidt, 22 Feb. 1996.

15. *LM*, 1 Mar. 1920, 5; *NN* 9 (June 1931): 213; *LM*, 6 Feb. 1933, 11.

16. SD 883.00/135, "Ladies of Egypt to the Diplomatic Agent and Consul-General of the U.S.," Cairo, 20 Mar. 1919.

17. Khalifa, *al-Haraka al-Nisa'iyya al-Haditha*, 60. Khalifa interviewed Zaynab 'Abduh as well as some Cairene housewives and students who remembered that period.

18. *LM*, 1 Mar. 1920, 5.

19. *LM*, 4 Apr. 1921, 12; 25 Apr. 1921, 6.

20. See, e.g., *NN* 1 (Oct. 1921): 84.

21. *NN* 5 (Feb. 1927): 67.

22. *NN* 2 (Oct. 1922): 61–62.

23. SD 883.00/431, enclosure: "Cairo's Goodbye to Madame Zaghlul: A Monster Demonstration," *Egyptian Mail,* 9 Oct.1922; *NN* 2 (Oct. 1922): facing p. 58.

24. *NN* 2 (Nov. 1922): 109.

25. *NN* 2 (Apr. 1923): 227; 2 (June 1923): 303; 3 (Sept. 1923): cover; 3 (Oct. 1923): 85.

26. *NN* 3 (Feb. 1924): insert; 3 (Mar. 1924): 253–55; 3 (June 1924): 387.

27. *LM*, 21 July 1924, 5, 9; *NN* 4 (Nov. 1926): 419.

28. *NN* 5 (Oct. 1927): 359; 8 (Sept. 1930): 316.

29. *NN* 1 (July 1922): 331; 2 (Feb. 1923): 194; 9 (Apr. 1931): 116–18.

30. *NN* 5 (Mar. 1927): cover; 2 (Dec. 1922): 125; 8 (Apr. 1930): 129; 10 (Mar. 1932): 100.

31. *NN* 3 (Nov. 1923): 141.

32. *NN* 5 (Feb. 1927): 68, back page; *Dhikrayat Faqid al-Watan: 'Ali Fahmi Kamil Bey* (Cairo, 1927).

33. *NN* 5 (Jan. 1927): 47.

34. On women's social welfare associations, see Beth Baron, *The Women's Awakening in Egypt: Culture, Society, and the Press* (New Haven, Conn., 1994), 169–75; Margot Badran, *Feminists, Islam, and Nation: Gender and the Making of Modern Egypt* (Princeton, N.J., 1995), chap. 6.

35. *NN* 1 (July 1921): 3.

36. *NN* 1 (July 1921): 3.

37. *NN* 1 (Sept. 1921): 35.

38. Baron, *Women's Awakening*, 28–29, 32–34, 176–79.

39. *NN* 1 (July 1921): 3; 1 (July 1922): 378. For background on orphanages, see Andrea B. Rugh, "Orphanages in Egypt: Contradiction or Affirmation in a Family-Oriented Society," *Children in the Muslim Middle East*, ed. Elizabeth Warnock Fernea (Austin, Tex., 1995), 124–41.

40. *NN* 1 (Dec. 1921): 129.

41. *NN* 1 (July 1921): 28.

42. *NN* 1 (July 1921): 17, 28; 1 (Oct. 1921): facing p. 68.

43. *NN* 1 (July 1921): 24.

44. *NN* 3 (Dec. 1923): 145–46; 3 (Jan. 1924): 209; FO 141/466/1415–26, Eastern Department to Chancery, London, 31 Jan. 1924; Hughes to Baker, Cairo, 3 Mar. 1924. According to Bruce Dunne, the Egyptian public prosecutor's office found no evidence of the kidnapping of girls and emphasized the voluntary nature of prostitution in Egypt. See Bruce W. Dunne, "Sexuality and the 'Civilizing Process' in Modern Egypt" (Ph.D. diss., Georgetown University, 1996), 250.

45. *NN* 3 (Dec. 1924): inside front cover; 3 (Feb. 1924): 252; 3 (Apr. 1924): 316.

46. *NN* 3 (June 1924): 387; 3 (July 1924): 419, 427; 4 (Oct. 1924): 103.

47. *SR* 5 (Nov. 1923): 306–7.

48. *NN* 4 (Nov. 1926): 399–401.

49. *NN* 3 (Feb. 1924): 252.

50. *NN* 3 (Apr. 1924): 316.

51. *NN* 1 (Sept. 1921): 55; 1 (Dec. 1921): 135; 1 (Jan. 1922): 159.

52. Badran, *Feminists*, 96; *NN* 8 (Jan. 1930): 9; 8 (Dec. 1930): 423; 9 (June 1931): 211. The broad contours of Labiba Ahmad's library can be surmised from book prizes offered in her journal. See *NN* 5 (Jan. 1927): 47.

53. *NN* 11 (Dec. 1933): 386.

54. *NN* 12 (Feb. 1934): back page; 12 (Mar. 1934): back page; 12 (Apr. 1934): back page. This group may have been the nucleus of the Cairo branch of the Muslim Sisters.

55. See Baron, *Women's Awakening*.

56. Ibid. See Ruz Antun's letter to Labiba Ahmad, and the article sent by Alexandra Avierino, editor of *Anis al-Jalis* (1898–1907), praising the journal when it first appeared. *NN* 5 (Feb. 1927): 65; 1 (May 1922): 266.

57. *MM* 7 (Feb. 1926): 42; Joseph T. Zeidan, *Arab Women Novelists: The Formative Years and Beyond* (Albany, N.Y., 1995), 239–41; Badran, *Feminists*, 102–8.

58. *NN* 10 (Jan. 1932): back page.

59. Baron, *Women's Awakening*, 28–29, 32–34.

60. *NN* 1 (July 1922): 379.

61. *NN* 1 (Apr. 1922): 255.

62. *NN* 1 (Mar. 1922): 218; 3 (Dec. 1923): 175.

63. *NN* 11 (Feb. 1933): 37; 12 (July 1934): 317.

64. Quotation from *NN* 9 (Aug. 1931): 255; see, e.g., *NN* 7 (Nov. 1929): 333–34; 2 (Feb. 1923): 169–70.

65. *NN* 2 (May 1923): 253–54.

66. *NN* 3 (Dec. 1923): 156; 3 (June 1924): 395; 14 (Mar. 1936): 88.

67. *NN* 12 (Oct. 1934): 326.

68. *NN* 16 (Sept. 1938): 289–91. On Dar al-'Ulum, see Lois A. Aroian, *The Nationalization of Arabic and Islamic Education in Egypt: Dar al-'Ulum and al-Azhar* (Cairo, 1983).

69. *NN* 1 (May 1922): 260.

70. See Lila Abu-Lughod, "The Marriage of Feminism and Islamism in Egypt: Selective Repudiation as a Dynamic of Postcolonial Cultural Politics," in *Remaking Women: Feminism and Modernity in the Middle East* (Princeton, N.J., 1998), 243–69.

71. *NN* 8 (Feb. 1930): 37–39, 61; 14 (June 1936): 184; 14 (Nov. 1936): 361–62.

72. *NN* 14 (Oct. 1936): 326–27; 16 (Apr. 1938): 109.

73. See, e.g., Muhammad Farid Wajdi's article on the occasion of Huda Sha'rawi's participation in the Rome Conference, *NN* 2 (June 1923): 283–85.

74. See, e.g., *NN* 6 (Oct. 1928): 347; 8 (Oct. 1930): 340–41; 8 (Dec. 1930): 430–31; 10 (Jan. 1932): 23–27; 11 (Apr. 1933): 120–21; 11 (May 1933): 166; 12 (Sept. 1934): 307. See Zeidan, *Arab Women Novelists*, 79–80; Issa J. Boullata, "Modern Qur'an Exegesis: A Study of Bint al-Shati's Method," *Muslim World* 64 (1974): 103–13.

75. *NN* 11 (Jan. 1933): 31.

76. *NN* 12 (Mar. 1934): 100; 14 (Mar. 1936): 96; 10 (Dec. 1932): 399; 11 (Feb. 1933): 66; 14 (Sept. 1936): 390.

77. *NN* 8 (May 1930): 251.

78. *NN* 5 (Jan. 1927): 47.

79. This is Arthur Goldschmidt Jr.'s characterization of the group. Correspondence from Goldschmidt, 23 May 1997.

80. *NN* 11 (Mar. 1933): 82, 90; 12 (Mar. 1934): 100; 16 (Jan. 1938): back page.

81. *NN* 4 (Mar. 1926): 136; 9 (Aug. 1931): 258.

82. *NN* 11 (Apr. 1933): 139.

83. *NN* 7 (Dec. 1929): 397.

84. *NN* 5 (Jan. 1927): 24.

85. *NN* 2 (Dec. 1922): 136; 3 (Sept. 1923): back page; 8 (Aug. 1930): back page; 11 (Aug. 1933): 277; 12 (May 1934): back page.

86. *NN* 6 (Oct. 1928): 346; 8 (Feb. 1930): 62–63; 12 (Mar. 1934): 101; 16 (Jan. 1938): 2.

87. Baron, *Women's Awakening*, 90–93; Ami Ayalon, *The Press in the Arab Middle East* (Oxford, 1995), 148–50; Gershoni and Jankowski, *Redefining the Egyptian Nation*, 61–65.

88. *NN* 5 (Jan. 1927): 3–4.

89. *NN* 4 (Oct. 1924): 103; 5 (Jan. 1927): 3; 6 (May 1928): 166–67; 11 (Oct. 1933): 329; 14 (Mar. 1936): 86.

90. *NN* 1 (Oct. 1921): 83–84; 14 (Jan. 1936): 29.

91. *NN* 1 (Nov. 1921): 110.

92. *NN* 3 (June 1924): 386.

93. *NN* 8 (Jan 1930): 12.

94. *NN* 4 (Mar. 1926): 118.

95. *NN* 4 (Mar. 1926): 136.

96. *NN* 4 (June 1926): 227; 6 (June 1928): 202; 8 (May 1930): cover; 10 (Apr. 1932): 127; 11 (Mar. 1933): cover; 12 (Feb. 1934): back page; 12 (May 1934): back page; 14 (Mar. 1936): 86.

97. *NN* 16 (Feb. 1938): 65.

98. *NN* 8 (May 1930): 146.

99. *NN* 12 (May 1934): back page; 12 (July 1934): 237.

100. *NN* 4 (Aug. 1926): 287–90; 8 (July 1930): 15; 8 (Aug. 1930): 259; 9 (Feb. 1931): 56–57; 9 (June 1931): 206; 10 (Nov. 1932): 365–67. See Gail Minault, *The Khilafat Movement: Religious Symbolism and Political Mobilization in India* (New York, 1982).

101. *NN* 6 (May 1928): 176; 6 (Aug. 1928): 278; 6 (Sept. 1928): 315; 6 (Oct. 1928): 357; 8 (Apr. 1930): 142; 8 (July 1930): insert; 8 (Aug. 1930): 282; 10 (Mar. 1932): 102, 107; 10 (Dec. 1932): 424, 429; 14 (Apr. 1936): 135. See also *LM*, 20 Mar. 1933, 25.

102. *NN* 8 (Aug. 1930): 283.

103. *NN* 8 (Nov. 1930): photo with friend.

104. *NN* 8 (Oct. 1930): 353; 8 (Nov. 1930): cover, 361–62, 379, 386, photo with friend; 9 (Apr. 1931): 138. See also Philip Mattar, *The Mufti of Jerusalem: al-Hajj Amin al-Husayni and the Palestinian National Movement* (New York, 1988).

105. *NN* 11 (Mar. 1933): 95.

106. *NN* 11 (Aug. 1933): 310.

107. *NN* 10 (Dec. 1932): 398.

108. *NN* 11 (Aug. 1933): 302; 14 (July 1936): 250; 16 (Sept. 1938): 291.

109. J. Heyworth-Dunne, *Religious and Political Trends in Modern Egypt* (Washington, D.C., 1950), 11.

110. Heyworth-Dunne, *Religious and Political Trends*, 11–14; *NN* 9 (Mar. 1931): 86; *NN* 9 (May 1931): 148.

111. *NN* 10 (May 1932): cover, and in subsequent issues.

112. *NN* 14 (Aug. 1936): 253–55, 269–72.

113. *NN* 9 (May 1931): 148.

114. Hasan al-Banna, *Memoirs of Hasan al Banna Shaheed*, trans. M. N. Shaikh (Karachi, 1981), 121–22.

115. Richard P. Mitchell, *The Society of the Muslim Brothers* (1969; repr. New York, 1993), 1–11.

116. Al-Banna, *Memoirs*, 189; Muhammad Shawqi Zaki, *al-Ikhwan al-Muslimun wa al-Mujtama' al-Misri*, 2d ed. (Cairo, 1980), 193; Mitchell, *Muslim Brothers*, 175.

117. Amal al-Subki, *al-Haraka al-Nisa'iyya fi Misr, 1919–1952* (Cairo, 1986), 118. Subki may have found evidence that Labiba Ahmad headed the Cairo branch in the legal files compiled to try the assassins of Mahmud al-Nuqrashi, dated 28 December 1948, which are stored at the High Court (p. 135 n. 36). Ghada Talhami draws almost exclusively on al-Subki for her account of Labiba Ahmad's activities in Ghada Hashem Talhami, *The Mobilization of Muslim Women in Egypt* (Gainesville, Fla., 1996), 46–49.

118. *NN* 12 (Mar. 1934): 91–92, 98; 12 (Apr. 1934): 114.

119. Zaki, *al-Ikhwan al-Muslimin*, 193–235; al-Subki, *al-Haraka al-Nisa'iyya*, 117–19; Mitchell, *Muslim Brothers*, 175, 288.

120. *NN* 16 (Sept. 1938): 317.

121. Zaynab al-Ghazali, *al-Da'iya Zaynab al-Ghazali* (Cairo, 1989), 196–97, 200, 218; *NN* 12 (Apr. 1934): 128–29.

122. Quotation from *NN* 16 (Sept. 1938): 317; Ghazali, *Daʿiya*, 196–97.

123. Al-Ghazali, *al-Daʿiya*, 18; id., *Ayyam min Hayati*, 10th ed. (Cairo, 1988), 23; id., *Return of the Pharaoh: Memoir in Nasir's Prison*, trans. Mokrane Guezzou (Leicester, U.K., 1994). For background, see Valerie J. Hoffman, "An Islamic Activist: Zaynab al-Ghazali," in *Women and the Family in the Middle East*, ed. Elizabeth Warnock Fernea (Austin, Tex., 1985): 234–41; Miriam Cooke, "Zaynab al-Ghazali: Saint or Subversive?" *Die Welt des Islams* 34 (1994): 1–20; id., "*Ayyam min Hayati*: The Prison Memoirs of a Muslim Sister," *Journal of Arabic Literature* 26, nos. 1–2 (Mar.–June 1995): 147–64.

124. *NN* 16 (Feb. 1938): 65.

125. *NN* 16 (Nov. 1938): 361–62.

126. The journal's demise may have been related to a new government policy under which the ministry of education no longer purchased blocks of subscriptions. See *NN* 16 (Jan. 1938): notice in front of issue.

127. Mitchell, *Muslim Brothers*, 175.

128. Al-Zirikli, *al-Alam*, 240; *al-Ahram*, 31 Jan. 1951, 7; *al-Misri*, 31 Jan. 1951, 7.

CONCLUSION

1. The statue appears on the jackets of countless Arabic and English books, including an Arabic translation by Lamis al-Naqqash of my book *The Women's Awakening in Egypt: Culture, Society, and the Press* (New Haven, Conn., 1994) under the title *al-Nahda al-Nisaʾiyya fi Misr: al-Thaqafa, al-Mujtamaʿ wa al-Sihafa* (Cairo, 1999), although the statue is not mentioned or discussed therein. The Egyptian government authorized the translation of the book, along with several others, for the convening of a conference to celebrate the centennial of Qasim Amin's *Tahrir al-Marʾa*.

2. Deniz Kandiyoti had already called for such studies in the early 1990s. In the meantime, studies of masculinity in other fields have taken off.

3. *Scott's Standard Postage Stamp Catalogue (1994)*, 150th ed. (Sidney, Ohio, 1993), 3: 137.

# Select Bibliography

ARABIC-LANGUAGE PERIODICALS

*Abu Naddara*

*al-'Afaf*

*al-Ahram*

*al-'Aila*

*al-Amal*

*Anis al-Jalis*

*al-'Arusa*

*al-Balagh al-Usbu'iyya*

*Fatat al-Sharq*

*al-Hilal*

*al-Hisan*

*al-Ikhwan al-Muslimun*

*al-Jins al-Latif*

*al-Kashkul*

*al-Lata'if al-Musawwara*

*al-Mar'a al-Misriyya*

*al-Mihrajan*

*Misr al-Fatat*

*al-Misri*

*al-Muqtataf*

*al-Musawwar*

*al-Nahda al-Nisa'iyya*

*Ruz al-Yusuf*

*al-Sayyidat wa al-Rijal*

*al-Sufur*

*al-Taliba*

*Tarqiyat al-Mar'a*

*al-Watani al-Misri*

ARCHIVAL MATERIAL

Rhodes House, Oxford. British and Foreign Anti-Slavery Society Papers.
St. Antony's College, Oxford. Private Papers.
United Kingdom. Foreign Office. Series FO 141, FO 371, and FO 407. Public
   Record Office, London.
United States. State Department. Series SD 883. National Archives, Washington,
   D.C.


DISSERTATIONS

Arnett, Mary Flounders. "Qasim Amin and the Beginnings of the Feminist Move-
   ment in Egypt." Ph.D. diss. Dropsie College, Philadelphia, 1965.
Dunne, Bruce W. "Sexuality and the 'Civilizing Process' in Modern Egypt." Ph.D.
   diss. Georgetown University, 1996.
Frierson, Elizabeth Brown. "Unimagined Communities: State, Press, and Gen-
   der in the Hamidian Era." Ph.D. diss. Princeton University, 1996.
Pollard, Clarissa Lee. "Nurturing the Nation: The Family Politics of the 1919
   Egyptian Revolution." Ph.D. diss. University of California, Berkeley, 1997.
Powell, Eve Marie Troutt. "Colonized Colonizers: Egyptian Nationalists and the
   Issue of the Sudan, 1875–1919." Ph.D. diss. Harvard University, 1995.
Russell, Mona L. "Creating the New Woman: Consumerism, Education, and
   National Identity in Egypt, 1863–1922." Ph.D. diss. Georgetown University,
   1997.


WORKS IN ARABIC CITED IN THE TEXT

'Abada, 'Abd al-Fattah. *Nahdat al-Mar'a al-Misriyya wa al-Mar'a al-'Arabiyya
   fi al-Ta'rikh.* Cairo: Matba'at Hilal, 1919.
'Abduh, Ibrahim. *Ruz al-Yusuf.* Cairo: Mu'assasat Sijill al-'Arab, 1961.
Abu Ghazi, Badr al-Din. *Maththal Mukhtar.* Cairo: al-Dar al-Qawmiyya li al-
   Tiba'a wa al-Nashr, 1964.
Amin, Ahmad. *Hayati.* Cairo: Lajnat al-Ta'lif wa al-Tarjama wa al-Nashr,
   1950.

Amin, Qasim. *Al-Mar'a al-Jadida*. 1900. Reprint. Cairo: al-Markaz al-'Arabi li al-Bahth wa al-Nashr, 1984.

_____. *Tahrir al-Mar'a*. 1899. Reprint. Cairo: al-Markaz al-'Arabi li al-Bahth wa al-Nashr, 1984.

Anis, Muhammad Ahmad. *Dirasat fi Watha'iq Thawrat 1919*. Cairo: Maktabat al-Anjilu al-Misriyya, 1963.

'Aqqad, 'Abbas Mahmud. *Sa'd Zaghlul: Sira wa-Tahiyya*. Cairo: Matba'at Hijazi, 1936.

Baha' al-Din, Ahmad. *Ayyam laha Ta'rikh*. Cairo: Dar Ruz al-Yusuf, 1954.

Baron, Beth. "Maghzan al-Tazahurat al-Nisa'iyya fi Thawra 1919 al-Misriyya" (The Meaning of Women's Demonstrations in the 1919 Egyptian Revolution). *Al-Nahj* 11, no. 41 (1995): 235–43.

_____. *Al-Nahda al-Nisa'iyya fi Misr: al-Thaqafa, al-Mujtama' wa al-Sihafa* (The Women's Awakening in Egypt: Culture, Society, and the Press). Translated by Lamis al-Naqqash. Cairo: Majlis al-A'la li al-Thaqafa, 1999.

al-Ghazali, Zaynab. *Ayyam min Hayati*. 10th ed. Cairo: Dar al-Shuruq, 1988.

_____. *Al-Da'iya Zaynab al-Ghazali*. Cairo: Dar al-I'tisam, 1989.

Goldberg, Ellis. "Al-Bigha' wa al-Tabshir wa al-Kiyan al-Siyasi al-Misri." *Abwab* 12 (Spring 1997): 64–73.

Hamza, 'Abd al-Latif. *Adab al-Maqala al-Suhuf fi Misr*. Cairo: al-Hay'a al-Misriyya al-'Amma li al-Kitab, n.d.

Hasan, Ilhami. *Dirasa Mukhtasara 'an Ta'rikh al-Sinima al-Misriyya, 1896–1976*. Cairo: al-Hay'a al-Misriyya al-'Amma li al-Kitab, 1976.

Ibrahim, Hafiz. *Diwan Hafiz Ibrahim*. Cairo: al-Hay'a al-Misriyya al-'Amma li al-Kitab, 1980.

al-Jundi, Anwar. *Adab al-Mar'a al-'Arabiyya*. Cairo: Matba'at al-Risala, n.d.

Kamil, 'Ali Fahmi. *Mustafa Kamil Basha fi 34 Rabi'an*. 9 vols. Cairo: Matba'at al-Liwa', 1908–11.

Khalifa, Ijlal. *Al-Haraka al-Nisa'iyya al-Haditha: Qissat al-Mar'a al-'Arabiyya 'ala Ard Misr*. Cairo: al-Matba'a al-'Arabiyya al-Haditha, 1973.

Mahfuz, Najib. *Bayna al-Qasrayn*. 1956. Reprint. Cairo: Dar Misr, 1979.

Musa, Salama. *Tarbiyat Salama Musa*. Cairo: Dar al-Katib al-Misri, 1947.

al-Nadim, 'Abd Allah. *Sulafat al-Nadim fi Muntakhabat*. Cairo: al-Hay'a al-'Amma li-Qusur al-Thaqafa, 1995.

Naji, Iffat, et al. *Muhammad Naji (1888–1956)*. Cairo: Kurrasat Shubramant, n.d.

al-Rafi'i, 'Abd al-Rahman. *Mustafa Kamil: Ba'ith al-Haraka al-Wataniyya, 1892–1908*. 5th ed. Cairo: Dar al-Ma'arif, 1984.

_____. *Thawrat Sanat 1919: Ta'rikh Misr al-Qawmi min 1914 ila 1921*. 1949. 2 vols., 3d ed. Cairo: Mu'assasat Dar al-Sha'b, 1968.

Ramadan, 'Abd al-'Azim. *Tatawwur al-Haraka al-Wataniyya fi Misr min Sanat 1918 ila Sanat 1936*. 2d ed. Cairo: Maktabat Madbuli, 1983.

Ramzi, Ibrahim. *Abtal al-Mansura*. 1915. Reprint. Cairo: M. al-Afandi, 1939.

Rashid, Bahija Sidqi, Tahiyya Muhammad Isfahani, and Samiyya Sidqi Murad. *Al-Ittihad al-Nisa'i al-Misri*. Cairo: Dar Mamun, 1973.

Rif'at Pasha, Ibrahim. *Mir'at al-Haramayn*. Vol. 1. Cairo: Dar al-Kutub al-Misriyya, 1925.

Sa'd, Malaka. *Rabbat al-Dar.* Cairo: Matba'at al-Tawfiq, 1915.

Sa'id, Naffusa Zakariyya. *'Abd Allah al-Nadim Bayna al-Fusha wa al-'Amiyya.* Alexandria: al-Dar al-Qawmiyya li al-Tiba'a wa al-Nashr, 1966.

Shafiq, Ahmad. *Hawliyyat Misr al-Siyasiyya.* Cairo: Matba'at Shafiq Basha, 1926.

Shafiq, Duriyya. *Al-Mar'a al-Misriyya.* Cairo: Matba'at-Misr, 1955.

Sha'rawi, Huda. *Mudhakkirat Huda Sha'rawi.* Cairo: Dar al-Hilal, 1981.

al-Subki, Amal. *Al-Haraka al-Nisa'iyya fi Misr, 1919–1952.* Cairo: al-Hay'a al-Misriyya al-'Amma li al-Kitab, 1986.

Thabit, Fahima. *Al-Za'im al-Khalid wa-Umm al-Misriyyin fi Manfan Jabal Tariq.* Cairo: Maktabat al-Shams al-Haditha, 1948.

'Urabi, Ahmad. *Hatha Taqriri.* Cairo: al-Markaz al-'Arabi li al-Bahth wa al-Nashr, 1981.

Wisa, Istir Fahmi. *Al-Qalb al-Tahir.* Alexandria: Matba'at al-Jihad, 1979.

al-Yusuf, Fatima. *Dhikrayat.* 3d ed. 1953. Reprint. Cairo: Ruz al-Yusuf, 1976.

Zaki, Muhammad Shawqi. *Al-Ikhwan al-Muslimun wa al-Mujtama' al-Misri.* 2d ed. Cairo: Dar al-Ansar, 1980.

al-Zirikli, Khayr al-Din. *Al-A'lam: Qamus Tarajim.* 7th ed. Beirut: Dar al-'Ilm li al-Malayin, 1986.

### WORKS IN OTHER LANGUAGES CITED IN THE TEXT

Abu-Lughod, Janet L. *Cairo: 1001 Years of the City Victorious.* Princeton, N.J.: Princeton University Press, 1971.

Abu-Lughod, Lila, ed. *Remaking Women: Feminism and Modernity in the Middle East.* Princeton, N.J.: Princeton University Press, 1998.

Abu-Odeh, Lama. "Crimes of Honour and the Construction of Gender in Arab Societies." In *Feminism and Islam: Legal and Literary Perspectives*, ed. Mai Yamani. London: Ithaca Press, 1996.

Agmon, Iris. "Women, Class, and Gender: Muslim Jaffa and Haifa at the Turn of the Twentieth Century." *IJMES* 30 (1998): 477–500.

Agulhon, Maurice. *Marianne into Battle: Republican Imagery and Symbolism in France, 1789–1880.* Translated by Janet Lloyd. Cambridge: Cambridge University Press, 1981.

Ahmed, Leila. *Women and Gender in Islam: Historical Roots of a Modern Debate.* New Haven, Conn.: Yale University Press, 1992.

Alessio, Dominic David. "Domesticating 'the Heart of the Wild': Female Personifications of the Colonies, 1886–1940." *Women's History Review* 6 (1997): 239–69

Amal-naguib, Saphinaz. "'Arusa: Doll, Bride or Fertility Symbol?" *Araby* 1 (1986): 3–10.

Amin, Ahmad. *My Life.* Translated by Issa J. Boullata. Leiden: E. J. Brill, 1978.

Anderson, Benedict. *Imagined Communities: Reflections on the Origin and Spread of Nationalism.* 1989. Rev. ed. London: Verso, 1991.

Antoun, Richard T. "On the Modesty of Women in Arab Muslim Villages: A Study in the Accommodation of Traditions." *American Anthropologist* 70 (1968): 671–97.

Armbrust, Walter. *Mass Culture and Modernism in Egypt*. Cambridge: Cambridge University Press, 1996.

Aroian, Lois A. *The Nationalization of Arabic and Islamic Education in Egypt: Dar al-'Ulum and al-Azhar*. Cairo: American University in Cairo Press, 1983.

Ayalon, Ami. *Language and Change in the Arab Middle East*. New York: Oxford University Press, 1987.

_____. *The Press in the Arab Middle East: A History*. New York: Oxford University Press, 1995.

Badawi, Muhammad Mustafa. *Early Arabic Drama*. Cambridge: Cambridge University Press, 1988.

Badran, Margot. *Feminists, Islam, and Nation: Gender and the Making of Modern Egypt*. Princeton, N.J.: Princeton University Press, 1995.

Badrawi, Malak. *Isma'il Sidqi (1875–1950): Pragmatism and Vision in Twentieth-Century Egypt*. Richmond, Surrey: Curzon, 1996.

Baer, Gabriel. *Studies in the Social History of Modern Egypt*. Chicago: University of Chicago Press, 1969.

al-Banna, Hasan. *Five Tracts of Hasan Al-Banna' (1906–1949)*. Translated by Charles Wendell. Berkeley: University of California Press, 1970.

_____. *Memoirs of Hasan al Banna Shaheed*. Translated by M. N. Shaikh. Karachi: International Islamic Publishers, 1981.

Baron, Beth. "The Construction of National Honour in Egypt." *Gender and History* 5 (1993): 244–55.

_____. "The Making and Breaking of Marital Bonds in Modern Egypt." In *Women in Middle Eastern History*, ed. Nikki R. Keddie and Beth Baron. New Haven, Conn.: Yale University Press 1991.

_____. "Mothers, Morality, and Nationalism in Pre-1919 Egypt." In *The Origins of Arab Nationalism*, ed. Rashid Khalidi et al. New York: Columbia University Press, 1991.

_____. "Nationalist Iconography: Egypt as a Woman." In *Rethinking Nationalism in the Arab Middle East*, ed. James Jankowski and Israel Gershoni. New York: Columbia University Press, 1997.

_____. "The Politics of Female Notables in Postwar Egypt." In *Borderlines: Genders and Identities in War and Peace, 1870–1930*, ed. Billie Melman. New York: Routledge, 1998.

_____. "Readers and the Women's Press in Egypt." *Poetics Today* 15 (1994): 217–40.

_____. "Unveiling in Early Twentieth Century Egypt: Practical and Symbolic Considerations." *Middle Eastern Studies* 25 (1989): 370–86.

_____. *The Women's Awakening in Egypt: Culture, Society, and the Press*. New Haven, Conn.: Yale University Press, 1994.

Beck, Lois, and Nikki Keddie, eds. *Women in the Muslim World*. Cambridge, Mass.: Harvard University Press, 1978.

Behrens-Abouseif, Doris. "The Political Situation of the Copts, 1798–1923." In *Christians and Jews in the Ottoman Empire*, ed. Benjamin Braude and Bernard Lewis. New York: Holmes & Meier, 1982.

Blom, Ida, Karen Hagemann, and Catherine Hall, eds. *Gendered Nations: Nationalisms and Gender Order in the Long Nineteenth Century*. London: Berg, 2000.

Blunt, Wilfrid Scawen. *Secret History of the English Occupation of Egypt: Being a Personal Narrative of Events*. London: T. F. Unwin, 1907. Reprint. New York: H. Fertig, 1967.

Booth, Marilyn. *Bayram al-Tunisi's Egypt: Social Criticism and Narrative Strategies*. Oxford: Ithaca Press, 1990.

_____. "Colloquial Arabic Poetry, Politics, and the Press in Modern Egypt." *IJMES* 24 (1992): 419–40.

_____. *May Her Likes Be Multiplied: Biography and Gender Politics in Egypt*. Berkeley: University of California Press, 2001.

Botman, Selma. *Engendering Citizenship in Egypt*. New York: Columbia University Press, 1999.

Boullata, Issa J. "Modern Qur'an Exegesis: A Study of Bint al-Shati's Method." *Muslim World* 64 (1974): 103–13.

Bracewell, Wendy. "Women, Motherhood, and Contemporary Serbian Nationalism." *Women's Studies International Forum* 19 (1996): 25–33.

Braude, Benjamin, and Bernard Lewis, eds. *Christians and Jews in the Ottoman Empire*. New York: Holmes & Meier, 1982.

Broadley, A. M. *How We Defended Arabi and His Friends*. London, 1884. Reprint. Cairo: Research and Publishing, Arab Centre, 1980.

Brown, Nathan J. "Shari'a and State in the Modern Muslim Middle East." *IJMES* 29 (1997): 359–76.

Brummett, Palmira. "Dogs, Women, Cholera, and Other Menaces in the Streets: Cartoon Satire in the Ottoman Revolutionary Press, 1908–11." *IJMES* 27 (1995): 433–60.

Buheiry, Marwan R., ed. *Intellectual Life in the Arab East, 1890–1939*. Beirut: American University of Beirut, 1981.

Cachia, Pierre. *Popular Narrative Ballads of Modern Egypt*. New York: Oxford University Press, 1989.

Cannon, Byron D. "Nineteenth-Century Arabic Writings on Women and Society: The Interim Role of the Masonic Press in Cairo—(al-Lata'if, 1885–1895)." *IJMES* 17 (1985): 463–84.

Çizgen, Engin. *Photography in the Ottoman Empire, 1839–1919*. Istanbul: Haset Kitabevi, 1987.

Cole, Juan. *Colonialism and Revolution in the Middle East: Social and Cultural Origins of Egypt's 'Urabi Movement*. Princeton, N.J.: Princeton University Press, 1993.

_____. "Feminism, Class, and Islam in Turn-of-the-Century Egypt." *IJMES* 13 (1981): 387–401.

Confino, Alon. "Collective Memory and Cultural History: Problems of Method." *American Historical Review* 102 (1997): 1386–1403.

Cooke, Miriam. "*Ayyam min Hayati*: The Prison Memoirs of a Muslim Sister." *Journal of Arabic Literature* 26 (1995): 147–64.

_____. "Zaynab al-Ghazali: Saint or Subversive?" *Die Welt des Islams* 34 (1994): 1–20.

Coury, Ralph M. "The Politics of the Funereal: The Tomb of Saad Zaghlul." *Journal of the American Research Center in Egypt* 29 (1992): 191–200.

Cuno, Kenneth M. "Ambiguous Modernization: The Transition to Monogamy in the Khedival House of Egypt." In *Family History in the Middle East: Household, Property, and Gender*, ed. Beshara Doumani. Albany: State University of New York Press, 2003.

———. "Joint Family Households and Rural Notables in Nineteenth-Century Egypt." *IJMES* 27 (1995): 485–502.

———. *The Pasha's Peasants*. Cambridge: Cambridge University Press, 1992.

Cuno, Kenneth M., and Michael J. Reimer. "The Census Registers of Nineteenth-Century Egypt: a New Source for Social Historians." *British Journal of Middle Eastern Studies* 24 (1997): 193–216.

Daly, M. W., ed. *The Cambridge History of Egypt*, Vol. 2: *Modern Egypt, from 1517 to the End of the Twentieth Century*. Cambridge: Cambridge University Press, 1998.

Davenport, Alma. *The History of Photography: An Overview*. Boston: Focal Press, 1991.

Deeb, Marius. *Party Politics in Egypt: The Wafd and Its Rivals, 1919–1939*. London: Ithaca Press, 1979.

Deringil, Selim. "The Ottoman Response to the Egyptian Crisis of 1881–82." *Middle Eastern Studies* 24 (1988): 3–24.

Douglas, Allen, and Fedwa Malti-Douglas. *Arab Comic Strips: Politics of an Emerging Mass Culture*. Bloomington: Indiana University Press, 1994.

Doumani, Beshara, ed. *Family History in the Middle East: Household, Property, and Gender*. Albany: State University of New York Press, 2003.

Duben, Alan, and Cem Behar. *Istanbul Households: Marriage, Family, and Fertility, 1880–1940*. Cambridge: Cambridge University Press, 1991.

Eley, Geoff. "Culture, Nation and Gender." In *Gendered Nations: Nationalisms and Gender Order in the Long Nineteenth Century*, ed. Ida Blom, Karen Hagemann, and Catherine Hall. London: Berg, 2000.

Eley, Geoff, and Ronald Grigor Suny. *Becoming National: A Reader*. New York: Oxford University Press, 1996.

English, Donald E. *Political Uses of Photography in the Third French Republic, 1871–1914*. Ann Arbor, Mich.: UMI Research Press, 1981.

Erdem, Y. Hakan. *Slavery in the Ottoman Empire and Its Demise, 1800–1909*. New York: St. Martin's Press, 1996.

Fahmy, Khaled. *All the Pasha's Men: Mehmed Ali, His Army and the Making of Modern Egypt*. Cambridge: Cambridge University Press, 1997.

Farag, Maged M. *1952, The Last Protocol: Royal Albums of Egypt*. Cairo: Max Group, 1996.

Farid, Muhammad. *The Memoirs and Diaries of Muhammad Farid, an Egyptian Nationalist Leader (1868–1919)*. Translated by Arthur Goldschmidt Jr. San Francisco: Mellen University Research Press, 1992.

Fay, Mary Ann. "Women and Waqf: Toward a Reconsideration of Women's Place in the Mamluk Household." *IJMES* 29 (1997): 33–51.

Feltus, Peter R. *Catalogue of Egyptian Revenue Stamps*. Southfield, Mich.: Postilion Publications, 1982.

Fernea, Elizabeth Warnock, ed. *Children in the Muslim Middle East*. Austin: University of Texas Press, 1995.

_____. *Women and the Family in the Middle East*. Austin: University of Texas Press, 1985.

Fleischmann, Ellen L. *The Nation and Its "New" Women: The Palestinian Women's Movement, 1920–1948*. Berkeley: University of California Press, 2003.

_____. "The Other 'Awakening': The Emergence of Women's Movements in the Modern Middle East, 1900–1940." In *Social History of Women and Gender in the Modern Middle East*, ed. Margaret L. Meriwether and Judith E. Tucker. Boulder, Colo.: Westview Press, 1999.

El-Gabalawy, Saad, trans. *Three Pioneering Egyptian Novels*. Fredericton, N.B.: York Press, 1986.

Gaitskell, Deborah, and Elaine Unterhalter. "Mothers of the Nation: A Comparative Analysis of Nation, Race and Motherhood in Afrikaner Nationalism and the African National Congress." In *Woman–Nation–State*, ed. Nira Yuval-Davis and Floya Anthias. London: Macmillan, 1989.

Gavin, Carney. "Imperial Self-Portrait: The Ottoman Empire as Revealed in the Sultan Abdul-Hamid II's Photographic Albums Presented as Gifts to the Library of Congress (1893) and the British Museum (1894)." *Journal of Turkish Studies* 12 (1988).

_____. *The Invention of Photography and Its Impact on Learning*. Cambridge, Mass.: Harvard University Library, 1989.

Gellner, Ernest. *Nations and Nationalism*. Ithaca, N.Y.: Cornell University Press, 1983.

Gelvin, James L. "Demonstrating Communities in Post-Ottoman Syria." *Journal of Interdisciplinary History* 25 (1994): 23–44.

Gendzier, Irene L. "James Sanua and Egyptian Nationalism." *Middle East Journal* 15 (1961): 25.

_____. *The Practical Visions of Ya'qub Sanu'*. Cambridge, Mass.: Harvard University Press, 1966.

Gershoni, Israel. "Between Ottomanism and Egyptianism: The Evolution of 'National Sentiment' in the Cairene Middle Class as Reflected in Najib Mahfuz's *Bayn al-Qasrayn*." In *Studies in Islamic Society*, ed. Gabriel R. Warburg and Gad G. Gilbar. Haifa: Haifa University Press, 1984.

Gershoni, Israel, and James P. Jankowski. *Egypt, Islam, and the Arabs: The Search for Egyptian Nationhood, 1900–1930*. New York: Oxford University Press, 1986.

_____. *Redefining the Egyptian Nation, 1930–1945*. Cambridge: Cambridge University Press, 1995.

al-Ghazali, Zaynab. *Return of the Pharaoh: Memoir in Nasir's Prison*. Translated by Mokrane Guezzou. Leicester, U.K.: Islamic Foundation, 1994.

Göçek, Fatma Müge. "From Empire to Nation: Images of Women and War in Ottoman Political Cartoons, 1908–1923." In *Borderlines: Genders and Identities in War and Peace, 1870–1930*, ed. Billie Melman. New York: Routledge, 1998.

Goldberg, Vicki, ed. *Photography in Print: Writings from 1816 to the Present*. New York: Simon & Schuster, 1981.

Goldschmidt, Arthur, Jr. *Biographical Dictionary of Modern Egypt*. Boulder, Colo.: Lynne Rienner, 2000.

———. "The Egyptian Nationalist Party: 1892–1919." In *Political and Social Change in Modern Egypt*, ed. P. M. Holt. London: University of London, 1968.

———. "The National Party from Spotlight to Shadow." *Asian and African Studies* 16 (1982): 11–30.

Gordon, Joel. "Film, Fame, and Public Memory: Egyptian Biopics from *Mustafa Kamil* to *Nasser 56*." *IJMES* 31 (1999): 61–79.

Graham-Brown, Sarah. *Images of Women: The Portrayal of Women in Photography of the Middle East, 1860–1950*. New York: Columbia University Press, 1988.

Gued Vidal, Fina. *Safia Zaghloul*. Cairo: E. Schindler, 1946.

Gupte, Pranay. *Mother India: A Political Biography of Indira Gandhi*. New York: Maxwell Macmillan International, 1992.

Hagemann, Karen. "A Valourous *Volk* Family: The Nation, the Military, and the Gender Order in Prussia in the Time of the Anti-Napoleonic Wars, 1806–15." In *Gendered Nations: Nationalisms and Gender Order in the Long Nineteenth Century*, ed. Ida Blom, Karen Hagemann, and Catherine Hall, London: Berg, 2000.

Hatem, Mervat. "Egyptian Upper- and Middle-Class Women's Early Nationalist Discourses on National Liberation and Peace in Palestine (1922–1944)." *Women and Politics* 9, no. 3 (1989): 49–70.

Hathaway, Jane. *The Politics of Households in Ottoman Egypt: The Rise of the Qazdaglis*. Cambridge: Cambridge University Press, 1997.

Haykal, Muhammad Husayn. *Zaynab*. 1914. Reprint. Cairo: Maktabat al-Nahda al-Misriyya 1963.

Herzfeld, Michael. "Honour and Shame: Problems in the Comparative Analysis of Moral Systems." *Man* 15 (1980): 339–51.

Heyworth-Dunne, J. *Religious and Political Trends in Modern Egypt*. Washington, D.C.: Author, 1950.

Hirsch, Julia. *Family Photographs: Content, Meaning, and Effect*. New York: Oxford University Press, 1981.

Hobsbawm, Eric. "Man and Woman in Socialist Iconography." *History Workshop* no. 6 (Autumn 1978): 121–38.

———. *Nations and Nationalism since 1780: Programme, Myth, Reality*. Cambridge: Cambridge University Press, 1990.

Hoffman, J. "An Islamic Activist: Zaynab al-Ghazali." In *Women and the Family in the Middle East*, ed. Elizabeth Warnock Fernea. Austin: University of Texas Press, 1985.

Holt, P. M., ed. *Political and Social Change in Modern Egypt*. London: University of London, 1968.

Hourani, Albert. *Arabic Thought in the Liberal Age 1798–1939*. Cambridge: Cambridge University Press, 1983.

———. *The Emergence of the Modern Middle East*. Oxford: Macmillan, 1981.

Hourani, Albert, Philip S. Khoury, and Mary C. Wilson, eds. *The Modern Middle East: A Reader*. Berkeley: University of California Press, 1993.

Hunter, F. Robert. "Egypt's High Officials in Transition from a Turkish to a Modern Administrative Elite, 1849–1879." *Middle Eastern Studies* 19 (1983): 277–91.

———. *Egypt under the Khedives, 1805–1879: From Household Government to Modern Bureaucracy.* Pittsburgh: University of Pittsburgh Press, 1984.

———. "The Making of a Notable Politician: Muhammad Sultan Pasha (1825–1884)." *IJMES* 15 (1983): 537–44.

Hutchinson, John, and Anthony D. Smith, eds. *Nationalism.* Oxford: Oxford University Press, 1994.

*Images d'Egypte: De la fresque à la bande dessinée.* Cairo: CEDEJ, 1991.

Iverson, Barry. *Garo Balian: An Ottoman Court Architect in Modern Egypt.* Cairo: American University in Cairo Press, 1994.

Jankowski, James, and Israel Gershoni, eds. *Rethinking Nationalism in the Arab Middle East.* New York: Columbia University Press, 1997.

Jerrold, Blanchard. *Egypt under Ismail Pacha.* London: S. Tinsley, 1879.

Kamel Pasha, Moustafa. *What the National Party Wants.* Cairo: Egyptian Standard, 1907.

Kandiyoti, Deniz, ed. *Gendering the Middle East: Emerging Perspectives.* New York: I. B. Tauris, 1996.

———. "Slave Girls, Temptresses, and Comrades: Images of Women in the Turkish Novel." *Feminist Issues* 8 (1988): 35–49.

———. "Some Awkward Questions on Women and Modernity in Turkey." In *Remaking Women: Feminism and Modernity in the Middle East*, ed. Lila Abu-Lughod. Princeton, N.J.: Princeton University Press, 1998.

———. *Women, Islam and the State.* Philadephia: Temple University Press, 1991.

Karnouk, Liliane. *Modern Egyptian Art: The Emergence of a National Style.* Cairo: American University in Cairo Press, 1988.

Katz, Sheila Hannah. "*Adam* and *Adama*, *'Ird* and *Ard*: En-gendering Political Conflict and Identity in Early Jewish and Palestinian Nationalisms." In *Gendering the Middle East: Emerging Perspectives*, ed. Deniz Kandiyoti. New York: I. B. Tauris, 1996.

Kazziha, Walid. "The Jaridah-Ummah Group and Egyptian Politics." *Middle Eastern Studies* 13 (1977): 373–85.

Keddie, Nikki R. *Women in the Middle East since the Rise of Islam.* Washington, D.C.: American Historical Association, forthcoming.

Keddie, Nikki R., and Beth Baron, eds. *Women in Middle Eastern History.* New Haven, Conn.: Yale University Press, 1991.

Kedourie, Elie. *The Chatham House Version and Other Middle-Eastern Studies.* London: Weidenfeld & Nicolson, 1970.

Kedourie, Elie, and Sylvia G. Haim, eds. *Essays on the Economic History of the Middle East.* London: Frank Cass, 1988.

Kelidar, Abbas. "Shaykh 'Ali Yusuf: Egyptian Journalist and Islamic Nationalist." In *Intellectual Life in the Arab East, 1890–1939*, ed. Marwan R. Buheiry. Beirut: American University of Beirut, 1981.

Khalidi, Rashid, et al., eds. *The Origins of Arab Nationalism.* New York: Columbia University Press, 1991.

Khater, Akram Fouad. *Inventing Home: Emigration, Gender, and the Middle Class in Lebanon, 1870–1920.* Berkeley: University of California Press, 2001.

Khouri, Mounah A. *Poetry and the Making of Modern Egypt (1882–1922).* Leiden: E. J. Brill, 1971.

Koester, David. "Gender Ideology and Nationalism in the Culture and Politics of Iceland." *American Ethnologist* 22 (1995): 572–88.

Kouloub, Out El. *Ramza.* Translated by Nayra Atiya. Syracuse, N.Y.: Syracuse University Press, 1994.

Koven, Seth, and Sonya Michel, eds. *Mothers of a New World: Maternalist Politics and the Origins of Welfare States.* New York: Routledge, 1993.

Kressel, Gideon M. "Sororicide/Filiacide: Homicide for Family Honor." *Current Anthropology* 22 (1981): 141–58.

Labib, Subhi. "The Copts in Egyptian Society and Politics, 1882–1919." In *Islam, Nationalism, and Radicalism in Egypt and the Sudan,* ed. Gabriel R. Warburg and Uri M. Kupferschmidt. New York: Praeger, 1983.

Landau, Jacob M. *Studies in the Arab Theater and Cinema.* Philadelphia: University of Pennsylvania Press, 1958.

Lazreg, Marnia. *The Eloquence of Silence: Algerian Women in Question.* New York: Routledge, 1994.

Lichtenstadter, Ilse. "The 'New Woman' in Modern Egypt: Observations and Impressions." *Moslem World* 38 (1948): 166–67.

Lockman, Zachary. "The Egyptian Nationalist Movement and the Syrians in Egypt." *Immigrants and Minorities* 3 (1984): 233–51.

———. "The Social Roots of Nationalism: Workers and the National Movement in Egypt, 1908–19." *Middle Eastern Studies* 24 (1988): 445–59

Mahfouz, Naguib. *Midaq Alley.* Translated by Trevor Le Gassick. 2d ed. Washington, D.C.: Three Continents Press, 1989.

———. *Palace Walk.* Translated by William Maynard Hutchins and Olive E. Kenny. New York: Doubleday, 1990.

Margolis, Eric. "Mining Photographs: Unearthing the Meanings of Historical Photos." *Radical History Review* 40 (1988): 33–48.

Mattar, Philip. *The Mufti of Jerusalem: al-Hajj Amin al-Husayni and the Palestinian National Movement.* New York: Columbia University Press, 1988.

McClintock, Anne. "Family Feuds: Gender, Nationalism and the Family." *Feminist Review,* no. 44 (Summer 1993): 61–80.

McIntyre, John D., Jr. *The Boycott of the Milner Mission: A Study in Egyptian Nationalism.* New York: Peter Lang, 1985.

Meeker, Michael. "Meaning and Society in the Near East: Examples from the Black Sea Turks and the Levantine Arabs." *IJMES* 7 (1976): 243–70.

Meital, Yoram. "Revolutionizing the Past: Historical Representation during Egypt's Revolutionary Experience, 1952–62." *Mediterranean Historical Review* 12 (1997): 60–77.

Melman, Billie. *Borderlines: Genders and Identities in War and Peace, 1870–1930.* New York: Routledge, 1998.

Meriwether, Margaret L., and Judith E. Tucker, eds. *Social History of Women and Gender in the Modern Middle East.* Boulder, Colo.: Westview Press, 1999.

Minault, Gail. *The Khilafat Movement: Religious Symbolism and Political Mobilization in India*. New York: Columbia University Press, 1982.

Mitchell, Richard P. *The Society of the Muslim Brothers*. 1969. Reprint. New York: Oxford University Press, 1993.

Moors, Annelies. "Embodying the Nation: Maha Saca's Post-Intifada Postcards." *Ethnic and Racial Studies* 23 (2000): 871–87.

Musa, Salama. *The Education of Salama Musa*. Translated by L. O. Schuman. Leiden: E. J. Brill, 1961.

Najmabadi, Afsaneh. "The Erotic *Vatan* (Homeland) as Beloved and Mother: To Love, to Possess, and to Protect." *Comparative Studies in Society and History* 39 (1997): 442–67.

_____. "*Zanha-y millat*: Women or Wives of the Nation?" *Iranian Studies* 26 (1993): 51–71.

Nakash, Yitzhak. "Reflections on a Subsistence Economy: Production and Trade of the Mahdist Sudan, 1881–1898." In *Essays on the Economic History of the Middle East*, ed. Elie Kedourie and Sylvia G. Haim. London: Frank Cass, 1988.

Nelson, Cynthia. *Doria Shafik, Egyptian Feminist: A Woman Apart*. Gainesville: University Press of Florida, 1996.

Ölçer, Nazan, et al. *Images d'empire: Aux origines de la photographie en Turquie*. Istanbul: Institut d'études françaises d'Istanbul, n.d.

Oren, Ruth. "Zionist Photography, 1920–41: Constructing a Landscape." *History of Photography* 19 (1995): 201–9.

Ostle, Robin. "Modern Egyptian Renaissance Man." *Bulletin of the School of Oriental and African Studies* 57 (1994): 184–92.

Özbek, Nadir. "Imperial Gifts and Sultanic Legitimation during the Late Ottoman Empire, 1876–1909." In *Poverty and Charity in Middle Eastern Contexts*, ed. Michael Bonner, Mine Ener, and Amy Singer. Albany: State University of New York Press, 2003.

Peirce, Leslie. *The Imperial Harem: Women and Sovereignty in the Ottoman Empire*. New York: Oxford University Press, 1993.

Perez, Nissan N. *Focus East: Early Photography in the Near East (1839–1885)*. New York: Harry N. Abrams, 1988.

Perlmann, M. "Memoirs of Rose Fatima Al-Yusuf." *Middle Eastern Affairs* 7 (1956): 20–27.

Philipp, Thomas. "Feminism and Nationalist Politics in Egypt." In *Women in the Muslim World*, ed. Lois Beck and Nikki Keddie. Cambridge, Mass.: Harvard University Press, 1978.

_____. "Nation State and Religious Community in Egypt: The Continuing Debate." *Die Welt des Islams* 28 (1988): 379–91.

Philips, Daisy Griggs. "The Awakening of Egypt's Womanhood." *Moslem World* 18 (1928): 402–8.

_____. "The Growth of the Feminist Movement in Egypt." *Moslem World* 16 (1926): 277–85.

Pierson, Ruth Roach. "Nations: Gendered, Racialized, Crossed with Empire." In *Gendered Nations: Nationalisms and Gender Order in the Long Nineteenth Century*, ed. Ida Blom, Karen Hagemann, and Catherine Hall. London: Berg, 2000.

Piterberg, Gabriel. "The Tropes of Stagnation and Awakening in Nationalist Historical Consciousness: The Egyptian Case." In *Rethinking Nationalism in the Arab World*, ed. James Jankowski and Israel Gershoni. New York: Columbia University Press, 1997.

Polk, William R., and Richard L. Chambers, eds. *Beginnings of Modernization in the Middle East: The Nineteenth Century*. Chicago: University of Chicago Press, 1968.

Pollard, Lisa. "The Family Politics of Colonizing and Liberating Egypt, 1882–1919." *Social Politics* 7 (2000): 47–79.

Powell, Eve M. Troutt. *A Different Shade of Colonialism: Egypt, Great Britain and the Mastery of the Sudan*. Berkeley: University of California Press, 2003.

Reid, Donald M. "Egyptian History through Stamps." *Muslim World* 62 (1972): 209–29.

_____. "The Symbolism of Postage Stamps: A Source for the Historian." *Journal of Contemporary History* 19 (1984): 223–49.

_____. *Whose Pharaohs? Archaeology, Museums, and Egyptian National Identity from Napoleon to World War I*. Berkeley: University of California Press, 2002.

Rosenblum, Naomi. *A World History of Photography*. New York: Abbeville Press, 1981.

Russell Pasha, Thomas. *Egyptian Service 1902–1946*. London: Murray, 1949.

Saadawi, Nawal El. *The Hidden Face of Eve: Women in the Arab World*. Translated by Sherif Hetata. London: Zed Press, 1980.

Sabri, Munira. "The Girl Guide Movement." Translated by A. Khaki. *The Bulletin* 29 (October 1948): 4–5.

Sabry, M. *La Revolution égyptienne*. 2 vols. Paris: J. Vrin, 1919–21.

Said, Hamed. *Contemporary Art in Egypt*. Cairo: Ministry of Culture and National Guidance, 1964.

al-Sayyid-Marsot, Afaf Lutfi. "The Cartoon in Egypt." *Comparative Studies in Society and History* 13 (1971): 2–15.

_____. *Egypt and Cromer: A Study in Anglo-Egyptian Relations*. New York: Praeger, 1969.

_____. "Egyptian Historical Research and Writing on Egypt in the Twentieth Century." *Middle East Studies Association Bulletin* 7, no. 2 (1973): 6–7.

_____. *Egypt's Liberal Experiment, 1922–1936*. Berkeley: University of California Press, 1977.

_____. "The Revolutionary Gentlewoman in Egypt." In *Women in the Muslim World*, ed. Lois Beck and Nikki Keddie. Cambridge, Mass.: Harvard University Press, 1978.

_____. *Women and Men in Late Eighteenth-Century Egypt*. Austin: University of Texas Press, 1995.

Schick, Irvin Cemil. "Review Essay: Representing Middle Eastern Women: Feminism and Colonial Discourse." *Feminist Studies* 16 (1990): 345–80.

Schölch, Alexander. *Egypt for the Egyptians! The Socio-political Crisis in Egypt, 1878–1888*. London: Ithaca Press, 1981.

_____. "The Egyptian Bedouins and the 'Urabiyun (1882)." *Die Welt des Islams* 17 (1976–77): 44–57.

Schuman, Howard, and Jacqueline Scott. "Generations and Collective Memories." *American Sociological Review* 54 (1989): 359–81.

*Scott's Standard Postage Stamp Catalogue (1994).* 150th ed. Vol. 3. Sidney, Ohio: Scott, 1993.

Sekula, Allan. "On the Invention of Photographic Meaning." In *Photography in Print: Writings from 1816 to the Present,* ed. Vicki Goldberg. New York: Simon & Schuster, 1981.

Seton, Grace Thompson. *A Woman Tenderfoot in Egypt.* New York: Dodd, Mead, 1923.

Seton-Williams, Veronica, and Peter Stocks, *Blue Guide Egypt.* New York: W. W. Norton, 1984.

Shaarawi, Huda. *Harem Years: The Memoirs of an Egyptian Feminist.* Translated and with an introduction by Margot Badran. London: Virago, 1986.

Shaham, Ron. "Jews and the Shari'a Courts in Modern Egypt." *Studia Islamica* 82 (1995): 113–36.

———. "Masters, Their Freed Slaves, and the *Waqf* in Egypt (Eighteenth–Twentieth Centuries)." *Journal of the Economic and Social History of the Orient* 43 (2000): 162–88.

Sivan, Emmanuel. "The Arab Nation-State: In Search of a Usable Past." *Middle East Review* 19, no. 3 (1987): 21–30.

Sklar, Katherine Kish. "The Historical Foundations of Women's Power in the Creation of the American Welfare State, 1830–1930." In *Mothers of a New World: Maternalist Politics and the Origins of Welfare States,* ed. Seth Koven and Sonya Michel. New York: Routledge, 1993.

Smith, Anthony D. *The Ethnic Origins of Nations.* Oxford: Blackwell, 1986.

———. "The Nation: Invented, Imagined, Reconstructed?" *Millennium* 20 (1991): 353–68.

———. "The Origins of Nations." *Ethnic and Racial Studies* 12 (1989).

Sonbol, Amira al-Azhary. "Adoption in Islamic Society: A Historical Survey." In *Children in the Muslim Middle East,* ed. Elizabeth Warnock Fernea. Austin: University of Texas Press, 1995.

Sontag, Susan. *On Photography.* New York: Farrar, Straus & Giroux, 1977.

Stewart, Frank Henderson. *Honor.* Chicago: University of Chicago Press, 1994.

Storrs, Ronald. *The Memoirs of Sir Ronald Storrs.* New York: Putnam, 1937.

Swedenburg, Ted. *Memories of Revolt: The 1936–1939 Rebellion and the Palestinian National Past.* Minneapolis: University of Minnesota Press, 1995.

Talhami, Ghada Hashem. *The Mobilization of Muslim Women in Egypt.* Gainesville: University Press of Florida, 1996.

Tamura, Airi. "Ethnic Consciousness and Its Transformation in the Course of Nation-Building: The Muslim and the Copt in Egypt, 1906–1919." *Muslim World* 75 (1985): 102–14.

Thompson, Elizabeth. *Colonial Citizens: Republican Rights, Paternal Privilege, and Gender in French Syrian and Lebanon.* New York: Columbia University Press, 2000.

Tignor, Robert L. *Modernization and British Colonial Rule in Egypt, 1882–1914.* Princeton, N.J.: Princeton University Press, 1966.

Toledano, Ehud R. "Forgetting Egypt's Ottoman Past." In *Cultural Horizons: A Festschrift in Honor of Talat S. Halman*, ed. Jayne L. Warner. Syracuse, N.Y.: Syracuse University Press, 2001.

———. "Late Ottoman Concepts of Slavery (1830s–1880s)." *Poetics Today* 14 (1993): 477–506.

———. *The Ottoman Slave Trade and Its Suppression: 1840–1890.* Princeton, N.J.: Princeton University Press, 1982.

———. "Slave Dealers, Women, Pregnancy, and Abortion: The Story of a Circassian Slave-girl in Mid-Nineteenth Century Cairo." *Slavery and Abolition* 2 (1981): 53–68.

———. *Slavery and Abolition in the Ottoman Middle East.* Seattle: University of Washington Press, 1998.

———. "Social and Economic Change in the 'Long Nineteenth Century.'" In *The Cambridge History of Egypt*, Vol. 2: *Modern Egypt, from 1517 to the End of the Twentieth Century*, ed. M. W. Daly. Cambridge: Cambridge University Press, 1998.

———. *State and Society in Mid-Nineteenth-Century Egypt.* Cambridge: Cambridge University Press, 1990.

Tomiche, Nada. "The Situation of Egyptian Women in the First Half of the Nineteenth Century." In *Beginnings of Modernization in the Middle East: The Nineteenth Century*, ed. William R. Polk and Richard L. Chambers. Chicago: University of Chicago Press, 1968.

Tucker, Judith E. *Women in Nineteenth-Century Egypt.* Cambridge: Cambridge University Press, 1985.

Tugay, Emine Foat. *Three Centuries: Family Chronicles of Turkey and Egypt.* London: Oxford University Press, 1963.

'Urabi, Ahmad. *The Defense Statement of Ahmad 'Urabi the Egyptian.* Translated by Trevor Le Gassick. Cairo: American University in Cairo Press, 1982.

Vatikiotis, P. J. *The History of Modern Egypt: From Muhammad Ali to Mubarak.* 4th ed. Baltimore: Johns Hopkins University Press, 1991.

Warburg, Gabriel R., and Gad G. Gilbar, eds. *Studies in Islamic Society.* Haifa: Haifa University Press, 1984.

Warburg, Gabriel R., and Uri M. Kupferschmidt, eds. *Islam, Nationalism, and Radicalism in Egypt and the Sudan.* New York: Praeger, 1983.

Warner, Jayne L., ed. *Cultural Horizons: A Festschrift in Honor of Talat S. Halman.* Syracuse, N.Y.: Syracuse University Press, 2001.

Wassef, Hind, and Nadia Wassef. *Daughters of the Nile: Photographs of Egyptian Women's Movements, 1900–1960.* Cairo: American University in Cairo Press, 2001.

Wehr, Hans. *A Dictionary of Modern Written Arabic.* Edited by J. Milton Cowan. 3d ed. Ithaca, N.Y.: Spoken Language Services, 1976.

Williams, Allen. "The Abdul Hamid II Collection." *History of Photography* 3 (1984): 119–45.

Wissa, Hanna F. *Assiout—The Saga of an Egyptian Family.* Lewes, Sussex: Book Guild, 1994.

Woodsmall, Ruth Frances. *Moslem Women Enter a New World.* New York: Round Table Press, 1936.

Yuval-Davis, Nira and Floya Anthias, eds. *Woman–Nation–State*. London: Macmillan, 1989.

Ze'evi, Dror. "*Kul* and Getting Cooler: The Dissolution of Elite Collective Identity and the Formation of Official Nationalism in the Ottoman Empire." *Mediterranean Historical Review* 11 (1996): 177–95.

Zeidan, Joseph T. *Arab Women Novelists: The Formative Years and Beyond*. Albany: State University of New York Press, 1995.

Zerubavel, Yael. *Recovered Roots: Collective Memory and the Making of Israeli National Tradition*. Chicago: University of Chicago Press, 1995.

Zevi, Filippo, and Sergio Bosticco. *Photographers and Egypt in Nineteenth Century*. Florence: Alinari, 1984.

# Index

Islamists and, 212–13; photography and, 97–101; settings of, 37–38; women's memoirs and, 165–66; Women's Wafd and, 162–63
women's political culture, maternalism and, 224n18
women's press: circulation of, 204; Copts and, 200; cult of domesticity in, 6; emergence of, 10; and "ladies' demonstrations," 118; Syrians and, 28, 199–200; veiling debated in, 248n63; and Woman Question, 32–33; WWII and, 211. *See also specific newspaper*
women's rights movement: Labiba Ahmad and, 189; "ladies' demonstrations" and, 117–18; male nationalists and, 177–78; Munira Thabit and, 165, 178–80; *Nahdat Misr* as symbol of, 215, 217; origins of, 9
women's suffrage, 11, 179
Women's Wafd, 11–12; establishment of, 166, 251n9; ethnic/religious/class backgrounds of members, 165; excluded from political ceremonies, 170; Labiba Ahmad and, 195; memoirs/memories of members of, 163–66; photographs of, 182–84; in political cartoons, 184–87; post-1919 political involvement of, 162–63, 166–70, 175–77; Safiyya Zaghlul and, 136–37, 151, 152, 159; Sha'rawi and, 170–74, 252n46; Wafd and, 168; Wisa and, 174–77, 217
Women's Wafd Central Committee (WWCC): factionalism in, 172–73; founding of, 121, 166, 174; goals of, 166–67; leadership of, 166, 167; post-1919 political involvement of, 167–70; reconfiguration of, 174, 218. *See also* Sa'dist Ladies' Committee
Woodsmall, Ruth, 68
Work for Egypt Society, 219
World War I, 29, 45, 52, 108
World War II, 52, 211–12

Yakan, 'Adli, 142, 194
Young Men's Muslim Association (YMMA). *See* Association of Muslim Youth
youth, Egyptian, photographs of, 94–95, 95
al-Yusuf, Fatima: government harassment of, 181; as journalist, 165, 180–82; memoirs of, 163, 186; political activism of, 54; in political cartoons, 78, 185, 185; and Wafd, 182; women's press and, 100. See also *Ruz al-Yusuf*
Yusuf, Muhammad, 90

Yusuf, Shaykh 'Ali, 34–35

Zaghlul, Sa'd: arrest/deportation of, 140, 168, 169; assassination attempt on, 151; death of, 132, 153; deteriorating health of, 146, 148–50; as exile, 141–45; funeral procession of, 97, 98, 153–54; historical significance of, 122, 219; house arrest of, 145; Labiba Ahmad and, 211; marriage of, 139–40; memorialization of, 153–56; Munira Thabit and, 165, 178; in nationalist iconography, 64; at Paris Peace Conference (1919), 48; photographs of, 85, 86, 90, 92, 93, 96–97, 139–40, 151–53; political partnership of, 151–53; as prime minister, 151–52, 170, 178; released from exile in Malta, 124–25, 129; return to Egypt, 150–51; and revolution, 145; Safiyya joins in exile, 146–50; Safiyya's influence on, 142; Sha'rawi's break with, 163, 170–74; Wisa and, 164; and women's rights, 178; Women's Wafd and, 168–69, 170. *See also* Wafd (Party)
Zaghlul, Safiyya, 130; biographies of, 137–38; in collective memory, 219; death of, 160; and feminism, 152; historical significance of, 160–61; influence on Sa'd, 142; joins Zaghlul in exile, 146–50, 194; and "ladies' demonstrations," 111, 120; marriage of, 139–40; and memorialization of Sa'd, 154–55; as mother of the Egyptians, 5, 11, 78, 135–36, 141, 147–48, 153, 158, 160–61; Mukhtar and, 215; Ottoman-Egyptian origins of, 138; photographs of, 85, 86, 90, 92, 96, 135, 136–37, 138, 139–40, 148, 149, 151–53, 154, 183; in political cartoons, 151, 157, 184, 184, 185, 216; political partnership of, 151–53; religiosity of, 138–39; Sha'rawi and, 152, 157–59; surveillance of, 143; unveiling of, 148, 150; and Wafd, 140–45, 156–60, 217; al-Wakil compared to, 250n123; as WWCC honorary president, 167
*al-Za'im al-Khalid wa-Umm al-Misriyyin fi Manfan Jabal Tariq* (*The Glorious Leader and Mother of the Egyptians in Exile in Gibraltar;* Thabit), 137–38
*zajals* (rhymed prose), 61
Zangaki brothers, 85
*Zaynab* (Haykal), 236n40
Ze'evi, Dror, 22
Zola, Mssr. (photographer), 151
*Zuqaq al-Midaqq* (*Midaq Alley;* Mahfouz), 52

| | |
|---:|:---|
| Text: | 10/13 Sabon |
| Display: | Sabon |
| Indexer: | Kevin Millham |
| Compositor: | IBT Global |
| Printer and binder: | IBT Global |